STUDIES IN CHRISTIAN HISTORY AND THOUGHT

The Extent of the Atonement

A dilemma for Reformed Theology from Calvin to the Consensus (1536–1675)

A full listing of titles in this series appears at the end of this book.

Series Preface

This series complements the specialist series of *Studies in Evangelical History and Thought* and *Studies in Baptist History and Thought* for which Paternoster is becoming increasingly well known by offering works that cover the wider field of Christian history and thought. It encompasses accounts of Christian witness at various periods, studies of individual Christians and movements, and works which concern the relations of church and society through history, and the history of Christian thought.

The series includes monographs, revised dissertations and theses, and collections of papers by individuals and groups. As well as 'free standing' volumes, works on particular running themes are being commissioned; authors will be engaged for these from around the world and from a variety of Christian traditions.

A high academic standard combined with lively writing will commend the volumes in this series both to scholars and to a wider readership.

Series Editors

STUDIES IN CHRISTIAN HISTORY AND THOUGHT

The Extent of the Atonement

A dilemma for Reformed Theology from Calvin to the Consensus (1536–1675)

G M Thomas

Wipf and Stock Publishers
199 W 8th Ave, Suite 3
Eugene, OR 97401

The Extent of the Atonement
A Dilemma for Reformed Theology from Calvin
to the Consensus (1536–1675)
By Thomas, G. M.

ISBN: 1-59752-742-4
Publication date 6/7/2006
Previously published by Paternoster, 1997

This Edition Published by Wipf and Stock Publishers
by arrangement with Paternoster

Paternoster
9 Holdom Avenue
Bletchley
Milton Keyes, MK1 1QR
Great Britain

Contents

Chapter 1 **Introduction** 2
The Problem of the Extent of Christ's Saving Work 2
Historical Background 4
The Patristic and Medieval Periods 4
The Early Reformation: Luther and Bucer 6
Notes 9

Part 1 The Sixteenth Century

Chapter 2 **John Calvin (1509-1564)** 12
Introduction 12
Predestination 12
The role of Predestination in Calvin's Theology 13
Christ and Election 16
The Promise of the Gospel 19
The Place of Election in God's Saving Will 21
The Two Wills of God 23
For Whom Did Christ Die? 26
The Nature of the Atonement 26
Universal Reconciliation 27
Accomplished Reconciliation 28
Effective Reconciliation 30
Sacrifice and Intercession 33
Conclusion 34
Notes 36

Chapter 3 **Theodore Beza (1519-1605)** 41
Introduction 41
The Bolsec Controversy 42
Letters to Bullinger 42
Letters to Calvin 44

The "Table" 45
Decree and Election 47
Beza and Calvin 47
The Controversy with Castellio 48
Beza's Letter to Calvin 49
Beza's Reply to Castellio: the Will of God 49
The Colloquy of Montbéliard 52
The Will of God 52
Election and Christ 55
The Extent of the Atonement 55
Faith and Assurance 58
Conclusion 59
Notes 60

Chapter 4 **Heinrich Bullinger (1504-1575)** **66**
Introduction 66
Theological Themes 66
The Nature and Will of God 66
Providence 68
Predestination 69
Election and Christ 70
Promise 72
Covenant 73
The Extent of the Atonement 74
Controversy 76
Moderation 77
The Bolsec Controversy and the Letter toTraheron 77
Theodore Bibliander 78
The Strasbourg Conflict 79
Conclusion 81
Notes 82

Chapter 5 **Girolamo Zanchi (1516-1590)** **87**
Introduction 87
The "Theses" 88
"Lecture on Predestination" 89
"Confession" - the Will of God 91
De Natura Dei - the Will of God 92
Predestination and Christ 94
The Extent of the Atonement 96

The Knowledge of Election 97
Conclusion 99
Notes 100

Chapter 6 **The Heidelberg School 104**
Zacharias Ursinus (1534-1583) 104
Introduction 104
Predestination 106
God's Covenant 107
The Extent of the Atonement 109
The Knowledge of Election 112
Conclusion 113
Caspar Olevianus (1536-1587) 113
Samuel Huber and Aegidius Hunnius 114
David Pareus (1548-1622) 115
Daniel Tossanus (1541-1602) 117
Jacobus Kimedoncius 117
Conclusion 118
Notes 119

Summary of Part I 124

Part 2 The Synod of Dort

Chapter 7 **The Synod of Dort (1618-1619) 128**
The Rise of Arminianism 128
The Arminian View of the Extent of the Atonement 131
Conclusions of the Synod 131
Predestination 132
The Extent of the Atonement 132
Submissions of the Deputations 134
Great Britain 134
The Palatinate 135
Geneva 136
Martinius of Bremen 137
Recurrent Themes 138
The Sufficient-Efficient Formula 138
Covenant 140
Covenant, Predestination and Christ 142
Actual or Potential Redemption 145
Conflict 147

Outstanding Problems 149
John Davenant (1572-1641) 150
Conclusion 152
Notes 153

Part 3 The Saumur Theology and its Opponents

Chapter 8 **John Cameron (1579-1625)** **162**
Introduction 162
Cameron Studies 163
Cameron's Theology 164
Predestination 164
The Will of God 166
The Threefold Covenant 167
Conditional Covenant 171
Conversion 172
The Nature of the Atonement 173
The Extent of the Atonement 174
Implications of Universal Conditional Covenant 177
The Nature of God 179
Cameron's Place in the Tradition 180
Conclusion 181
Notes 182

Chapter 9 **Moïse Amyraut (1596-1664)** **187**
Introduction 187
Amyraut's Theology 189
Predestination 189
The Will of God 192
Covenant 194
Conversion 197
The Nature of God 198
The Nature and Extent of the Atonement 200
Conclusion 203
Notes 205

Chapter 10 **The Roots of Amyraldism** **210**
Introduction 210
Amyraut and Arminianism 210
Amyraut and Lutheranism 212
Amyraut and Calvin 213

The German Tradition 218
Humanism 218
Conclusion 220
Notes 221

Chapter 11 **Amyraut's Opponents and the Swiss Consensus of 1675** **224**
Introduction 224
Biographical Background 224
Pierre du Moulin (1568-1658) 224
Friedrich Spanheim (1600-1649) 225
John Owen (1616-1683) 225
Francis Turretin (1623-1687) 226
The Charges against Amyraut 226
Absurdity 226
A Threat to Divine Freedom and Grace 230
A Distortion of the Covenant 231
An Empty Atonement 232
Novelty 236
Reliance upon Reason 237
Universal Saving Revelation 237
Separation of Christ and Predestination 237
The *Formula Consensus Helvetica* (1675) 238
Conclusion 240
Notes 242

Part 4 Conclusion

Chapter 12 **Conclusion** 248
Summary: a Reformed Dilemma 248
Reformulation: Barth's Doctrine of Election 252
Notes 253

Abbreviations **256**

Bibliography **257**

Index **273**

Introduction

Chapter One

Introduction

THE PROBLEM OF THE EXTENT OF CHRIST'S SAVING WORK

In 1675 theologians representing the Swiss Reformed Churches prepared the *Formula Consensus Helvetica,* a statement designed to exclude the view that Christ died for all. This controversial and short-lived agreement was the culmination of over a century of discussion and conflict about this point among the Reformed. Recent scholarship has been divided on the interpretation of the course of Reformed theology in the sixteenth and seventeenth centuries, some writers seeing it as a steady departure from the approach and content of the teaching of John Calvin, while others have regarded it as a legitimate and faithful development of the Genevan reformer's thought.[1] At the heart of the matter is the question of the place of predestination in the thought of Calvin and his successors. Consideration of the way the extent of the atonement was understood leads directly towards answers to this question, because it exposes the degree to which Reformed theologians allowed important elements of their teaching to be shaped by predestination.

With reference to the Synod of Dort (1618–1619), P. White has recently written, "At perhaps no point were the tensions within international Calvinism more acute than on the extent of the atonement".[2] In fact, this statement holds good for much of the seventeenth century, with its long-running controversy over the "hypothetical universalism" propounded by Moïse Amyraut. In the course of pursuing not only the seventeenth-century debate, but also its sixteenth-century beginnings, we aim to show that these debates were an expression of fundamental stresses within Reformed doctrine itself, from the very early days of its formulation. In the process, it will become clear that, in view of the early diversity within the Reformed constituency, any approach that would judge the development of Reformed theology according to the standard of conformity to Calvin must be regarded as somewhat suspect.

While a wholly impartial approach is unlikely to be found in any study of Christian doctrine, much work on the extent of the atonement in Reformed theology seems tinged with an obvious eagerness to prove that Calvin held a certain position and that later "Calvinism" either did or did not depart from him. It is certainly striking that R.T. Kendall can assert without hesitation Calvin's "belief that Christ died indiscriminately for all men", while J.H.Rainbow can give his own work on this theme the subtitle, "An historical theological study of John Calvin's doctrine of limited redemption". This divergence, in which these two writers are representative of a number of other contemporary scholars,[3] at least suggests that further work needs to be done. It also indicates that it is important to see the extent of the atonement not as an isolated doctrine, but in its relation to other doctrines within the thought of each theologian studied. Furthermore, it puts us on guard against seeking to categorize theologians in a simple way, by posing to them questions framed according to terms and concepts they did not use themselves.

Among works dealing with aspects of the atonement controversy, two call for attention at the outset. The first is B.G.Armstrong's influential, *Calvinism and the Amyraut Heresy.*[4] It is Armstrong's contention that the humanistic theology of Calvin was distorted by the scholastic approach of his successors, to be revived a century later by theologians of the French Academy of Saumur, John Cameron and Moïse Amyraut. Although not concentrating on the extent of the atonement, Armstrong claims, as illustrative of his contention, that there was a transition from Calvin's teaching of universal atonement to the assertion of limited atonement by Theodore Beza and the Reformed orthodoxy of the late sixteenth and early seventeenth centuries, challenged by the return of the Saumur theologians to Calvin's universal perspective. Armstrong concludes his work with the suggestion that a closer comparison of the theologies of Calvin and Amyraut would be fruitful.[5] It was with the aim of making such a comparison that the research behind the present work was commenced. However, because of the danger that a comparison between theologians belonging to distinct periods would be artificial if undertaken without reference to the theological development between them, this study traces the theology of the extent of the atonement between, as well as in, Calvin and Amyraut. In doing so, it sheds light on Armstrong's claim that the heirs of Calvin were unfaithful to their heritage.

The other work is S.Strehle's unpublished thesis, "The Extent of the Atonement within the Theological Systems of the Sixteenth and Seventeenth Centuries".[6] This work is valuable in many respects, not least for its tracing of the pre-Reformation background. It is dominated by Strehle's contention that Luther's and Calvin's understanding of the atonement combined the classical concept of Christ as victor with the penal theory, and was radically different from the later Lutheran and Reformed expositions in terms of penal substitution only. According to Strehle, Luther and Calvin held that Christ was victor in his death and resurrection over all evil, and therefore the question of whether he died for the sins of only some people could not arise. The divide between people comes, for these two reformers, not at the cross or in the divine will, but at the point of union by faith with the risen Christ, through which we participate in his victory and unlimited power to save. Later theologians, however, not only made room, through their exclusive concentration on penal suffering, for the question, "Did Christ die for me?", but they were also guilty of reviving the medieval Nominalist preoccupation with the will of God. So they had to ask, "Whom did God will to benefit from the atonement?" Strehle includes an appendix in which he expounds his own view of "Dynamic Atonement",[7] which coincides with the views attributed to Luther and Calvin, and by which the other theologians have been judged throughout the work. In our view, Strehle's very distinctive angle is fresh and interesting, but not entirely persuasive, and imposes a too rigid framework upon the subject matter. There is a need for further investigation of the debate on the extent of the atonement, especially as Strehle does not consider in depth the Reformed-Lutheran divide, and he deals only briefly with the teaching of Bullinger, Zanchi and the Heidelberg theologians, and the Amyraldian debates.

HISTORICAL BACKGROUND

The Patristic and Medieval periods

Because the question of the extent of the atonement through the patristic and medieval period has been examined in some detail by Strehle, W.R.Godfrey and Rainbow,[8] only enough attention will be given to it here to provide a background to the Reformation and post-Reformation debates.

Issues of predestination and human free will came to the fore in the fifth-century controversies between Augustine and Pelagius and their followers. Augustine opposed the Pelagian teaching that human beings have a natural ability to obey God and so achieve salvation, and that they are able to choose salvation because his will is free from internal constraint. On the contrary, he taught that human nature is so corrupted by sin that only by the intervention of an inner-working divine grace can the will be set free to choose salvation. He reinforced this position by maintaining that God eternally, without respect to any foreseen merit, chose to whom he would give this grace. With this doctrine of the predestination of certain individuals to salvation, it was inevitable that the question would be raised, "Did Christ come into the world for the elect only?" There are indications that Augustine's answer was, in some sense, affirmative. For example, he interpreted 1 Timothy 2.4-6, "[God] wants all men to be saved and to come to a knowledge of the truth...Christ Jesus...gave himself as a ransom for all men", as referring to all classes of people, or to all those who would in fact be saved, rather than all individuals without restriction. However, the controversies in which Augustine engaged did not centre on the extent of Christ's work, for his main concern was to establish the inability of human beings to save themselves, and to attribute salvation entirely to the grace and omnipotence of God.

Through the fifth century there was, according to P.L.Barclift, a process of moderating the extreme positions taken in the initial conflict over grace and predestination.[9] So, on the extent of the atonement, writers like Prosper, Primasius and Leo stated that Christ died for all, but pointed out that not all receive the benefit of his death. Thus it was a moderate form of Augustinianism, not anxious to place limitations upon the extent of the atonement, which emerged, and was sanctioned by the Council of Orange in 529.

Controversy was initiated again by Gottschalk, a ninth-century monk who, appealing to Augustine, maintained a strict doctrine of double predestination. He argued that the design of Christ's redeeming work must be understood, in accordance with divine predestination, to have been for the elect only. Gottschalk was imprisoned by Hincmar, Archbishop of Rheims, who took the opposite view, but Gottschalk's teaching struck a chord, and much debate ensued. To resolve the conflict, six synods were held between 849 and 860, but their pronouncements were at variance with each other or unclear.

In the eleventh century, Anselm of Canterbury made a contribution to thought about the atonement that would have a lasting influence. His *Cur Deus Homo* developed the satisfaction theory, according to which sin is an offence of infinite proportions, because committed against the infinite majesty of God, and requires an infinite satisfaction. Christ, as God, was capable of offering such an infinite satisfaction and, as man, was a fitting representative of the human race.

When, in the twelfth century, Peter Lombard wrote,

> "He offered himself for all as far as the sufficiency of the price is concerned, but, as far as efficacy is concerned, for the elect only,"[10]

he was expressing the broad consensus that had arisen in considerations of the extent of the atonement from Augustine onwards, that in some sense Christ's work is adequate for and can be made available to all, but that, however the connections between divine predestination, faith, the human will and the ministrations of the church may be understood, not all receive benefit from it. Thomas Aquinas (c.1224–1274) also used the distinction between universal sufficiency and limited efficacy. The formula presented difficulties for John Duns Scotus (c.1265–1308), with his interest in the will of God. Scotus was not prepared to grant to the work of Christ an infinite intrinsic merit, but maintained that the merit of his death was dependent on the acceptance of God. Thus, the question of the extent of the atonement was for him a question of for whom Christ's work was accepted by God, and his answer was "the elect". It was characteristic of Nominalist theology, for which Duns laid a foundation, to be preoccupied with God's will rather than God's nature or the nature of things. God's power is absolute, and only limited in practice by his will, which is not predictable by reference to his nature. Thus, in Nominalism, God's will was the sole category by which the value and extent of the atonement was to be judged.[11]

In the following pages, it will be seen that Augustine's interpretation of God's will to save "all", Anselm's theory of the atonement, the distinction between the sufficiency and the efficacy of Christ's work, and the question of whether the merit of Christ is to be located in the dignity of his divine nature or in the ordination and acceptance of God, were considered and variously estimated by the theologians of the Reformation and post-Reformation. The question of the extent of the atonement did not originate in their minds, nor did they approach it wholly unaware of the patristic and scholastic background.

The Early Reformation: Luther and Bucer

Martin Luther (1483-1546)

Luther's stand for salvation by the grace of God alone entailed not merely a new formulation of the doctrine of justification through faith, but a protest against the notion of free will. In The *Bondage of the Will* (1525)[12] directed against Erasmus, he asserted the Augustinian view of predestination in the sometimes extreme language he was given to. Later Reformed predestinarians like Beza and Zanchi would never tire of pointing Lutherans to statements found in that work. However, it is questionable whether Luther continued to maintain this early stark form of predestination. It is not that there is any evidence that he abandoned it, but rather that he seems to have developed a strong instinct to warn people against searching into God's secret counsels, and to direct them to Christ instead. In his lecture dealing with Genesis 26.9, for example, Luther represented God as saying,

> "I will reveal my foreknowledge and predestination to you in an extraordinary manner...This is how I will do so: from an unrevealed God I will become a revealed God...I will be made flesh."[13]

In Christ we have to do with *Deus revelatus.* If we seek to know God as the *Deus absconditus* of predestination apart from Christ we will bring fear and damnation upon ourselves.[14]

It was certainly the approach of Melanchthon, Luther's colleague and successor at Wittenberg, to warn people against speculation on predestination, and to direct them to Christ. Trusting in him they could be sure of their election, and need search no further into the eternal counsels. It was typical of his practice of keeping election and faith in Christ very close together when he wrote,

"Election to eternal salvation is...*for the sake of Christ through faith.*"[15]

As a consequence of the christocentric orientation, and of the fear of speculation about predestination, on the part of Luther and Melanchthon, Lutheranism developed a doctrine of predestination that did not embody the more stark assertions of The *Bondage of the Will.* The Formula of Concord of 1577 was to sum up the Lutheran position:

> "We are not to investigate this predestination in the secret counsel of God, but it is to be looked for in his Word, where he has revealed it...In Christ we should seek the eternal salvation of the Father, who has decreed in his eternal counsel that he would save no-one except those who acknowledge his Son, Christ, and truly believe on him. The Christian should banish all other opinions."[16]

It is outside the scope of the present work to explore Luther's complex theology. It is simply necessary here to indicate firstly that he did not formulate a doctrine of limited atonement, secondly that he gave his followers scope to overshadow his more speculative and deterministic predestinarian comments by reference to his christological emphasis, and thirdly that it was not difficult for theologians of the sixteenth century, engaged in controversy over predestination, to find justification for their opposing views in his works.

Martin Bucer (1491-1551)

The young Bucer was won over by Luther to the cause of reformation, and became in time the leader of the Reformed Church of Strasbourg. Like Luther, and with the same intention of defending salvation by grace alone, Bucer adopted a strong, Augustinian view of predestination. According to W.P.Stephens, "The doctrine of predestination or election is one that shapes the whole of Bucer's theology", and he notes several places where Bucer confines the death of Christ to the elect alone.[17] At the same time Bucer was convinced that the gospel should be proclaimed to all, and is good news for all. His way of reconciling particular predestination and a universal gospel was to call upon all people to believe in their election. This appears to be a logically inconsistent procedure, in that it amounted to requiring people to believe something that was not necessarily true in every case. At the same time, within Bucer's own terms of reference, it had an experiential consistency, in that no-one who actually believed in his own election would be believing a falsehood, for such faith could only come as a gift from God, in accordance with his electing will. Bucer drew upon Melanchthon to assert that,

> "The first duty you owe to God is to believe that you have been predestined by him."

He continued,

> "We must reject as the source of every damaging temptation the question, 'Are we predestined?'...We must confidently trust, therefore, as the foundation of faith, that we have all been foreknown, predetermined...chosen by God."[18]

The implication for the atonement was that Christ died for the elect, but the gospel calls on every person to believe in his election and that Christ died for him.

It is noteworthy that the extent of the atonement featured in the debates Bucer had with the Anabaptists. In the 1520s, Strasbourg was home to many radicals, thanks to the degree of tolerance shown them there. The Anabaptists generally held to the universality of Christ's saving work, and maintained that Christ won for all mankind the grace and freedom to turn to God in repentance and faith for salvation. Some, like Hans Denck, held out the hope of ultimate universal reconciliation. A public debate was held between Bucer and Denck, on December 22 and 23, 1526, after which Denck was expelled from Strasbourg. In 1533 Melchior Hoffman was opposed by Bucer, and in the statement drawn up as a basis for Hoffman's examination and expulsion, the restriction of the redemptive work of Christ to the elect was prominent.[19]

Between 1538 and 1541, John Calvin worked alongside Bucer in Strasbourg, after his first brief and apparently unsuccessful period in Geneva had come to an abrupt end. It is not possible that Calvin could have worked in Strasbourg without being aware of the debates that had taken place just a few years before with the Anabaptists. Calvin did not follow Bucer's understanding of predestination in every respect. He rejected Bucer's idea that the elect have within them from birth a "seed of election",[20] and he does not seem to have reproduced the call to all who hear the gospel to believe in their own election. He surely would have gained from Bucer, however, an awareness that a doctrine of eternal, unconditional, predestination of certain individuals to salvation can engender a tendency to place restrictions on the scope of the atonement. It is with this background in mind that we begin to examine the teachings of the Genevan reformer.

Chapter One

Notes

1 See below, pp.12,41.

2 P.White, *Predestination, Policy and Polemic: conflict and consensus in the English Church from the Reformation to the Civil War*, Cambridge 1992, p.187.

3 R.T.Kendall, *Calvin and English Calvinism to 1649*, Oxford 1979, p.13; J.H.Rainbow, *The Will of God and the Cross: an historical theological study of John Calvin's doctrine of limited redemption*, Allison Park 1990.

4 B.G.Armstrong, *Calvinism and the Amyraut Heresy: Protestant scholasticism and humanism in seventeenth-century France*, Madison 1969.

5 Ibid, p.265.

6 S.Strehle, "The Extent of the Atonement within the Theological Systems of the Sixteenth and Seventeenth Centuries", Th.D.Dallas 1980. Strehle has also made much of the influence of Nominalism in Reformed theology in his *Calvinism, Federalism and Scholasticism: a study of the Reformed doctrine of covenant*, Bern 1988.

7 "The Extent", op.cit, pp.280–293.

8 The following exposition draws on Strehle, "The Extent", op.cit., pp.4–62; and Rainbow, op.cit., pp9–48. J.Davenant, "A Dissertation on the Death of Christ as to its Extent and Special Effects", appended to *An Exposition of the Epistle of St. Paul to the Colossians*, (ed. J. Allport), London 1831, contains valuable material. See also, M.S.Freeman, "The Doctrine of Predestination from Augustine to Peter Lombard (430–1160)", *BS* 47(1890), no.188, pp.645–668.

9 P.L.Barclift, "Predestination and Divine Foreknowledge in the Sermons of Pope Leo the Great", *CH* 62(1993)1 pp.5–21. See also J.N.D.Kelly, *Early Christian Doctrines*, New York 1960, pp.366–374.

10 Peter Lombard, *Libri Sententiarum Quatuor*, in J.Migne (ed.), *Cursus Completus Patrologiae*, Paris 1845. For the scholastics and the atonement, see A.Ritschl, *A Critical History of the Christian Doctrine of Justification and Reconciliation*, Edinburgh 1872, pp.22–90; P.Vignaux, *Justification et Prédestination au XIVe. Siècle: Duns Scot, Pierre D'Auriole, Guillaume D'Occam, Grégoire de Rimini*, Paris 1934; J.Rivière, *La Dogme de la Rédemption au Début du Moyen Age*, Paris 1934. For Gottschalk, see D.E.Nineham, "Gottschalk of Orbais: reactionary or precursor of the Reformation?", *JEH* 40(1989)1 pp.1–18.

11 For the main principles of Nominalist theology see, in addition to the above, H.A.Oberman, *Forerunners of the Reformation: the shape of late medieval thought*, London 1967, and "*Facientibus Quod In Se Est Deus Non Denegat Gratiam*: Robert Holcot O.P., and the beginnings of Luther's theology", in S E Ozment (ed), *The Reformation in Medieval Perspective*, Chicago 1971; A.E.McGrath, *The Intellectual Origins of the European Reformation*, Oxford 1987, pp.69–92.

12 M.Luther, *The Bondage of the Will*, trans. J.I.Packer and O.R. Johnston, London 1957.

13 *Lectures on Genesis*, in *Works*, ed. J.Pelikan, St. Louis 1968, vol.5 pp.44–46.

14 On Luther and the concept of *Deus absconditus*, see W.Elert, *The Structure of Lutheranism*, St. Louis 1962, vol.1 pp.117–140; I.D.K.Siggins, *Martin Luther's Doctrine of Christ*, New Haven 1970, pp.79–87; B.A.Gerrish, "'To the Unknown God': Luther and Calvin on the hiddenness of God", in *JR* 53(1973)3 pp.263–292; E.Brunner, *The Christian Doctrine of God*, London 1949, pp.168–174; G.C. Berkouwer, *Divine Election*, Grand Rapids 1960, pp.104–132; G.Adam, *Der Streit um die Prädestination im*

ausgehenden 16. Jahrhundert, Neukirchen 1970 pp.46–47; F. Brosché, *Luther on Predestination: the antinomy and the unity between love and wrath in Luther's concept of God*, Uppsala 1978.

15 C.L.Manschreck (ed), *Melanchthon on Christian Doctrine: Loci Communes 1555*, New York 1965, pp.187–191.

16 T.G.Tappert (ed), *The Formula of Concord: The Confessions of the Evangelical Lutheran Church*, Philadelphia 1959, p.495.

17 W.P.Stephens, *The Holy Spirit in the Theology of Martin Bucer*, Cambridge 1970, p.106; ibid, p.23, and see A.Lang, *Der Evangelienkommentar Martin Butzers und die Grundzüge seiner Theologie*, Leipzig 1900, pp.164–166, cited in Rainbow, op.cit. For Bucer on the atonement, see also Rainbow pp.48–63.

18 M.Bucer, *Common Places*, (ed) D.F.Wright, Abingdon 1972, pp.98–100.

19 Details of the 1533 debate between Bucer and Hoffman are found in G.Zanchi, *Opera* (7 books in 3 vols.), Geneva 1613, 7.1.342–345; A.J.Beachy, *The Concept of Grace in the Radical Reformation*, Nieuwkoop 1977, pp.16–20; K.Deppermann, *Melchior Hoffman: social unrest and apocalyptic visions in the age of the Reformation*, Edinburgh 1987, pp.268–311.

20 F.Wendel, *Calvin: the origins and development of his religious thought*, London 1974, p.276 n.131.

Part One

The Sixteenth Century

Chapter Two

John Calvin (1509–1564)

INTRODUCTION

In recent years a number of scholars have given attention to John Calvin's view of the extent of the atonement. Among those concluding that Calvin held to a "limited atonement" position have been P.Helm, R.Nicole, W.R.Godfrey, R.A.Muller and J.H.Rainbow. Others, such as P.van Buren, B.Hall, B.G.Armstrong, R.T.Kendall, M.C.Bell, J.W.Anderson, C.Daniel, S.Strehle and A.C.Clifford have presented Calvin as a teacher of universal atonement.[1] This division of opinion may be explained partly by the difficulty, indeed impropriety, of attempting to fit the views of an original thinker into a framework developed after his own time. It also suggests that a more nuanced presentation of Calvin's thought on the extent of the atonement may be called for.

Among those who have maintained that Calvin believed Christ died for the elect only, it has been found necessary to claim not so much that he put forward this view, but that he would have done so had it been a controverted point, as it was later in the disputes with the Arminians.[2] It should not be forgotten, however, that the question of the extent of the atonement had already been touched on in the wake of the controversy between Augustine and Pelagius and in the debates connected with Gottschalk, and had been addressed by the medieval scholastics. Calvin would have known something of this background, and, having worked alongside Bucer in Strasbourg between 1538 and 1541, would have been aware that the issue had figured in the disputes there in 1533. Moreover, Calvin was challenged to pursue the theme of the extent of the atonement in his debates over predestination with Pighius and Georgius,[3] which to some degree anticipated the later divide between "Calvinists" and Arminians. The fact that Calvin did not, as all concede, present a developed, explicit doctrine of limited redemption in the face of the attacks on his predestination teaching makes it at least questionable that he would have done so had he faced the threat of Arminianism.[4] Furthermore, the fact that he never, except in a polemical context, treated the extent of the atonement as a subject in its own right is significant in itself, for it indicates that he regarded it as capable of proper consideration only in relation to other themes. Therefore, any investigation into Calvin's views on the scope of Christ's saving work must of necessity be set firmly in the context of other, more prominent, aspects of his theology.

This chapter aims to avoid an approach that would identify Calvin too simply as either "universalist" or "particularist" in his doctrine of redemption. It seeks to provide a nuanced exposition, setting his statements on the scope of Christ's death in the context of related teaching.

PREDESTINATION

Calvin's concise definition of predestination was as follows:

> "We call predestination God's eternal decree, by which he determined with himself what he willed to become of each man. For all are not created in equal condition; rather eternal life is preordained for some, eternal damnation for others."[5]

This definition indicates a fundamental particularism in Calvin's thought. To understand it more fully it is necessary to consider the role played by predestination in his theology.

The Role of Predestination in Calvin's Theology

It was once widely held that predestination was the *Centraldogmen* of Calvin's theology, a concept to which all other doctrines were subordinate. This view was set out by Alexandre Schweizer in 1844. A different approach was taken by H.Bauke in 1922. He drew attention to Calvin's adherence to biblical themes, and his willingness to follow them through even to the point of holding positions that seem logically incompatible. He thus called Calvin's theology a *complexio oppositorum.* Another perspective was adopted by P.Jacobs and W.Niesel, who drew attention to the christocentric heart of Calvin's theology.[6] In spite of this variety of interpretation, certain facts about Calvin's placing of the doctrine of election emerge clearly from the reformer's writings.

a) Election, as the positive aspect of predestination, was a significant part of Calvin's doctrine of the church. In the first edition of the *Institutes* (1536), following the outline of Luther's *Little Catechism,* election is introduced in discussing the fourth article of the Creed, concerning the "holy catholic church", which is understood to be identical with "the whole number of the elect". In its final form the *Institutes,* in book 4 concerning the church, often refers to the church as the company of God's elect.[7]

b) The close connection of predestination and providence in Calvin's thought should be observed. For twenty years from 1539, predestination and providence shared a chapter of the *Institutes.* In the definitive 1559 edition, issued when Calvin thought his life might be drawing to a close, the treatment of providence was removed and placed at the end of the doctrine of God, the treatment of predestination coming after sanctification and justification.[8] The fact that this separation in the treatment of predestination and providence took place, though significant, need not be taken as a sign that Calvin had abandoned his commitment to the close connection of these two concepts.

To Calvin, providence is the effective care God exercises over the whole of his creation, down to the last detail. Like predestination, it entails an eternal decree:

> "What he had from eternity foreseen, approved, decreed, he pursues in uninterrupted tenor."[9]

Providence and predestination depend upon an absolute and hidden will of God, which is "the cause of all things" and is different, as far as it appears to humans, from the will revealed in Scripture for the direction of their faith and obedience. Inferior causes are used by providence, the chief cause. Providence employs human beings, but without removing their own responsibility, since they are acted upon in accordance with their own nature. It is so active that the concept of "permission" is inadequate to describe it. Thus, while predestination differs from providence in that it involves the sending of the Spirit to change our natures from bad to good, and so works in opposition to, instead of in accordance with, the existing order, it still shares the same basic character as a pretemporal, causal decision of God, omnipotently fulfilled in time.[10]

Indications of the inseparability of predestination and providence are found in the records of the Bolsec controversy.[11] The Geneva pastors' *Registres* for 1551 show that Jerome Bolsec perceived that the two doctrines were of a piece according to Calvin, and he began his attack on Calvin's doctrine of predestination by opposing his providence teaching. In reply, Calvin and his fellow pastors were perfectly willing to defend the two doctrines as one.

The *Registres*, Friday 16 October 1551, record that Bolsec began to put forward "his false propositions about election and reprobation". He vigorously asserted "that those who place an eternal will in God by which he has ordained some to life and others to death make a tyrant of him". He claimed that this concept of predestination was supported by twisting certain passages of Scripture, and referred especially to Proverbs 16.4, "God has made all things for his own glory, even the wicked for the day of wickedness". Bolsec questioned Calvin's use of this text to teach a providential rule of God in which God's will is the necessity of all things, which, to Bolsec, implied divine authorship of sin. In the first point of their report of what Bolsec had said, the pastors stated that he had claimed that a new opinion was being propagated in Geneva, namely that before the creation of the world, without foresight of who would or would not believe, God had determined that some would be saved and some condemned. Bolsec was attacking the notion of a pretemporal, absolute, causal decree of God, whether understood in terms of a general providence, or a predestination to salvation or condemnation.

Several days later, developing his criticism of Calvin's doctrine of predestination-providence in a series of written questions addressed directly to the reformer, he demanded to know how God, who is good, could will the sin of Adam, or any other sins. Challenging Calvin's doctrine of two divine wills (expounded under both providence and predestination in the *Institutes*) Bolsec wrote,

> "He should explain how God can be said to be simple, seeing he says that there are two wills in God, and how there can be a union in him between two contraries, to will and not to will, to have pleasure and not to have pleasure, to ordain and to forbid the same thing."

Calvin's response to Bolsec's articles commenced with a defence of Zwingli's *De Providentia*, which Bolsec had assailed. It continued with an attempt at giving a metaphysical explanation of how God can ordain sin without being the author of it. Calvin then proceeded to insist on the priority of election over faith. Thus it was evident throughout Bolsec's attack and Calvin's defence that the Genevan reformer's doctrines of providence and predestination were perceived as belonging, and standing or falling, together.

Concerning the Eternal Predestination of God (1552) was directed against the arguments of Pighius and Georgius, and, with Bolsec in mind, concludes with a section on providence. This is a further confirmation that Calvin's position was close to that of Thomas Aquinas, who held that, "Predestination is a part of providence". Consequently F. Wendel can state that, in Calvin, "Predestination can in fact be regarded as in some respects a particular application of the more general notion of Providence."[12]

A noteworthy instance of the merging of predestination and providence can be seen in Calvin's view of those who do not hear the gospel. God's providential deprivation of such people is to be viewed as an expression of the predestination which has destined salvation for a part only of the human race:

> "The covenant of life is not preached equally among all men...This variety...also serves the decision of God's eternal election."[13]

The significance of the predestination-providence connection, in that both are traced back to an eternal, absolute and causal decree which is infallibly revealed in history, is that election cannot be understood in this way as a divine decision regarding the human race, revealed uniquely and surprisingly in Christ. It must also be a matter of causal determination of individual destinies revealed by effects (the conversion of some and non-conversion of others). Scope is thereby given for understanding God's intention concerning the scope of redemption in terms of its effects in time. As will be seen, Calvin was capable of sometimes measuring the scope of Christ's death by observable effects. Many of his followers would do so without inhibition.

c) The relocation of predestination in the 1559 *Institutes*, to follow the work of Christ as mediator, sanctification and justification, shows Calvin's final decision as to the best place for the consideration of this theme. It belongs to the doctrine of salvation. This placing of predestination reinforced the Reformation insistence that salvation is by grace alone. The believer is justified by God's grace, through faith, not by his own works. This faith is God's gift, granted to some rather than others, not on account of any superior quality of doing or willing, but in accordance with God's eternal and free election. Thus in his opening paragraph in the section on predestination, Calvin explained:

> "We shall never be clearly persuaded, as we ought to be, that our salvation flows from the wellspring of God's free mercy, until we come to know his eternal election, which illumines God's grace by this contrast:- that he...gives to some what he denies to others."

Indeed the chief concern of the whole section on election is evidently to assert election as the final answer to any who would attempt to give to human merit even the tiniest place. The enormous pastoral value of election, in destroying pride and building assurance of the final salvation of believers, is constantly emphasized.[14]

Christ and Election

The efforts of scholars like Niesel to establish the christocentricity of Calvin's theology have been referred to already. The reformer certainly made a great effort to relate his doctrine of election to Christ. Christ is presented as the elect one. Repeating Augustine, Calvin asserted the gratuitous election of the humanity of Christ and pointed to it as "the clearest mirror of free election". As God, Christ can also be said to be the author of election, along with the Father, though this insight is not developed.[15]

More prominent is the insistence that our election is "in Christ". Basing his comment on Ephesians I.4, he explained,

> "Since among all the offspring of Adam, the Heavenly Father found nothing worthy of his election, he turned his eyes upon his Anointed, to choose from that body as members those whom he was to take into the fellowship of life."

Similarly,

> "Those whom God has adopted as his sons, are said to have been chosen not in themselves, but in his Christ (Eph.I.4); for unless he could love them in him, he could not honor them..."[16]

God could not love us in and of ourselves, because we were unworthy, but he loved and accepted his incarnate Son, who sustains the office of mediator, ("his Anointed") and extends this favour to us.

In the above citation, and frequently elsewhere, love and election are equated by Calvin. He returned several times to the problem of how we can be said to have been loved and elected by God and at the same time to have his wrath resting on us. For, he pointed out, on John 3.16 and Ephesians I.4, God's love precedes our reconciliation through Christ, and, on 2 Corinthians 5.19, he presented the relationship between love and redemption as one of "cause" producing "effect". However, God's love must not be considered in abstraction from Christ.

> "My answer is that we were loved from before the foundation of the world, but not apart from Christ."[17]

Thus redemption can be viewed as an expression of the love and election of God. Election necessitates Christ, in that a mediator is required in order to bring sinners to God. But this does not mean that there has to be a mediator simply as a means to save the elect, for it pleased God that Christ should have a people to be his body. The elect constitute the body of which Christ is the head. Election and Christ are inseparable. There is eternally in the mind of God a bond between the elect and Christ,

> "the Head, in whom the Heavenly Father has gathered his elect together, and has joined them to himself by an indissoluble bond."

Christ is not presented, then, as simply subordinate to, or executor of, election, the fulfiller of a decree made independently of him.

Calvin treated Christ and election together because they belong together in the purpose of God, and also because they cannot be separated in human knowledge and experience: we can neither comprehend the love and election of God, nor consciously participate in them, except by looking to Christ. Thus the path to speculation about the love of God is blocked. It can only be considered and enjoyed in Christ. In this sense Christ is the "mirror of election".

Perhaps the chief use Calvin makes of the concept of "election in Christ" is to exclude human merit from the appropriation of salvation. To be chosen in Christ is made to stand opposite to being chosen on the basis of our own worthiness. In this sense too, Christ is the mirror of election, for we cannot find meritorious grounds for our election in ourselves, but only when we look to Christ.

> "Therefore when he would adopt us before the worlde was made, it was requisite that Jesus Christ should be as it were betwixt us, and that wee shoulde be chosen in his person, for he is the welbeloved sonne...he is ye true looking glasse wherein we must behold our election...without Jesus Christ, if we hear speaking of his everlasting purpose, we cannot but be afraid...But when we knowe that all grace resteth in Jesus Christ, then we may assure our selves, that God loved us, even though we were unworthy."[18]

In every way, then, the love of God, election and the person and work of Christ belong together. God's election is expressed in the person and work of Christ. The elect are loved with the love the Father has to Christ, and could not be loved apart from him. Their election constitutes them one body with Christ. They are elected to a salvation to be secured by the Mediator. It might be thought that such close co-ordination between Christ and election would lead Calvin to restrict the extent of the redeeming work of Christ to the elect. Indeed, Rainbow, having convincingly demonstrated Calvin's linkage between election and Christ, states, "This all points logically at the doctrine of limited redemption."[19] It will be shown below, however, that the position was not so straightforward.

In spite of Calvin's evident concern to present a christocentric doctrine of election, it must be said that he was not able to make Christ the key to, or revelation of, the whole meaning of election. For it was basic to his understanding that election involves a selection of certain individuals to be saved. Why some have been chosen as opposed to others is not revealed in Christ any more than it is explained by reference to human merit. For all Calvin's pointing to Christ and warning against speculation, he nevertheless believed the theologian to be in possession of knowledge about the existence of a "dreadful decree", above and beyond Christ, a decree rendering inevitable the salvation of some and condemnation of others. So sometimes Calvin could say that behind Christ lay not only love but also a hidden will:

> "Many testimonies of Scripture...place the first foundation of the divine love towards us in Christ...But we should remember...that the secret love in which our heavenly Father embraced us to Himself is, since it flows from His eternal good pleasure, precedent to all other causes."

The terms "secret", "good pleasure" and "cause" are all used often by Calvin in connection with the inscrutable divine decree.[20] This element of his thought, according to which the destinies of all have been fixed before the world began, might be expected to point towards a limited scope of the work of Christ.[21] Before coming to that conclusion, however, it is necessary to consider what Calvin taught about the promise of the gospel.

THE PROMISE OF THE GOSPEL

For Calvin, election implied particularism. When he came to speak of the application of Christ's saving work, however, there was a universalistic element in his teaching.[22] The work of Christ is for the human race, we are told. At the same time, in and of itself, it benefits no-one. It must first be applied.

> "As long as Christ remains outside of us, and we are separated from him, all that he has suffered and done for the salvation of the human race remains useless and of no value to us."[23]

Faith is that which unites us to Christ, by the Spirit, and the message of the gospel is that to which faith responds.[24] This message has the character of promise to everyone who hears. The promise is founded on Christ, and all the promises of God to us are comprehended in Christ. They are for all, not for those only who embrace them, and their character as testimony to the grace of God is not nullified by human unresponsiveness:

> "For although the effectiveness of the promises only appears when they have aroused faith in us, yet the force and peculiar nature of the promises are never extinguished by our unfaithfulness and ingratitude. Therefore, since the Lord, by his promises, invites man not only to receive the fruits of his kindness but also to think about them, he at the same time declares his love to man."[25]

In an external sense the word is universally sufficient, and its lack of effect in some is to be attributed to their own resistance to it:

> "This bare and external proof of the Word of God should have been amply sufficient to engender faith, did not our blindness and perversity prevent it."

That for Calvin the promise of the gospel is genuinely addressed by God to all is convincingly demonstrated in his own evangelistic preaching. His sermons on Isaiah 53 contain abundant evidence of his understanding of the universality of the promise:

> "God does not wait for us to ask him to sprinkle us; He takes the initiative and offers Himself freely and sets before us His only Son with His teaching. And in this He shows Himself so worthy of love, that He ought to be received without any argument. Should we not all be inflamed with zeal that makes us despise everything else and embrace this Redeemer who has appeared? But far from that being the case, hardly one in ten of those who hear are touched to the quick."[26]

Although, unlike Bucer, Calvin did not teach that all should believe themselves to be elect, he clearly urged all to consider themselves loved, called and in receipt of the promise. The fact that nine out of ten could be said to spurn the love held out to them in Christ demonstrates that Calvin did not confine the promise to the elect only. It also shows that he did not consistently equate "love" and "election". However, he often went on to say that God sends his Spirit to the elect alone, to enable them to respond to the promise in faith. In the light of this, it could even be said:

> "By so promising he merely means that his mercy is extended to all, provided they seek after it and implore it. But only those he has illumined do this. And he illumines those he has predestined to salvation."

Calvin was well aware that his opponents asserted that "the universality of the promise removes the distinction of special grace". His answer was not to deny this universality, but simply to assert the evidence of experience, "that all are called to repentance and faith by outward preaching, yet that the Spirit of repentance and faith is not given to all."[27]

The apparent contradiction between a sincere universal promise and an unchangeable decree of particular election was maintained. The two are held together in Christ, since he is the Christ of divine election and divine promise. The love of God, because manifested in Christ, can be seen in both election and the promise. Beyond Christ as the unifying factor in this apparent contradiction, however, an ultimate harmony between the two is hinted at in the assertion that the very genuineness of the offer of Christ, with the correspondingly real ingratitude of the reprobate, ultimately serve the decree of predestination:

> "God's boundless goodness is already manifesting itself but not to the salvation of all; for a heavier judgement remains upon the wicked because they reject the testimony of God's love. And God also, to display his glory, withdraws the effectual working of his Spirit from them."[28]

Furthermore, the fact that particular election in Christ is said to be eternal, whereas the promise of Christ simply operates within time suggests a priority of the former over the latter.

The themes of particular election and universal promise are basic elements in Calvin's thought. They meet, but can hardly be said to be harmonized, in Christ. A tendency to point towards the resolution of the tension in the direction of an absolute and particularistic decree has been observed, and will be seen again.

THE PLACE OF ELECTION IN GOD'S SAVING WILL

In approaching Calvin's presentation of the extent of the atonement it is useful to ask whether he saw election as God's first or last act in the matter of salvation. In other words, is eternal election the source from which Christ, the preaching of the gospel, faith and all else in the work of salvation flow, or is it that which merely explains the existence of faith in some individuals as opposed to others? Is it that which lies at the root of all the saving grace of God, or does it enter in only at the point of application, to be understood as the *ex post facto* explanation of conversion? This question was to become crucial in the debates about the extent of the atonement after Calvin, coming to the fore in the Amyraldian controversy of the mid-seventeenth century. For if the person and work of Christ are subordinate to an election which embraces part of mankind only, the whole redeeming work of Christ is bound to be perceived as limited in intent. If, however, particularism enters in only at the stage of application, the work of Christ can be seen as having a wider reference. Commenting on the seventeenth-century controversy, Armstrong has maintained that just as for Calvin, so for Amyraut, election was merely the explanation of conversion.[29] It is necessary to examine this claim.

A first impression from the *Institutes* may be that Calvin adopted an *ex post facto* view, for he begins his treatment of predestination with the facts of experience, pointing to the observable inequality in the response to the gospel. Positive responses are not due to the good will of some. Rather, left to themselves, all would reject the gospel, because of the corruption of human nature. The same pattern can be found elsewhere:

> "We are all of us so contrarie...to God, that we cannot but resist him. So then, how can it be that we may be partakers of...salvation...unlesse God draw us to it by his holie spirit?"

To have given Christ for our salvation, and even to have sent the word to us, is inadequate to accomplish our conversion:

> "Therefore GOD must goe further to bring us to salvation, he must not onely appoint men and send men to teach us faithfully, but he must play ye maister within our heartes."[30]

As can be seen, Calvin felt comfortable in presenting election as the explanation of why some believe, taking as his starting point the facts of experience, coupled with the doctrine of the will's bondage. Indeed, there are passages in which he can speak of God's approach to people as entirely equal, right up to the point where he gives to some, but not others, the ability to respond. Notable among these is the following, written against Pighius:

> "That it [the gospel] is salvific for all I do not deny. But the question is whether the Lord in His counsel here destines salvation equally for all. All are equally called to penitence and faith; the same mediator is set forth for all to reconcile them to the Father - so much is evident. But it is equally evident that nothing can be perceived except by faith....the greater part remain unbelieving because God honours with his illumination none but those whom He will...The mercy of God is offered equally to both kinds of men, so that those who are not inwardly taught are rendered only inexcusable...we are always forced back on the question whether an equal power to believe is conferred upon all...Now experience teaches that the Spirit is not bestowed on all."[31]

In such statements as these it is difficult to discern any significant difference between Calvin's doctrines of predestination and effectual calling. What does election add to effectual calling, if election only functioned in his theology as a way of attributing conversion to the grace of God, and ruling out free will ?

After this presentation of Calvin's teaching on election as if it were God's last act in the plan of salvation, an act which reckons with the human inability to respond to the gospel, it must be said that this was not the whole of Calvin's understanding. Effective calling is not synonymous with election, but "displays" the election hidden behind it and "serves the decision of God's eternal election". There are times when election is that which governs not only man's response to the work and word of Christ, but that work and word themselves. Indeed, the experiential starting point, referred to above, concerns not only the response to the gospel, but also the fact that only some hear it, and this too is attributed to election. The fact that there is a gospel to be preached at all is dependent on election, for "the preaching of the gospel springs from the fountain of election". Satanic opposition to the doctrine of election is not to be wondered at, "seeing it is the foundation of our salvation."[32]

Moreover, Calvin's doctrine of reprobation and his teaching of God's foreordination of the fall are conclusive proof that for him election can be seen as standing at the head of all God's purposes. While he commences his exposition of reprobation in the *Institutes* in such a way as to lead the reader to think that his sole concern is to cut off the possibility of salvation by merit, he proceeds further. Reprobates are not merely left to themselves:

> "The fact that the reprobate do not obey God's Word when it is made known to them will be justly charged against the malice and depravity of their hearts, provided it be added at the same time that they have been given over to this depravity because they have been raised up by the just but inscrutable judgement of God, to show forth his glory in their condemnation."

The fall of Adam was a step along the road of the reprobate to condemnation, and of the elect to salvation, since it was necessary for there to be a corrupt human race out of which some could be elected:

> "The decree is dreadful, indeed I confess. Yet no-one can deny that God foreknew what end man was to have before he created him, and consequently foreknew because he so ordained by his decree."[33]

Here predestination is presented not merely as related to helpless man's response to the gospel, but as determining the fall and willing the depravity of mankind. Calvin's exposition of Romans 9 is restrained in comparison with later "Calvinistic" exegesis, nevertheless it proceeds on the assumption of an eternal decree fixing the destiny of all people with the ultimate aim of declaring God's glory, the glory of his justice in the case of the reprobate, and of his mercy in the case of the elect.[34] It is clear that, for Calvin, election is more than that which distinguishes between persons at the point of their response to the gospel. It is part of a larger absolute decree, embracing reprobation, the fall, and indeed everything that takes place in the world.[35]

It has been shown, then, that Calvin often approached election as the *ex post facto* explanation of conversion. This understanding left room for a logically prior universal promise and was capable of being combined with a doctrine of universal atonement. However, Calvin was not confined to this perspective. Although election could be presented as God's "last" act, it was also the fountain and foundation of the whole work of salvation.[36] As such, it was the grace which constituted Christ as mediator, a synonym for the love of God. Seen as a decree to save part of humanity only, and occupying this primary position, it would seem to imply a limited scope to the whole of God's saving activity in Christ. In fact, Calvin's two ways of relating election to soteriology do not harmonize easily and ensured that an uncomfortably dual approach would emerge when he tried to define for whom Christ had died.

THE TWO WILLS OF GOD

The tension between God's universal and particular provisions for salvation was explained, though not resolved, in terms of the apparent existence of two wills in God.[37] This distinction was by no means original to Calvin, for the division of God's will into the *voluntas beneplaciti* and the *voluntas signi* was an established feature of the scholastic theology of the Middle Ages.[38] The twofold nature of the will of God in the *Institutes* appears, significantly, in the section on providence. It is explained that, while God's will is found in his law, "he has another hidden will which may be compared to an abyss". This will is:

> "His wonderful method of governing the universe...rightly called an abyss, because while it is hidden from us, we ought to reverently adore it...we see how he [Moses] bids us not only to direct our study to meditate upon the law, but to look up to God's secret Providence with awe."[39]

The concept of two wills is necessary because there are many things done by God's providence which are forbidden by God's law.

In the section on predestination, Calvin returned to the same distinction.[40] The fact that he did so should dispel any doubts as to the close interrelation of predestination and providence in his theology. In asserting that the eternal appointment of elect and reprobate proceeds from the will of God, Calvin had to explain why certain texts of Scripture appear to teach that God wills the salvation of all. These texts were Ezekiel 18.23, 1 Timothy 2.4, 2 Peter 3.9 and Matthew 23.34.[41] We will examine the last of these.

In Matthew 23.37-39 Christ's lament over Jerusalem and his willingness to gather its people is recorded in moving terms. Calvin did not seek to eliminate the difficulty of an unfulfilled will of God by asserting that Christ was speaking only according to his human nature, but specifically rejected that solution. The key to Christ's words is to be found in remembering that, although God's will is essentially one, there are "many passages in which God clothes himself with human affections and descends beneath his proper majesty". Consequently, "to our apprehension the will of God is manifold". Thus Christ was revealing a will other than the "counsel of God" in his lament, and although this will remained unfulfilled, "it does not follow that by the wickedness of men the counsel of God was frustrated". The *Harmony of the Gospels* elaborates considerably.[42]

> "Whenever the Word of God is put before us He bares His breast to us with maternal kindness... Accordingly our rough nature is quite monstrous, if we do not let ourselves be gathered by Him."

Turning to those who used the passage to teach free will and abolish God's secret predestination Calvin explained his "two wills" device at length:

> "Seeing that in His Word He calls all alike to salvation, and this is the object of preaching, that all should take refuge in His faith and protection, it is right to say that he wishes all to gather to Him. Now the nature of the Word shows us that here there is no description of the secret counsel of God - just His wishes [*Non ergo hic nobis arcanum Dei consilium, sed voluntas quae perspicitur ex verbi natura, describitur*]."

In view of the glowing terms in which Calvin speaks of the love and tenderness of God revealed to all through the gospel, it is impossible to doubt his concern to maintain a genuine universal promise. However, it continually becomes apparent that his concern to safeguard the eternal, hidden will of God is even greater. For in the process of expounding Matthew 23.37-39 he lets us know what our ultimate frame of reference must be in considering difficult biblical statements about the will of God.

> "The will of God as mentioned here must be judged by the result."

Furthermore, at the end of this exposition, the reader is informed that the need to speak of two wills is due to our incapacity for understanding the secret will.

> "Because our minds cannot plumb the profound depths of His secret election to suit our infirmity, the will of God is set before us as double."

Thus while the tension between the hidden and revealed will of God is maintained, Calvin lets it be known that for him, the secret will stands not so much on an equal footing with the revealed, but behind it, in an incomprehensible way, as the ultimate truth about the will of God. As confirmation of this it can be pointed out that in leading up to his exposition of the lament over Jerusalem, Calvin explains to the critic who demands to know why God should send his messengers to the reprobates, that his secret plan is to render them inexcusable and so bring them to ruin. Thus, the whole discussion is set in a context in which the revealed will is ultimately subsidiary to the secret decree.

The fact that he opens his exposition of Ezekiel 18.23 in the *Institutes* with the following assertion indicates further which will of God had priority in Calvin's thought:

> "This passage is violently twisted, if the will of God, mentioned by the prophet, is opposed to His eternal plan, by which he has distinguished the elect from the reprobate."[43]

It becomes clear that Calvin could not use the concept of two wills to explain difficult texts about God's will, but only to classify them into two groups. Into one category went all statements that present God's saving will as limited in scope and effective. Into the other went those that portray God's saving will as universal and ineffective. By maintaining that reconciliation between these two groups of statements is humanly impossible, although in itself and beyond human comprehension God's will is one, he felt justified in maintaining both positions. To Calvin it was the way to do justice to the biblical data, but it left a grave difficulty, never convincingly addressed by him: how can Christ be regarded as an adequate revelation of God, if what is seen and heard in Christ has to be so severely qualified by considerations of a secret will? To his opponents the "two wills" device was an avoidance of the issues. To some of his successors, such as Theodore Beza, it was a solution entailing too sharp a contradiction. They found it necessary to resolve the problem firmly in favour of the secret will. It is possible to detect already in Calvin certain leanings in that direction. On the other hand, we cannot accept Rainbow's thesis that Calvin was so consistently governed by God's predestinating will that to him the universal offer of the gospel was "only and simply the public preaching of the gospel to all men".[44] The fact is that there was a deep and uncomfortable dualism in Calvin's thought, which made itself abundantly clear in his comments relating to the extent of the atonement.

FOR WHOM DID CHRIST DIE?

It is now possible to assess Calvin's teaching on the scope of Christ's work. The strains between promise and election, between secret and revealed will of God, and between election regarded as the first or last act in God's plan of salvation, all contribute to an absence of consistency at this point. It is not surprising that both those who have invoked Calvin on behalf of "limited atonement" and those who have claimed him for "general redemption" have been able to find support in his writings.

The Nature of the Atonement

There are some basic similarities between Calvin's and Anselm's explanation of the cross. The *Institutes* (2.12.3) describe humanity as owing God both obedience, and punishment for his sin. Christ appeared in order to suffer the penalty of death due to us. Since God cannot suffer death, and since the debt was owed by the human race, it was necessary that Christ should appear in human nature. In view of this explanation of the incarnation, and the understanding of the atonement in terms of payment of an outstanding debt, Wendel claims that "we have good right to regard this last passage as a classic expression of the doctrine of satisfaction as it had been current ever since St. Anselm". Indeed, Calvin frequently used the terms "satisfaction" and "merit", drawn from the Anselmic tradition.[45]

While the Anselmic elements in Calvin's doctrine of the atonement are not to be denied, there is a significantly different emphasis in the reformer. P. van Buren has demonstrated the more thoroughly substitutionary nature of Calvin's doctrine.[46] Ideas of justice and penal substitution generally predominate over the Anselmic categories of honour and debt. To preserve God's freedom, Calvin echoed Nominalist thought and asserted that God might have found other ways to save us, though he added that the incarnation was the most fitting way. The trend of his teaching, however, was to present the death of Christ as a divine necessity for the expiation of human sin, without which we could not be saved. Christ took our nature, assumed our guilt, suffered our punishment and so reconciled us to God. Unlike Anselm, who derived the value of Christ's satisfaction from his divine nature, Calvin traced it to the will of God in his appointment, and his corresponding obedience.

> "In discussing Christ's merit, we do not consider the beginning of merit to be in him, but we go back to God's ordinance, the first cause. For God solely of his own good pleasure appointed Him Mediator to obtain salvation for us."[47]

J.F.Jansen rightly pointed out, in contrast to Gustaf Aulen, that the classical theory of the atonement, with its theme of Christ as victor over all the powers of darkness, is prominent in Calvin. This fact is developed by Strehle, who maintains that, because Calvin gave prominence to this interpretation, he did not need to ask for whom Christ died. It is not apparent, however, that, in the framework of Calvin's predestinarian theology, there is no reason to ask for whom Christ was victorious. Moreover, the substitutionary element in Calvin's atonement doctrine, amply described by Van Buren, was not less prominent than the "victory" motif. It is helpful, however, to be reminded that Calvin considered Christ's work under the offices of prophet, priest and king, and not only as sacrificial victim.[48]

Universal Reconciliation

Calvin's freedom in presenting redemption in universal terms is undeniable, and is grounded in the person of Christ, in that, through his incarnation, Christ bears a relation to the whole human race:

> "The salvation provided by Christ is common to all mankind, for Christ, the Author of salvation, was begotten of Adam, the common father of us all."

It also relates to the universality of sin:

> "From the very fall of man He was needed by all...It would have done no good...if He had not been available to all without distinction."[49]

It may be granted that citations referring to "all", "the world", "mankind" and "the human race", do not prove that Calvin intended to speak of an unlimited universality, since he sometimes could assert that the terms "all" and "world" should be understood of "all sorts", "all peoples" or the church throughout the world.[50] Nevertheless, there are numerous places where an unrestricted universality must be intended. Among these are:

> "*To bear the sins* means to free those who have sinned from their guilt by his satisfaction. He says 'many' meaning 'all', as in Romans 5.15. It is of course certain that not all enjoy the fruits of Christ's death, but this happens because their unbelief hinders them."

> "The word 'many' is often as good as equivalent to 'all'. And in fact our Lord Jesus was offered to all the world. For it is not speaking of three or four when it says: 'God so loved the world, that he spared not his only Son'...Our Lord Jesus suffered for all and there is neither great nor small who is not inexcusable today, for we can obtain salvation in him. Unbelievers who turn away from Him and who deprive themselves of Him by their malice are today doubly culpable, for how will they excuse their ingratitude in not receiving the blessing in which they could share by faith?"

> "He willed in full measure to appear before the judgement seat of God His Father in the name and in the person of all sinners, being then ready to be condemned, inasmuch as He bore our burden."

> "He was there, as it were, in the person of all cursed ones and all transgressors, and of those who had deserved eternal death. Since then, Jesus Christ has this office, and He bears the burden of all those who had offended God mortally, that is why He keeps silence."[51]

In addition to such clear statements, it is significant that in his "Antidote to the Acts of the Council of Trent" Calvin wrote that he "would not touch" the assertion of the Council's Sixth Session that, "Though He died for all, all do not receive the benefit of His death". Furthermore, he showed no hesitation in repeating, without modification, the biblical statements about the possibility of some for whom Christ died perishing.[52]

Accomplished Reconciliation

In line with the whole thrust of the Protestant Reformation, Calvin regarded the work of redemption as performed *extra nos*. It is a work of God complete in itself and to which we can add nothing. He described it, therefore, in terms of actual accomplishment. In explaining how Christ performed the office of Redeemer, Calvin stated that, although God loved us from eternity, restoration, expiation and the cessation of separation from God were actually accomplished in the sacrifice of Christ.

> "The Spirit usually speaks in this way in the Scriptures: 'God was men's enemy until they were reconciled to grace by the death of Christ' (Rom.5.2). 'They were under a curse until their iniquity was atoned for by his sacrifice' (Gal.3.10,13)..."[53]

This manner of speaking has led some to conclude that Calvin must have held a limited atonement position. For since only the elect experience reconciliation with God through faith, it would have been inappropriate for Calvin to speak of the atonement in terms of actual reconciliation with reference to any other than the elect. Thus R.Nicole interprets Calvin's position: "What Christ has accomplished on the cross is not so much to secure the salvability of all humans, as actually to accomplish the salvation of those he does redeem."

Van Buren adopted the opposite approach to Calvin's description of the atonement in terms of actual accomplishment. Believing that Calvin taught universal atonement, he pointed out the apparent inconsistency of Calvin's teaching that only by faith does Christ's saving work, accomplished *extra nos*, have any benefit for anyone. He saw it as a weakness in Calvin's theology that, having stated universal atonement in absolute terms, he should make salvation conditional on faith.[54]

There are many passages in Calvin where the atonement is presented as something already wholly accomplished, and where it is hard to deny that Calvin was thinking in universal terms. To the extracts given above some further examples may be added:

"This redemption was procured by the blood of Christ, for by the sacrifice of His death all the sins of the world have been expiated."

"By His mediation God is satisfied and appeased, for He bore all the wickedness of all the sins of the world."

At the same time, however, Calvin could speak of reconciliation with God being accomplished in the experience of the individual through faith:

"God is reconciled to us as soon as we put our trust in the blood of Christ, because by faith we come to the possession of this benefit...Having just stated that God has been reconciled in Christ, he now adds that this reconciliation is brought to pass by faith."[55]

Some scholars have identified conditionalism in Calvin's theology, and have asserted that he had a concept of a conditional covenant between God and human beings, an embryonic form of later covenant theology. While it is true that Calvin occasionally called faith a condition, he did not regularly designate it in that way, nor does the notion of conditional covenant form a central plank in his theology. It appears a number of times in his expositions of God's covenant with Israel, and is extended to Christians because God's covenant is essentially one, but, significantly, the concept of conditional covenant does not receive distinct treatment in the *Institutes*. Even in his sermons Calvin was careful to stress that the covenant depends upon God's love and not upon us.[56] It is important to appreciate that Calvin frequently spoke of reconciliation in absolute terms, to emphasize that the work of Christ requires no addition from us. Accordingly, faith is a matter of being persuaded of, and accepting, the objective reality of the work of Christ, in no way supplementing that accomplished work. Calvin's considered definition of faith was,

"A firm and sure knowledge of the divine favour toward us."[57]

The fact that unbelief can prevent us from entering into the reconciliation accomplished by Christ does not call into question the reality and objectivity of that work. Rather,

"The moment we turn away even slightly from him, salvation, which rests firmly in him, gradually vanishes away. As a result, all those who do not repose in him voluntarily deprive themselves of all grace."[58]

R.A.Muller has rightly argued that Calvin used the terms 'expiation' and 'propitiation' to refer to the work of Christ in itself, but the terms redemption and reconciliation to denote both the work of Christ and the application of salvation.[59] Calvin could speak of reconciliation as objective and subjective, as indicated above, and even of "daily reconciliation"[60]. However, Muller's claim that on this basis Calvin spoke of a universal expiation and propitiation, but of a particular redemption and reconciliation cannot be substantiated, for the terminology of redemption and reconciliation is often applied in a universal context, for example on Mark 10.45.

> "He declares that His life was the price of our redemption. From this it follows that our reconciliation with God is free...'Many' is used, not for a definite number, but for a large number...And this is its meaning also in Romans 5.15, where Paul is not talking of a part of mankind but of the whole human race."

On the other hand, it is in commenting on a verse about "propitiation" that he feels it necessary to query whether "the sins of the whole world have been expiated?" It is in that place that one of his strong statements about the particularism of the atonement is to be found: "Under the word 'all' he does not include the reprobate."[61] While Muller is right to detect both universal and particular aspects in Calvin's teaching on the atonement, it is not possible to categorize Calvin's use of words in this respect, and he over-simplifies when he concludes that "this distinction well fits what is loosely called 'limited atonement' not only in Calvin's thought but in later Reformed theology".

Effective Reconciliation

Just as it is possible to give many examples of Calvin speaking of atonement in universal terms, so it is possible to give many references where Christ is described as redeeming his elect, his church, his people, his body.[62] These are usually incidental references, but there are a few places where Calvin explained why he sometimes saw the work of Christ in restricted terms. The explanation is that it does not bear fruit in all people, due not to any inherent lack in the work of Christ, but to the absence of faith in those who hear the gospel. While Calvin sometimes stops his explanation at this point, it is standard practice with him to go on to add that, faith being the gift of God, the effectiveness or non-effectiveness of the cross is ultimately dependent on the election or non-election of God.

That the effective application of Christ's work was a primary concern with Calvin is shown in the way he treated the summary of the extent of the atonement handed down from the medieval scholastic theologians. It had been stated by Peter Lombard that the work of Christ was sufficient for all, but effective only for the elect. Calvin could give formal assent to this formula, and could make occasional use of the concept of Christ's all-sufficiency. For example, he exhorted his hearers,

> "Let us not fear to come to Him in great numbers, and each one of us bring his neighbours, seeing that he is sufficient to save us all."[63]

Nevertheless, he was not attracted to the formula as such, for he scarcely ever mentioned it, and when he did, it was with qualified approval only. This was probably because he was concerned about the will of God in the application of redemption. Georgius had appealed to 1 John 2.2, where Christ is described as the propitiation for our sins "and not for ours only, but for the sins of the whole world". He had argued that "world" must include the reprobate. Calvin replied that the scholastic formula was an inadequate one to answer Georgius, and went on to explain why:

> "For this, the common solution does not avail, that Christ suffered sufficiently for all, but efficaciously only for the elect...For the present question is not how great the power of Christ is or what efficacy it has in itself, but to whom He gives Himself to be enjoyed. If possession lies in faith and faith emanates from the Spirit of adoption, it follows that only he is reckoned in the number of God's children who will be a partaker of Christ; the evangelist John sets forth the office of Christ as nothing else than by his death to gather the children of God into one (Jn.11.52). Hence, we conclude that though reconciliation is offered to all through him, yet the benefit is peculiar to the elect, that they may be gathered into the society of life."[64]

The reason why the traditional formula was inadequate was that it did not explicitly recognize the sovereign will of God in the application of salvation. It must be borne in mind that the word "elect" in the formula was open to interpretations other than Calvin's and that his opponents could happily use the same formula, understanding "elect" as those foreseen by God as exercising faith through the power of free will. Thus Calvin found the formula insufficiently clear about the very issue at stake between himself and his opponents: whether the acceptance or rejection of the benefits of Christ's death is to be attributed ultimately to human or divine will.

From Calvin's comments on this formula it is plainly apparent that he was willing to place the work of Christ in conjunction with the electing purpose of God, and so present the atonement as having a particular as well as a universal aspect. Which of these facets was more prominent at any time depended on the context. Particular redemption appears in the context of election, while universal atonement is usually set forth in the context of the promise. This double aspect is illustrated in the reference to "reconciliation...offered to all through him" and "the benefit...peculiar to the elect" in the above citation.

Calvin's exposition of several crucial passages of Scripture brings these two facets to light repeatedly.

a) 1 John 2.2

Just as in his explanation of this passage in the *Eternal Predestination*, so in his *Commentary*,[65] Calvin cited, and then left to one side, the sufficient-efficient formula, with the explanation:

> "Although I allow the truth of this, I deny that it fits this passage, for John's purpose was only to make this blessing common to the whole Church. Therefore, under the word 'all' he does not include the reprobate, but refers

> to all who would believe and those who were scattered through various regions of the earth."

For reasons he did not, and perhaps could not, make clear, Calvin chose to interpret this passage from the perspective of election ("reprobate") and effective application ("whole Church") and accordingly restricted the scope of Christ's propitiation. It must not be forgotten, though, that at the outset he had granted the truth of the "sufficient for all" position, although denying it to be suitable to this passage.

In contrast to this explanation of Christ's death "for the world" in 1 John 2, is Calvin's exposition of John 1.29, in which he co-ordinated the universality of redemption with the universality of sin:

> "And when he says *the sin of the world* he extends this kindness indiscriminately to the whole human race, that the Jews might not think the Redeemer has been sent to them alone. From this we infer that the whole world is bound in the same condemnation, and that since all men without exception are guilty of unrighteousness before God, they have need of reconciliation."[66]

Here Calvin could speak of the world which is guilty and for which Christ is the sacrificial lamb, as "all men without exception" because he was thinking of the universal promise, for he continued:

> "Now it is for us to embrace the blessing offered to all, that each may make up his mind that there is nothing to hinder him from finding reconciliation in Christ, if only, led by faith, he comes to Him."[67]

Again, Calvin's choice of whether to expound such passages from the point of view of particular election or universal promise often appears arbitrary, and reveals a serious weakness in his approach.

b) 1 Timothy 2.3-6

In his *Commentary* Calvin did not place much emphasis on the universality of Christ's ransom according to this passage, except to state that,

> "The universal term "all" must always be referred to classes of men but never to individuals."[68]

This caution was given on the basis of the doctrine of election. It has already become clear that Calvin frequently departed from his own rule, and he did not provide an exegetical justification of why he felt compelled to understand the word as "all without distinction" rather than "all without exception" in 1 Timothy 2. The answer may well be that this text had been so interpreted by Augustine against the Pelagians and Calvin may simply have been loyally continuing a predestinarian exegetical tradition.[69] Certainly he approached the passage with a view to combating "the beastliness of them that abuse this place of Paule, to make the election of our

God, a thing of naught".[70] In his *Sermons* on the passage Calvin seems to swing back and forth between generic and unrestricted universality. He was at pains to assert that "all" means "all classes" and so the obvious conclusion is that he was maintaining that Christ ransomed only the elect, or at least, believers. Yet he also made many statements about the offer of salvation through Christ to all, where "all" includes those who reject it. The clearest of these is:

> "Behold the Turkes, which cast away the grace which was purchased for all the world by Jesus Christ: ...the Jewes...the Papistes... And all they are as well shut out, and banished from the redemption that is purchased for us, as if Jesus Christ had never come into this world. And why so? For they have not this witnesse, *That Jesus Christe is their Redeemer*...And thus we see now, howe men are not partakers of this benefite, whiche was purchased them by our Lorde Jesus Christ."[71]

How is it that Calvin could teach limited and universal redemption in the same place? Only by appreciating that he viewed the atonement from two vantage points can this apparent confusion be understood. From the perspective of election, Christ died for "all sorts" but not all individuals. From the perspective of the promise of the gospel, he died for all the world, even for those who do not participate in the purchased benefit. This interpretation is confirmed in that, in his sermon on v.4 concerning God's will to save all people, Calvin dwelt on his distinction between the secret and revealed will of God. In this double will, corresponding to the particular election and universal promise, is to be found the basis for speaking of Christ's work as both particular and universal.

Calvin's statements limiting the extent of the atonement are concerned with its effective application, which itself is dependent on the electing purpose of God. This concern is conveyed, in a positive way, in the following words, which may serve as a conclusion to this section:

> "God will win the victory by His infinite goodness. In short, the Prophet wanted in this passage to say that not only were the death, cross and passion of our Lord Jesus Christ sufficient for the salvation of the world, but that God will make them efficacious and that we shall see the fruit of them and even feel and experience it."[72]

Sacrifice and Intercession

It is difficult to accept R.T.Kendall's theory that Calvin taught that Christ's sacrifice was for all, but his intercession for the elect.[73] Examples of the intercessory work of Christ presented by Calvin as both particular and universal can be found,[74] in just the same way as with the atonement, and for the same reasons, namely that sometimes the intercession of Christ is set within the electing purpose of God, and sometimes set forth as an element of the promise on which all sinners are called to rely. In the same way, the kingship of Christ, founded upon his work of redemption, is presented as having reference to the elect and to all people, indeed, to all creation. It is true, however, that as the focus moves from the cross to the resurrection, so it moves from the accomplishment of redemption to its application by the exalted Lord, and accordingly the particularistic elements become more prominent.[75]

CONCLUSION

Several stress points in Calvin's theology have been identified. A tension between universal promise and particular election lay behind his comments bearing on the extent of the atonement. This tension need not have caused any qualification to his teaching of universal atonement had he understood election merely as an *ex post facto* explanation of effectual calling. It has been shown that, although he frequently presented election in that way, he also viewed it as God's first act in the plan of salvation, the cause of Christ's coming into the world. Thus sometimes he spoke of redemption as limited by election, while at other times as unrestricted. In this way the reformer left to his successors a theology that was indeed a *complexio oppositorum*, and therefore inherently unstable. They, like contemporary interpreters, would find it difficult not to ease the tensions in one way or another.

It has also been shown that there are elements in the way Calvin handled these strains which foreshadowed the direction in which his successors would resolve them, namely in a particularistic direction. These elements are as follows:

a) Predestination and providence are closely allied, and in matters of both providence and predestination God's will may be judged from its result. From the fact that not all hear the gospel, and of those that hear not all believe, Calvin read the particularism of God's ultimate intentions.

b) Of the "two wills" of God, the absolute and particular will is the more basic. The revealed, universal will has something of the nature of an appearance, whilst the absolute is that which is certain and unquestionable. In the end, the universal promise and revealed will of God serve the decrees of election and reprobation by manifesting the wickedness and inexcusability of the wicked in their rejection of the same.

c) The fact that election is presented as that which is eternal, whereas the promise has its place in God's temporal dealings with the world seems to locate election more firmly than the promise in the character of the eternal God.

d) While election and promise are both tied to Christ, Christ is not the whole meaning of election as he is of the promise, for there is no revelation in Christ as to why one should be chosen as opposed to another. The election of certain persons lies behind Christ, and so, in election, we have to do with *Deus absconditus*.[76] It was hardly possible that any number of warnings against investigating the secret will of God could hold back Calvin's successors, in seeking to understand a doctrine so prominent in his theology, from that dangerous but fascinating exercise. In the scope thus given for speculation and logical deduction, a theology more consistently particularistic than Calvin's own was almost bound to emerge.

So, in developing elements in Calvin's theology further, many of his successors would define the extent of the atonement in strictly limited terms, believing that they were adhering to Calvin's own position in doing so.

Chapter Two

Notes

1 P. Helm, *Calvin and the Calvinists*, Edinburgh 1982; R.Nicole, "John Calvin's View of the Extent of the Atonement", *WTJ* 47(1985) pp.197-225; Godfrey, op.cit., pp.80-82; R.A.Muller, *Christ and the Decree: christology and predestination in Reformed theology from Calvin to Perkins*, Durham (N. Carolina) 1986, pp.33-35; Rainbow, op.cit.; P. van Buren, *Christ in Our Place: the substitutionary character of Calvin's doctrine of reconciliation*, Edinburgh 1957, pp.102-106; B. Hall, "Calvin against the Calvinists", in G.E.Duffield (ed.), *John Calvin*, Abingdon 1966, pp.19-37; Armstrong, op.cit., pp.137-138 n.58; Kendall, op.cit., pp.13-18; M.C. Bell, *Calvin and Scottish Theology: the doctrine of assurance*, Edinburgh 1985 pp.13-19; J.W.Anderson, "The Grace of God and the Non-elect in Calvin's Commentaries and Sermons", Th.D. New Orleans Baptist Theological Seminary 1976, pp.104-146; C.Daniel, "Hyper-Calvinism and John Gill", Ph.D. Edinburgh 1983, pp.777-828; Strehle, op.cit., pp.84-94; A.C.Clifford, "Geneva Revisited or Calvinism Revised: the case for theological reassessment", *Churchman* 100(1986)4, pp.323-334, and *Atonement and Justification. English Evangelical Theology 1640-1790: an evaluation*, Oxford 1990, pp.142-161. See also M.Jinkins, "Calvin and the Extent of the Atonement", *EQ* 64(1992)4 pp.333-355.

2 E.g. Helm, op.cit., p.18; F.S.Leahy, "Calvin and the Extent of the Atonement", RTJ 8(1992) pp.54-64.

3 Albert Pighius was a Catholic polemicist, whose writing on free will had already drawn forth an opposing work from Calvin in 1543. Georgius was a lesser known Sicilian monk.

4 Georgius had specifically addressed the question of the extent of the atonement, see Calvin, *Concerning the Eternal Predestination of God*, trans. J.K.S.Reid, London 1961, p.148.

5 *Institutes of the Christian Religion*, 3.21.5. The version of the *Institutes* cited throughout is that edited by J.T. McNeill, Library of Christian Classics vols.20-21, Philadelphia 1954, based on Calvin's 1559 edition. In these notes, figures unaccompanied by further explanation refer to the Institutes.

6 A. Schweizer, *Die Glaubenslehre der evangelisch-reformierten Kirche*, 2 vols. Zurich 1844-5; H. Bauke, *Die Probleme der Theologie Calvins*, Leipzig 1922 pp.16-19; P. Jacobs, *Prädestination und Verantwortlichkeit bei Calvin*, Neukirchen 1927; W. Niesel, *The Theology of Calvin*, Philadelphia 1956, especially pp.159-181. Bauke's view has found support from G. Rist, "Modernité de la Methode de Calvin", *RTP* 18(1968)1 pp.19-33, esp. p.30; similarly, A. Ganoczy, *The Young Calvin*, Edinburgh 1987, pp.181-187, refers to the "dialectical structure" and "profound bipolarity" of Calvin's thought. W.J.Bouwsma, "The Quest for the Historical Calvin", *ARG* 77(1986) pp.47-57, and B.G.Armstrong, "Duplex Cognition Dei Or? The problem and relation of structure, form and purpose in Calvin's theology", pp.135-153 in E.A. McKee and B.G.Armstrong (eds.), *Probing the Reformed Tradition*, Louisville 1989, caution against looking for systematic theology in Calvin. C.Partee, *Calvin and Classical Philosophy*, Leiden 1977, has written, "...predestination is not the basic doctrine from which Calvin deduces a theological system." (See also Partee, "Calvin's Central Dogma Again", *SCJ* 18(1987)2 pp.191-199). But for a recent contrary conclusion, see D.N.Wiley, "Calvin's Doctrine of Predestination: his principal soteriological and polemical doctrine", Ph.D. Duke 1971, esp. pp.299-312.

7 *Christianae Religionis Institutio*, Basel 1536, p.137. 4.1.7: Sometimes...the term 'church'...includes...all the elect from the beginning of the world."

8 1.16.1; 1.17.13. For the successive editions of the *Institutes*, see F.Wendel, *Calvin: the origin and development of his religious thought*, London 1974, pp.112-122.

9 1.18.2, cp. *Eternal Predestination*, pp.169,176-178.

10 1.17.5,9; 1.18.1 cp. *Eternal Predestination*, pp.170-174.

11 Jerome Bolsec, ex-Carmelite, and theologian of Paris, had fled to Geneva because of his Reformation sympathies and taken up the practice of medicine. In the *congregation* of 16 October 1551, after an exposition of Jn. 8.47, he had spoken in opposition to Calvin's understanding of providence and double predestination as resting upon an absolute, eternal, divine decree. He was arrested, and subsequently banished from Geneva. See T.H.L.Parker, *John Calvin*, London 1975 pp.132-136; F.Wendel, op.cit., p.264; P.C.Holtrop, *The Bolsec Controversy on Predestination, from 1551 to 1555; statements of Jerome Bolsec and the responses of John Calvin, Theodore Beza and other Reformed theologians*, Lewiston 1993. Our account is based on *Registres de la Compagnie des Pasteurs de Genève au Temps de Calvin*, ed. R.M.Kingdon and J.F.Bergier, Geneva 1964 vol.l pp.80-118.

12 For Zwingli's De Providentia, see A.E.McGrath, *Intellectual Origins of the European Reformation*, Oxford 1987, p.51. Thomas Aquinas, *Summa Theologica*, London 1922, 1.23.2; Wendel, op.cit., p.178.

13 3.21.1, cp. Thirteene Sermons of Maister John Calvine, *Entreating of the Free Election of God in Jacob, and of Reprobation in Esau*, London 1579, p.19b.

14 3.21.1.

15 3.22.1, 2.17.1; 3.22.7.

16 3.22.1; 3.24.5.

17 *Commentary on 2 Corinthians* (ed. D.W. and T.F.Torrance), Edinburgh 1964, ch.5 v.19, p.78. See also 2.16.4 and 2.17.2. Daniel, op.cit., p.795 n.43, notes that Calvin frequently conflates Jn.3.16 and Rom.8.32, an interesting observation in that the former became a favourite text of proponents of universal atonement, the latter of those who stood for particular redemption.

18 3.21.7; *Sermons of M. John Calvin on the Epistles of S. Paule to Timothie and Titus*, London 1579, 2 Timothy 1.8-10, p.709a.

19 Rainbow, op.cit., p.87 (and see ibid., pp.64-88).

20 3.23.7; *Commentary on John* (ed. D.W. and T.F.Torrance), Edinburgh 1959, ch.3 v.16, pp.73-74. See also 2.17.2.

21 Wiley, op.cit., pp.254-263,297, concludes that Calvin adapted the role of Christ to a presupposed doctrine of predestination, rather than making the election of Christ his genuine starting point. See also J.K.S. Reid, "The Office of Christ in Predestination", *SJT* 1(1948) pp.1-19,166-183. V.A. Shepherd, *The Nature and Function of Faith in the Theology of John Calvin*, Macon 1983, p.95, has gone so far as to say, "The most distressing feature of Calvin's understanding of election is that it is not an implication of his christology; it is a surd."

22 On the universality of the promise in Calvin, see Anderson, op.cit., pp.62-96.

23 3.1.1.

24 3.2.29: "We make the freely given promise of God the foundation of faith."

25 3.2.32.

26 3.2.33, cp.3.2.34; *Sermons on Isaiah's Prophecy of the Death and Passion of Christ*, London 1956 p.41, cp. *A Harmony of the Gospels* (ed. D.W. and T.F.Torrance), Edinburgh 1972, vol.1, Lk.2.10, p.75.

27 3.24.17; 3.22.10.

28 3.24.2.

29 Armstrong, op.cit., pp.142-143.

30 3.21.1; *Sermons on Timothy*, 1 Tim.2.3-5, p.151a; p.156a.

31 *Eternal Predestination*, p.103.

32 3.11.21; 3.24.1; "An Answeare to Certaine Slaunders and Blasphemyes", appended to *Thirteene Sermons*, 171b.

33 3.24.14; 3.23.7.

34 *Commentary on Romans* (ed. D.W. and T.F.Torrance), Edinburgh 1961, ch.9 esp. vv.23-24, pp.210-212.

35 E.A. Dowey, *The Knowledge of God in Calvin's Theology*, New York 1965, pp.210-220, argues that reprobation was substantially less significant than election, both systematically and practically, in Calvin's theology. However the significance of Calvin's making reprobation the other side of election within the eternal decree cannot be overlooked. See Wiley, op.cit., pp.239-249.

36 Calvin's dual approach to predestination was recognized by H.Otten, *Calvins Theologische Anschauung von der Prädestination*, Munich 1938, pp.131-135. He referred to his theological (working from the decrees) and soteriological (dealing with fallen man) perspectives.

37 On the relationship between the "two wills" and the promise, see Anderson, op.cit., pp.97-103. Parallel to the "two wills" motif, and with similar purpose and problems, was Calvin's concept of "double justice" (secret and ordinary), see R. Stauffer, *Dieu, la Création et la Providence dans la Prédication de Calvin*, Bern 1987, pp.116-124.

38 See R.A.Muller, *Dictionary of Latin and Greek Theological Terms - drawn principally from Protestant scholastic theology*, Grand Rapids 1989 pp.331-333, on *Voluntas Dei.*

39 1.17.2.

40 The "two wills" device is also used in the exposition of the third petition of the Lord's Prayer in 3.20.43.

41 3.24.15-17. The 1 Timothy snd Ezekiel texts are also dealt with in *Eternal Predestination*, op. cit, pp.105-109.

42 *Harmony*, op.cit., vol.3, Matthew 23.34-37, pp.63-70, upon which the following exposition is mainly based. Latin citation from *Harmonia ex Tribus Evangelistis Composita*, Geneva 1560, p.351.

43 3.24.15.

44 Rainbow, op.cit., pp.148-158. A tendency in Calvin to lean towards reconciling the two sides of his thought in favour of the absolute has been detected by Otten, op.cit., pp.80-87; E. Fuchs, *La Morale Selon Calvin*, Paris 1986, pp.119-124, writes of the threat, in Calvin, from providence and predestination to an ethic of law and the cross.

45 Wendel, op.cit., p.219. For surveys of Calvin's teaching on the nature of the atonement, see Van Buren, op.cit.; J.F. Jansen, *Calvin's Doctrine of the Work of Christ*, London 1956; R.A. Peterson, *Calvin's Doctrine of the Atonement*, Phillipsburg 1983. For Calvin on merit, see E.D.Wallis, "The Influence of Laelius Socinus on Calvin's Doctrines of the Merit of Christ and Assurance", in *Italian Reformation Studies in Honour of Laelius Socinus*, ed. J.A.Tedeschi, Florence 1965, pp.231-241.

46 Van Buren, op.cit., esp. pp.49, 76-78. See also Ritschl, op.cit., pp.207-233; L.W. Grensted, *A Short History of the Doctrine of the Atonement*, Manchester 1920, pp.209-220; R.S.Paul, *The Atonement and the Sacraments; the relation of the atonement and the sacraments of baptism and the Lord's supper*, London 1961, pp.98-109.

47 2.17.1. Sections 1-5 of this chapter were inserted by Calvin from his work against Socinus, *Responsio ad aliquot L. Socini Senensis Quaestiones.* Socinus had asked how salvation could have been achieved by the merit of Christ, and still depend upon the free mercy of God. See also van Buren, op.cit., p.49; Wendel, op.cit., pp.227-32; Ritschl, op.cit., pp.207-209; J.Wawrykow, "John Calvin and Condign Merit", *ARG* 83(1992) pp.73-90; Muller, *Dictionary*, op.cit., pp.190-191, on *Meritum Christi.*

48 Jansen, op.cit., pp.86-91, Strehle, op.cit.

49 2.13.3; *Harmony*, op.cit., vol.1, Luke 2.23-38 (and see below, p.32).

50 *Commentary on 1 John* (ed. D.W. and T.F.Torrance), Edinburgh 1961, ch.2 v.2, p.244, "...all refers to all

who would believe." *Commentary on 1 Timothy* (ed. D.W. and T.F.Torrance), Edinburgh 1964, ch.2 v.5, p.210, "The universal term all must always be referred to classes of men but never to individuals."

51 *Commentary on Hebrews* (ed. D.W. and T.F.Torrance), Edinburgh 1963, ch.9 v.27, p.131; *Sermons on Isaiah*, p.141; *Sermons on the Saving Work of Christ*, Welwyn 1960, p.52; ibid., p.95. These examples may be supplemented from the extensive range provided by Daniel, op.cit., pp.777-828.

52 "Acts of the Council of Trent, with the Antidote", in, *Tracts and Treatises*, trans. H. Beveridge, Grand Rapids 1958, vol.3 pp.93,109. *Sermons on Isaiah*, p.126, "For how many unbelievers do we see perishing, for whom the death and passion of our Lord Jesus Christ serves only for more severe condemnation, because they trample underfoot His sacred blood and reject His grace offered to them?"

53 2.16.2.

54 Nicole, op.cit., p.220; van Buren, op.cit., p.50.

55 *Commentary on Colossians* (ed. D.W. and T.F.Torrance) Edinburgh 1965, ch.1 v.14, p.308; *Sermons on Isaiah*, p.74; *Commentary on Romans*, ch.3 v.25, p.76; cp. 2.16.13, "In his death we have an effectual completion of salvation, because by it we are reconciled to God, satisfaction is given to his justice, the curse is removed, and the penalty paid."

56 D.A.Stoute, "The Origins and Early Development of the Reformed Idea of the Covenant", Ph.D. Cambridge 1979, pp.190-243 and P.A.Lillback, "The Binding of God: Calvin's role in the development of covenant theology", Ph.D.Westminster Theological Seminary 1985, have sought to demonstrate continuity between Calvin and later (conditional) covenant theology, and Clifford, *Atonement*, op.cit., esp. p.239 n.76, has compared Calvin's references to faith as a condition to the conditionalism of the English "Neonomian" Richard Baxter (1615-1691). See also J.F.Veninga, "Covenant Thought and Ethics in the Thought of John Calvin and John Preston", Ph.DRice 1974, pp.14-112. Among those who have denied that Calvin maintained a conditional, two-sided covenant are: J.G.Møller, "The Beginnings of Puritan Covenant Theology", *JEH* 14(1963) pp.46-67; J.B.Torrance, "Covenant or Contract? A study of the theological background of worship in seventeenth-century Scotland", SJT, 23(1970) pp.51-76, and "The Concept of Federal Theology: was Calvin a federal theologian?" in W.H.Neuser, Calvinus Sacrae Scripturae Professor: Calvin as Confessor of Holy Scripture, Grand Rapids 1994, pp.15-40; R.W.A.Letham, "Saving Faith and Assurance in Reformed Theology: Zwingli to the Synod of Dort", Ph.D. Aberdeen 1979; J.W.Baker, *Heinrich Bullinger and the Covenant: the other Reformed tradition*, Athens (Ohio) 1981. Armstrong's different, but relevant, argument, that there is a "hypothetical structure of Calvin's thought" is worthy of consideration in this respect, see "Duplex Cognitio", in McKee and Armstrong, op.cit. Faith is described as a condition by Calvin in 1.17.14, 3.21.6, *Sermons on Deuteronomy*, London 1583, ch.7 vv.7-10, ch.26 vv.16-19, ch.32 vv.44-47 (pp.317a-317b, 913b, 1028a-1029b).

57 3.2.7. See Niesel, op.cit., pp.169-181; Kendall, op.cit., pp.13-28; J.R.Beeke, *Assurance of Faith: Calvin, English Puritanism and the Dutch Second Reformation*, New York 1991, pp.47-49; though contrast R.A.Muller, "Fides and Cognitio in Relation to the Problem of the Intellect and Will in the Theology of John Calvin", *CTJ* 25(1990)2 pp.207-234.

58 2.16.1. Proponents of limited atonement have made much of a remark of Calvin to the Lutheran Heshusius on the subject of the Lord's Supper (e.g. Nicole, op cit., p.222), in "The Clear Explanation of Sound Doctrine Concerning the True Partaking of the Flesh and Blood of Christ in the Holy Supper" (1561), in *Theological Treatises*, ed. and trans. J.K.S.Reid, Library of Christian Classics vol.22, London 1954, pp.258-324: "I should like to know how the wicked can eat the flesh of Christ which was not crucified for them" (p.285). There is no need, however, to understand this in any other way than to imply that the benefits of the atonement are only intended to be effective in the case of those who believe. Over against the Lutheran view that participation in the bread and wine invariably means

participation in the body and blood of Christ, Calvin taught that participation in Christ is only through faith. The promise of the gospel is to all, but is only intended to benefit those who believe. Calvin's many statements of the atonement as being for believers are in full harmony with his view that the atonement is for all, in the context of promise, and for some, in the context of election. For belief is the response both invited by the promise, and given by election. Bell, op.cit., pp.16-17, convincingly expounds this remark of Calvin to Heshusius. Cp. *Commentary on John*, ch.1.v.29, p.33, "Let us therefore learn that we are reconciled to God by the grace of Christ if we go straight to His death and believe that He who was nailed to the cross is the only sacrificial victim by whom all our guilt is removed."

59 *Christ and the Decree*, op.cit., p.33-34.

60 *Commentary on 2 Corinthians*, ch.5 v.20; *Harmony*, vol.2, Mark 10.45, p.277.

61 *Commentary on 1 John*, ch.2 v.2.

62 E.g.*Harmony*, vol.1, Matthew ch.2 v.19, p.104, "...the cross...was to be His means of redeeming the Church"; *Sermons on Timothy and Titus*, 1 Tim.4.9-11, p.403b, "For the word Saviour is not taken here in his proper and necessary signification, as they call it, in respect of everlasting salvation which God promiseth his elect". *Eternal Predestination*, p.102, "Christ was so ordained for the salvation of the whole world that He might save those who are given to Him by the Father". And see Harmony, vol.1, Matt.4.1, p.135; 3.4.30; n.50, above.

63 *Sermons on Isaiah*, p.144.

64 *Eternal Predestination*, pp.148-149.

65 *Commentary on 1 John*, ch.2 v.2.

66 Commentary on John, ch.1. v.29.

67 Ibid.

68 *Commentary on 1 Timothy*, ch.2 v.5.

69 See ante, p.39 n.51.

70 *Sermons on 1 Timothy*, p.150b.

71 Ibid., pp.148-185, esp.p.149b; 177b.

72 *Sermons on Isaiah*, p.116.

73 Kendall, op.cit., pp.16-17.

74 See, for example, *Sermons on Isaiah*, pp.143-8. While Calvin says, "...He prays for His own" and "He does not pray for all" (p.145), the statement, "Let us not fear to come...seeing He is sufficient to save us all", occurs in the same section, and in the same context of Christ's intercession (p.144).

75 M.P.Hoogland, *Calvin's Perspective on the Exaltation of Christ, in comparison with the post-Reformation doctrine of the two states*, Kampen 1966, pp.194-197, argues that, for Calvin, the death of Christ is of value only when joined to the power of his exaltation.

76 See ante, p.9 n.14.

Chapter Three

Theodore Beza (1519–1605)

INTRODUCTION

Having been under the influence of humanism and the movement for religious reform in France for many years, and having hesitated for a long time to take the costly step of identifying himself openly with the reform, Theodore Beza finally fled France for Geneva, arriving there on 24 October 1548. He was invited by Pierre Viret to go to Lausanne, where he became professor of Greek. Prolonged disputes with the Bernese rulers of Lausanne, over predestination and the support by Viret and Beza of Calvin and the Genevan church, eventually led to the two men leaving in 1558. Beza went to Geneva and was quickly appointed first rector of its new Academy, where he also assisted Calvin in lecturing in theology. On Calvin's death the leadership of the Genevan Church fell to him. Throughout his life he was deeply involved in political and ecclesiastical affairs on an international scale.[1]

Recent scholarship has often contrasted Calvin's "biblical", "humanistic" and "christocentric" theology with Beza's scholastic and systematic approach. Beza has been portrayed as the father of Reformed scholasticism[2] by such scholars as B.Hall, J.Dantine, B.G.Armstrong, and R.T.Kendall. W.Kickel has argued at length that Beza introduced a rationalism and a deductive logic, foreign to Calvin's methodology, into Reformed theology. More recently, J. Raitt, J.S. Bray, T. Maruyama and M. Delval in their studies of Beza's teaching on the eucharist, predestination, the church, and salvation respectively, have found it necessary to modify this position, and have viewed Calvin's successor as a transitional figure between the first wave of Reformation thought and the scholastic orthodoxy of the seventeenth century.[3]

In one of the few thorough comparisons between Calvin's and Beza's predestination teaching, I.McPhee contends that Calvin's theology was not so christocentric as to be free of important rationalistic elements, and demonstrates continuity in this respect from Calvin to Beza.[4] Our previous chapter has shown that Calvin's theology contained different and apparently irreconcilable elements. It was in seeking to cope with these elements, without ever wanting to be other than a faithful follower of Calvin, that Beza constructed his theology of predestination.

According to Raitt, the place of predestination in Beza's doctrinal development is the major question in current Beza scholarship.[5] The present study aims to address this issue, taking account of continuity with Calvin, as well as observing signs of departure from him, in Beza's teaching on the scope of Christ's saving work, and its background in the doctrine of predestination.

Beza will be followed through three predestination controversies: with Bolsec, with Castellio, and with the Lutherans at and after the Colloquy of Montbéliard. The danger of this approach is that the emphases made in controversy may well not present Beza's theological thought in true proportion. It is not easy to avoid the danger, since Beza produced no work comparable to Calvin's *Institutes* that would enable the researcher to gain ready access to the wholeness of his thought. However, some comparison with Beza's less polemical works[6] will indicate that he held consistently to the positions defended in these three controversies. At the same time it must be borne in mind that history cast Beza in the role of polemicist. In the field of predestination, the controversies which had begun to rage in response to Calvin's teaching were inherited by him. Moreover it was during Beza's ascendancy that predestination was firmly added to the sacraments as matters of disagreement between the Reformed and the Lutherans. Furthermore, the Roman Church, having recovered from the first shock of "schism", was better placed to counter attack. Yet another source of trouble was the rise of Socinianism.[7] As someone attempting to adhere to theological positions established by his predecessor, and defend them against increasingly determined opposition, Beza's thought was hardly likely to escape the influence of controversy. The outline of his theology would be, almost inevitably, more stark, its structure more systematic, its positions more rigid.

THE BOLSEC CONTROVERSY[8]

The Letters to Bullinger

Calvin spent a great deal of labour in defending and asserting his predestination teaching against Bolsec. Beza, in Lausanne, stood with him as a staunch ally in this, when other churches were showing a certain lack of enthusiasm for his strong doctrine, especially his unambiguous assertion of reprobation. On 29 October 1551 Beza wrote to Heinrich Bullinger at Zurich, seeking to win his support for Calvin. Bolsec had made election dependent on foreseen faith, and reprobation dependent on foreseen lack of faith. He had concentrated on reprobation, regarding it as the most offensive and vulnerable aspect of Calvin's predestination teaching. Beza, following both Calvin and Bolsec, took for granted a certain parallelism between election and reprobation, and addressed himself to it without embarrassment. The issues were:

> "Whether anyone is reprobated from eternity, and therefore created by God to be a vessel of wrath? Whether they are reprobates because they are unbelieving or, on the contrary, unbelieving because reprobates, although they are condemned because they are unbelieving?"[9]

Beza pointed out to Bullinger that if reprobation was based on foresight of unbelief, then there would be no defence against the view that election was based on foresight of faith, and so the human will would be the pivot on which salvation turned. Beza's anxiety to exclude free will and corresponding human merit, was fully in line with Calvin's *Eternal Predestination* and, indeed, with Luther's *Bondage of the Will.* Beza was also in accord with Calvin's definition of predestination, and with Calvin's stronger statements about reprobation, in which he saw the ultimate cause of reprobation not as unbelief or sin but the secret judgement of God. However, whereas Calvin often presented election as the explanation for the conversion of the corrupt will of some people, without going further, Beza, in the letter to Bullinger, concentrated directly on the double decree. This was because Beza saw that logical consistency demanded that one could not argue for unconditional election on the basis that God's will is free, and that his decree governs his foreknowledge, and then seek to qualify the freedom of God's will, and make foreknowledge (of sin) "prior" to the decree in dealing with reprobation.

So the demands of the Bolsec controversy led Beza to outline a supralapsarian understanding of predestination, according to which election is not God's response to the human race as fallen, but his reason for creating it and ordaining the fall.[10] Reprobation is not simply the passing by of some who have no claim on mercy, but the creation of some in order that they may be sinful and condemned. Recognizing that his construction would seem wholly unjust to human apprehension, Beza cautioned against the attempt to measure God's ways by human understanding. The only proper response to the mystery is the apostle Paul's, "Oh, the depth!" (Romans 11.33). Furthermore, it must be held as an unquestioned basic principle that "the will of God is the sole rule of justice". We may not form a concept of justice and then measure God by it, but must accept what the Bible says about God's ways, and then believe that they are just. In order that it may not seem that God is the author of sin, Beza insisted that causes must be distinguished. Man is the blameworthy cause of sin; God's decree is the blameless cause of man sinning. The whole scheme is unified under the final cause of the glory of God.

The letter to Bullinger is startling in that it reveals a developed, deliberate and logical supralapsarianism, and an Aristotelian preoccupation with causality, that would be put forward frequently through the rest of Beza's life. A further letter to Bullinger on 12 January 1552 repeated the main points.[11]

Letters to Calvin

It was during the Bolsec controversy that Calvin produced his *Eternal Predestination*, and he invited Beza's comments upon it in advance of publication. Beza responded in a letter from Lausanne on 21 January 1552.[12] Whilst expressing admiration for the work, Beza gave his opinion that something more methodical would be necessary for the total overthrow of the adversary, and said that he himself had prepared some headings. These were almost certainly the beginnings of his "Table", a diagrammatic representation of predestination and its execution.[13]

In a letter of July 29 1555[14] he told Calvin that he was willing for the publication of the "Table" to go ahead at Geneva. It had been circulated in manuscript and Peter Martyr Vermigli had advised the addition of explanatory notes.[15] However, Beza was wrestling with a problem, which he unfolded to Calvin at length. His logical supralapsarian construction had made him ponder the relation of Christ to election, and ask the following:

> "I ask first whether election is to be taken as the eternal plan of God by which he destined us to adoption, or the execution of that plan. Indeed, the execution (if it is considered not in us who are born and called at a certain moment, but in God) is not less eternal than the first, although, with respect to order, is subservient to it. Then I also ask this, how we are said to be elect in Christ. Is it because God had regard to Christ when he predestined us, or because, since he had already decided in himself to save us, afterwards (if we look at the order of causes) he ordained Christ, through whom his plan would be carried out in us?"

In these words, Beza showed that he was fully aware of the implication of his supralapsarian view of election, namely that Christ must be subordinated to the decree, as a means to an end. He stated that this was indeed the presentation he had chosen in his "Table".[16]

Beza revealed the place of Aristotelian logic in his construction of his doctrine when he explained that part of the reason for it was that,

> "...as they say, the end should be first in intention",

although he stated that the main factor was that he could not accept that election, or reprobation, should be made posterior to God's foreknowledge of sin.

Next Beza disagreed with Augustine's understanding of the "lump of clay" in Romans 9.21. To Augustine it had represented humanity corrupted by the fall. To Beza it was "the human race not yet made". Out of this lump God decided to make people in two ways, to declare his glory.

While the decree has the declaration of God's glory as its end, its "material cause" cannot be assigned to anything beyond "the will of God". Likewise the question of why certain ones are chosen and others rejected can only be answered by pointing to the will of God. No second causes, not even Adam or Christ, must be assigned as causes to the decree. They belong to its execution.

This letter is of immense significance. It demonstrates once again all the leading features of a supralapsarian system uniting predestination and providence on the basis of an eternal, causal decree.[17] It shows a commitment to the use of Aristotelian categories of causality. Furthermore, it is important in that it recognizes the implications for christology. The most basic assumption of the letter is that the doctrine of predestination must not be built on any concept of foreknowledge that would imply human action independent of God's decree. Neither foreknowledge of faith nor of corruption are to be admitted as undergirding the decree. However, because Scripture says that election is "in Christ", the foreknowledge of sin is implied, for provision of the remedy (Christ) implies knowledge of the disease (sin). Thus, in order to ensure that the decree is prior to the foreknowledge of sin it must also be prior to the ordination of Christ, and election in him.[18] The divine order, then, is that God first decrees that certain persons shall be saved, he then ordains the fall, then Christ is ordained to be the mediator and the elect are chosen in him. Election in Christ becomes, in effect, election to the means of salvation for those already elected to salvation itself.[19] The consequence of this order, as will be seen, was that the work of Christ was consistently viewed by Beza as defined and delimited by the plan of God to reprobate and elect. It would have meaningful reference to the elect only. The "Table" starkly shows the subordinate position of Christ.

The "Table"

The "Table" is reproduced overleaf.[20] In the explanation which accompanied it, the way in which double predestination works for the glory of God is elaborated: the divine mercy is displayed in saving the elect, and the divine justice in condemning the reprobate.[21] There is full agreement between the correspondence and the "Table", including the placing of the mission of Christ firmly in subordination to the decrees of predestination.

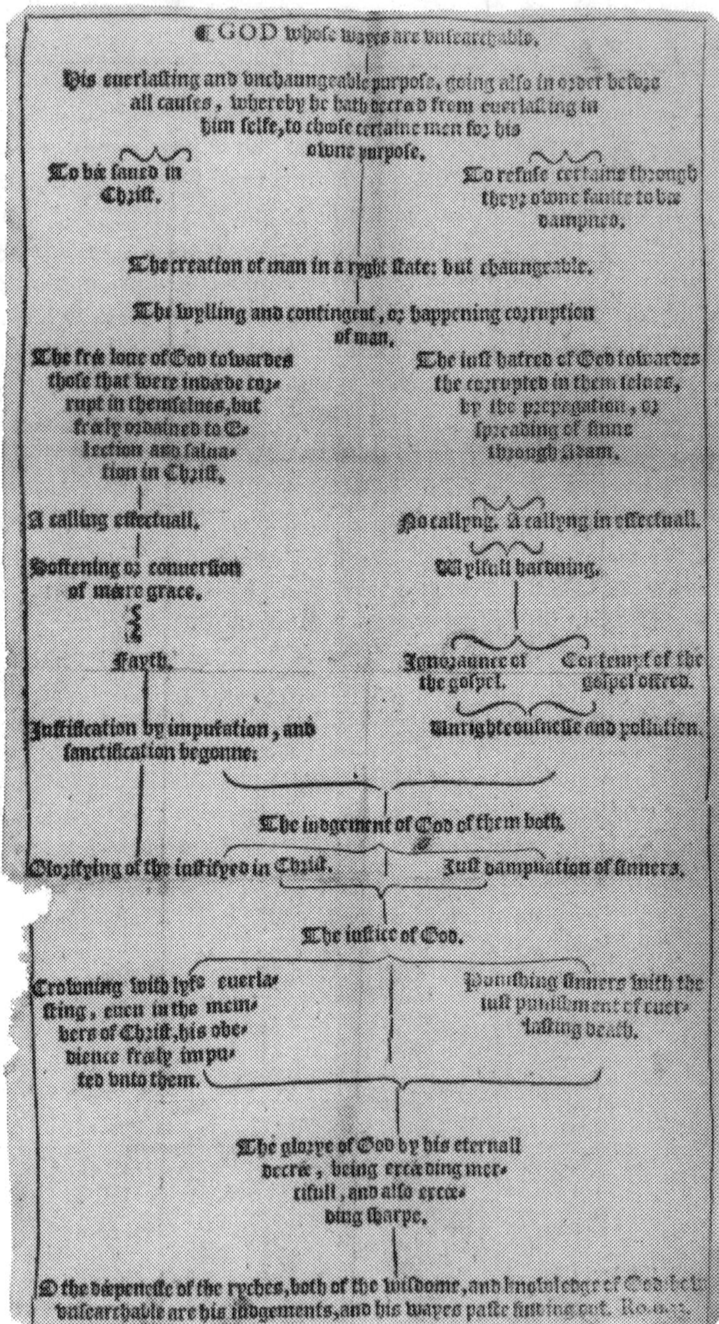

GOD whose wayes are unsearchable,

His everlasting and unchaungeable purpose, going also in order before all causes, whereby he hath decreed from everlasting in him selfe, to chose certaine men for his owne purpose,

To be saved in Christ. | To refuse certaine through theyr owne faulte to be dampned.

The creation of man in a right state: but chaungeable.

The wylling and contingent, or happening corruption of man.

The free love of God towardes those that were indede corrupt in themselves, but freely ordained to Election and salvation in Christ. | The iust hatred of God towardes the corrupted in them selves, by the propagation, or spreading of sinne through Adam.

A calling effectuall. | No callyng. A callyng in effectuall.

Softening or conversion of mere grace. | Wyllfull hardning.

Fayth. | Ignoraunce of the gospel. Contempt of the gospel offred.

Iustification by imputation, and sanctification begonne. | Unrighteousnesse and pollution.

The iudgement of God of them both.

Glorifying of the iustifyed in Christ. | Iust dampnation of sinners.

The iustice of God.

Crowning with lyfe everlasting, even in the members of Christ, his obedience freely imputed unto them. | Punishing sinners with the iust punishment of everlasting death.

The glorye of God by his eternall decree, being exceading mercifull, and also exceading sharpe.

O the depenesse of the ryches, both of the wisdome, and knowledge of God: [illegible] unsearchable are his iudgements, and his wayes paste finding out. Ro. [illegible]

Beza's *Table* reproduced by permission of the British Library from *The Treasure of Trueth* (shelfmark 4256a14)

Decree and Execution

The distinction between the decree and its execution lies behind Beza's "Table". In one sense the decree and execution are inseparable, in that the decree is infallibly carried out through the exercise of divine omnipotence. On the other hand, the two are carefully distinguished. The decree is first cause, dependent on God alone.[22] The execution employs second causes, chief among which are Adam and Christ.[23] This distinction between decree and execution has been accorded great importance by Bray, who maintains that it was a means by which the limits of human enquiry were drawn.[24] The decree is inaccessible to human reason, its execution is comprehensible in terms of second causes. Without doubt, this structure is intended to uphold both the sovereignty of God and human responsibility. Perhaps its most frequent use by Beza was in distinguishing between reprobation and condemnation. To the adversary who would object that it was unjust for God to make someone in order to condemn him, Beza could reply that God would not condemn without the intervention of sin, and sin intervened by means of Adam's free and responsible fall. Thus the fall and subsequent corruption of the human race were "without the blame of God", and the responsibility for sin lies firmly with humanity.[25] God's justice in the execution of the decree can be recognized, even if the justice of the decree itself is incomprehensible.[26] Bray calls Beza's decree-execution distinction, "Beza's most significant original contribution to theology".[27] It should be understood, however, that the originality did not lie in giving a new content to Calvin's teaching on divine sovereignty, nor, since Thomas Aquinas had explained providence in terms of primary and secondary causality, in the method of explanation, but in the imposition, for apologetic purposes, of a Thomist framework upon Calvin's doctrine of absolute sovereignty. The rigorous application of the decree-execution, or primary-secondary causality, framework is apparent in the way Christ is seen as a means, albeit chief among other means, for the execution of the decree of God to glorify himself by saving an elect portion of mankind. This subordination of Christ to the decree pointed the way to a doctrine of limited atonement.

Beza and Calvin

The letter to Calvin of July 1555, and the "Table", present Beza's views on predestination in a precise and systematic way, views that would undergo no significant alteration through the remaining fifty years of his life. He put his thoughts to Calvin with an expression of some reticence, appealing to Calvin, "*mi pater*", to correct him and the "Table" if he was going astray.[28] The reply, if reply there was, is not extant. The fact that the published "Table" fully reflected the views in the letter indicates that Calvin did not feel it necessary to make changes.

How could Calvin have sanctioned a presentation of predestination so systematically supralapsarian and which explicitly subordinated Christ to the decree of election? The only explanation is that these elements were already to be found in his own teaching. From material provided by Calvin, Beza was able to fashion his own more coherent system. The same Calvin who presented election and reprobation as being so out of symmetry that reprobation sometimes appeared to be just the shadow of election could, in his very definition of predestination, make election and reprobation sound as if they were two equal sides of the same reality. Although Calvin warned against going beyond the corruption of the reprobate in order to explain reprobation, he sometimes said that the ultimate cause of reprobation was the hidden judgement of God ordaining the reprobate's wickedness. Calvin who often approached particular election as the *ex post facto* explanation of conversion, also presented it as the very beginning of all God's saving work. While Calvin made much of the actualization of election in faith, he also classified election as a branch of providence, an aspect of a causal decree lying behind every event in history. The same Calvin who strove to understand election as being "in Christ" could also concede that God's electing love, being founded upon his good pleasure, is precedent to all other causes, including Christ. Calvin, too, could use the Aristotelian causal framework. He also quashed objections to his predestination teaching by asserting that the incomprehensible will of God is the rule of all justice.[29] It could be said, therefore, that Beza aligned himself with the logical rather than the homiletic and apologetic Calvin. Whilst Beza was undoubtedly giving greater definition to Calvin's teaching, he was seeking thereby only to give it greater coherence. Calvin's apparent approval of Beza's relevant work strongly suggests that he saw his own concerns reflected there.

THE CONTROVERSY WITH CASTELLIO

As in the case of Bolsec, the controversy with Sebastian Castellio[30] was one that arose as a reaction to the doctrine of Calvin. Castellio published some observations on Calvin's *Eternal Predestination.* Both Calvin and Beza answered these "calumnies", Beza's response being the longer of the two. Once again there is evidence that Calvin was satisfied with Beza's work. The two men corresponded while preparing their publications, and Beza sought Calvin's comments. Moreover, Calvin recommended his own readers to consult Beza's work for a fuller refutation of Castellio.[31] This is not to say that there were no differences of approach between the two men, and some of these are revealed in the letter Beza sent to Calvin.

Beza's Letter to Calvin (22 January 1558)[32]

Beza's observations on Calvin's manuscript show him anxious to make Calvin's teaching on predestination a little more consistent. Calvin had planned to include the following statement:

> "I concede that the apostate angels, like men, were created for salvation, but with respect to their future falling away were destined to perish."

Beza warned that to suggest that reprobates were in some sense created for salvation would cast doubt upon the decree of reprobation.[33] It is apparent that Beza was pressing Calvin to follow a consistently supralapsarian line, and the published version, omitting this, and altering a similar statement,[34] shows that Calvin was willing to accept his advice. Whereas different emphases can be found in the two men, the agreement and continuity between them at this point is apparent.

Beza's Reply to Castellio: the Will of God

In Beza's *Ad Sebastiani Castellionis Calumnias...Responsio*, the same points already noted in his polemic against Bolsec are prominent.[35] Much attention is devoted to Castellio's charge that Calvin posited two contradictory wills in God, and it is that aspect of the *Ad Calumnias* that will be highlighted here. Castellio rejected Calvin's use of the two wills concept in his expositions of Ezekiel 33.11 and Matthew 23.37.

With reference to Ezekiel 33.11,[36] in which the Lord declares that he does not will the death of the sinner, Beza states that this text is not directly relevant to the subject of predestination. Ezekiel refers to God's word, not his decree.

> "The prophet disputes with men who were complaining they had incurred the wrath of God according to what they call his *potentia absoluta*, as if God should deal with them tyrannically, that is, without reference to their righteousness or unrighteousness. What, though, is the Lord doing through the prophet? He is bringing them back to the cause of perishing, residing in themselves, which we also do daily...the prophet I say is not rising up to the eternal decree of God."[37]

Beza asserted that this method of the prophet is fully in accord with his own constant practice of telling his hearers:

> "We ought not to scrutinize the hidden recesses of the decree concerning ourselves, but to trust what is placed before us in the word."

So, just as Beza had a dichotomy between the decree and its execution, he also had a dichotomy between decree and word. We are to believe in the decree, but not to consider it when anxious about our own salvation, but rather to turn our eyes to the word. This is parallel to the distinction between God's revealed and secret will.

Addressing Christ's statement that he had willed to gather unwilling Jerusalem (Matt. 23.37),[38] Beza departed from Calvin in not taking Christ to be speaking in his divine nature. Rather, Christ speaks as minister of the circumcision, and as such sets a pattern for Christian ministers, who are to be guided by God's revealed will or word. Their duty is

> "plainly to invite all promiscuously to salvation...they leave the hidden judgements to God until he reveals them."

There is a difference of motivation between God and ministers in this matter,

> "since often they [ministers] wish to gather those whom they do not know do not belong to the flock of God."

Bearing in mind that some might find difficulty with this sharp division between divine and human nature in Christ, but probably mainly through awareness of his own difference from Calvin in this exposition, he added that it is acceptable to understand Christ as speaking in his divine nature, provided it is remembered that, in such cases, God "lisps" with men.[39] If Christ were understood to be speaking in his divine nature, without qualification, the unthinkable implication would be that God could fail.

There are major similarities between Calvin's and Beza's expositions of these two passages. Both men had recourse to a dichotomy within God so that he can be said to will what he does not will. Neither was entirely comfortable in presenting what seemed to be a contradiction in God, and we have already detected hints that Calvin regarded the revealed will of God as being ultimately subservient to the hidden. In Beza this lack of satisfaction with paradox is more obvious, in that, on the whole, he avoided speaking bluntly of two wills, preferring to refer to God's will (hidden) and his word (revealed). An obvious difference from Calvin is that Beza was reluctant to see Christ as speaking in his divine nature, lest there should be even a hint of a real divine will that fails. In short, while a tendency can be detected in Calvin to give the absolute will of God precedence over the revealed, in Beza that tendency is marked.

Beza's reluctance to speak of the revealed will as "will" at all is seen in his comment on the father of the prodigal son.[40] Castellio had asked whether it had been the father's will that the son should live in luxury. Beza replied that he would rather say the father had not approved it, than that he had not willed it.

With reference to the law of God, Beza pointed out that in a sense God wills that everyone should keep it. But God did not give the law with the intention that we should actually keep it and be saved by so doing, but rather that we should be convicted of sin and led to Christ. This he regarded as illustrative of a principle:

> "Thus there are not two wills where two seem to appear."

In response to Castellio's pointing out the apparent contradiction between God's absolute will and his precepts, Beza explained that it is the same with human beings who may will something they do not approve as such in order to achieve a higher end: a prince who approves of peace may decide on war, for certain good reasons. At that point Beza seems to have conceded the reality of the revealed will as will, for he wrote:

> "The will of God is not to be sought otherwise than in his word."

However, almost immediately, responding to Castellio's next "calumny", he again drew back from attributing the description "will" to God's commands. The case of Pharaoh shows that God can command what he does not will. He commanded Pharaoh to let the Israelites go, "But he did not will it". Similarly,

> "Daily he calls many, whom however he does not draw to himself. But we deny that he therefore is a dissimulator. For to command and to be unwilling are not contrary."

Rather, the contrary of "to will" is "not to will", while the contrary of "to command" is "not to command". God commands *serio* but he does not always grant the ability to obey, and therefore he does not always will the response. Likewise, the gospel call does not imply that God wills the call to be heard in faith.

Calvin's tendency to see the hidden will of God as more fundamental than the revealed is seen in the way the revealed will ultimately serves the hidden will of election and reprobation. Beza's thought moves in the same direction but goes further, in that he shows distinct reluctance to give weight to the revealed will as will. A further reason for Beza's use of the decree-execution dichotomy may therefore be suggested: it was more consistent than the two wills device of Calvin. Whereas the two wills device could seem to imply contradiction in God, the execution of the decree is one step removed from God, through secondary causality. Harmony is preserved in that the preaching of the word strictly furthers the execution of the decree by gathering the elect and increasing the condemnation of the reprobate.

The reply to Castellio does not deal with the extent of the atonement because it was not an issue Castellio directly addressed. However, the tendency to subordinate the revealed will to the absolute will would have its repercussions in that area. For the universal revealed will or promise of God in Christ, which enabled Calvin to have a prominent universal dimension in his doctrine of the extent of the atonement, was weakened by Beza. Thus nothing of consequence stood between Beza's supralapsarianism and its logical outworking in a doctrine of limited atonement. This application of his doctrine of predestination came to the fore in the Colloquy of Montbéliard.

THE COLLOQUY OF MONTBÉLIARD

Following its publication in 1577, Duke Frederick of Württemberg attempted to impose the Lutheran Formula of Concord upon the territory of Montbéliard. Meeting with considerable resistance, he agreed to call a conference of Lutheran and Reformed theologians. Beza was chief spokesman for the Reformed. Following the publication of the acts of the Colloquy, with notes, by the leader of the Lutheran representatives, Jakob Andreae, Beza thought it necessary to publish his own version, with a response to Andreae's notes, the *Ad Acta Colloquii Montisbelgardensis Tubingae Edita Theodori Bezae Responsio.*[41]

The main subject of debate at Montbéliard was the eucharist, and it is no coincidence that it was in connection with this debate that the Lutherans and Reformed came to disagree on the meaning of divine predestination.[42] The Lutherans wished to stress the reality of the grace presented to all in word and sacrament.[43] The Reformed were anxious to insist that the effectiveness of word and sacrament is dependent on faith, which in turn is the sovereign gift of God. Beza did not want the Colloquy to worsen this division by taking up the theme of predestination. However, Andreae insisted on pushing the discussion into that area.[44] The Lutherans accused the Reformed of undermining the gospel, and the Reformed insisted that the Lutheran position either opened the door to free will, or made God inconsistent with himself, in that he willed the salvation of all, but granted the gift of faith only to some.[45]

The Will of God

In opposition to the Lutherans, Beza argued from his by then well-defined supralapsarianism, stating that God's decision to show or not to show mercy is based on his will alone, election and reprobation being two sides of the predestinating purpose.[46] From all eternity God planned to illustrate his own glory, and this must be understood as the final cause of destining some to be loved and some to be hated, for thus mercy and justice are revealed. Underpinning this system was a fixed concept of the divine attributes, particularly of immutability and omnipotence. The immutability of God was held by Beza to imply that the divine decree must be fixed and causal: enacted by divine omnipotence it moves all things but cannot itself be moved.

> "How absurd it is to think that there is mutability in God himself.... What sort of God is it whose decree and judgement is uncertain in itself and dependent on the will of man?"[47]

In this Beza was arguing in a scholastic fashion. He took the attributes of omnipotence and immutability as independent first principles, possibly derived by inductive reasoning from Scripture, and then reached a series of conclusions about the divine decrees and actions, by deductive logic from these principles.[48]

Beza understood God's will as his determination to glorify himself. To explain it any further, or to give any further criterion for election and reprobation, is impossible. The divine will, because united with immutability and omnipotence, is that which cannot be withstood:

> "The will of God...is the necessity of all things."[49]

Consequently this will of God is read with absolute clarity in the event, so that we know God does not will all to be saved because it is clear that all are not. Thomas Aquinas was cited as support for the position that the will of God is necessarily followed by its outcome, and the "schools" were pronounced correct in teaching that there is no firmer conclusion than *a posteriori*:

> "This has been done, therefore God willed that it should be done."[50]

The foreknowledge of God does not operate passively (*otiose*). It is to be connected to his will, even with respect to the fall. Though the fall resulted from the free choice of Adam, it had been willed by God to take place precisely in that way:

> "Nothing more absurd can be said about God than that there will be something God has not willed, or that something he has willed will not be."

This will can therefore be equated with providence.[51]

Beza referred approvingly to the scholastic distinction, also relied upon by Calvin, between the *voluntas signi* or *patefacta* and the *voluntas beneplaciti* or *secreta*.[52] He told Andreae that he took this distinction from the scholastics, especially Thomas. Although there is only one will in God, it is permissible to consider it in two ways. In the light of his emphasis on the secret will, what content could Beza give to the revealed? His exposition was twofold. The revealed will is

> "what God simply approves, as being good in its own nature and agreeable to God's nature."

In this sense God wills good, does not will evil, and does not will people's death, and in this sense both law and gospel can be called, "will".

> "For in them he shows that he approves what is done well and rightly."

The revealed will also covers whatever God commands.[53]

From his understanding of the *voluntas signi* as indicating what does and does not, in and of itself, please God, and from his application of this not only to the law but also to the gospel, it might be expected that Beza would have developed a doctrine of a universal promise of the gospel, as Calvin had done. Beza, however, was more consistent than Calvin, and much more thorough in giving the *voluntas signi* only secondary importance. He was careful to warn that the name "will" must not lead us to think of it as God's will, strictly speaking. For the second, and probably more important, element in Beza's thought about the revealed will was that it indicates human duty. Thus when Abraham was ordered to sacrifice Isaac,

> "God by the will of the sign...not so much willed but rather ordered Isaac to be sacrificed."

> "He...even orders to be done what he does not will to be done, and also promises what he does not will to fulfil."

In the gospel, according to the revealed will, the power and goodness of the Saviour are made known to all hearers. The word and sacraments constitute in themselves an invitation to all hearers and spectators.

> "But if he willed [sc. to gather all] he would give faith to all."[54]

The revealed will in the gospel shows us that

> "God has decided to save men in Christ, apprehended by true faith."

Beza spoke for himself and fellow Reformed ministers when he went on to say that this will was daily made plain. In saying this, however, he immediately felt the need to add the qualification:

> "Not however universally, that is without exception to all peoples, much less to every man, but promiscuously and indefinitely..."

The absolute will, as providence, sets limits to the scope of the revealed will, and enables us to understand that its intended extent is not universal. The revealed will is eventually resolved into the secret will, in that the word increases the guilt of those who do not heed it, and so furthers the condemnation of the reprobates.[55] Beza conceded that the gospel is conditional - its very conditionality meaning to him that it could not be universal - but the saving will of God is absolute. It is impossible that God should will people to fulfil a condition which they do not and cannot perform.[56]

Following Calvin and Augustine, Beza understood the will of God for the salvation of all, in 1 Timothy 2.4, to refer to "all sorts" rather than all individuals.[57] As in the controversies with Castellio, he interpreted Ezekiel 33.11 and Matthew 23.37 in terms of the distinction between revealed and secret will,[58] repeating, on the Matthew passage, that Christ's human and divine natures are to be carefully distinguished:

> "Thus, therefore, Christ as minister of the gospel willed and applied himself to gather all his hearers promiscuously, leaving with God his hidden will, as all God's ministers have been accustomed to do."[59]

Perhaps there is no better gauge of Beza's view of which will of God is the more fundamental than his comment that the revealed will of God is appropriate to Christ's humanity but not his divinity, a position that was wholly unacceptable to the Lutherans with their view of the profound interpenetration of the two natures in Christ.[60] While the above citation shows that the revealed will could and even should be prominent pastorally and practically, the secret will predominates theologically. Indeed the theological inevitably colours the pastoral, for the preacher has only to see to it that his proclamation is "promiscuous and indefinite" - a phrase frequently repeated by Beza in this context.[61]

Election and Christ

To the Lutherans, the Reformed concept of two wills was unacceptable. They insisted that the will of God must be understood "in Christ", and as set forth in the universal promise, which they accused Beza of undermining. According to them,

> "Election is not defined by an absolute decree of God, but in Christ, who calls all men to repentance."

At Montbéliard, the Lutheran understanding of election as "in Christ" was that, according to the will of God, all are called to believe in Christ, and those who comply with this call are "elect in Christ". This was the position laid down in the Formula of Concord.[62]

Beza, accused of separating election from Christ, replied with his distinction between decree and execution. In the decree, Christ had a role in election: as God he is the predestinator, along with the Father. But in the execution of the decree, as head of the elect, and mediator, he is the predestinated. As God, his role is in the decree, as God-man in its execution. As God he is efficient cause of election. As man, he is the first effect of it, and subordinate cause. In this sense Beza admitted to not a separation, but a subordination, of Christ as mediator, to the decree. Christ is the medium through which the decree of election is accomplished. Indeed, Beza blamed the Lutherans for confusing that decree with the decree of sending his Son.[63]

The Extent of the Atonement

It is now possible to approach Beza's teaching on the extent of the atonement, bearing in mind his subordination of the revealed will of God to the hidden, and his subordination of Christ as mediator to the decree of election. The detailed debate with Andreae made it necessary for Beza to deal directly with the implications of his doctrine of predestination for the extent of the atonement, and the *Ad Acta...Responsio* is the fullest source for Beza's answer to the question, "For whom did Christ die?"

A preliminary consideration must be that Beza was working with essentially the same understanding of the nature of the atonement, namely as penal substitution, as Calvin, but that Beza went further in trying to give it a logical explanation. At the beginning of his *Christian Questions and Answers* Beza stated that the justice and mercy of God are united in saving us through the satisfactory work of Christ. He suffered in body and, especially, in soul, and to the point of death, bearing the wrath of God for us. Echoing Calvin, Beza said that this was not the only means by which God could have saved us, but was,

> "The moste convenient meane for him to shew, as well his singular justice, as his singular mercy."[64]

The display of justice and mercy required the dual nature of Christ as God and man, so that mercy would be seen in the Father's willingness to give his divine Son, and justice in the fact that the penalty was paid by man, the guilty party. The divinity of Christ also enabled him to discharge the wrath of God as no mere human could have done. The same divine concern for the demonstration of justice and mercy noted in Beza's doctrine of predestination can be observed here.[65]

The Anselmic theory of the atonement had left its mark on Beza. The necessity for the divinity of the Mediator is placed in the need for due proportion between the offence and penalty. An infinite satisfaction was required because the offence was infinite, being committed against the infinite majesty of God. Hence the need for an infinite, divine Mediator.

There is no argument about the nature of the atonement in the *Ad Acta...Responsio*, but sharp exchanges over its extent. To Andreae's enquiry about John 3.16 Beza replied that the world God loves is not to be understood universally, but indefinitely, with reference to those who believe in Christ, just as Christ said that he did not pray for the world but for those given him by his Father. "The world" in John 3.16 means the elect throughout the world. A will of God to save all individuals cannot be meant, because what God decrees, he also performs, since he cannot be impeded or changed.

1 John 2.2 was expounded similarly. In its statement that Christ is the propitiation for the sins of the whole world, "the world"

> "...is to be understood of the sole universality of the elect and believing".

The same text refers to the intercession of Christ, which, on the basis of John 17.9, cannot be "for the world", in an unrestricted sense. Other verses mentioning "the world" or "all" are similarly interpreted as referring to a restricted universality.[66]

Andreae's concept of universal atonement was repudiated as "intolerable", for it implied that Christ died for those already damned, and so had failed.[67] Andreae maintained:[68]

> "He has satisfied sufficiently for the sins of all individuals, so that there would be no need for a new or additional sacrifice if a thousand worlds, so to speak, remained to be reconciled to God. One drop of the blood of the Son of God would suffice for them."

This led Beza to consider the sufficient-efficient formula. As Calvin had done, Beza accepted the formula as true in a sense, but regarded it as inadequate.

> "It is said very roughly and ambiguously, as well as barbarously."

The reason given for this criticism was that the preposition "for" (*pro*) declares a plan and effect, and so the statement "Christ died for..." can only be properly completed by "the elect" or an equivalent term. So, although there is no need to deny that Christ's satisfaction could have been sufficient for an infinite number, it is necessary to add the proviso,

> "...if God willed to have mercy on all".

Thus the statement that Christ died sufficiently for all could only be accepted in a hypothetical sense, which, to Beza, made it irrelevant. Andreae's appeal to it was therefore "a mere subterfuge". For the dispute was not about whether only believers benefit from Christ's work. It was about God's intention behind the atonement.[69]

It was suggested in the previous chapter that Calvin's dissatisfaction with the sufficient-efficient formula was that it did not explicitly trace the effectiveness of the atonement to the divine predestination. It can be seen that Beza dismissed it at Montbéliard for the same reason. Beza's observations on it seem to amount to a total dismissal, however. It is not surprising to find him even less interested in the formula than Calvin was, for, lacking any doctrine of a real universal saving will or promise, he had no need to maintain any kind of universality in the atonement. Indeed, it was in his interest, in defending his logical system of predestination, to deny it.[70]

Beza took Andreae's position on the universality of the atonement to imply that people cannot be condemned for their sins, but solely for failing to believe in Christ. So he pointed out that unbelief is a sin and thus Andreae should maintain that unbelief is also expiated, and the unbelieving saved. Beza held that if sins are expiated, salvation must follow. According to his system, particular atonement guarantees the salvation of the elect.

> "Satisfaction necessarily abolishes all blame."[71]

This argument represents a departure from Calvin. Calvin had spoken of the atonement in terms of actual accomplishment, and yet stated that without faith the benefit could be lost. Beza said that application is certain for all those for whom Christ died, namely the elect. Beza's famous advice to the believer who is fearful of God's condemnation, to tell the devil that God "is content with one payment" may be compared with the position he adopted at Montbéliard. Although that pastoral advice was given in the context of faith, not election, and was not presented as an argument for limited atonement in the way that it would be in later Reformed theology, it did express Beza's conviction that the work of Christ must be effective for all for whom it was performed.[72]

Andreae explained that he meant that failure to believe in Christ is not the only, but the greatest, reason for condemnation, for it is the rejection of the only means of forgiveness of all sins. Christ may have died for one's sins, but one could still perish through unbelief. Beza was unwilling to accept this apparent negation of the work of Christ, regarding it as unthinkable that Christ could have died for the damned no less than for the saved.[73]

Faith and Assurance

In the *Ad Acta...Responsio* Beza conceded that a different method should be adopted in preaching and pastoral counselling than that used in doctrinal formulation.[74] As part of the counsel of God, predestination must be preached, but viewed *a posteriori* rather than *a priori.* Rather than attempt to scrutinize predestination directly, we must first exercise faith in Christ. Then, from the reality of our faith, we may conclude our election.[75] Scholars have pointed out that Beza did not place assurance, as Calvin did, primarily in the act of believing.[76] He constructed and concentrated on the *syllogismus practicus* by which believers may deduce the presence of faith from the presence of sanctification. The reason for this shift in the doctrine of assurance may well be due to the fact that, for Beza, the Mediator can have significance only for the elect. Calvin had preserved the significance of Christ for all, by means of his teaching of a universal atonement and promise of the gospel, and thus could place assurance in the act of faith exercised towards a personally applicable Christ. By contrast, Beza, however much he may have wished, for pastoral reasons, to exclude election from the first stages of seeking assurance, preached a Christ who could not be a pledge of the loving-kindness of God to all. Thus it was to be expected that his hearers would not find assurance through a direct act of faith. It is not difficult to see that the *syllogismus practicus* had to replace the direct assurance of faith. Thus limited atonement shaped both the preaching of an indefinite and promiscuous, but not universal, gospel, and the pastoral direction of those who lacked assurance.

CONCLUSION

Beza produced a tight system of supralapsarian predestination, according to which predestination and providence were virtually identified. His understanding of predestination was dominated by Aristotelian concepts of causality, so that the will of God could be read from events, being related as cause to effect. Divine attributes of immutability and omnipotence supported the causal series. Though Beza thought that by use of the concept of secondary causality, otherwise described as the execution of the decree, he could ascribe the guilt of sin to mankind and not God, he always looked for the theological significance of the person and work of Christ, of history and of human acts, in their nature as "effects" of the first cause, namely the divine decree. Consistently, he found little room for a universal promise, indeed the promise was characterized by him as "promiscuous and indefinite" rather than universal. Christ, as an effect of, and in subordination to, the decree could not be a mediator with genuinely universal significance within this system, and so his atoning death was seen as being for the elect alone. It would be going too far to say that Beza's theology was totally dominated by predestination, and it is worth taking into account that at the end of the Colloquy of Montbéliard Beza maintained that, in spite of differences over predestination, the Reformed and Lutherans were agreed on the "fundamentals of the Christian religion": it was Andreae who refused to shake Beza's hand because of the latter's "errors and heresies".[77] Nevertheless, Beza's theology, if not dominated, was shaped at every point, by predestination. The limitations he placed upon the promise of the gospel and the extent of the atonement indicate the all-pervasive influence of his predestinarianism.

Much within Beza's system, including the particularism of the atonement, can be found in Calvin's theology.[78] However, in striving for coherence within a polemical context, Beza eliminated or subdued other, apparently contradictory, elements in Calvin's thought. Notable among these were the universal saving will and promise of God and the universal aspect of the atonement.

Chapter Three
Notes

1 For biographical information, see H.M.Baird, *Theodore Beza, the counsellor of the French Reformation*, New York 1899; P-F.Geisendorf, *Théodore de Bèze*, Geneva 1949; J.Raitt, "Theodore Beza 1519-1605", in J.Raitt (ed.), *Shapers of Religious Traditions in Germany, Switzerland and Poland, 1560-1600*, New Haven 1981, pp.89-104; H.Vuilleumier, *Histoire de l'Eglise Reformée du Pays de Vaud sous le Régime Bernois*, (4 vols.), Lausanne 1928-1933, vol.1 pp.417-423, 474-489, 646-648, 663-666.

2 Hall, in Duffield, op.cit., pp.19-37; J.Dantine, "Les Tabelles sur la Doctrine de la Prédestination par Théodore de Bèze", *RTP* 16(1966), pp.365-377: "*...il faut nommer Bèze le père de l'orthodoxie calviniste*" (p.365). This article is based on Dantine's 1965 Göttingen dissertation, "Die Prädestinationslehre bei Calvin und Beza"; Armstrong, op.cit., pp.41-42, 136-138; Kendall, op.cit., pp.29-38; W.Kickel, *Vernunft und Offenbarung bei Theodor Beza: zum Problem des Verhaltnisses von Theologie, Philosophie und Staat*, Neukirchen 1967; and see D.Steinmetz (ed.), *Reformers in the Wings*, Philadelphia 1971, pp.162-171.

The definition of "scholasticism" has proved difficult. Several scholars use the four criteria suggested by Armstrong, (op.cit., p.32), but recognize their inadequacy (e.g. Bray, op.cit., p.119), as does Armstrong himself. It is also important to be alert to the dangers of setting scholasticism and humanism in direct opposition. P.O.Kristeller has shown that the two were not necessarily incompatible as they dealt with largely separate fields. See Kristeller, *Renaissance Thought, the classic, scholastic and humanistic strains*, New York 1961, esp. pp.8-23, 100-111; J.H.Overfield, *Humanism and Scholasticism in Late Medieval Germany*, Princeton 1984, esp. pp.329-330; McGrath, *Intellectual Origins*, op.cit., pp.33-58. Indeed Beza had a humanistic training, displayed the humanist commitment to exploring source literature in his editions of the New Testament in Greek and Latin, pursued the favourite humanist occupation of writing poetry, plays and biographies, and was thus a man in whom the humanist passion for rhetoric and the scholastic devotion to dialectical reasoning combined. Thus Kickel, op.cit., p.10, refers to the influence of a "*rationalistischen Humanismus*". See also K.M.Summers, "Theodore Beza's Classical Library and Christian Humanism", *ARG* 82(1991) pp.193-207. For a sympathetic view of Reformed scholasticism, see R.A.Muller, *Post Reformation Reformed Dogmatics*, vol.1: Prolegomena to Theology, Grand Rapids 1987, pp.1-40.

3 J.Raitt, *The Eucharistic Theology of Theodore Beza: development of the Reformed doctrine*, Chambersburg 1972, p.71; J.S. Bray, *Theodore Beza's Doctrine of Predestination*, Nieuwkoop 1975: "Theodore Beza was not a Protestant scholastic" (p.142, and see pp.86-106), "Beza is best viewed as a transitional figure who bridged the gulf between the biblical-Christocentric position of Calvin and the scholasticism of those who followed him" (p.21); T.Maruyama, *The Ecclesiology of Theodore Beza: the reform of the true church*, Geneva 1978, pp.139-148; M.Delval, "Orthodoxie et Prédication: Théodore de Bèze", in *BSHPF* 134(1988), pp.693-697, based on his Lille thesis, "La Doctrine du Salut dans L'Oeuvre Homéletique de Théodore de Bèze"; Muller, *Christ*, op.cit., calls Beza "a transition figure" (p.95) and goes so far as to say, "Beza's role in the development of the Reformed system may...be described as a generally successful attempt to clarify and to render more precise the doctrinal definitions he had inherited from Calvin" (p.96). Cp. R.W.Letham, "Theodore Beza: a reassessment", *SJT* 40(1987)1 pp.25-40.

4 I.McPhee, "Transformer or Conserver of Calvin's Theology? A study of the origins and development of Theodore Beza's thought", Ph.D. Cambridge, 1980, esp. pp.42-43, 82-83; cp. M.Jinkins, "Theodore Beza: continuity and regression in the Reformed tradition", *EQ* 64(1992)2 pp.131-154.

5 Raitt, in Raitt, op.cit., p.104.

6 The following are non-polemical works: *A Briefe and Pithie Sum of the Christian Faith*, London 1572 (English translation of Confession de la Foi, Geneva 1559); *Cours sur les Epîtres aux Romains et aux Hébreux 1564-66; d'après les notes de Marcus Widler*, ed. P. Fraenkel and L. Perrotet, Geneva 1988; "De Praedestinationis Doctrina et Vero Usu Tractatio Absolutissima, ex praelectionibus in nonum epistolae ad Romanos caput a Raphaele Eglino Tigurino", in *Tractationes Theologicae* (3 vols.), vol.3, Geneva 1582, pp.402-447; *Propositions and Principles of Divinitie, propounded and disputed in the universitie of Geneva...under M. Theod. Beza, and M. Anthonie Faius*, Edinburgh 1591.

7 The Council of Trent sat in 1546. For the development of Socinian thought, see M.Martini, *Fausto Socino et La Pensée Socinienne: un maître de la pensée religieuse (1539-1604)*, Paris 1967; Z.Ogonowski, "Faustus Socinus 1539-1604", in Raitt, *Shapers*, op.cit.

8 For the Bolsec Controversy see ante, p.37 n.11, and *Correspondance de Théodore de Bèze*, ed. H.Aubert, F.Aubert and H.Meylan, Geneva 1960- , vol.1 pp.71-73, on which the following exposition is based.

9 Cp. *Cours*, p.377, "Election cannot stand in any way other than in opposition to reprobation."

10 Cp. *Cours*, p.362, "God did not create men and then afterwards decree what they would be...God decreed not only that there should be men, but what kind of men they should be."

11 *Correspondance*, pp.76-80.

12 Ibid., pp.81-84.

13 Ibid., p.84 n.5.

14 Ibid., pp.169-173. The following exposition is based on this letter.

15 See ibid., pp.153-155 (letter of March 1555 from Vermigli at Strasbourg to Beza). See esp. p.155 n.3.

16 "I...in my table, have subordinated all these [sc. creation, the fall and Christ] first to God's plan of electing and reprobating, to which I make absolutely nothing superior."

17 Beza's identification of predestination and providence is seen in the Thomistic definition in *Propositions and Principles*, pp.19-20: "First in generall, Praedestination is that aeternal and immovable decree of GOD, whereby, as it pleased his Majestie; he hath decreed all things, both universalie and particularlie...to the laying open of his owne glory. Secondlie, applying this decree in speciall unto mankind. Wee call Praedestination, that aeternall decree...whereby, he hath immutably purposed from all aeternity, by saving some of his great mercie, and by damning others in his most just severitie, to manifeste himselfe...namely, that he is most merciful and most just."

18 Similarly God's love to the elect, and hatred towards the reprobate, are subsidiary to and flow from the decree. Cp. *Cours*, p.362.

19 The same distinction between God's decision to elect ("*non tam elegit quam eligere constituit*"), and "election in Christ" is made elsewhere, e.g. *Ad Sebastiani Castellionis Calumnias, Quibus Unicum Salutis Nostrae Fundamentum, id Est Aeternam Dei Praedestinationem Evertere Nititur Responsio*, in *Tractationes*, vol.1 (1570), (pp.337-424) p.342; *The Treasure of Trueth*, trans. John Stockwood, n. pl. 1576, ch.2.4. (This work is an English translation of the *Summa Totius Christianismi* of 1555, the first printed work in which the "Table" appeared. See F. Gardy, *Bibliographie des Oeuvres Théologiques, Littéraires, Historiques et Juridiques de Théodore de Bèze*, Geneva 1960, for this and other bibliographical details).

20 Reproduced from *The Treasure*. A similar chart and explanation are given in the "De Praedestinationis Doctrina", in *Tractationes*, vol.3, pp.402-447.

21 *The Treasure*, op.cit., ch.2.2.

22 Ibid., ch.4.2, "God therefore the most gentle Father of the elect and chosen...appointed his onely sonne...should be made a verie, or true man."

23 The explanation of the "Table" in *The Treasure* constantly refers to causality, cp. Correspondance, vol.1 p.171, and *Ad Acta...Responsio* (see below, p.63 n.43), pp.167-168. Beza's continual use of causality to categorize the works of God is perhaps the most obvious example of his commitment to Aristotelian scholastic method. The comment in Beza's *Novum Testamentum*, London 1574, on Ephesians 1 states that the first part of the letter contains "all the causes of our salvation". This comment is explained as follows: "The efficient cause of our salvation is God, not universally and confusedly considerd, but as the Father of our Lord Jesus Christ. The proximate final cause, with respect to us, is our salvation...The material cause of our salvation is Christ...He (Paul) explains the efficient cause...because he says he chose us from eternity in the Son". Though the concept of causality is much more prominent in Beza, Calvin had already applied it in his exposition of the same passage. Beza understood the *prae* of *praedestinatio* in a causal sense. It cannot, he explained, be a statement of chronology, since, all time is present to God. Rather than indicating temporal sequence it denotes a causal sequence: He understands the particle *"non significare tempus, sed ordinem causae"* (*Cours*, p.135).

24 Bray, op.cit., p.92. Dantine, "Les Tabelles", op.cit., p.367, states that Beza considered that in this distinction he had found the key to maintaining that God is the author of salvation but not of sin.

25 *Ad Calumnias...Responsio*, *Tractationes*, vol.1, p.360.

26 "De Praedestinationis Doctrina", *Tractationes*, vol. 3 pp.406b,438b.

27 Bray, op.cit., p.140.

28 *Correspondance*, vol.1 p.82.

29 Raitt, *Shapers*, op.cit., p.99, points out that Calvin did not correct, but approved, Beza's supralapsarian doctrine.

30 Castellio was a Savoyard humanist Calvin had come to know at Strasbourg, and had appointed master of the school in Geneva. His subsequent request to enter the pastoral ministry was refused, however, when it was found that he questioned the canonical status of the Song of Songs, and took a literal view of the descent into hell. This was the start of a fierce antagonism between the two men. For Castellio, see Parker, John Calvin, op.cit., p.102; Wendel, op.cit. pp.81-83, 90-91; S.E.Ozment, *Mysticism and Dissent; religious ideology and social protest in the sixteenth century*, New Haven 1973, pp.168-202.

31 *Correspondance*, vol.2 p.168; *An Answeare*, op.cit. p.173b.

32 *Correspondance*, vol.2 pp.168-171.

33 "You see the sophisms prepared: if created for salvation, why are they not destined for salvation...if destined to perish with respect to their future defection, therefore their foreseen defection will be the cause why they were destined to destruction. The hidden decree of reprobation will not therefore be the cause."

34 Calvin had planned to refer to "those who, created for salvation, perish through their own fault." See *Correspondance*, vol.2 p.170 n.4.

35 Op.cit. First published in 1558 as *Praefatio Calumniorum adversus Doctrinam Ioannis Calvini, aut potius fidelium ecclesiarum de occulta Dei providentia.* Castellio's main charges against Calvin were that he distorted the loving character of God, made God the author of sin and posited two contradictory wills within God (*Tractationes*, vol.1 pp.341,388-394,396a). Beza set out his supralapsarian predestination doctrine, defending it by appeal to the inscrutability of God's will, which is the rule of all justice (p.342). Scholastic concepts abound, particularly in the causal structure of Beza's doctrine, and in the concept of God as the First Mover (p.401).

36 Ibid., pp.353-354, contains Beza's discussion of Ezek.33.11.

37 The reference to the *potentia absoluta* indicates a familiarity with the *Via Moderna* of scholastic theology.

38 The discussion of Matt.23.37 is found in pp.397-398.

39 Calvin himself had used the verb *balbutire* in *Institutes* 1.13.1.

40 The following exposition is based on *Ad Calumnias...Responsio*, pp.386-396.

41 For Montbéliard, see P.Pfister, *Le Colloque de Montbéliard*, Geneva 1873; A.Lods, "Les Actes Du Colloque de Montbéliard 1586: une polémique entre Théodore de Bèze et Jacques Andreae", *BSHPF* 1897 pp.192-215; Vuilleumier, op.cit., pp.125-131; Adam, op.cit., pp.19-49; J.Raitt, *The Colloquy of Montbéliard: religion and politics in the sixteenth century*, New York 1993. The Lutherans were represented by Jacob Andreae, one of the authors of the Formula of Concord, and Lucas Osiander. For Andreae, see R.Kolb, "Jacob Andreae 1528-1590", pp.53-68, in Raitt (ed.) *Shapers*, op.cit. The Reformed deputation consisted of Abraham Musculus and Peter Hubner of Bern, Claudius Alberius of Lausanne, Antonius Faius and Beza of Geneva.

42 See A.E.McGrath, *Iustitia Dei: a history of the Christian doctrine of justification*, Cambridge 1986, vol. 2, "From 1500 to the present day", pp.28-32, for an account of the way Lutheranism departed from the absolute predestinarianism of the early Luther's *Bondage of the Will*.

43 *Ad Acta Colloquii Montisbelgardensis Tubingae Edita Theodori Bezae Responsio pars altera*, Geneva 1588, pp.192,211,215,231

44 See Adam, op.cit., pp.31-33, and Raitt, *The Colloquy*, op.cit., pp.147-156,160-164, for accounts of how predestination was introduced into the discussions at Montbéliard, and for background to the publication of the *Ad Acta*. Pp.147-156 of Raitt, *The Colloquy*, contain an excellent summary of the debate on predestination.

45 *Ad Acta*, pp.161, 147. Lengthy extracts from Luther's *Bondage of the Will* were printed at the end of the *pars prior* of the *Ad Acta* to show that the Lutherans were departing from their mentor.

46 Pp.166-167.

47 Pp.154,165,175: "If that decree is of God, therefore it is eternal, and therefore it is immutable." Kickel, op.cit., pp.136-146, maintains that sovereignty and immutability have a purely philosophical character in Beza's thought, guaranteeing the causal system.

48 See Kickel, op.cit., p.121, for Beza's inductive and deductive logic.

49 Pp.204,208.

50 Pp.159,185.

51 Pp.152-156; pp.204-206, "We also understand by that term, 'the will of God' that part of providence which directs all human affairs, and even individual men...to that ultimate end, namely his glory...some by way of mercy and some by the way of justice."

52 P.173; p.185. Dantine, op.cit., p.372, points out parallels between Beza and Thomas Aquinas, in that Thomas, starting with the distinction between primary and secondary causes, developed a distinction between providence and its execution. He asserts that, even though Beza does not speak of the link with Thomas, "It cannot be doubted that Thomas had a certain influence on Beza in this". However, Beza does explicitly claim the support of Thomas "and the scholastics" for his doctrine of absolute predestination at this point in the *Ad Acta*. He also explains that "there is no firmer conclusion than *a posteriore*, as the schools say: *hoc factus est, ergo Deus voluit ut fieret*." See Thomas Aquinas, *Summa Theologica*, London 1922, 22.3.

53 *Ad Acta*, op.cit., pp.173,152-3,168,204.

54 P.225; p.174; p.226; p.174; pp.225-226; pp.174-175.

55 P.204; p.175.

56 P.10, "God wishes all to come to the knowledge of the truth, but conditionally, if they will believe". On the conditionality of the gospel, see *Sum*, 14a-26a, *Tractationes*, vol.3, 405a-406a.

57 *Ad Acta*, p.192.

58 Beza echoed Calvin in appealing to Proverbs 16.4, a verse ranking with Romans ch.9, in the frequency of its use by Beza, e.g. *Tractationes*, vol.3, 403a; *Ad Acta*, op.cit., pp.168,176.

59 Ibid., pp.170-171.

60 M.P.Hoogland, *Calvin's Perspective on the Exaltation of Christ: in comparison with the post-Reformation doctrine of the two states*, Kampen 1966, pp.207-211, accuses the Reformed after Calvin of veering towards Nestorianism in separating the divine and human natures of Christ. See also E.D.Willis, *Calvin's Catholic Christology: the function of the so called 'Extra Calvinisticum' in Calvin's Theology*, Leiden 1966.

61 *Ad Acta*, p.208 states that it cannot be said that God wills the conversion of any except those who are in fact converted. Cp. p.196. See also p.2LL, which says that 'the world' God is said to love in John 3.16 is to be understood indefinitely, not universally, and p.214, on John 1.29 where, in contrast to Calvin's universalistic comment on the same text, Beza explains the world as the gathering of the elect of all races.

62 *Ad Acta*, p.196; cp. p.156, "[Election is] not understood as an absolute decree but is to be limited and described in Christ: Eph.1.4"; p.230, "The predestination of the elect cannot be judged by reason...but from the gospel alone"; p.192, "God does not will all men to be saved by an absolute will. For thus all would certainly be saved...But by a restricted will IN CHRIST, out of whom he wills no-one to be saved. He offers Christ to all through the preaching of the Gospel and the use of the Sacraments." See ante, p.7.

63 *Ad Acta*, pp.156,199-200.

64 *A Booke of Christian Questions and Answers*, London 1572, pp.1-8 (p.6). Beza sometimes distinguished Christ as *mediator* and *medium*:. As *mediator* he stands between God and the human race, as *medium* he stands between the decree and its accomplishment, see e.g. *Ad Acta*, p.195-6; *Questions and Answers*, op.cit., p.14.

65 Ibid., pp.5-7; p.93; *Sum*, 8a-10a.

66 *Ad Acta*, op.cit., pp.211,213,214,192. 1 Tim. 2.4-6 is to be understood "according to all the orthodox fathers, especially Augustine" as meaning "*non singulos generum, sed genera singulorum*". The same explanation appears in the annotations of Beza's *Novum Testamentum*, on the same verse.

67 *Ad Acta*, pp.215-16, "It is impious and blasphemous...to say that those whose sins have been expiated through the death of Christ, or for whom Christ has satisfied, can be condemned."

68 For the sufficient-efficient discussion, see pp.214-221.

69 Pp.217-218. For an example of the way Beza could happily apply the term "sufficiency", see *Cours*, p.406, "The one and only sacrifice of Christ once made, is sufficient for the abolishing of all the sins of all the faithful."

70 The concept of the merit of Christ as "ordained" rather than intrinsic, typical of the *Via Moderna*, was held by both Calvin and Beza. This common ground with the *Via Moderna* may go some way to explain why both he and Calvin had little interest in the potential sufficiency of Christ's atonement, but concentrated upon its ordained effectiveness. For Duns Scotus, "As the merit was in itself finite, so the reward in accordance with justice that awarded it was also finite. Wherefore also Christ did not earn merit for an infinite number of persons in respect of the sufficiency of that merit to be accepted by God" (cited by A.Ritschl, op.cit., see pp.65-70).

71 *Ad Acta*, p.219.

72 *Sum*, pp.21a-21b; cp. *Treasure*, ch.6.

73 *Ad Acta*, 218-221. For an overview of Beza on the extent of the atonement, see Bray, op.cit., pp.111-112, and, for a more extensive treatment, see Strehle, "The Extent", op.cit., pp.125-134.

74 Pp.64-68,150,230.

75 Cp. *Cours*, p.376, "True sanctification, since it is fruitful in the elect alone, is a certain evidence of our election....The testimony of our election is not to be sought by us in the hidden counsel of God, but rather from the apprehension of calling and faith."

76 Kendall, op.cit., pp.29-38, "Fundamental to the doctrine of faith in Theodore Beza...is his belief that Christ died for the elect only." (p.29); Bray, op.cit., pp.107-111. In fact, sometimes Beza spoke as Calvin did of faith as a persuasion, and a knowledge that Christ died for me, at other times he defined it as "assent" and "embracing Christ" (e.g. *Sum*, ch.14a-26a; *Questions and Answers*, pp.23-24). These various ways of speaking are understandable in terms of degrees of faith (*Propositions*, p.46).

77 See *Ad Acta*, p.251. See R.M.Kingdon, "Barriers to Protestant Ecumenism in the Career of Theodore Beza", pp.237-251, in McKee and Armstrong, op.cit., esp. p.247.

78 Kickel concedes that all Beza's predestination teaching was in Calvin, op.cit., p.47, the difference being that, for Calvin, predestination was not the *Centraldogmen*. We accept the statement of W.J.Bouwsma, *John Calvin: a sixteenth-century portrait*, New York 1988, with regard to the debate about whether Beza and the other heirs of Calvin departed from him: "The existence of two rather different Calvins suggests that this way of dealing with the relationship between Calvin and his successors misses the essential point. Later Calvinists were the heirs of the philosophical and systematic Calvin..."

Chapter Four
Heinrich Bullinger (1504–1575)

INTRODUCTION

Heinrich Bullinger was the leading pastor of Zurich from 1531, after the death of Zwingli. His theology has suffered some neglect by scholars, overshadowed by his contemporary, Calvin. However, his influence and importance are being recognized increasingly.[1] Although studies of Bullinger's theology are still comparatively few, there has been a growing interest, especially in connection with the search for the origins of covenant theology.[2]

With reference to the extent of the atonement, considerable interest attaches to Bullinger. Arminians were later to claim him in support of their views, so that J.J.Breitinger, the leader of the Zurich delegation at the Synod of Dort, found it necessary to defend his orthodoxy.[3] Subsequently, Moïse Amyraut and his supporter Jean Daillé maintained that their modification of seventeenth-century orthodoxy was in full accord with the teaching of Bullinger. They appealed to him in their attempt to prove that the Reformed fathers had taught a universal atonement dependent for its effectiveness on the fulfilment of the condition of faith.[4]

This chapter will draw widely upon Bullinger's writings to examine some of his theological themes. It will then concentrate on writings produced in controversy to highlight distinctive emphases.

THEOLOGICAL THEMES

The Nature and Will of God

Pre-eminent in Bullinger's treatment of the nature of God is the divine goodness. He often calls God the *Summum Bonum*,[5] and derives the German *Gott* from *gut*[6]. In places where he lists the divine attributes, goodness is nearly always to the fore.

> "Notwithstanding amongst all things which are attributed to God his bountefulnes or love, fayth and mercy are the chiefe. For he is our Father..."

> "God is the sovereigne, eternal and onlie god, the fountaine and head of all goodnesse, almightie, bountefall, loving, merciful, righteous and true, a trustie father over the things that he hath made."[7]

In dealing with difficult questions he frequently laid it down as fundamental that no conclusion may be reached that may conflict with the goodness of God. Thus, for example, God cannot be the author of sin, because God is good.

> "This is an argument of greatest force and probability, because God is said to be good naturally."

In fact, the divine goodness seems to occupy the place in Bullinger's theology that the omnipotent will does in Beza's. For although Beza also wished to maintain the goodness of God, he conducted his enquiry into the origin of sin on the principle that no conclusion was permissible which seemed to threaten absolute divine omnipotence. Bullinger's sensitivity to the danger of casting a shadow upon the goodness of God is seen in his treatment of the fall. He insisted firmly that God was not the author of the fall, which is rather to be attributed to human free will, and the temptation of the devil. Further than this Bullinger refused to go.[8]

The omnipotent will of God, so important to Calvin and Beza, was understood by them to be hidden. Bullinger's supreme principle of the goodness of God is, by contrast, declared in and learned from Christ.

> "So then the cause of God's love to us-wards must of necessity be not in us..., but even in God himself. Moreover the most true scripture doth teach us, that God is of his own inclination naturally good, gentle, and, as Paul calleth him, philanthropon, a lover of us men, who hath sent his own Son, of his own nature, into the world for our redemption: whereupon it doth consequently follow, that God doth freely, of himself and for his Son's sake, love man..."[9]

In Christ God is revealed as *philanthropon,* and this love, which is part of the divine nature, extends to all.

> "For God is not onelie the Father of Christe from everalastinge, but the father of us all, not onelie because he created us, but also bycause hee beareth everie one of us good will, is loving and mercifull unto all men, and gyveth us all thinges necessarie...and defendeth us."[10]

Part of Bullinger's understanding of God as the *Summum Bonum* was that God's will must be a good will. In fact Bullinger used the term *beneplacitum* ("good pleasure") to emphasize the goodness of the divine will revealed in the gospel, whereas Beza and Calvin used it as a technical term for the unknowable absolute will of God. Christ is the perfect expression of the good will of God. It was according to this *beneplacitum* of God that

> "it pleased our Lord God that his Son should suffer for us".

Furthermore,

> "The will of God is that beneplacitum of God, from which...he wills that the world should be saved through the innocent death of Christ. This will of God is proclaimed in the gospel."[11]

Like the Genevans, and in harmony with the medieval tradition, Bullinger recognized a need to speak of the will of God in two ways, even though he could make the beneplacitum synonymous with the gospel. A hidden will regarding the destiny of each individual remains, but the will revealed in Christ takes pride of place. The secret will is to be acknowledged, and we are to trust that it is good. Since, however, it is an abyss too deep for us to fathom, attention is quickly to be redirected to the revealed will, which we can see is good.[12]

> "The godly do not curiously dispute about election at all. For they do not break into the hidden will, but concern themselves with the mystery of the incarnation and seek their salvation in the cross, where, if they feel themselves inserted into Christ by faith, they believe that they are chosen by God."[13]

Bullinger's comments on 1 Timothy 2.3-6, contradicting the Genevan exposition, can be summarized as follows:

a) It is inadequate to explain "all men" in this verse as "all sorts of men".
b) That all are in fact not saved is the fault of those who refuse to believe.
c) God genuinely desires the salvation of the heathen.[14]

The prominence Bullinger gave to the revealed and universal saving will of God is apparent in what he did not say in his comments on Ezekiel 18.23 and Matthew 23.37, texts frequently cited in his writings. He did not feel a need to qualify the biblical statements concerning God's not wanting the death of the sinner, and Christ's will to gather unwilling Jerusalem, by reference to a hidden will, as Beza and Calvin did. He pointed, however, to human unbelief in response to God's revealed will, which is both universal, and conditional upon faith. He wanted to let God's hidden will remain hidden.[15]

Providence

The theme of providence had been important to Zwingli. A similarity between Zwingli's doctrine of providence and the Stoic concept of fate has been pointed out by some scholars. Jerome Bolsec, in fact, singled out Zwingli's *De Providentia* for attack as being fatalistic.[16] Bullinger, with all the Reformed, shared Zwingli's basic conviction that all things are governed by the providence of God, but he was also at pains to point out that God works through instruments, and therefore responsible human action is not nullified.[17] Moreover, by constantly presenting providence as a matter of God's goodness towards creation, and the human race in particular, he ensured that his doctrine did not conjure up a picture of a heartless deity inexorably pursuing his own ends. In fact he went so far as to assert,

> "Bicause God of himself is of such nature and goodwill towards us...of right and woorthely he hath rule over all men."[18]

For Bullinger the goodness of God made it unthinkable that God could have been in some sense responsible for the fall. In refusing to present the fall as ordained by God, he was accepting a more circumscribed understanding of the omnipotence of God than either Calvin or Beza would allow. The fall was indeed foreseen by God, but with a foresight that imposed no necessity.[19] In answering a point which could have come directly from the writings of Beza or even Calvin, that sin was necessary "that by that means the glory of God might shine more brightly", Bullinger stated that God is glorious, irrespective of the human race or its sin. Similarly, he did not share the Genevan hesitation about the concept of divine permission as an aspect of providence. The fall and all evil actions must be understood as permitted by God, who chooses for his own good reasons to allow certain evil things to be done by human beings, in such a way that the responsibility rests entirely with their evil will, not with God.[20]

If Bullinger's account of providence seems less complete and logically satisfying than that of his Genevan counterparts, it is because he was dedicated to keeping the goodness of God to the fore. Omnipotence was not to swallow up the divine goodness.

Predestination

Predestination was dealt with by Bullinger in close association with providence. Both are aspects of the omnipotent will of God, providing an explanation, in divine-causal terms, of human experience. Providence and predestination are also related because both are outstanding demonstrations of the goodness of God. The title of the *Decades* sermon, which, significantly, deals with both providence and predestination, is:

> "That God is the creator of all things, and governeth all things by his providence: where mention is also made of the goodwill of God to usward, and of predestination."

Bullinger's caution about understanding providence simply as the irresistible outworking of an omnipotent will is observable in his handling of predestination in the *Decades* sermon. His definition is:

> "The predestination of God is the eternal decree of God, whereby he hath ordained either to save or destroy men; a most certain end of life or death being appointed unto them."[21]

This may seem stark, but it becomes clear that it was not intended to be taken in a supralapsarian sense. Rather than creating the human race in order to display his justice and mercy by dividing it into two parts with different destinies, God's one plan from the beginning was that man would bear his image.

> "Now the will of God is, that man should be like unto his image, that is, that he should be holy, innocent, and so consequently saved. This will of his did God express, first by the law of nature, then by the law which he writ in two tables of stone, and lastly by the preaching of his holy gospel.

> "God ...ordeyned by his eternal purpose to declare his grace unto the world in Chryste at certeyne times by him appointed. For as he foresaw from everlasting the fall of man, so also hee prepared from everlasting remedies whereby the lost worlde should be restored, and appointed to send his Sonne in to the world, which should take upon him mannes nature, by whom the fall of man should bee restored."

Indeed, upon the fall,

> "God here again, as it were, of fresh began the work of salvation."[22]

No eternal plan of condemnation is set forth by Bullinger other than God's foreknowledge of man's sin, and refusal to come to Christ.

Election and Christ

Bullinger was insistent that election is christocentric: *in Christo, per et propter Christum.*[23]

Frequently Bullinger stated in general terms that the eternal purpose of God is the good of humanity, through conformity to the divine image. The fall being foreseen, this plan is formulated more specifically as the restoration of the human race, through Christ.

> "God, of his eternal goodness and liberality...did from everlasting determine to create man to his own similitude and likeness: but for because he did foresee that he would fall headlong into a filthy and miserable bondage, he did therefore by the same his grace and goodness ordain a deliverer to bring us out of thraldom."

Christ was foreordained by the Father:

> "God our faithfull and loving father...hath ordained Jesus Christ his onely Sonne...to be advocate, meane, intercessor and patrone or helper for mankind."[24]

Thus, supremely, Christ is the predestinated one, and Bullinger embarked upon his doctrine of predestination with the stated intention of basing it upon Christ:

> "The end of predestination, or fore-appointment, is Christ, the Son of the Father. For God hath ordained and decreed to save all, how many soever have communion and fellowship with Christ...."

> "If thou be a stranger from Christ...thou art predestinate to death...Higher and deeper I will not creep into the rest of God's counsel."[25]

According to G.W.Locher, Zwingli had also maintained that Christ's ordination precedes the election of individuals.[26] Moving on from this foundation, Bullinger could speak of election as if it presupposes faith, just as reprobation presupposes sin, the very comparison feared by Beza in the conflict with Bolsec.

> "God hath ordained and decreed to save all, how many soever have communion and fellowship with Christ and to destroy and condemn all, how many soever have no part in the communion or fellowship of Christ; now the faithful only have communion or fellowship with Christ and the unfaithful are strangers from Christ. Therefore whosoever are in Christ are chosen and elected."

The predestination of Christ, revealed in his historical coming and work, has a universal significance in that it provides a basis for calling all to faith in him, who is "the looking glass in whom we may contemplate our predestination"[27]. Those who become united to Christ by faith are the elect.

> "In Christ, by and through Christ, hath he chosen us ...Therefore whosoever are in Christ are chosen and elected."

> "We knowe that the elect are only saved, and that the elect in Christ: in Christ to be they that beleve."[28]

Accordingly, the doctrine of election in Christ allows the gospel to be viewed as a testimony of election, gives grounds to hope well of all and provides a motive to pray for faith in Christ.[29]

It is remarkable that throughout the sermon on predestination, election is presented as God's will and choice to give eternal life to believers in Christ, and not as an unfathomable decree to cause certain persons to become believers. In similar vein, the Second Helvetic Confession, of which Bullinger was author, speaks ambiguously of an election of those who are "saints" or "in Christ", without specifying whether they have been chosen as such or to be such. It also says:

> "God has elected us, not directly, but in Christ, and on account of Christ, in order that those who are now ingrafted into Christ by faith might also be elected."[30]

It will be appreciated that Bullinger could often be taken to imply that persons are elected on the basis of foreseen faith. He denied that position, aware that his mode of expressing himself could be open to criticism. Nevertheless, it is plain that he was convinced that, theologically and pastorally, election, Christ and faith should be held together. By stating that all who believe are elected to salvation, he could, as preacher and pastor, call upon all not to doubt their election, but rather believe.[31] This concept of election gave no room for speculation upon the eternal decrees or the attendant danger of uncertainty and despair.

Bullinger did not stop at relating election to believers in Christ, however. Standing in the Augustinian tradition, he had from very early in his career opposed Erasmus' advocacy of free will. Bullinger asserted that the will is corrupt and cannot choose the good unless set free by the Holy Spirit. To the question, "Why are some thus freed while others are not?", his answer was that faith is the gift of God, granted to those whom God chooses. After passionately insisting, in a sermon on Revelation 3.20, on the sincerity of God's call and on the human duty to be active in "opening the door to Christ", he nevertheless added:

> "The Lord illumineth his elect...They therefore that open, do open by the grace of God."[32]

Bullinger's doctrine of predestination, then, begins with God's determination that the human race will bear his image, and a decision to send Christ so that, in spite of the fall, this determination will be accomplished. When it comes to the election of individuals, the doctrine has two levels. On one, it is an election to salvation of those who are in Christ by faith, and it is at this level Bullinger preferred to deal with it. In order to oppose free will, however, he acknowledged, but would not dwell upon, a hidden level, at which election is a choice concerning those to whom faith will be granted. In both senses "election in Christ" is made to stand in opposition to any assertion that we are chosen on the basis of our own merit.[33] The ambiguity of this position gave succour to Bolsec[34], troubled Calvin and Beza and foreshadowed the Saumur doctrine of twofold predestination.

It should be observed that, even defined as that which is causally determinative of faith, election, according to Bullinger, enters into the purposes of God at the point of application of salvation. It logically follows the mission of Christ, and is subordinate to him. Therefore, it does not require a doctrine of limited atonement.

Promise

For Bullinger, the content of the gospel and the object of faith is Christ.[35] In the promise of the gospel, Christ is for all. The title of the eighth chapter of the *Commonplaces* states, "That Christe calleth all sinners unto him, and offereth unto them grace and all good things."

The promise is portrayed in such a universal manner as almost to displace the causal aspect of election.

> "Christ and the preaching of Christ his grace declared in the gospel doth belong unto all. For we must not imagine that in heaven there are laid two books, in the one whereof the names of them are written that are to be saved, and so to be saved, as it were of necessity, that, do what they will against the word of Christ and commit they never so heinous offences, they cannot possibly choose but be saved; and that in the other are contained the names of them which, do what they can and live they never so holily, yet cannot

> avoid everlasting damnation. Let us rather hold that the holy gospel of Christ doth generally preach to the whole world the grace of God, the remission of sins and life everlasting."[36]

Whilst Bullinger was opposing, in this passage, an understanding of election that would dispense with the use of means, the final sentence of the citation shows that he was anxious that the doctrine of election should in no way curtail the universality of the gospel promise. This universality does not imply that the promise becomes effective for all, for it is dependent for its effectiveness on the faith of the hearer.

> "He who came for the salvation of all does not benefit all, because through their own blame and vice they do not all believe. For by faith the good things offered by God through Christ are perceived...those however do not believe because they prefer darkness to light."[37]

Covenant

An investigation of the origins and development of Bullinger's covenant thought is beyond the scope of this work. Undoubtedly it was an important and distinctive element in his theology.[38] His interest in the covenant has been attributed to three factors: the need to find justification for the practice of infant baptism in his conflict with the Anabaptists, the related desire to understand the city state of Zurich as being in covenant with God after the manner of Old Testament Israel, and the likewise related search for a hermeneutical principle to establish the unity of the Old and New Testaments.[39] As well as these specific concerns there was a desire to stress the reliability of God and human responsibility within a "theology of history".[40]

Bullinger's concept of the covenant of God stood for the unity of God's dealings with the human race through the ages. It consists of divinely given promises and obligations, as in the covenant with Abraham.

> "First, the passage explains who bound themselves together, namely, God and the descendants of Abraham. Second, the text states the conditions under which they bound themselves together, specifically that God wished to be the God of the descendants of Abraham and that the descendants of Abraham ought to walk uprightly before God."[41]

The covenant had its original revelation in the promise of God to fallen Adam and Eve, but was repeatedly promulgated to Noah, to Abraham, in the law, and through the coming of Christ. Though limited for a time, in its revelation, to Israel, it is essentially universal, having been made known first to Adam.[42]

> "And this is that covenaunt which in holy scriptures god is sayd to have made with mankynde, which first was begun with Adam."[43]

It is a covenant of grace, resting upon God's goodness and the free and merciful movement of God towards sinful mankind,[44] but bilateral in giving promises from God and demanding faith and obedience from us.[45] Faith, however is simply a trusting response to the promise, and obedience the inevitable spontaneous outgrowth of true faith.

> "Yet on oure syde is all unfruteful, where faith is not. But where faith is, it ceaseth not throwe love to worke good accordynge to the law: all honoure and prayse beynge referred unto God, to men nothyng but unperfectnesse."[46]

Therefore there is no question of salvation by works.

Because faith is the condition of the covenant, Bullinger sometimes spoke of the essentially universal covenant as being made with believers, "Abraham with all his seed, that is, with all the faithful".[47] It is proclaimed, promised and commanded to all: its benefits are received only by believers.

There is no conflict between Bullinger's doctrines of election and covenant. It fully accords with his understanding of the covenant that God should elect believers to be his covenant partners.[48] And on the "hidden" level, it is necesary that some of mankind be elected to receive the gifts of faith and obedience in order to fulfil the conditions of the covenant. The covenant underscores the universality of the promise of the gospel. Behind it, guaranteeing its success, lies eternal, particular election. In terms of emphasis, the prominence of the covenant motif in Bullinger ensures that his theology concentrates on the dealings of God with all mankind in time and through Christ, rather than on the election of some within a pretemporal decree. It constitutes a theology of history, in harmony with Bullinger's pastoral concern to avoid distressing preoccupation with the eternal decrees.

The Extent of the Atonement

Bullinger's understanding of the nature of the atonement is essentially the same as that of Calvin and Beza. Christ bore divine wrath and satisfied divine justice, standing in the place of sinners. Through his sufferings he has ransomed and redeemed them and reconciled them to God. Surprisingly, though, in view of his avoidance of speculation about the divine will and omnipotence, he agreed with the Genevans that, in theory, God could have found a way to redeem the world apart from Christ.[49]

Nothing has been found in Bullinger's concept of election that would necessitate the subordination of the work of Christ to particular election. All that has been stated about the promise of the gospel and the covenant of God would lead us to expect a universal dimension to be prominent in his understanding of the work of Christ, and this expectation is not disappointed. In fact he was frequently at pains to stress the universality of Christ's saving work:

> "The Lord made to meet on him, as an expiatory sacrifice, not one or another or most sins of one or other man, but all the iniquities of all of us. Therefore I say, the sins of all men of the world of all ages have been expiated by his death."[50]

Passages like the above abound,[51] often with the purpose of urging the applicability of the gospel upon everyone who hears it. Every individual should understand that there are ample grounds for receiving the promise in faith. In the *Decades* sermon on predestination the doubter is urged,

> "Thou canst not complain that he will not give unto thee his Son, or that he is not thine, who, as the apostle saith, was given for us all."[52]

For Bullinger, faith is more than assent to general propositions. It must involve the recognition that the work of Christ avails for "me". So it is necessary for the exercise of faith that it have as its object a Christ who is significant for every individual.

> "For you believe in vain that Jesus Christ suffered, unless you believe he suffered on account of you, that is, for the remission of your sins."

Therefore the reason why not all are saved is not to be sought in any limitation within the atonement, but in human unbelief. The writer of Isaiah 53

> "says many and not all, not because Christ the Saviour did not die for all, but because not all believe".

> "He is born the Saviour for all generations, he wills all men to be saved and come to the knowledge of the truth. Therefore no-one is excluded unless he excludes himself by unbelief and rebellion...No-one is left out."[53]

The orientation of Bullinger's theology created no necessity to adopt Augustine's generic interpretation of "all" in texts like 1 Timothy 2.4-6. On the contrary, he explained that "world" in John 3.16 means "all men of all sorts". The only limitation on such universality of grace is that unbelievers exclude themselves from it.[54]

Underlying the universality of the atonement is the incarnation, in which Christ shares the nature of the whole human race.

> "For as, by this taking of flesh, he joined man to God; so, by dying in the flesh, with sacrifice he cleansed, sanctified and delivered mankind."[55]

The universality of redemption meets the universality of sin. The cause of universal death is that all are sinners, and so,

> "God placed on him all the sins of the world...We confess we, each and all, are sinners...the Son of God was sent into the world and bore in himself our sins."[56]

As has been seen, Bullinger taught that behind the incarnation and atonement of Christ lie the love and goodness of God: not a love that arises from the hidden electing will of a *Deus absconditus*, but a love that is part of his nature, and is fully revealed in the person and work of Christ.

Bullinger's stress on the universality of Christ's work could be thought to diminish its character as accomplished. Nevertheless, he did portray the atonement as a finished work.[57] Commencing the chapter in the *Commonplaces* entitled, "After what sort Christes Satisfaction is made ours", he moves from the position that Christ "hath delivered us by his death" to ask how we may partake of this deliverance.[58] Reconciliation has been accomplished. Nevertheless it still has to be appropriated. At this point, Calvin and Bullinger are at one, although Bullinger, in accordance with the centrality of his covenant motif, referred more frequently to faith as the "condition" of the application of reconciliation:

> "God the Father of heaven...in him [Christ] hath given us all things belonging to a blessed life and eternal salvation, as he that for us men was incarnate, dead and raised from the dead again, was taken up into heaven, and is made our only Lord and Saviour, upon condition that we, acknowledging our sins, do soundly and surely believe in him...."[59]

Holding that Christ died for all certainly did not lead Bullinger to maintain that all will be saved, for not all believe. He could speak of the atonement in particularistic terms, in that it is designed for those who fulfil the condition: Christ died for the believing and faithful, for "the church" and for "the elect", not exclusively, but in that its effect reaches them alone.[60] The description of the atonement in particularistic terms by Bullinger is never undergirded by any explanation that would cancel its universality as accomplished fact, content of the promise and object of faith.

CONTROVERSY

Moderation

Bullinger often recommended moderation, especially concerning predestination. At the beginning of his 1536 speech on providence and predestination he noted that both scholastics and contemporaries had examined these themes minutely, and announced that he himself would rather simply teach the Scriptures and so deal with the subject with "moderation", a word that recurs in the speech several times. Indeed, the speech was entitled, "A Speech on Maintaining Moderation in the Matter of Providence, Predestination, Grace and Free Will."[61]

Similarly, his *Decades* sermon on the same themes commences by deploring the philosophical approach, and by claiming that he would rather give a simple, scriptural and comforting treatment of the subject. His stated refusal to speculate has already been observed.[62]

This approach is an outstanding example of the Reformed determination to draw theology from the Scriptures, reinforced by the aversion Bullinger developed during his education, to scholastic theology.[63] It also accords well with the humanist concern to have a practical piety as opposed to a speculative theology. Furthermore, Bullinger's concern for peace in the church, and for the comfort of the believer and the seeker alerted him to the danger of predestinarian speculation. These perspectives enabled him to produce a warm and practical theology. It may be asked however, whether "moderation" is an appropriate criterion in the construction of theology. With regard to predestination, it led him to the scarcely satisfactory position of sometimes seeming to say that the doctrine is true and important, but generally best avoided. Calvin and Beza gave similar warnings about prying into predestination, but, unlike their counterpart in Zurich, they were often compelled by a sense of theological consistency, to ignore their own warnings. In controversy over predestination, Bullinger followed the lines laid down in his systematic and biblical works.

The Bolsec Controversy and the letter to Traheron[64]

Bullinger wrote four letters, in response to the appeal from the ministers of Geneva to support their opposition to Bolsec, making it clear that he could not adopt as rigid an approach as Calvin. He also replied to a letter he had received from the Englishman Bartholomew Traheron, asking him about apparent differences between himself and Calvin over providence and predestination, and expressing anxiety that he seemed to be favouring Melanchthon's rather than Calvin's approach. As these letters were written within a short space of each other, and as they contain substantially the same points, they are dealt with together here.

The first letter, addressed to the Genevan ministers, was written by Bullinger on behalf of his Zurich colleagues on 27 November 1551.[65] It expressed the opinion that the Genevan ministers had lacked moderation in their proceedings against Bolsec. Zurich's position was that election is to be attributed wholly to the mercy of God and not to human effort or will, and that faith is the gift of God. On the other side, the sin of the condemned is to be attributed to themselves and not to God. This moderate and imprecise reply fell significantly short of the Genevan position, especially on reprobation, and was not advanced upon in the remaining correspondence.

The letter to Traheron,[66] written early in 1553, also refused to concede that the sin of the condemned has its cause in the decree of God. It put forward the concept of permission as a way of ensuring that God is not seen as the author of sin. Predestination was set in the context of the goodness of God to the human race in general, and of the universal offer of the gospel:

> "We urge the universal promises and urge all to hope well. The predestination hidden in the will of God and revealed by the prophets, Christ and the apostles, is that God is the lover of mankind..."

Bullinger reasserted his concept of the election of believers:

> "God is the lover of mankind, wishes well to mankind, and elects to life all those who believe in Christ, in such a way that he wills all to be saved. Accordingly he commands the gospel to be preached to all creatures...all those who believe in Christ will be saved, because all believers are preordained to eternal life."

These comments were accompanied by reference to a number of the universal texts of Scripture,[67] and continued by the statement,

> "I hold that these things are to be urged in the church, without superfluous disputes about God's hidden judgements concerning the predestination and election of God. Otherwise there would be doubts, hatred of God, blasphemies and desperation, as if God were joking in offering his gifts. In this way the divine promise and truth would be endangered."

Bullinger claimed that he himself handled predestination "moderately, religiously and orthodoxly".

Setting forth an election of "believers", within the context of a universal saving will and promise of God could easily seem like an espousal of Bolsec's teaching. But Bullinger had a double concept of election. It could enable him to write not only,

> "God therefore chose whom he willed from eternity. God willed, however, according to his plan and decree, those who believe",

but also,

> "We have not decided that faith as our work is the cause of election or predestination, as if God had elected us on account of faith that he foresaw in us, but we have attributed election and salvation to the grace of God, and indeed faith in Christ is the gift of this grace of God."

Bullinger concluded the letter to Traheron by saying that he could not blame Calvin for attempting to assert the purity of divine grace. Coupled with a comment about his own unwillingness to speculate about God's hidden judgement, it is obvious that Bullinger was implying that, in the attempt, Calvin had gone too far![68]

Theodore Bibliander[69]

When Peter Martyr Vermigli went to Zurich to replace Konrad Pellikan as professor of Old Testament, Zurich already had a reputation for being weak on predestination. Girolamo Zanchi expressed to Calvin his hope that Martyr would succeed in correcting errors about faith and election held by some in the Zurich church.[70] This wish was soon granted in the dispute which arose between Martyr and Theodore Bibliander. As early as 1535, Bibliander had expressed to Myconius of Basel his aversion to a doctrine of predestination that seemed to make the good God the author of evil and desirous of the death of sinners, and had set forth a doctrine of predestination to life or death on the basis of faith or unbelief. When, much later, Myconius pointed out to him the similarity of his own position and that of Bolsec, he replied protesting that he regarded faith as the gift of God, but maintaining as before that faith "is the basis of that comforting election by which we have been chosen in Christ". Such statements as these could have been made by Bullinger himself, and the extent of agreement between the two men is illustrated by their ability to co-operate amicably for thirty years. Bullinger, however, unlike his colleague, had room for an election to faith itself, whilst Bibliander, it seems, was not prepared to go beyond describing faith as a gift of God.

Impending crisis may have been sensed in Zurich in the midst of the Bolsec affair, when Calvin reported to Bullinger that he had heard that Bibliander was hostile to him over the doctrine of predestination,[71] making it necessary for Bullinger to reassure Calvin of Bibliander's friendliness. Clearly, as a result of the Bolsec affair, the issue of predestination was becoming more sensitive among the Reformed, but it was the arrival of the uncompromisingly predestinarian Martyr that proved Bibliander's downfall. The differences between Bibliander and Martyr became apparent in their lectures, to the point when it became necessary for the Zurich ministers to choose between them. As a result, on 8 February 1560, Bibliander was relieved of his position and given a pension. Bullinger continued to regard him highly.[72]

There is no need to interpret Bullinger's repudiation of Bibliander as a movement towards a more "Calvinistic" theology on his part. Bibliander's views were less predestinarian than Bullinger's, and, at a time when the Reformed churches were becoming increasingly sensitive about their distinctive doctrine of predestination, the need for solidarity made it impossible for Bullinger to continue to tolerate his views. It is noteworthy that the Second Helvetic Confession, prepared by Bullinger in 1561, embodied the same moderation that had marked his teaching throughout his life.

The Strasbourg Conflict[73]

The controversy in Strasbourg between Lutherans and Reformed will be described in the following chapter. At present it is sufficient to note that predestination was one of the two main subjects of disagreement. The Reformed Girolamo Zanchi appealed to other Reformed churches for help, and a number of letters of support were sent. Among them was one from Zurich. It was only natural that the task of writing on behalf of Zurich had fallen to Zanchi's friend and one time teacher, Martyr, who also had been theology professor at Strasbourg. In asking Martyr to do this, Bullinger indicated that his own main aim was to support Zanchi's eucharistic teaching. He also confided that some of Zanchi's theses, and we suspect that he had those on predestination in mind, could have been expressed better.

The Zurich letter or "Gutachten"[74] contained nothing opposed to the main lines of what Bullinger had long been teaching. Even where a difference seems to emerge, it is expressed in such cautious terms as to fall short of identifying Zurich fully with Zanchi's view. For example, Zanchi's interpretation of 1 Timothy 2.4, as meaning "all the elect" was accepted as "distorting Scripture least". This phraseology allowed Bullinger to hold that Zanchi's position was better than that of the Lutherans, but not the best. The conclusion to the "Gutachten" gave rather less than a full endorsement, when it said that the theses Zanchi had circulated contained nothing "either heretical or absurd", and added, "We embrace them partly as necessary, partly as defensible".

Bullinger's support for Zanchi's extreme and scholastic predestinarianism must not be taken as implying identity of doctrine, and certainly not as evidence of a change of view on Bullinger's part. In signing the "Gutachten" his aim was to assert the Reformed doctrine of predestination over against the Lutheran, without implying that Zanchi's framing of the doctrine was ideal. It was perceived as vital for the Reformed to make a united stand against the encroachments of Lutheranism, in the wake of the agreement by German princes at the Diet of Augsburg (1555) that Catholic and Lutheran states should co-exist peacefully, a tolerance not extended to the Reformed.[75] Bullinger's distinctive doctrine of election was largely a matter of emphasis, and the "Gutachten", by its very nature, could not have been expected fully to state Bullinger's own concerns. In a letter to Martyr, he pointed out that he would not normally say things in the way they were being said in this controversy:

> "The proposition about those to be damned and those to be saved by necessity seems hard, and, if proposed so nakedly to the people, would cause more offence than edification."[76]

While none of the controversies described here concentrated on the extent of the atonement, they all showed that Bullinger's view of predestination was more moderate and more successfully christocentric than that of Calvin, Beza and Zanchi, and so help to explain how it was that he had no inclination towards a doctrine of limited atonement.

CONCLUSION

There was a basic agreement between Bullinger and all thc Reformed, in tracing faith to a pretemporal, causal electing decree of God. Nevertheless, in his concern to give precedence to the goodness of God over the omnipotent and incomprehensible divine will, his determination to focus on Christ and his deliberate avoidance of speculation and extremism, he did not develop a doctrine of double predestination to the same extent as Beza or even Calvin. Rather, although he held that faith was a result of election, he frequently spoke of the election of those who are "in Christ". This was a mode of speaking anti-Calvinists could seize upon, but which Bullinger was not prepared to drop.

Central to Bullinger's theology was a universal covenant. The prominence of the universal promise and condition rendered it possible, even necessary, for him to teach universal atonement. Election did not threaten universal atonement. Understood as an election of those who are united to Christ by faith, it is clearly subordinate to Christ. Even as an election of certain individuals to faith, it was seen as the means of overcoming human inability to believe, rather than as the divine motivation for, and therefore limitation of, the mission of Christ.

J.W.Baker, concentrating on the covenant, has presented Bullinger as the initiator of "the other Reformed tradition"[77]. As the present study pursues the theme of the extent of the atonement, it will be seen that there is considerable justification for maintaining the existence of another Reformed tradition, and for tracing it back to Bullinger.

Chapter Four
Notes

1 A measure of Bullinger's influence is his vast and widely disseminated correspondence (11,000 extant letters), and the 119 works published during his lifetime. See P.Walser, *Die Prädestination bei Heinrich Bullinger: im Zusammenhang mit seiner Gotteslehre*, Zurich 1957, pp.14-16; R.Walton, "Heinrich Bullinger 1504-1575", in Raitt, *Shapers*, op.cit., pp.69-87 (p.85); J.W.Baker, *Heinrich Bullinger and the Covenant: the other Reformed tradition*, Athens (Ohio) 1980, p.xi.

2 Major works are A.Bouvier, *Henri Bullinger, réformateur et conseilleur oecuménique: le successeur de Zwingli, d'après sa correspondance avec les reformés et les humanistes de langue française*, Neuchâtel 1940; F.Blanke and I.Leuschner, *Heinrich Bullinger: Vater der reformierten Kirche*, Zurich 1990: Walser, op.cit.; J.Staedtke, *Die Theologie des jungen Bullinger*, Zurich 1962; J.Koch, *Die Theologie der Confessio Helvetica Posterior*, Neukirchen 1968; U.Gäbler and E.Herkenrath (eds.), *Heinrich Bullinger 1504-1575; gesammelte Aufsätze zum 400. Todestag*, (2 vols.), Zurich 1975; Baker, op.cit.; C.S.McCoy and J.W.Baker, *Fountainhead of Federalism: Heinrich Bullinger and the Covenantal Tradition*, Louisville 1991. Bullinger's works are in the process of publication: F.Busser (ed.), *Heinrich Bullinger Werke*, Zurich 1972- .

3 Breitinger's speech is printed in *Historiae Ecclesiasticae Novi Testamenti*, J.H.Hottinger, Zurich 1667, Tom. viii, Seculi xvi, Pars iv, pp.959-976.

4 See for example J.Daillé, *Apologia pro Duabus Ecclesiarum in Gallia Protestantium Synodis Nationalibus*, Amsterdam 1655, pp.1097-1108.

5 H.Bullinger, *Isaias Excellentissimus Dei Propheta...expositus homiliis cxc*, Zurich 1567, sermon 153 p.268a.

6 H.Bullinger, *Commonplaces of Christian Religion*, London 1572 p.185b; *Isaiah*, p.268a, Hottinger, op.cit., p.784 (Hottinger, pp.763-827, reproduces a speech given by Bullinger at the anniversary of the Zurich Karlsschule, on Jan.28 1536).

7 *Commonplaces*, p.33a; p.70a.

8 *The Decades of Henry Bullinger*, trans. H.I. (1587 edition), ed. T. Harding (Parker Society), London 1849-51, (5 books in 4 vols.), 3 pp.366-384; *Commonplaces*, pp.48b-51a; Hottinger, op.cit., pp.788-795. The "Second Helvetic Confession", in A.C.Cochrane (ed.), *Reformed Confessions of the Sixteenth Century*, London 1966, pp.224-361, labels the issue of "whether God willed Adam to fall" as a "curious question" (p.237). (The Confession was drawn up by Bullinger in 1561, and attached to his will. Cochrane regards it as "evidence of the degree to which Bullinger embodied the Reformation in his own life and thought", ibid., p.221).

9 *Decades*, 4 pp.7-8. Cp. p.146, where God's proclamation of his name to Moses is understood to mean, "I do not abuse my might, for I am gentle and merciful; I love my creatures, and man especially, on whom I do wholly yearn in the bowels of love and mercy", and Bullinger goes on to point out that we do not have a more full revelation of this than in Christ. Cp. "Second Helvetic Confession", ch. 10, "Predestination", in Cochrane, op.cit., p.242.

10 *Commonplaces*, p.123a.

11 *Isaiah*, pp.268b-269a.

12 *Commonplaces*, pp.142a-144a, illustrates Bullinger's usual procedure. After asserting that God's eternal decree of election results in an effective work of the Holy Spirit, without which the external word would be ineffective, he hastens to discourage speculation, "But rather we muste comforte

our selves with the moste sweete promises of God, and hope and looke for all goodness at Gods hande."

13 H. Bullinger, *In Divinum Iesu Christi Domini Nostri Evangelium secundum Ioannem, Commentariorum Libri x*, Zurich 1548, p.162b, on the beginning of Jn.17.

14 The explanation of 1 Tim.2.4 given by Ambrose, rather than that of Augustine. See Walser, op.cit., p.152.

15 E.g.Hottinger, pp.786,800; Bullinger, *A Hundred Sermons on the Apocalipse of Jesu Christe*, 1561, sermons 22, 28, pp.135 & 173; Bullinger, *Inluculentum et Sacrosanctum Evangelium Domini Nostri Iesu Christi secundum Lucam*, Zurich 1548 p.26a, on Lk.2.11; *Commonplaces*, p.144b.

16 McGrath, *Iustitia*, op.cit., vol.2, p.33; E.Brunner, *The Christian Doctrine of God*, op.cit., pp.321-323, sees Bullinger as the corrector of Zwingli's Stoic error. G.W.Locher, however, in *Zwingli's Thought: new perspectives*, Leiden 1981, esp. pp.113-114, does not share this view of Zwingli.

17 "We believe that all things in heaven and on earth, and in all creatures, are preserved and governed by the providence of this wise, eternal and almighty God.... Nevertheless, we do not spurn as useless the means by which divine providence works...", "Second Helvetic Confession", in Cochrane, op.cit., pp.232,233.

18 *Commonplaces*, p.72a. Walser, op.cit., p.73, sees continuity from Zwingli in Bullinger's stress on the goodness of God in providence.

19 Ibid., p.106a: "He foresaw from everlasting the fall of manne". *Decades*, 3 p.377: "Upon God's foreknowledge there followeth no necessity"; cp. Hottinger, op.cit., p.795.

20 *Decades*, 3 pp.378-379; *Apocalipse*, p.531, sermon 76. Walser., op.cit., pp.71-82, demonstrates the close connection between providence and predestination, resting upon God's goodness, within Bullinger's doctrine of God. Koch, op.cit., pp.91,102, indicates how, for Bullinger, the goodness and philanthropy of God are fundamental to predestination.

21 *Decades*, 4 pp.173; p.185.

22 *Decades*, 3 pp.406; *Commonplaces*, pp.106a-106b; *Decades*, 1 p.42, cp. Hottinger, op.cit.,p.788. Consistently, the blinding and hardening spoken of in Scripture is viewed not as a means of fulfilling a decree of reprobation, as in Calvin and Beza, but purely as a judgement of God upon sin, cp. *Decades*, 3 p.380-381. Walser, op cit., p.135-136, states that he knows of no use of the word *reprobatio*, in the context of predestination, by Bullinger, who spoke only of *condemnatio* or *damnatio*, as a consequence of sin.

23 *Decades*, 4 p.186, "God hath chosen us; and he hath chosen us before the foundations of the world were laid; yea, he hath chosen us that we should be without blame, that is, to be heirs of eternal life: howbeit, in Christ, by and through Christ..."

24 *Decades*, 3 p.379; *Commonplaces*, p.174b, cp. pp.142b-143b; *Decades*, 1 p.112; *Apocalipse*, p.447; "Second Helvetic Confession", in Cochrane, op.cit., ch.11, "Of Jesus Christ" begins, "Our Lord Jesus Christ was predestinated or foreordained from eternity by the Father to be the Saviour of the world" (p.242). Here, as elsewhere, Bullinger did not formulate the decree of sending Christ in particularistic terms.

25 *Decades*, 4 pp.185-7.

26 Locher, op.cit. p.135.

27 *Decades*, 4 pp.185-187. Cp. 1 p.112: "The eternal and unchangeable will of God is, that he will give eternal life unto the world. But he will give the life through Christ, who is naturally life itself, and can give life. The very same God also wills that we obtain and have life in us, and that we have it in no other ways than by faith." "Second Helvetic Confession", ch.10 "Predestination", in Cochrane., op.cit., p.242. After referring to the greatness of the love the Father has revealed in Christ, and

citing Matt. 11.28, Jn.3.16 and Matt.18.14, texts speaking of the universal invitation to Christ, Bullinger concludes, "Let Christ, therefore, be the looking glass, in whom we may contemplate our predestination". Cp. ibid., p.251, "He has disclosed to the world through the gospel this his predestination."

28 *Decades*, 4 p.186; *Apocalipse*, pp.134-135, sermon 22.

29 *Decades*, 4 p.187: "Faith therefore is a most assured sign that thou art elected; and whiles thou art called to the communion of Christ and art taught faith, the most loving God declareth towards thee his election and good will", cp. *Isaiah*, p.130a; *Commonplaces*, p.144b; *Decades*, 4 p.192: "Let us keep it deeply printed in our breasts, that God hath chosen us in Christ, and for Christ his sake predestinated us to life; and that therefore he giveth and increaseth faith to Christ-ward in them that ask it."

30 "Second Helvetic Confession", ch.10 "Predestination", in Cochrane, op.cit., pp.240-242. The fact that Beza could produce a French translation of the Confession in 1566 must have been due to the fact that its language concerning predestination was sufficiently imprecise to bear different shades of Reformed interpretation. For Bullinger's frequent presentation of election as an election of believers, see Walser, op.cit., pp.149-162.

31 See *Decades*, 4 pp.186-187 for Bullinger's answer "if thou ask me whether thou art elected to life or predestinate to death"; Koch, op.cit., pp.88-105, stresses the centrality of Christ and faith to Bullinger's doctrine of predestination.

32 *Apocalipse*, pp.134-135, sermon 32. Cp. Hottinger, op.cit., pp.781-782.

33 *Decades*, 4. p.188: "Freely therefore, of his own mercy, not for our deserts, but for Christ's sake, and not but in Christ, hath he chosen us, and for Christ's sake doth embrace us, because he is our Father and a lover of men." Cp. Hottinger, p.778.

34 See *Registres*, op.cit., p.90 for Bolsec's claim that Bullinger, Melanchthon and Brenz taught election on the basis of faith.

35 *Decades*, 4 pp.36: "Christ doth offer himself in the gospel"; *Commonplaces*, p.176a.

36 *Decades*, 4 pp.32-33.

37 *Luke*, p.26b (on Luke 2.10-11).

38 See G. Schrenk, *Gottesreich und Bund im älteren Protestantismus - vornehmlich bei Johannes Cocceius*, Gütersloh 1923, pp.40-44; Koch, op.cit., pp.387-430; Baker, op.cit.

39 See Baker, op.cit. pp.1-25, 107-140; Koch, however, op.cit., p.423, denies that the origin of Bullinger's covenant thought is to be found in the conflict with the Anabaptists. See also J.W.Cottrell, "Is Bullinger the Source for Zwingli's Doctrine of the Covenant?", in Gäbler and Herkenrath (eds.), op.cit., pp.75-83. See also Steinmetz, op.cit., pp.133-143. For social, political and theological background to the covenant idea, see Baker and McCoy, op.cit., pp.14-17.

40 Walton, in Raitt, op.cit., sees Bullinger's covenant motif as a means of concentrating on divine reliability and human responsibility. The phrase "theology of history" is used in this connection by M.McGiffert, "Grace and Works: the rise and division of covenant divinity in Elizabethan Puritanism", *HTR* 75(1982)4, pp.463-502 (p.470).

41 H.Bullinger, *The One and Eternal Testament and Covenant of God*, 1534, in McCoy and Baker, op.cit., pp.99-138 (p.104).

42 An overview of Bullinger's use of the covenant, and particularly his retracing of God's covenantal dealings with mankind throughout history, may be gained from *The One and Eternal*, op.cit., and *The Olde Fayth*, n.pl. 1547.

43 *Commonplaces*, p.44a, cp.71a-71b. See Koch, op.cit., p.397.

44 Koch, op.cit., pp.390-391 shows that Bullinger rooted his covenant doctrine in the goodness of

God. He also maintains that, in Bullinger's thought, it reflected the original relationship between God and mankind. See ibid., pp.424-427.

45 "It is our duty to adhere firmly by faith to the one God..., and to walk in innocence of life", *The One and Eternal*, op.cit., p.111, cp. *Decades*, 2 p.170.

46 *The Olde Fayth*, op.cit., pages unnumbered.

47 *Decades*, 3 p.170. Cp. 1 p.44: "God by a certain legue hath joined himself to mankind, that he hath most straitly bound himself to the faithful."

48 *Commonplaces*, p.192b: "wee are adopted or chosen of God for his sonnes, and receyved into the covenaunt."

49 Ibid., pp.109a-109b; p.142a.

50 *Isaiah*, p.266b, sermon 151.

51 *John*, p.36b, on Jn.3.16; *Decades*, 1 pp.110,148,151,154; 2 pp.181,184,189, 199,216,265,269,270; 3 pp.32,219,286,376; 4 pp.432,553.

52 Ibid., 3 p.188.

53 *Isaiah*, p.264a, 269b (sermons 150,153), cp. *Apocalipse*, p.173, "For the Lord hath died for al: but that all are not made pertakers of this redemption, it is through their owne faulte. For the Lord excludeth no man, but him only whiche, by his owne incredulitie...excludeth him selfe"; *Luke*, pp.26a-26b (on Luke 2.10-11).

54 *John*, p.36b, on Jn.3.16.

55 *Decades*, 1 pp.42-43. Cp. *Commonplaces*, p.106a: "his Sonne...which should take upon him mannes nature, by whom the fall of man should be restored and repayred."

56 *Isaiah*, p.266b, sermon 151; cp. *The Olde Fayth* , op.cit., (pages unnumbered), "For he dyed for us all, inasmuche as god sayd: in what day soever thou eatest thereof, thou shalte dye the deathe. Therefore dyed Christ for us all..."; *In Sanctissimam Pauli ad Romanos Epistolam Commentarius*, Zurich 1533, p.54a-54b; Decades, 4 p.40.

57 *Isaiah*, p.265b, *Decades*, 3 p.265.

58 *Commonplaces*, p.109a-112A.

59 *Decades*, 4 pp.3-4. Cp. *Commonplaces*, p.156a: "...god receyved us into grace, and redeemed and saved us through Christ, if so be that we beleeve in him."

60 *Isaiah*, p.266b; *Decades*, 1 p.107, 3 pp.184,205,249; 4 p.29; 5 p.415; *Commonplaces*, pp.132b,240b; *Decades*, 3 pp.184,199; *Isaiah*, p.268b.

61 See ante, p.82 n.6, and Walser's analysis of the speech, op.cit., pp.163-167. Hottinger p.765, cp. pp.774,776,777.

62 *Decades*, 4 p.181.

63 See Staedtke, op.cit., pp.27-39, for Bullinger's education, his espousal of humanism and criticism of scholastic theology and philosophy.

64 For description and analysis of the correspondence regarding Bolsec and with Traheron, see W.Kolfhaus, "Der Verkehr Calvins mit Bullinger", in J.Bohatec (ed.), *Calvinstudien: Festschrift zum 400. Geburtstag Johan Calvins*, Leipzig 1909, pp.27-125, (pp.74-84); C.P.Venema, "Heinrich Bullinger's Correspondence on Calvin's Doctrine of Predestination", *SCJ* 17(1986)4 pp.435-450; Walser, op.cit., pp.95-104, 124-130, 168-181; Baker, op.cit., pp.34-39.

65 The second official letter (1 Dec. 1551) was addressed to the Geneva City Council. The third and fourth were personal letters from Bullinger to Calvin.

66 Traheron, who was Dean of Chichester at the time of the corrrespondence, had been taught by Bullinger in Zurich (1536-37). Traheron's letter (10 Dec. 1552) is in *CO* 14.359-360 and Bullinger's reply 480-490.

67 Jn.3.16, 2 Pet.3.9, 2 Cor.5.14.

68 Early in the letter Bullinger suggested that the reason his teaching appeared to resemble Melanchthon's by comparison with Calvin's, was that Calvin had written "so absolutely". For a discussion of the relationship between Calvin's and Bullinger's thought, see G.W.Locher, "Bullinger und Calvin: Probleme des Vergleichs ihrer Theologien", in Gäbler and Herkenrath (eds.), op.cit., pp.1-33, esp. (for predestination) pp.23-28.

69 For an account and analysis of the Bibliander controversy, see J.Staedtke, "Der Zürcher Prädestinationsstreit von 1560", *Zwingliana*, 9(1953) pp.536-546; Baker, op.cit., pp.39-41.

70 *CO* 16.246 contains a letter from Zanchi to Calvin of July 1556 expressing the hope that "he [sc. Martyr] may unteach many in that church [sc. Zurich] of that pestilential doctrine...of free will against predestination and God's grace. You know what I am talking about."

71 In a letter of April 1553, in *CO* 14 513-514.

72 Baker cites Bullinger's *Diarium* to illustrate his continuing esteem for Bibliander, op.cit., p.41 n.54.

73 For an account and analysis of Zurich's contribution to the Strasbourg controversy, see Walser, op.cit., pp.181-193, and Baker, op.cit., pp.41-44.

74 The Zurich "Gutachten" can be found in H. Zanchius, *Opera*, Geneva 1613, 7.I.72-73.

75 G.R.Elton, *Reformation Europe 1517-1559*, London 1972, pp.265-266.

76 Bullinger stated, "I do not deny that these propositions could have been in some cases put forward more properly...but since they have been proposed, it is certain, in order that a bad interpretation might not be added, that they cannot be rejected", Letter to Martyr of 27 Dec 1561, in Hottinger, pp.833-834.

77 Baker's subtitle.

Chapter Five

Girolamo Zanchi (1516–1590)

INTRODUCTION

In October 1551 Girolamo Zanchi[1] fled from the community of regular canons at Lucca in Northern Italy to the Graubünden. Under the influence of Peter Martyr Vermigli the Lucca community had become something like a Reformed academy, and for the first 15 months of his time there, in 1541-42, Zanchi had been influenced considerably by Vermigli, until the latter found it necessary to flee from the Inquisition. While at Lucca, Zanchi had studied such works as Melanchthon's *Loci Communes*, Bullinger's *De Origine Erroris* and Bucer's Gospel commentaries. He also had abridged Calvin's *Institutes* for his own private study.

From the Spring of 1552 Zanchi spent 9 months in Geneva, becoming personally acquainted with Beza while there. He also visited Bullinger in Zurich. A shortage of teachers in the School at Strasbourg led to his being offered a post there, which he accepted, becoming a canon of the St. Thomas Church on 10 April 1555. When Vermigli had come for the second time to Strasbourg, in October 1553, he refused to sign the Lutheran Augsburg Confession, but agreed to teach in accordance with it "when rightly understood". Zanchi had to give the same undertaking.

The ecclesiastical situation in Strasbourg was delicate. Its position in the Rhineland plain made it more vulnerable than the cities of the Swiss Republic, and, after the defeat of the Schmalkaldic League, the city was compelled by Emperor Charles V in 1548 to sign the Augsburg Interim, which granted tolerance to Lutheran, but not Reformed, doctrine.[2] Martin Bucer refused to do so and went into exile in England. After his departure, the city moved steadily towards Lutheranism. This movement was promoted by, among others, Johan Marbach, the new presiding pastor of the city.[3] Against this background a controversy developed which resulted in Zanchi's leaving to become a pastor in the Graubünden, and subsequently professor of theology in Heidelberg and then Neustadt.

The controversy which took place between Zanchi and Marbach in 1561-3 has been variously explained.[4] The theological issues were eschatology, the Lord's Supper, predestination, the perseverance of the saints, and the extent to which the regenerate may sin. Whilst eschatological questions were prominent at the commencement of the controversy, the other issues soon predominated.

Some credence may be given to Zanchi's explanation of the controversy as a personal attack on himself, for a somewhat pro-German, anti-Italian, note enters into Marbach's comments.[5] Due weight must also be attached to Kittelson's observation of a power struggle between church and school in Strasbourg, in the absence of clearly defined roles for the two institutions.[6] Nevertheless, predestination emerged, alongside the Lord's Supper, as an acute problem in Lutheran-Reformed relationships.

Lutheran thought on predestination was evolving to the stage where the 1577 Formula of Concord required that it should be interpreted only through Christ, who earnestly desires the salvation of all. Lutheranism was, in fact, on a pathway that would lead its seventeenth-century theologians to teach that predestination to life is on the basis of foreseen faith in Christ. Reformed theology, especially the Genevan variety, was taking a very different direction.[7]

In the present chapter, Zanchi's writings from or about the controversy with Marbach relating to predestination will be examined, using his *Miscellanea*, a record of that troubled period.[8] It will be seen that he felt it necessary to discuss and determine the extent of the atonement under predestination, and that no aspect of Zanchi's predestinarianism was more objectionable to the Lutherans than the restrictions upon the work of Christ implied by this approach.

THE "THESES"

In his "Theses...objected to by some as partly novel, partly heretical",[9] Zanchi set out three theses on eschatology, two on the Lord's Supper and nine on predestination and perseverance. Among these were the positions that there is a definite and unalterable number of elect and reprobate; that there are both external and visible bonds (word and sacraments) and internal and invisible bonds (election and the Spirit) between the church and Christ, the invisible bonds being indissoluble; that, bound to Christ in this way, the elect must surely persevere for final salvation; and that,

> "The promises regarding the free mercy of God concerning certain and eternal salvation, although they are universally proposed to all, and ought to be preached to all, pertain in fact to the elect."[10]

While acknowledging election and reprobation (the latter according to foreknowledge of sin, however) Marbach requested Zanchi not to teach election *a priori*, but *a posteriori*. This request was motivated not only by a desire to understand election correctly but also by the conviction that Zanchi's contrast between the indissoluble, "invisible bonds" of election and the Spirit, and the dissoluble bonds of word and sacrament, undervalued the divinely ordained ministry of the church.

> "I urged him that in the explanation of this question he should rather lead his hearers to the word of the gospel. For the *a priori* way is dangerous, and leads the common man into many inscrutable questions, leading to contempt of the ministry of the church, and atheism, rather than piety and penitence."[11]

The Consensus, intended to bring the controversy to a close, was widely regretted at the time by the Reformed, and was undoubtedly a victory for Marbach,[12] who wanted predestination to be considered only in so far as it was revealed in the gospel:

> "Since it is an abyss and, considered outside Christ, leads to an infernal downfall, it should not be enquired into except in Christ...There is however an eternal decree of God revealed in the word of the gospel i.e. that all who believe will have eternal life."[13]

"LECTURE ON PREDESTINATION"

The second section of the first part of the *Miscellanea* contains lectures to which Marbach had taken exception. The "Praelectio de Praedestinatione"[14] commences with the assertion that all theologians agree that predestination is part of providence. Predestination is a species of the genus providence. Its scope may be understood in three ways. Firstly, as relating to all things, secondly as relating to human beings elect and reprobate, and thirdly as relating to those elected to eternal life. In the second sense, predestination may be defined as,

> "The most wise, eternal and immutable decree, by which God first decided with himself, of his own free will, from eternity, to create all men and allow them to fall into sin and perish in death; then to give grace to some of them in Christ and not to honour others with this grace, but to blind, harden and destroy them with Satan in eternal condemnation, in order that in some the divine goodness mercy, and in others the divine power and justice, should be declared, and so in all things God would be glorified."[15]

Zanchi went on to point out that his definition contained all relevant causes: the acting cause (God), the material cause (predestined man), the formal cause (man uncreated) and the impulsive cause (God's free will loving some and hating others). He could have added the glory of God as the final cause. Zanchi explained that the decree was described as eternal because all that God wills is from eternity, and as unchangeable because mutability would imply imperfection.

The definition assumes the necessity of the fall, and Zanchi explained that the fall is indeed to be assigned to predestination, but not as if God imposes sin on anyone. The fact of reprobation is evident from observation, for plainly not all believe. Reprobation, like election, is for the glory of God, the proof text being the familiar Proverbs 16.4. Election is not in any sense based on any merit of human works or will, but on the good pleasure of God alone. In predestination, Zanchi continued, it is important to understand cause and effect. Creation and the fall are effects of the causal decree common to elect and reprobate, redemption and regeneration effects special to the elect, hardening and blinding effects special to the reprobate.

Zanchi pointed out that two orders of predestination can be presented. The first is: creation, permission of the fall, grace or abandonment. Zanchi said that this infralapsarian, or, as he called it, *a posteriori*, order, cannot be disproved. He continued, however, to propose an alternative supralapsarian order, putting election and reprobation before creation and the fall. The first order is patterned upon the execution of predestination, the second is according to God's intention, understood from the "ultimate effect". Although there is no former or latter in God, the decree has a natural order, according to which we can say that God decreed the end and then the means, following the axiom that "what he does now he willed from eternity to do". The conclusion of this discussion of the order of predestination was that the supralapsarian order is "how the matter is". However the first is also true, and offends the simple less.[16]

Two points should be specially noted in this presentation of predestination by Zanchi. First, he considered predestination as part of God's providential rule over all things, understood in a causal sense. Thus events in time are to be treated as revelation of God's eternal will and purpose. One of Zanchi's favourite principles was,

> "God neither knows nor wills anything now which he did not know or will from eternity."[17]

Second, predestination is built on the doctrine of the divine attributes. In the "De Praedestinatione" divine eternity and immutability were used. In other works Zanchi also used divine omnipotence and simplicity as foundations of the predestination doctrine. The exaltation of divine grace through the exclusion of human merit in salvation, far from being the *raison d'être* of the doctrine of predestination plays a comparatively minor role as an almost incidental "use" of a scheme logically deduced from the attributes of God.

Both these points support Grundler's contention that Zanchi continued, as a Reformed theologian, to perpetuate the Thomism and Aristotelianism in which he had been trained.[18] Thomas had defined predestination as *pars providentiae*,[19] and had made Aristotelian causal theory integral to his theology, with God as the eternal first cause of all "effects" in time. He had also made the attributes of God, philosophically defined, basic to his theological enterprise.

«CONFESSION» - THE WILL OF GOD

During the controversy with Marbach, Zanchi presented a "Confession"[20] on the themes of predestination, perseverance and the Lord's Supper to the Council of Strasbourg. It covers at length the will, immutability and constancy, omnipotence, justice, mercy and love of God by way of laying a foundation for the predestination doctrine proper. It is apparent again here that Zanchi deduced his doctrine of predestination from his doctrine of God. It will be useful to focus on his treatment of the will of God.

Zanchi recognized a duality in God's will. The human task is to follow the revealed will without scrutinizing the hidden. The revealed will is often conditional in character. Thus, when 1 Timothy 2.4 says that God wills all to be saved, it is to be understood, as Ambrose understood it, that God wills all to be saved if they repent. Similarly it is correct to say that Christ died for all, according to the conditional will of God.[21]

The hidden will of God is absolute, or omnipotent. It is the uncaused efficient first cause of all things. It lies behind even human sin, in that God permits sin to be done, and therefore cannot be wholly unwilling that it should be. To grant that possibility would be to deny the first article of the Creed, "I believe in God the Father Almighty". Any apparent injustice in the exercise of the omnipotent will is not to be admitted, since God, and therefore the will of God, is the rule of all justice. 1 Timothy 2.4 can therefore be understood not only, with Ambrose, in an entirely universal and conditional sense, but also, with Augustine, as referring to the omnipotent will of God, in the sense that God effectively wills the salvation of all sorts of people.

An interesting feature of Zanchi's division of the will of God is that he included election under both hidden and revealed will. Election belongs to the absolute will, as the foundation of our salvation, guaranteeing the final outcome. But since the Scriptures teach, and the gospel proclaims, election, it also belongs to the revealed will. Even though the identity of the elect is hidden, even this becomes revealed in human experience upon the exercise of faith.[22]

The treatment of the will of God continues under the heading of the immutability and constancy of God. The section commences by stating that God is unchangeable both in his essence and in his decrees and promises. Expounding this proposition, Zanchi used Gregory's distinction that God's counsels do not change but only his pronouncements (*sententiae*). Under God's counsels are to be included the decrees to create, give the law, and send Christ. God's threats of punishment and promises of reward are classed as *sententiae.* These are subject to change in so far as they are conditioned upon the human response. This conditionality must be qualified, however, by the proviso that it is God who, according to his unchanging purpose, grants the ability to the elect to fulfil the conditions.

Under the heading of omnipotence, Zanchi identified God's absolute will with all that takes place in time. There is no passive power in God. All events result from the exercise of God's active power and therefore may be identified with his will.

The "Confession" proceeds to the mercy, then love and hatred of God. Mercy is defined as a propensity of God's will, and God's love is traced to the good pleasure *(beneplacitum)* of God as its "efficient cause". A general mercy, not leading to salvation, is conceded, but redeeming mercy and love are directed solely towards the elect. Having approached God's will through the philosophically understood attributes of omnipotence and immutability, Zanchi then interpreted the attributes of mercy and love through the concept of will. Thus, not only is Zanchi's theology built up on the basis of the initially defined attributes of God, but the hidden divine will is made superior to the attributes of love and mercy - God is truly *Deus absconditus.*[23]

DE NATURA DEI - THE WILL OF GOD

Zanchi's exposition of the will of God in the midst of the Strasbourg controversy of the early 1560s foreshadowed the positions he would set out in his *De Natura Dei,*[24] published in 1577. The method of the *De Natura* is to deduce the attributes of God from recognized principles.[25] Conclusions are always supported by scriptural texts, but the argument proceeds by logical deduction. Thus the simplicity of God is asserted on the basis of Aristotelian philosophy, the eternity of God is then asserted on the basis of divine simplicity (change involves movement which is incompatible with absolute simplicity, therefore God is exempt from all change and must be eternal), and so on. The existence of will in God is maintained on the ground that it is an axiom of philosophy that God is the mover of all things, and as such, and as a being of supreme intelligence, he must have will. Since God is most simple act, his will must be identical with his essence. Since there is no succession in God his will must be an eternal, unchangeable and simple action. The first object of the will of God is himself and his glory.[26]

Developing the theme of the duality of the divine will Zanchi pointed out various ways theologians had divided it: antecedent and consequent (John of Damascus), of good-pleasure and of sign (Lombard and the scholastics), revealed and hidden, absolute and conditional, a will concerning us and a will to be done by us, omnipotent and ineffective. None of these distinctions are rejected, but to Zanchi the absolute will has pre-eminence. It is to be regarded as an attribute of God. He defines the divine will as,

> "The free, eternal, most wise and unchangeable decree of God of leading each and all things he has made, to certain uses and ends, through certain means."[27]

Attempting to explain that much called the will of God does not accord with his definition, he takes up the distinction between what is willed concerning us and, on the other hand, what is willed to be done by us. God's favour, love and grace, and all the promises of grace are included in the former will, the *beneplacitum* of God. The command to believe in Christ, however, belongs to the latter.

Furthermore, God wills things in different ways. According to his complacent will he wishes all the elect to be saved. According to his permissive will he wishes all people to be saved on condition that they believe. As for the names *voluntas beneplaciti* and *signi*, Zanchi explained that the former is used because it refers to that which pleases God simply, and

> "consequently it is called the will of God properly",

whereas the *voluntas signi* refers only to an external divine command, such as when God commanded Abraham to sacrifice Isaac, but not to a divine decision about the outcome of the command. He observed that Augustine had said that there was a will "not so properly called the will of God".

Having made the above distinctions, Zanchi felt able to say that God's will

> "is one decree concerning all things".

Furthermore,

> "It is granted that he seems to wish many things absolutely, others conditionally, in fact however, if it is spoken of properly, all things whatever God wills he wills absolutely and simply. Consequently all that he wills is done. For whatever he is said to will conditionally refers to the revelation of his will. For there is no conditional will in God."

In fact, the conditional "will" serves the absolute will in that it reveals that God wills absolutely that the way to be saved is to have faith in Christ. Thus the absolute will of God concerning election and reprobation is accomplished, for through the revealed "will" the elect are saved and the reprobate rendered inexcusable. The conditional gospel does not imply a conditional predestination.[28]

The subordination of the conditional will, which has reference to all, to the absolute will which, in its positive side, has reference to the elect only, is a necessary adjunct to Zanchi's doctrine of God, inseparable from the concepts of divine simplicity, immutability and omnipotent all-causality. The primacy of the absolute will ensured that the scope of the work of Christ would be viewed by Zanchi as limited by the decree of election.

The central role granted by Zanchi to the absolute will of God must modify Grundler's picture of him as dominated by the Thomistic tradition.[29] Furthermore, his frequent use of the concept of God's conditional will raises the question of whether students of covenant theology have been right virtually to ignore him, especially in view of his association at Heidelberg with Olevianus and Ursinus, whose status as early covenant theologians is beyond dispute. For the purposes of the present work, it is enough to recognize that Zanchi's espousal of a "two wills" model, with the emphasis on the omnipotent will, provided the framework for his understanding of the extent of the atonement.

PREDESTINATION AND CHRIST

In the conclusion to his study of Zanchi's theology, Grundler states, "The key to Zanchi's theology and its unifying principle is the concept of causality. It dominates his doctrine of God; it determines the relationship between Creator and creature....In fact, it would be quite possible to present Zanchi's entire doctrines of Scripture, God, creation, providence and predestination without ever mentioning Christ, and they would suffer little or no distortion from doing so."[30] The present study has so far served to reinforce this judgement. However, there is another side to Zanchi's theology, emerging in the way he related predestination to Christ.

Zanchi explained that the Bible says that election is "in Christ" because without the work of Christ no-one can be saved.

> "As many as are predestined to eternal life are predestined in Christ, that is, through and on account of [*per et propter*] Christ."
>
> "God the Father decrees to save no-one except through Christ."[31]

This perspective does not mean, however, that Zanchi understood Christ to be merely the executor of election. In the theses to which Marbach had originally taken exception, he had presented election as the invisible indissoluble bond between Christ and the church. Election in Christ is the first link in a chain in which Christ features throughout, for we are chosen in Christ, called to Christ, justified through Christ and glorified with Christ. The concept of election in union with Christ may be filled out by reference to Zanchi's *Commentary on Ephesians.* On the phrase, "He chose us in Christ" (Eph.l.4), he observed, perhaps with Beza in mind, that some interpret this as implying a distinct order, namely that God first chose whom he would save, and then chose Christ as the one through whom they would be saved. However,

> "It seems better to me that we were elected in Christ as head, that we should be his members...God the Father willed that his Son should become head of the church; he therefore chose members for him."[32]

In this way, Zanchi made the election of Christ logically prior to the election of others.[33] Thus he differed from Beza, but without the introduction of any universal dimension to the election of Christ that would have brought him into line with Bullinger. To this extent, Zanchi's doctrine of election was christocentric. However, the concept of "a certain number" governs Zanchi's definition of election, and his approach to it, and the question of why some as opposed to others are chosen remained inexplicable in terms of Christ: it could only be referred to the hidden will of God:

> "What God has predestined about who will have eternal life, and what the apostles preached about eternal salvation in the gospel, are two different things. The gospel was not and is not a manifestation of to which persons God wills to give eternal life, but of the sort of persons to whom he wills to give eternal life, namely, believers in Christ."[34]

Furthermore, as has been seen, election was only one species of predestination according to Zanchi. Therefore the christocentric election has to be set within the larger scheme of double predestination designed to glorify God by the manifestation of his justice and mercy. Nevertheless, it would be unfair to ignore Zanchi's attempts to teach a christocentric doctrine of election. In answer to Marbach's demand that he should not teach predestination, or that, if a passage of Scripture demanded it, he should teach it *a posteriori*, Zanchi answered,

> "To abstain from preaching election would be to abstain from preaching the love of God towards us."

> "I say therefore that the gospel is the glad preaching of the eternal and free divine love in Christ the beloved Son. It was by this love that God chose us from eternity to eternal life and salvation."

> "The first part of the gospel is the preaching of the eternal, free and constant love of God towards us in Christ, that is, election."[35]

The mission of Christ and election spring from the same grace. To avoid teaching predestination a priori would be to neglect the first part of John 3.16.

Outside the controversy with Marbach Zanchi granted to Christ a role as the electing God:

> "Christ, as he is one with God the Father...and the Spirit...has blessed us, and chosen us."

However, he did not pursue this statement far enough to make it a key element in his doctrine.[36]

Zanchi's doctrine of election was both christocentric and particularistic. As such it necessarily left little room for universalistic elements in the will of God regarding the work of Christ.

THE EXTENT OF THE ATONEMENT

It would not be unfair to say that the Lutherans sought to understand the will of God through the unrestricted proclamation of the cross, whilst Zanchi sought to understand the cross through the already understood will of God. The difference in approach ensured that the extent of the atonement would be a major element in the conflict that raged in Strasbourg.

In the relationship Zanchi saw between Christ and election, election is enclosed within Christ in so far as he is the elect head for whom a body is also chosen. At the same time, Christ is enclosed within election, in so far as election involves a decree to save a certain number. For,

> "Christ, according to the plan and will of the Father, neither prayed nor suffered except for the elect."

Zanchi usually placed those Scriptures that speak of Christ's death as being for all under the heading of conditional will. 1 Timothy 2.6 could be understood in this way.

> "It is not false that Christ died for all men, regarding the conditional will: namely, if they want to be partakers of his death by faith. For the passion of Christ is offered to all in the gospel. No-one is excluded from it unless he excludes himself."

This, Zanchi said, is the meaning of the scholastic distinction between Christ dying for all sufficiently and for the elect efficiently. However, since the will of God, strictly considered, cannot be conditional,

> "It cannot be said that it was properly and simply the will of God that Christ should die for the salvation of all... and...that Christ, according to the Father's plan, died for all...sufficiently."

Experience proves this:

> "The elect alone are saved...therefore God wills simply to save only them, and for them alone Christ died and for them alone he intercedes."[37]

The *Commentary on Ephesians* confirms Zanchi's acceptance of the sufficient-efficient formula. Approving this saying of "the schools", he acknowledged universal sufficiency "respecting the power of the blood of Christ" as well as "as far as preaching is concerned." As far as efficacy is concerned, though,

> "regarding the plan and counsel of the Lord, and eternal will of God, he died for the elect alone."

Had the blood of Christ been shed for the reprobate, then all would be saved.[38]

In the "Tractatio de Christo Advocato", based on 1 John 2.1, Zanchi maintained, on the basis of John 17.9 and Romans 8.34, that Christ is the advocate for the elect only, and that the limited extent of his intercession indicates the scope of his propitiation. The use of the "whole world" in 1 John.2.2 does not contradict this, for, by synecdoche, the whole is taken for a part, namely the church. For this reason the efficient-sufficient formula appealed to by some, although true, is not relevant to the exposition of this text.

Zanchi could say, then, that Christ died for all, and that Christ died for the elect only, but it is not difficult to find where his emphasis lay. Whilst the statement that Christ died for all is "not to be condemned", the statement that he died for the elect only is made "properly and simply". Since he held that the absolute will of God is the only will truly worthy of the name, it was inevitable that Zanchi would determine the extent of the atonement, properly and simply, by reference to the absolute decree of election.[39] In doing so he was able to appeal to the stance Bucer had taken in the same city against Hoffman in 1533.[40]

The conditional universality of the atonement has its place in preaching, but was not of ultimate significance to Zanchi. His respect for Thomas Aquinas would have predisposed him to keep a place for the "sufficient-efficient" formula. It did not, however, play a vital role in his theology.

THE KNOWLEDGE OF ELECTION

Zanchi claimed that Marbach's only real cause of disagreement with him over predestination had to do with the question of assurance.[41] The Lutheran pastor accused him of robbing people of the consolation of the gospel by restricting its applicability to the elect only, which, since election is part of the hidden will of God, was bound to lead to uncertainty and even despair. Zanchi argued that predestination conveys supreme assurance, since the elect can be sure that, come what may, they are bound to persevere in God-given faith. To Marbach, that kind of assurance was dangerous, in that it would create "carnal security" in some, and useless, in that it left the individual unsure that he was in fact elect. Marbach wanted predestination to be taught *a posteriori*, so that assurance would be continually found in the gospel through the ministry of the church.[42] Zanchi could not comply because, to him, the *a priori* presentation of election was the only way of presenting the love and goodwill of God, without which there could be no assurance. So sure was he that the gospel reveals election (though not which specific persons have been chosen) that he said he did not know what Marbach meant by asking him to confine himself to the revealed will of God. He claimed, indeed, that Marbach himself did not understand what he was talking about either! He became utterly exasperated by the church president's "old song" about *a priori* and *a posteriori* method, which, he said, was so puerile it had often made him laugh.[43]

Zanchi allowed that the *a posteriori* approach did have a use in conveying assurance. But even in assurance, the *a priori* approach was primary. Thus, because the gospel is a declaration of electing love, it is itself an assurance of election to the person who receives it, with the witness of the Spirit, in faith. To confirm the initial assurance, the new believer reflects on the fact that he now exercises faith and, knowing that faith is the fruit of election, receives a supplementary, *a posteriori* assurance. *Persuasio* comes already from the *a priori* method, the *a posteriori* approach simply adding *confirmatio.* In relation to the *a posteriori* method, Zanchi, like Beza, had a *syllogismus practicus.* However, by giving pride of place to the *a priori* approach, Zanchi gave less incentive than Beza to introspection, with its twin dangers of self-righteousness and despair.

Regarding the content of the message a person is called to believe, Zanchi had no hesitation in saying that it is that Christ died for him. Since Christ died for the elect only, this entails the hearer in believing in his own election. Zanchi referred to Bucer on this point.

> "We are ordered to believe the gospel, and the gospel both assumes that we have been redeemed through Christ and proclaims that we have been predestined in Christ. So, just as we are required simply to believe we have been redeemed by Christ, so we are commanded to believe simply that we have been predestined in Christ from eternity to obtain redemption."[44]

Zanchi found it necessary to insist in this context that there is a big difference between believing in one's election and presuming upon it.[45]

Zanchi's logical approach seems to have broken down entirely in this teaching. For, according to him, not all who hear the gospel are elect, and yet they are all expected to believe that they are. The fact that, according to this system, no-one actually does believe erroneously in his election, since only the elect are enabled to comply with the call to faith, does little to remove the distinct impression of a sleight of hand. Zanchi the scholastic appears, astonishingly, as the proponent of an extremely experiential and non-logical concept of faith at this point. Beza, though so similar to Zanchi in his theological method, would not follow his Italian friend's abandonment of logic in his own debates with the Lutherans 20 years later.

CONCLUSION

Zanchi's doctrine of predestination was constructed on the basis of his doctrine of God and of Aristotelian concepts of end, cause and effect. The doctrine of God itself was shaped according to axioms of Aristotelian philosophy, mediated through the theology of Thomas Aquinas. At the same time, stressing so heavily the omnipotence of God (understood in an all-causal sense), and so interpreting the absolute will of God according to experienced reality, led inexorably to an understanding of the work of Christ in terms of perceived results, and so to the position that Christ died for the elect only.

Alongside this scholastic approach, a christocentric impulse has been identified, leading to an identification of election with the gospel of Christ, and equating faith in Christ with faith in election. Given the foundations he had laid for his theology, this identification tended to modify, at least in theory, the extent of the gospel by the particularism of election rather than shape the concept of election according to the universality of the gospel. The presupposition of a predetermined number of the elect and reprobate, and the claim that, strictly speaking, the work of Christ was, and the promises of God are, for that certain number only, robbed of credibility, in Lutheran eyes, Zanchi's conviction that the gospel calls upon everyone to believe himself to be elect.

In both Geneva and Strasbourg, the logic of the Reformed system was producing a doctrine of limited atonement. Beza's clearest statements on the subject would not be made until his debates with the Lutherans at Montbéliard in the 1580s. Zanchi was openly contending for that doctrine in Strasbourg as early as 1561. To him belongs the dubious distinction of being its first public champion from the Reformed camp.

Chapter Five

Notes

1 For biographical details, see O.Grundler, "Thomism and Calvinism in the Theology of Girolamo Zanchi (1516-1590)", Th.D. Princeton 1961 (this work is published as *Die Gotteslehre Girolamo Zanchis und ihre Bedeutung für seine Lehre von der Prädestination*, Neukirchen 1965); P.McNair, *Peter Martyr in Italy, an anatomy of apostacy*, Oxford 1967 pp.227-229; C.J.Burchill, "Girolamo Zanchi: portrait of a Reformed theologian and his work", in *SCJ* 15(1984)2 pp.185-207.

2 E.G.Rupp, "The Reformation in Zurich, Strassburg and Geneva", in *The New Cambridge Modern History: The Reformation 1520-1559*, vol.2, second edition, ed. G.R.Elton, Cambridge 1990, pp.105-111.

3 Marbach was born in 1521, studied at Strasbourg from 1536 and in 1543 received his doctorate at Wittenberg, where he had studied under and been known to Luther. From 1545 he was pastor of the St. Nicholas church in Strasbourg. Prior to leaving for England in 1549, Bucer appointed him to share the leadership of the Strasbourg church with the aged Hedio. On Hedio's death he was appointed as president of the church council (1552). See A.Trensz, *Situation Intérieure de l'Eglise Evang.-Luthérienne de Strasbourg, sous la Direction de J. Marbach, Président du Convent Ecclésiastique (1557-1581)*, Strasbourg 1857.

4 Accounts of the controversy can be found in C.J.Burchill, "Girolamo Zanchi in Strasbourg 1553-1563", Ph.D. Cambridge 1979, and "Le Dernier Théologien Reformé. Girolamo Zanchi: de officio docentium et discentium in scholis", *BSHPF* 135(1989), pp.54-63; J.M.Kittelson, "Marbach versus Zanchi: the resolution of controversy in late Reformation Strasbourg, *SCJ*, 8(1977)3 pp.31-44; W.Neuser, "Dogma und Bekenntnis in der Reformation: von Zwingli und Calvin bis zur Synode von Westminster", pp.167-352, in C.Andresen (ed.), *Handbuch der Dogmen- und Theologiegeschichte* (3 vols.), Göttingen 1980, vol.2, pp.303-305.

5 E.g. *Opera Theologica* (7 books in 3 vols.), Geneva 1613, 7.2.222,305.

6 Kittelson, op.cit., pp.36-40,44; J. Moltmann, *Prädestination und Perseveranz: Geschichte und Bedeutung der reformierten Lehre 'de perseverantia sanctorum'*, Neukirchen 1961, pp.81-90; Zanchi, *Opera*, 7.2.296. Kittelson p.34 concludes that, to those in the conflict, predestination was the most important of the theological issues.

7 See ante, pp.6-7. See *Opera* 7.2.348 for Zanchi's interpretation of Luther. See McGrath, *Iustitia Dei*, op.cit., vol.2, pp.28-32. Predestination was defined by the Lutheran John Gerhard (1582-1637) as follows: "God determined from eternity to save those who would believe in Christ", and by David Hollaz (1646-1713): "Predestination is the eternal decree of God to bestow salvation on all of whom God foresaw that they would finally believe in Christ", cited by H. Schmid, *The Doctrinal Theology of the Evangelical Lutheran Church*, Minneapolis 1961, pp.272,275.

8 Zanchi attempted to publish the *Miscellanea*, containing lectures, theses and other material relating to the controversy, anonymously in Zurich during the course of the dispute itself. He was dissuaded by Bullinger who feared exacerbating the situation. Zanchi eventually signed an agreement in 1563, and felt the need to defend himself for having done so, by publishing the *Miscellanea*. The *Miscellanea* published in 1566, and in the 1613 edition in the *Opera* (7.1), contains material edited by Zanchi. Fuller records of the course of the dispute are found in 7.2 of the *Opera*. Further original material is to be found in the Strasbourg Archives. Kittelson, who consulted these Archives, does not seem to have brought forward any theological points on Zanchi's part, which cannot be found in the published material. See Kittelson, op.cit., pp.31-32.

9 "Theses aliquot Hieronymo Zanchio, Argentinae, cum ibi theologiam profiteretur, a quibusdam obiectae, atque partim ut novae, partim ut haereticae damnatae: ab academiis vero & ecclesiis aliqot, doctisque & piis theologis in Germania, partim ut probabiles, partim ut piae & orthodoxae, datus & scriptis suis iudiciis comprobatae" (7.L.63-64). Zanchi had sent the theses to various theologians and academies, and prints their favourable responses at the end. They are from the academies and churches of Marburg, Heidelberg, Schaffhausen, Zurich and Basel. There are also a number of individual letters.

10 7.L.64.

11 7.2.340. Marbach accused Zanchi of Schwenkfeldianism, because he seemed to be separating the activity of the Spirit from the word (7.2.349).

12 Kittelson, op.cit., p.43, concludes that the Consensus truly continued the direction of Luther's thought: "...the disagreement between the two men concerned matters of theological substance, in which Zanchi truly represented the orthodox Reformed tradition and Marbach that of Luther". This is in contrast with the view of J.P. Donnelly, "Italian Influences on the Development of Calvinist Scholasticism", *SCJ* 7(1976)1 pp.81-108. Donnelly claims, "The Strasbourg quarrel marks an important stage in the gradual retreat of later Lutheranism from Luther's *De Servo Arbitrio* to a milder position", p.99. Both could be correct, if the later Luther indeed modified his own earlier position on predestination. The Consensus, found in *Opera* 7.2.439-442, was signed by Zanchi (15 March 1563) thus: "*Hanc doctrinam formulam, ut piam agnsoco, ita etiam recipio.*" Zanchi subsequently produced an explanation of his understanding of the Consensus (7.1.45-62), thereby ensuring further strife and his own departure from Strasbourg. Calvin, Beza and Bullinger all disapproved of Zanchi's acceptance of the Consensus, which referred to the Augsburg Confession's teaching on the Lord's Supper, and ruled out the *a priori* approach to predestination. See Kittelson, op.cit., p.40; Beza's *Correspondance*, op.cit., p.271, letter of Beza to Bullinger (5 June 1563); J.N.Tylenda, "Girolamo Zanchi and John Calvin", *CTJ* 10(1975) pp.101-141.

13 7.2.440. This definition is strikingly similar to that of the Formula of Concord. Zanchi tried to escape the force of this article by subsequently explaining it, "Here the eternal decree of God concerning the salvation of certain men in Christ, which we call predestination...is not defined, but rather the decree concerning the mode by which God willed and wills the gospel to be preached." (7.L.56).

14 "Praelectio de Praedestinatione", 7.L.183-203, on which the following exposition is based.

15 7.1.188.

16 Grundler, "Thomism", op.cit., p.143, and Strehle, The "Extent", op.cit., p.103, regard Zanchi as a supralapsarian, whilst Muller, *Christ and the Decree*, op.cit., pp.112-113, and P.K.Jewett, *Election and Predestination*, Grand Rapids 1985, p.94, classify him as infralapsarian. Although Grundler seems to have correctly identified Zanchi's preference, Zanchi allowed that both constructions were possible. It was characteristic of him to accept apparently conflicting positions as valid, when appropriately interpreted, e.g. his acceptance of both Augustine's and Ambrose's expositions of 1 Tim.2.4-6, his assertion that the atonement is for the elect only and for all men, and his view that God's stated will can be conditional, but that there is no conditional will in God.

17 7.1.188, cp.7.1.288.

18 See Grundler, "Thomism", op.cit., esp. pp.121-159. For Zanchi's scholasticism see also J.P.Donnelly, op.cit.

19 *Summa*, op.cit., 1.23.1,2.

20 "De Praedestinatione Sanctorum: deque eorundem in fide perseverantia, & de coena Domini, olim Senatui Argentinensi exhibita confessio", 7.1.279-346.

21 7.1.280-281; 284-286.

22 7.1.281, "The absolute will of God is the primary cause of all things in such a way that nothing is the cause of it". 284, "...the first cause of all things and of all other causes"; 7.1.285-8, cp.303-4; 7.1.289-90.

23 7.1.293-306; 295, "Therefore the conditional promises are immutable not only in God and in themselves but in the elect themselves, because in them the immutable effect follows"; 323, "All the ministrations of the church are means God uses in those to be led to eternal life...(and by which) reprobates are rendered inexcusable."

24 *De Natura Dei seu de Divinis Attributis...* (Bk.2 of *Opera*).

25 The fifth of the five books of the *De Natura* deals with providence and predestination, and the fact that these themes are dealt with, in Thomist fashion, as part of the doctrine of God is significant. The length of the chapters reflects the emphases of Zanchi's theology: 84 columns are devoted to the will of God, compared to only 100 on the goodness, grace, love, mercy, righteousness, wrath and hate of God, combined. 163 columns are devoted to providence and predestination.

26 2.3.245-246: "Who doubts that things are moved by God? This is also an axiom of the philospher. And also who does not know that God is an intelligent mind? Therefore since God moves all things and is the greatest intelligence of all it cannot be denied that there is free will in him, free, I say, touching all those things which are not God himself."

27 2.3.251; 2.3.253-4.

28 2.3.254-6; 2.3.485.

29 Muller, *Christ and the Decree*, op.cit., p.111 notes that, although Zanchi seemed to be following the pattern of Thomas Aquinas' *Summa* in commencing his own projected (but never completed) *Summa* with the attributes of God, his emphasis on the will of God suggests a Scotist influence. See *Opera* 1.342-345, where Zanchi gives explicit approval to the Nominalist *potentia absoluta* and the dictum that God's will is the rule of all justice.

30 Grundler, "Thomism", op.cit., pp.158-159.

31 7.1.311; 189, cp.29L.

32 7.1.63,95; 312; "Commentary on Ephesians", 6.1.12

33 It is true that Zanchi calls Christ "the first effect of predestination", but this description must be understood according to the author's own explanation, namely that Christ was appointed as mediatorial head, in order that he might have members. See 2.3.535.

34 2.3.484.

35 7.2.258; 362. The idea of predestination meeting us in Christ was fully in accord with Luther's view cited above, p.6. But Zanchi could not let this be the end of the matter - he had to theorise about predestination apart from Christ, on the basis of the attributes of God.

36 2.5.495; 6.1.11.

37 7.1.285-286.

38 6.1.15; 7.1.239.

39 *Commentary on 1 John*, 6.2.46, cp.7.1.285; "Tractatio de Christo Advocato", 7.1.234-238, cp.7.1.239; "Confessio", 7.1.291, "Those who, looking at the revealed will of God, teach that God both wills that all be saved and that Christ died for the salvation of all, cannot be condemned." Zanchi's teacher, Vermigli, also dealt with the extent of the atonement by reference to the sufficient-efficient distinction, the latter part of which was set by him within the framework of a strong doctrine of particular predestination. See Peter Martyr Vermigli, *The Common Places*, n. pl. 1574, 3.44 (p.31).

40 See 7.1.342-345, for reference to the Bucer-Hoffman debate.

41 7.2.436.

42 7.2.229.

43 7.2.355-61; 7.2.341, "...*tuam antiquam catalinam*..."

44 7.2.359-364, ESP. 362; 7.2.278.

45 Marbach accused Zanchi that he "orders everybody to presume simply that he has been eternally elected", his objection to this being that "he does not make any mention in this of the ministry of the church" (7.2.340). Zanchi's defence was, "There is a difference between presuming and believing. I have taught everyone ought to believe himself predestined in Christ to eternal salvation. Who is able to believe, however, without the preached word?" (7.2.342).

Chapter Six
The Heidelberg School

ZACHARIAS URSINUS (1534-1583)

Introduction

Early in his reign, which began in 1559, Frederick III, the Elector of the Palatinate, set out to make the University of Heidelberg a Reformed school. Thus Heidelberg became a centre of Reformed theology equal in importance to Geneva during the latter half of the sixteenth century, and characterized by certain emphases of its own.[1] Zacharias Ursinus[2] became professor of dogmatics at Heidelberg in 1562. He was chiefly responsible for the production of the influential Heidelberg Catechism (1563).

Ursinus was capable of a giving a practical and pastoral slant to his work, as typified in the Catechism, whose first question is,

> "What is your only comfort in life and death?"[3]

At the same time, he frequently demonstrated a scholastic approach and methodology, as is apparent in his exposition of the Catechism, issued posthumously in several editions and under different titles, based on lecture notes taken by his students.[4] This work employs the *loci* method, after the example of Philip Melanchthon, under whom Ursinus had studied. Under each *locus* it follows the scholastic approach of asking questions like *an sit*, *quid sit* and *qualis sit*, even dealing with God himself in this way.[5]

Interest in Ursinus has concentrated on the question of his role in the development of covenant theology. Heinrich Heppe viewed the Heidelberg treatment of covenant as a movement away from the predestinarianism of Geneva.[6] This thesis has met with considerable acceptance, but its tendency to set Geneva and Heidelberg in opposition has been questioned. So D.A.Weir draws attention to the close relations between the Heidelberg theologians and Beza, and also demonstrates his essential oneness with them in his view of predestination.[7] Weir points to their shared preoccupation with the fall, understanding that their predestinarian theology both required the fall of Adam, and also rendered it incapable of comprehension.

He concludes that, "For the Calvinist of whatever variety, the prelapsarian covenant with Adam did not "soften" the decree of God concerning the Fall; rather, it affirmed it, expanded it, explained it, and worked it out."

This citation indicates what Weir identifies as the key element in covenant theology: the pre-fall covenant with Adam, viewed as a legal relationship, establishing a basic and continuing partnership between God and the human race, and promulgated a second time in the "moral law" of Moses.[8] Theological use of the covenant motif was frequent, before and after the Reformation. Among the early Reformed, Bullinger, W.Musculus and Calvin,[9] for example, made use of it. The distinctiveness of the covenant theology arising from Heidelberg was the two-covenant scheme, with the "covenant of works"[10] established with Adam in Eden. A system was constructed in which God's dealings with the human race in nature and grace were radically opposed, and yet in which grace operated largely in accordance with the legal-covenantal pattern of pre-fall nature.

Weir's emphasis on the importance of Ursinus' references to the covenant of nature can be disputed,[11] in that he is able to provide only a few relevant and specific citations, and these are taken from a work Ursinus himself did not see fit to publish. There can be no dispute, however, that covenant theology became a well established feature of German Reformed thought, and that Ursinus played a part in preparing its way.

A feature of covenant theology to which Weir devotes less attention is the fundamental role of the concept of conditionality. Earlier studies have sought to distinguish two sorts of covenant theology, the bilateral-conditional and unilateral-unconditional, but attempts to divide theologians sharply according to this distinction have proved unconvincing, since Calvin, for example, can be cited in such a way as to place him on both sides.[12] The two models are not necessarily mutually exclusive, since theologians could understand predestination according to the unconditional covenant model, and at the same time present the gospel as embodying a conditional covenant. Weir's criterion of the presence or absence of the pre-fall covenant is a more incisive tool, distinguishing between more or less developed covenant theologies. Building upon Weir's work, it may be said that, by introducing a pre-fall, legal covenant, and tuning the covenant of grace to it, Ursinus made the conditionality of the gospel, which all Reformed theologians acknowledged to some degree, approximate to a formal legal obligation. The present chapter will demonstrate the importance of conditionality to Ursinus and his colleagues and successors at Heidelberg and Neustadt (to which, when the Lutheran Louis VI became the Elector Palatine, the Reformed theologians of Heidelberg had to move until 1583), and will show how it was important in their treatment of the extent of the atonement.

Predestination[13]

Predestination was understood by Ursinus to be a part of providence:

> "Predestination differeth from providence, as a speciall from a generall."

In fact, in *The Summe*, the first definition of predestination occurs in the section on providence:

> "Predestination is the most wise, eternall and unchangeable decree of God, whereby he deputed and destined every man, before he was created, to his certain use and end."[14]

Predestination is divided into election and reprobation, as two sides of the same decree. In terms reminiscent of Beza, Ursinus explained that the cause of both is nothing other than the incomprehensible good pleasure of God, having as its final cause the display of his glory in the manifestation of goodness and mercy in the elect and justice and severity in the reprobate. As faith is a consequence of the decree of election, rather than its cause, so sin, although the cause of damnation, is not the cause of reprobation, for the divine decision about whom to elect and whom to reprobate is attributable to the good pleasure of God alone.[15]

In the passage of *The Summe* just expounded, as in the definition given in the section on predestination itself, it is taken for granted that predestination is chiefly concerned with discrimination between people:

> "Predestination is the eternall...counsell of God...of converting some...and of leaving the rest."
>
> "The efficient cause of this distinction is the election of God."[16]

The same points are made to "a friend" in a "Letter concerning Predestination": God is the *Prima Causa*; predestination is that aspect of God's providence which determines which individuals are to be saved and which condemned; God's omnipotence guarantees the execution of his predestinating will; the love of God which sent his Son into the world was his love to the elect.

As well as being placed in relation to providence as a way of attributing the facts of experience to the eternal will of God, predestination functions soteriologically as a guarantee of the entirely gracious character of salvation.[17] Defined as that which comes, in the plan of God, before all human activity, it rules out the view that God chooses people on the basis of their good works.

Ursinus also related predestination to the church.[18] The Heidelberg Catechism, following the outline of the Creed, has no section devoted specifically to predestination, but *The Summe* introduces it as a commonplace which "ariseth out of the former place of the Church, and is joyned with it". Predestination is related to the church in the sense that the true, invisible church is defined as a body of elect individuals.

> "The invisible Church is a company of those which are elected to eternal life."

Ursinus regarded election as a guarantee that there would in fact be a church, so that the first of four effects of predestination is given as

> "the creation and gathering of the church."

It is disappointing to find that, having brought predestination and ecclesiology into proximity, he was unable to unite the two other than by teaching that the church is composed of elect individuals.

Ursinus did not devote much attention to the relationship between Christ and predestination. He gave the explanation that the Pauline "chosen in Christ" means "chosen to be in Christ". It is true that Ursinus makes Christ's election prior to ours: Christ was chosen to be head and mediator, then we were chosen to be in him, then Christ was sent into the world. Thus God's (electing) love preceded the mission, though not the election, of Christ.

> "He first chose the head...Afterwards he also chose us as members in that head...God's love, that is his free election, is the cause of the sending of the Son."

These points, however, were not developed very far by Ursinus.

This brief survey of Ursinus' teaching on predestination is enough to show that, as far as the doctrine in itself was concerned, Heidelberg was not far removed from Geneva.

God's Covenant

Ursinus portrayed the plight of man in terms of a covenant broken, and man's restoration in terms of a covenant kept. His "Major Catechism" asks:

> "What is the difference between the Law and the Gospel?"

and answers,

> "The Law contains the covenant of nature [*foedus naturale*], initiated in creation by God with men, that is, known to men naturally; and it requires from us perfect obedience to God, and it promises eternal life for those who keep it, and threatens eternal punishments for those who do not keep it. But the gospel contains the covenant of grace....It shows to us the fulfilment in Christ of his righteousness, which the law requires, and its restoration in us through the Spirit of Christ; and it promises eternal life freely because of Christ, to those who believe in him."

The above answer shows the covenant of grace understood as a fulfilment for us and in us, by Christ, of the law or covenant of nature. For this reason the office of Mediator is described as being,

> "To reinstate the covenant between God and men."[19]

Ursinus defined covenant (*foedus* and *testamentum*) as a mutual agreement, and believed that as such it could provide a category for understanding the work of Christ:

> "This reconciliation in the Scriptures is termed, The Covenant and Testament."

This is further defined as,

> "A mutuall promise and agreement between God and men, whereby God giveth men assurance, that he will be gracious and favourable to them, remit their sins, bestow new righteousnesse, his holy Spirit, and life eternall for and by his Son our Mediatour: And on the other side, men bind themselves to faith and repentance; that is to receive this so great a benefit with true faith, and to yeeld true obedience unto God."

This covenant of grace is the same in substance under both old and new dispensations, though different in administration. In particular,

> "the principall conditions...are the same."[20]

It should be clear, not simply that Ursinus regarded a covenant as conditional in itself, but that he carried over the conditionality of the pre-fall covenant into the covenant of grace. This did not mean that the demand for obedience under the new covenant is a demand for perfect obedience with a view to justification. For,

> "The law promiseth life...with a condition of our own righteousnesse...The Gospel promiseth the same...with condition of another's righteousnesse, to wit, Christs, applied unto us by faith".

Nevertheless both faith and obedience are still expected as covenant conditions. Only God can give the ability to fulfil the conditions, for the covenant has "its restoration in us through the Spirit of Christ". Without the Spirit "we should have been unable to stand to the conditions".

The conceptual subservience of the covenant of grace (gospel) to the covenant of nature (law) is matched by a pragmatic subservience.

> "Their order in preaching must be observed: First the law is to be proposed...Then...the gospel...Thirdly...the law is to be taught again."[21]

The idea of conditional covenant features in Ursinus' teaching on the sacraments. Over against the Lutheran view that the sacraments effectively convey God's promise to all, "worthy" or not, who participate in them, he maintained that they seal the promise only to those who fulfil the condition of faith.[22]

> "Unto whom nothing is promised in the word, to him the Sacraments seale nothing: To the wicked nothing is promised in the word; (for all promises in the word have a condition of faith and repentance annexed to them)."[23]

As Weir rightly points out, the Genevan teaching on predestination left the problem of how Adam could have been responsible for a fore-ordained fall. Weir also perceives that it left the question of the basis on which a Christian state can expect moral and law-abiding behaviour from its non-elect citizens, and in the Palatinate, where the theologians were given an extraordinarily large share in government, this question was far from academic.[24] It should be added that the Genevan doctrine of predestination had also raised the questions, whether the work of Christ was for the elect only, and how the gospel could be sincerely preached to the non-elect. Ursinus' covenant teaching provided a basis for dealing with all these difficulties, for it laid a basis for God's dealings with human beings as human beings, in which their moral and evangelical obligations were set out independently of predestination, and God's promises were made dependent on them playing their part.

Thus Ursinus espoused a two-sided system of predestination and covenant. When seeking to stress divine sovereignty and the gratuitous nature of salvation, or the perseverance of the saints, he could speak in terms of predestination. When wishing to make room for God's dealings with the human race in history, to present God's ethical and evangelical demands as binding upon all, and to defend God from the charge of being the author of evil, he could refer to the covenant. This was very convenient, but did not make for an integrated theology. It could be judged to be more a symptom of than a cure for a Reformed dilemma.

Ursinus' one convincing meeting point between predestination and covenant was in the way that predestination ensures that the elect are given the ability to fulfil the covenant condition. The integration of predestination and covenant at this point exalted the human fulfilment of conditions to a very high place within Ursinus' total system. It did not save the system, however, from appearing to have two virtually independent halves, as his teaching on the extent of the atonement shows.

The Extent of the Atonement

Ursinus drew heavily on Anselm for his explanation of the death of Christ, and his usual term for it was "satisfaction". In characteristic Reformed fashion he combined the idea of penal substitution with the Anselmic view. Ursinus' scholasticism is evident in his endeavour to prove the logical necessity of every aspect of Christ's satisfaction.[25]

The version of Ursinus' exposition of the Heidelberg Catechism which became standard was produced by David Pareus in 1591. It was Pareus' edition which was reproduced in the *Opera Theologica*, ed. Quirinius Reuter, Heidelberg 1612. Pareus included a section under "The Death of Christ", entitled, "Whether Christ died for all". His marginal note states that Ursinus never addressed this question directly, and that the section, put together on the basis of scattered comments, has been included because the subject had come into contention. He offers to take responsibility for the insertion if the reader should think it insufficiently "Ursinian". The Henry Middleton edition (1586) and Henry Parry translation (1587), based on versions earlier than Pareus', have in the same position a section entitled "The fruit of Christ's death". In the light of this uncertainty about what Ursinus actually said, in our exposition of Ursinus' teaching we will not use Pareus' insertion.[26]

At the beginning of his treatment of predestination, Ursinus anticipated the objection that "the promise of grace is universall". His answer to this was in terms of the usual two-wills teaching. He wrote,

> "God willeth that all be saved, as he is delighted with the salvation of all...[and] inasmuch as he inviteth all to repentance: but he will not have all saved, in respect of the force and efficacy of calling."[27]

In this God is not acting deceitfully, for he has given no promise to work in all who are externally called. Furthermore, "A promise on an impossible condition" is not useless, for by it God seriously shows to all the way to be saved, and he also grants to his elect the ability to fulfil the condition. The conditionality of the promise explains why the two wills are not contradictory: God does not have an unqualified will for the salvation of all, but for all who believe. Thus, in the "Letter concerning Predestination", Ursinus denied what he elsewhere seems to grant concerning the universality of the promises:

> "It is absurd to say they are universal. They are restricted to believers, and those God elects, he calls."

Ursinus was prepared to grant that the "all" in 1 Timothy 2.4 may refer to all individuals with respect to (external) calling, but he preferred the exposition of Augustine in terms of the efficacy of God's saving will among all classes.[28]

Under the heading of The Gospel, the question of the extent of the atonement is considered in terms of its reception or non-reception through faith. The end of the section on the Mediator asks whether salvation has been restored to all, and answers,

> "Not at all, but to those only who by a true faith are engraffed into him, and receive his benefits."[29]

Ursinus rejected the unqualified proposition,

> "Whomsoever Christ hath fully satisfied for, they are to be received by God into favour",

explaining that,

> "All are received into favour for whom Christ satisfied, with this condition, if they apply the satisfaction of Christ unto themselves by faith."

Repeatedly Ursinus maintained that there are two sides to the satisfaction of Christ, its merit and its application. As far as merit is concerned,

> "He satisfied for all regarding satisfaction, but not with respect to application."[30]

Unaided, people fall short by failing to fulfil the condition of faith, but the risen Christ supplies the condition to his elect.

> "For it is not sufficient for our Mediatour to be made a sacrifice for us...but it is necessary also that he promise on our behalf that we shall imbrace the decree concerning our redemption by our Mediatour, and cease at length to offend God through our sins; which is the other part of the Covenant made between God and us, and is performed by us, that the Covenant may remain firme and ratified."

Dealing with the same problem, Ursinus cited the familiar scholastic dictum:

> "The cause why all are not saved by Christ, is not the insufficiency of the merit and grace of Christ (for Christ is the full propitiatory sacrifice for the sinnes of the whole world, as concerning the worth and sufficiency of the ransome and price which he paid) but it is the infidelity of men, whereby they refuse the benefits of Christ offered in the Gospel..."

This sufficiency is dependent upon the infinite value of the divine nature of Christ, which was a match for the infinite (eternal) punishment deserved by sin. The extremity of the penalty coupled with the worth of the person amounted to a sacrifice of infinite value.The other side of the traditional formula was equally acceptable to Ursinus:

> "Christ was ordained by God the Father...to offer himself a sacrifice propitiatory for the sins of all mankinde...and lastly to apply effectually his sacrifice unto us...by enlightening and moving the Elect."[31]

At times it seems as if Ursinus would go no further than to maintain that the universality of the atonement is only limited by human unbelief, as when he said,

> "Now the reason why all men do not believe, nor apply this Christs benefit unto themselves, is a question of higher and deeper speculation, impurtinent to this place."

Unable to resist a little speculation, however, he added,

> "This may suffice for an answer herein",

and directed his readers to Romans 9.18.

In fact, Ursinus regularly went "higher and deeper". Since for him faith is given in accordance with the decree of election, and Christ is mediator not only to provide satisfaction but also to apply it to the elect, the work of Christ is to be seen ultimately in terms of the decree of election. Thus Ursinus interchangeably referred to the atonement as being for "the faithful" or "the elect", and could make statements like the following:

> "God verily decreed from everlasting to pardon in Christ, for his satisfaction, the sins of the elect."[32]

Ursinus, then, had a double explanation of the extent of the atonement. In terms of the merit of Christ and the conditional promise, it is universal. In terms of God's eternal plan, its extent is restricted. This plan is revealed at the point of application, in the exercise of faith as a gift of the risen Mediator through the Holy Spirit. To put it differently, the work of Christ on the cross can be viewed in isolation as merely potential, or in connection with election and the work of the risen Christ as an effective accomplishment.

Ursinus' double-sided doctrine of the extent of the atonement resembles Bullinger's position, as does his use of the conditional covenant theme. It also bears a strong resemblance to that of the Bernese theologian Wolfgang Musculus (1497-1563). In his *Common Places*, Musculus set out a covenant theology in which there is a "generall covenant" of God's goodness to all creation, and a "speciall and everlasting covenant...with his elect and believing". As far as the latter is concerned, its condition of faith means that it can be regarded as either particular or universal.

> "If a man will have it called Generall and universall, forasmuch as it...comprehendeth universally all and lone, which cleave in beleving to our Lord Christe...he may also so far me."

This perspective enabled him to maintain that, in a sense, Christ died for all.

> "We know that all be not partakers of this redemption, but yet the loss of them which be not saved, doth hinder nothing at all, why it is called an universall redemption...It is not for the lacke of the grace of God, that the reprobate...do not receave it."[33]

Musculus saw a direct link between universal sinfulness and a universal redemption. At the same time he said that the work of the Mediator involved both "to purchase and dispense" redemption, and that, though redemption is "perfect in itself" it may be "rightly deemed unperfect" until it has been applied.[34]

Knowledge of Election

In the light of all the above, we would expect Ursinus to define faith in terms of personal reception of Christ as the universally sufficient and offered Saviour, with assurance of election flowing from the exercise of faith, on the basis that faith is the gift of God to the elect alone. In fact, an echo of the teaching of Bucer and Zanchi seems to be heard in Ursinus, in that he maintained,

> "Of himself every man ought certainly to believe that he is an elect; for we have a generall commandment, that all believe the gospel and repent."

Ursinus did not express himself in this way often. His statement probably should be taken to mean that everyone should first repent and believe the gospel and then consequently believe in his own election. Indeed, the instruction cited above followed a statement that,

> "We should be sure of our election by the effects thereof, namely by conversion, that is, by true faith and repentance."[35]

Thus, election is known in consequence of the fulfilment of the conditions of the covenant.

Conclusion

Predestination was a major theme of Ursinus' theology, but so was the covenant and the related concept of conditionality. His main way of asserting the universality of the atonement was to say that it was sufficient for all, and his main way of asserting its particularity was to teach that it is applied only to those, namely the elect, who fulfil the condition of faith.

CASPAR OLEVIANUS (1536-1587)

To what extent Olevianus[36] contributed to the preparation of the Heidelberg Catechism is uncertain, but there can be little doubt that his *De Substantia Foederis Gratuiti Inter Deum et Electos*[37] was a significant contribution to the development of covenant theology. The way he used the covenant motif was distinct from his colleague Ursinus' mode of dealing with it.

Two of Olevianus' major emphases are contained in the title of his work. The first is his insistence, reminiscent of Calvin, that the covenant is wholly free and undeserved, arising solely from God's grace:

> "The whole of this covenant is entirely free, and without condition from us men, but from the free mercy of God in Christ through faith."[38]

God's covenant, Olevianus often claimed, is to be equated with his promise. For the covenant to be entirely of grace, Christ as Mediator was appointed both to make satisfaction for sin and to obtain the Spirit, through whom the elect can become participants in him. God

> "willed the incarnate Son to be the foundation of his great and eternal covenant".[39]

Everything, therefore, is provided by the covenant and through Christ: faith is the gift not the condition of the covenant, won by Christ crucified and imparted by Christ risen. Clearly not everyone is included in this eternal covenant, nor can Christ, in putting the covenant into effect, have died for everyone, for not all receive the Spirit and faith. Christ's *impetratio* and *applicatio*, or, to put it another way, his sacrifice and intercession belong together as two sides of the same work belonging to the same group of people.[40] Thus, as the title indicates, the covenant concerns the elect.

Olevianus had no hesitation whatsoever in teaching that the work of Christ was for God's elect alone. Indeed,

> "In the eternal counsel of God...this ransom was not destined for any other than those who believe...that is, those whom the Son of God makes or will make believers."
>
> "If he had made intercession and sacrifice for reprobates too, then clearly, their sins having been paid for by the sacrifice of the Son of God, the justice of God would not allow him to require a debt already paid by the Son, nor would the justice of God be able to punish them with eternal death for their sins inasmuch as satisfaction has been made by him."[41]

Here was a Genevan type of theology, starting, as Calvin did, with grace and election, and then following it through, further than Calvin did, to an extremely particularistic conclusion. Olevianus seems to have been travelling the same road as Beza, and managing to do so even without the help of Beza's scholasticism.

If the positive side of Ursinus' covenant theology was its universal openness, while its shadow side was the conditionalism it introduced, and if the positive side of Olevianus' covenant theology was its emphasis on the initiative of grace, while its shadow side was its severe particularism, it is ironic that the main stream of seventeenth-century Reformed theology would manage to combine and give prominence to Ursinus' conditionalism and Olevianus' particularism. This, however, was what the covenant theology of such men as John Owen and Francis Turretin would succeed in doing.[42]

SAMUEL HUBER AND AEGIDIUS HUNNIUS

In the wake of the Colloquy of Montbéliard of 1586, controversy developed at Bern.[43] Samuel Huber accused Abraham Musculus (son of Wolfgang) and Peter Hubner, the Bernese representatives, of departing from accepted Bernese teaching by agreeing to Beza's theses on predestination. The first of the four positions with which Huber found fault was "that Jesus Christ did not die for all men". The ensuing friction led to the calling of a Colloquy at Bern on 14 April 1588, attended by representatives from Basel, Schaffhausen and Zurich, as well as by Beza. The gathering issued a statement that nothing had been signed at Montbéliard contrary to the Bernese Confession, against the position of the other Reformed churches or against Scripture, and Huber was ordered to cease his protestations. For failing to do so, he was exiled, and sought a home among the Lutherans of Württemberg, from where he continued his attacks on the Reformed doctrine of predestination, maintaining that Christ had redeemed the whole human race. According to Huber, universal redemption is not merely conditional but actual and effective, though he allowed for the possibility of losing salvation through unbelief.[44]

Also in the wake of Montbéliard, the Lutheran Aegidius Hunnius attacked both the "Calvinists" and Huber for making redemption absolute, either for the elect or for all, and so, in his estimation, devaluing the preached word of God and ministry of the church. Hunnius' writings, rejecting the absolute particular redemption of the "Calvinists" and the absolute universal redemption of Huber, are based on the view that election is dependent on foreseen faith.[45] Hunnius was instrumental in drawing up the 1592 Saxon Visitation Articles, designed to root out Crypto-Calvinism from Electoral Saxony. One of the four sections of the Articles covered predestination and providence, and had as its first statement, "That Christ died for all men". The Articles explicitly identified "the false and erroneous doctrine of the Calvinists", and, under predestination and providence, listed first the error "that Christ did not die for all men, but only for the elect".[46] Thus, in the 1590's, Reformed theologians, especially those in German states, felt it necessary to deal with the extent of the atonement, which had been shown to be a point of disagreement between Lutheran and Reformed at Strasbourg and Montbéliard, and was now being kept to the fore by Huber and Hunnius.

DAVID PAREUS (1548-1622)

Pareus was a colleague of Ursinus at Heidelberg and later the editor of Urisinus' exposition of the Catechism. He made a speech in Heidelberg in 1590 concerning the extent of Christ's saving work.[47] With Huber in mind he ridiculed the notion that Christ can be said to have saved all absolutely, when all are not in fact saved. He denied that all have been received into God's favour through Christ's work, since Scripture makes this status dependent on faith. Pareus accepted the sufficient-efficient formula, and was reluctant to speak without qualification of Christ having died for all. Granting that he died absolutely for all as regards sufficiency, he added,

> "But the question is properly of the efficiency and participation."[48]

Accordingly he pointed out that evangelical promises

> "have annexed expressly or tacitly the condition of faith and repentance."

On the understanding that the death of Christ belongs to "the universalitie of the faithfull", people discover whether Christ died for them by employing the syllogism:

> "Christ prayed and died for all believers;
> I believe;
> Ergo, Christ prayed and died for me."

Pareus rejected the alternative:

> "Christ died for all men;
> I am a man:
> Ergo, Christ died for me."

Huber's position that unbelief is the only sin that can condemn a person is countered by the assertion that, if, as Huber maintained, only unbelief can bring condemnation, then Christ must have died for all sins except unbelief. But this would be to maintain the foolish position that Christ died for all sins except the greatest of all.[49]

Pareus' speech does little more to link limited atonement to predestination than to refer to believers as "elect". His crucial point was that the atonement has the condition of faith attached to it, that none are reconciled to God without faith, and that the exercise or non-exercise of faith determines how far the work of Christ is effective.[50]

In his *Irenicum*,[51] Pareus was seeking to counter a Roman Catholic claim that the Lutherans had more in common with Catholicism than with the Reformed. Therefore, in that work, while recognizing the Lutheran-Reformed division over the extent of the atonement, he placed more emphasis on the universality of Christ's work, still relying on his basic distinction between sufficiency and efficacy:

> "Christ carried, dissolved, expiated the sins of all, if we consider the magnitude of the price or sufficiency of the ransom, but only of the faithful and not of all, if we consider the efficacy, fruit and application of the ransom."

In the letter he wrote to the Synod of Dort,[52] the elderly Pareus again based his approach to the extent of the atonement on the distinction between sufficiency and efficacy.

DANIEL TOSSANUS (1541-1602)[53]

Another Heidelberg professor, Daniel Tossanus, who came from Montbéliard, was engaged in a literary battle with Huber and Hunnius during the 1590s. In 1600 he preached, and then published, three sermons, the first of which directly addressed the question, "For whom did Christ die?". Bound with the *Drei Christliche Predigten*, in a volume in the Bodleian Library, Oxford, is the *Gegenbeweisung*, and the *Gülden Kleinot vom Todte Christi.*[54] Both are anonymous, but were probably by Tossanus. All three works maintain that Christ came into the world for his people, and pour scorn on the idea that Christ could have died for those now damned. The "all"s of the Bible are to be understood as referring to all believers. The sufficiency of the death of Christ for all is freely granted, but the fruit or effect limited to believers, so that it is said that Christ both did and did not die for all, depending on the sense in which the assertion is made. The discussion ranges around faith rather than predestination, which is hardly touched upon, and the position espoused is, in summary, that Christ died for believers.

JACOBUS KIMEDONCIUS[55]

In his *Theses de Universalitate Redemptionis et Gratiae per Christum*, of 1591, the Dutch Heidelberg professor Kimedoncius directed his arguments against Huber.[56] He used the sufficient-efficient distinction to forward his aim of showing that effective redemption is limited to those who by faith receive it. He also pointed out the uselessness of a universal atonement to those already damned before Christ died.[57]

In his larger *Concerning the Redemption of Mankind*,[58] Kimedoncius pointed once more to Huber as the one who had made it necessary to address the extent of redemption. He appealed again to the sufficient-efficient distinction.

> "The blood of Christ was shed for those only that are predestinated, as touching efficacie: but for all men as touching sufficiencie."

Kimedoncius was sensitive to Huber's charge that limited redemption was a novelty introduced by Beza at Montbéliard, and cited fathers and schoolmen to "prove" the antiquity of the position. Calvin, Beza, Grynaeus and other Reformed leaders were also cited as favouring the sufficient-efficient distinction. According to Kimedoncius, when the Reformed have said that Christ did not die for all, and Beza is specially singled out for this "defence", they are not to be taken "absolutely and without restraint" but as following "the old distinction". The Reformed,

Kimedoncius maintained, agree that if all would believe, all would be saved. This defence of Beza cannot be regarded as more than wishful thinking.[59]In fact, it tends to point up the fact that the Heidelberg theologians were at least as close to Hunnius in their view of the extent of the atonement as they were to Beza, in that the limitation they placed on its extent had to do with the suspension of its effectiveness upon the exercise of faith. Hunnius, convinced that an absolute and particularistic predestination must have a limited atonement as a logical consequence, preferred to take the stricter Bezan doctrine as representative of the Reformed view.

As well as acknowledging universal sufficiency, Kimedoncius indicated other legitimate understandings of universal redemption. It is universal in the sense that the whole church is redeemed, and that all who are saved are saved only through Christ, and that Christ is a ransom for all classes.[60]

Of the Redemption has a treatise on predestination appended to it, but it is noteworthy that in his treatment of the extent of the atonement Kimedoncius made little use of predestination, and in the treatise on predestination he did not develop the theme of limited atonement. To him and to the other immediate successors of Ursinus, limited atonement was related primarily to the conditionality of the gospel.[61]It had to do with the application of Christ's work in time, and only secondarily with the eternal predestination that determined this application.

CONCLUSION

While there are no grounds for asserting that the Heidelberg school departed from the main lines of the established Reformed doctrine of predestination, its teachers, with the possible exception of Olevianus, ensured that attention was also given to God's dealings with mankind in history, by stressing God's covenant, and the conditional nature of the gospel and, indeed, of the atonement itself. Conditionalism was essential to Ursinus' concept of a two sided covenant, and, shortly after his death, came to the fore even more, in response to the "unconditionalism" of the atonement according to Huber.

Heidelberg conditionalism,[62] though it may have saved Reformed theology from preoccupation with eternal decrees, carried within itself its own threats to other elements of that theology. It could make faith seem like a work, being bracketed together with "true obedience" as part of our fulfilment of a covenant of grace, whose main lines were patterned on a legal covenant of nature. The other danger was that the atonement of Christ could seem to be emptied of any objective content, being entirely suspended upon the subjective fulfilment of a condition. In this way the Reformation focus on the grace of God in Christ and outside ourselves could move to the grace at work in the individual fulfiller of conditions. Awareness of these dangers would give rise to lively debate in the following century.

Chapter Six
Notes

1 For historical background, see J.T.McNeill, *The History and Character of Calvinism*, New York 1954, pp.268-280; C-P.Clasen, *The Palatinate in European History 1559-1660*, Oxford 1963; D.Visser, *Zacharias Ursinus: the Reluctant Reformer. His life and times*, New York 1983; H.J. Cohn, "The Territorial Princes in Germany's Second Reformation, 1559-1622", in M.Prestwich (ed.), *International Calvinism 1541-1715*, Oxford 1985, pp.135-165; D.A.Weir, *The Origins of the Federal Theology in Sixteenth-Century Reformed Thought*, Oxford 1990, pp.116,117.

2 For Ursinus, see E.K.Sturm, *Der junge Zacharias Ursin: sein Weg vom Philippismus zum Calvinismus (1534-1562)*, Neukirchen 1972; Visser, op.cit.; C.J.Burchill, "On the Consolation of a Christian Scholar: Zacharias Ursinus (1534-1583) and the Reformation in Heidelberg", *JEH* 37(1986)4 pp.565-583; Zacharias Ursinus", in Raitt, *Shapers*, op.cit., pp.121-139; D. Visser, "Zacharias Ursinus and the Palatinate Reformation", in D.Visser (ed.), *Controversy and Consolidation : the Reformation and the Palatinate*, Allison Park 1986, pp.1-20.

3 "The Heidelberg Catechism", pp. 307-355, in P.Schaff, *The Creeds of Christendom*, vol.3, "The Creeds of the Evangelical Protestant Churches", London 1877, p.307. See F.H.Klooster, "The Priority of Ursinus in the Composition of the Heidelberg Catechism", in Visser, *Controversy*, op.cit., pp.73-100; M.E.Osterhaven, "The Experientialism of the Heidelberg Catechism", in ibid., pp.198-203.

4 Weir lists the main editions and versions, op.cit., p.111 n.9. Also J.M.Platt, *Reformed Thought and Scholasticism: the arguments for the existence of God in Dutch theology 1575-1650*, Leiden 1982, pp.49-50. We use here *The Summe of Christian Religion, delivered by Zacharias Ursinus*, trans. H.Parry, London 1645, unless stated otherwise.

5 For Ursinus' scholasticism, see E. Bizer, *Frühorthodoxie und Rationalismus*, Zurich 1963, pp.16-32, and Platt, op.cit., pp.49-59. Instances of Ursinus' scholasticism are: his use of the *quaestio* method throughout *The Summe*; his frequent use of syllogisms; his frequent use of causal distinctions (e.g. *The Summe*, pp.64-74, 355-356; *Opera* [3 vols.], ed. Q. Reuter, Heidelberg 1612, 3.601); his explanation of the incarnation and atonement in terms of what was "necessary" (*The Summe*, pp.107-118); the scope he gives to reason in understanding God through general revelation, and on this basis investigating the attributes of God (*The Summe*, pp.149-170); his concept of God as Unmoved Mover ("Miscellanea", in *Opera*, 3.29). Ursinus' opposition to Ramism was possibly the outcome of his respect for scholastic logic (see Weir op.cit., pp.108-111). Letham, "Saving Faith", op.cit., p.192, finds the later Ursinus the most thorough-going of the early Reformed scholastics.

6 H.Heppe, *Dogmatik des deutschen Protestantismus im sechzehnten Jahrhundert*, (3 vols.), Marburg 1857, vol.1 pp.158-160. L.D.Bierma, "The Role of Covenant Theology in Early Reformed Orthodoxy", *SCJ* 21(1990)3 pp.453-462, claims that the tendency, following Heppe, to set predestination and covenant theology in opposition has been losing ground.

7 Weir, op.cit., p.16, see pp.15-18,107-108.

8 Schrenk, op.cit., pointed to the pre-fall covenant as an essential ingredient of the kind of covenant (*Doppelbund*) theology that found its clearest expression in the theology of J.Cocceius, who published his *Summa Doctrinae de Foedere et Testamento Dei* in 1648. Schrenk (pp.57-59) also regarded Ursinus as the first to make any systematic use of this scheme. Weir, op.cit., pp.22-35, gives a thorough survey of research into the development of covenant theology, and, pp.160-195, a very full chronological

bibliography. For the relationship of God to humanity before the fall, see M.W.Karlberg, "The original state of Adam: tensions within Reformed theology", *EQ* 59(1987)4 pp.291-309.

9 For W.Musculus' views, see *Common Places of Christian Religion*, London 1563, pp.120a-123b. D.A.Stoute, "The Origins and Early Development of the Reformed Idea of the Covenant", Ph.D. Cambridge 1979; M.W.Karlberg, "The Mosaic Covenant and the Concept of Works in Reformed Hermeneutics: a historical-critical analysis with particular attention to early covenant eschatology", Th.D. Westminster 1980, P.A.Lillback, "The Binding of God: Calvin's role in the development of covenant theology", Ph.D. Westminster 1985, and S.Strehle, *Calvinism, Federalism, and Scholasticism: a study of the Reformed doctrine of covenant*, Bern 1988, have traced the covenant idea through the Middle Ages and Reformation. They build on foundations laid by H.A.Oberman's attention to medieval covenant thought, e.g. in *The Harvest of Medieval Theology: Gabriel Biel and Late Medieval Nominalism*, Cambridge (Mass.) 1963, and *Forerunners*, op.cit.

10 Ursinus' term was *foedus naturale*. The term *foedus operum* is later. Since P.Althaus, *Die Prinzipien der deutschen reformierten Dogmatik im Zeitalter der aristotelischen Scholastik*, Leipzig 1914, pp.155-163, Melanchthon's doctrine of natural law has been seen as the source for Ursinus' covenant of nature. P.A.Lillback, however, in "Ursinus' Development of the Covenant of Creation: a debt to Melanchthon or Calvin", *WTJ* 43(1980-81) pp.247-288, traces Ursinus' ideas to Zurich and Geneva. Visser, "The Covenant in Zacharias Ursinus", *SCJ* 18(1987)4 pp.531-544; and R.W.Letham, "The *Foedus Operum*: some factors accounting for its development", *SCJ* 14(1983)4, pp.457-467, warn against over-emphasising the importance of the pre-fall covenant to Ursinus, and insist that it was no more than a foil to the covenant of grace. While this caution has some justification, the significance of the underlying similarities between both of Ursinus' covenants, and the accompanying stress on the conditionality of the covenant of grace, must not be overlooked.

11 Weir admits this weakness, op.cit., p.103. The work Weir draws on is the "Summa Theologica" (or "Catechesis Major"), in *Opera*, 1.10-33. The "Catechesis Major" should not be confused with the Heidelberg Catechism.

12 L.J.Trinterud, "The Origins of Puritanism", *CH* 20(1951) pp.37-57, divided covenant theology into the Genevan (maintaining a unilateral covenant with an unconditional promise) and the Rhineland (holding to a bilateral and conditional covenant). Others have used the same distinction, e.g. K.Hagen, "From Testament to Covenant in the Early Sixteenth Century", *SCJ* 3(1972)1 pp.1-24; R.W.Letham, Saving Faith, op.cit.; J.B.Torrance, "Covenant or Contract", *SJT* 23(1970) pp.51-76; McCoy and Baker, op.cit., pp.29-30,34-39. Thus Letham and Torrance regard Calvin as a supreme example of a unilateral covenant theologian, while Lillback and Stoute insist on his adherence to a conditional covenant.

13 For treatments of Ursinus on predestination see Bizer, op.cit., pp.31-32; Sturm, op.cit., pp.287-291; Muller, *Christ*, op.cit., pp.111-113.

14 *The Summe*, p.355; p.197. In the "Loci Theologici", *Opera*, 1.427-733, there is no treatment of predestination as a locus in its own right, but it is alluded to in the section on providence, e.g. col.574, where it is called special, as opposed to general, providence, and cols.586-7 on the will of God.

15 *The Summe*, pp.352. Muller, *Christ*, op.cit., pp.106-108, notes the affinities between Ursinus' and Beza's predestinarian teaching. He points out that predestination can be found presented in both infralapsarian and supralapsarian modes by Ursinus. The use of both schemes was observed in Zanchi, see ante, p.90, who was Ursinus' colleague at Heidelberg from 1568. Commencing his "Epistola de Praedestinatione", Ursinus referred his correspondent to the treatments of the subject by Beza, and Zanchi's mentor Peter Martyr Vermigli, "Miscellanea" col. 28, in *Opera* 3.

16 *The Summe*, pp.355,352.

17 "Epistola...de Praedestinatione", dated Sept 11 1573, in "Miscellanea", *Opera*, 3. 28-37. Ibid., 347-357.

18 The following exposition of Ursinus' teaching on predestination is based on *The Summe*, pp.347-357.

19 "Catechesis Major", in *Opera*, 1.10-33. The opening question of the "Catechesis Major", in *Opera*, 1.10, gives pride of place to the covenant motif: "Q.What firm consolation do you have in life and death? A.That God has made me in his image and for eternal life: and after I willingly lost this in Adam, God of his immense and free mercy received me into the covenant of his grace...."

20 It is called "the covenant between God and believers" in *Opera*, 3.427; *The Summe* p.124, cp. p.126, "In all Covenants, their conditions are ever to be considered". For Ursinus' covenant terminology, see Weir, op.cit., pp.51-58.

21 Ibid., pp.125-131. On p.131 the gospel is said to require faith and repentance, or "new obedience".

22 The Heidelberg theologians were in the front line of debate with Lutheranism, in view of the unstable political-ecclesiastical conditions of the Palatinate, as well as its proximity to the German Lutheran states. Consequently virtually the whole of vol.2 of the 3 vols. of Ursinus' *Opera* are taken up with anti-Lutheran controversial writings, mainly on the sacraments.

23 *The Summe*, p.401, cp. *Opera*, 2.1669, cp. 2.1670, dealing with the sacraments: "Universally, in every stipulation when the condition is violated by one party, the promise of the other party is rendered void". Cp. 2.1231: "A divine promise, whether proposed in the sacraments or otherwise, always has the command of faith annexed as a condition, whether expressed or understood."

24 See Weir, op.cit., p.67; J.Torrance, "Interpreting the Word by the Light of Christ or the Light of Nature?", in R.V.Schnucker (ed.), *Calviniana: the ideas and influence of Jean Calvin*, Kirksville 1988, pp.255-267.

25 See especially the discussion at the beginning of the section in *The Summe*, entitled "Of Man's Delivery" pp.107-119. W.Metz, *Necessitas Satisfactionis? Eine systematische Studie zu den Fragen 12-18 des Heidelberger Katechismus und zur Theologie des Zacharias Ursinus*, Zurich 1970, pp.185-218, contrasts Anselm's rationalistic construction with the scriptural content of Ursinus' thought. But see Bizer, op.cit., pp.28-29. See also Sturm, op.cit., pp.266-272.

26 See above, n.4.

27 *The Summe*, p.353; Opera, 1.653.

28 "Miscellanea", cols.35-36, in *Opera* 3.

29 *The Summe*, p.131 (Ursinus also uses the distinction between the *voluntas signi* and *beneplaciti* in discussing providence, *The Summe*, p.213, *Opera*, 1.643.

30 *The Summe*, pp.131-132; *Doctrinae Christianae Compendium*, London 1586 (An edition of Ursinus' explanation of the Catechism), p.406.

31 *The Summe*, pp.116-117 (cp.pp.118,122); pp.132,232.

32 Ibid., p.133 (Rom.9.18: "God has mercy on whom he wants to have mercy, and he hardens whom he wants to harden"); p.364, cp.p.224.

33 W.Musculus, *Common Places*, op.cit., pp.120a-122a,128a-129b.

34 Ibid., pp.139b-140a. For Musculus' thought, see R.B.Ives, "The Theology of Wolfgang Musculus, 1497-1563", Ph.D. Manchester 1965.

35 *The Summe*, p.358, cp.p.295, where faith in Christ who suffered is said to be "To believe that he suffered..for my sake; that is, that by his passion and death he hath satisfied for my sins, hath merited for me remission of sins, the holy Ghost, and life everlasting". Cp. "Miscellanea", col.37 in *Opera* 3. Letham, "Saving Faith", op.cit., pp.194-6, finds the syllogismus practicus in Ursinus, and claims that he was the first to fully work out the consequences of a bilateral conditional covenant in the realm of faith and assurance. See "Miscellanea", col.33 in *Opera* 3, for the syllogism. See J.R.Beeke, "Faith and

Assurance in the Heidelberg Catechism and its Primary Sources: a fresh look at the Kendall thesis", *CTJ* 27(1992)1 pp.39-67.

36 For Olevianus, see K.Sudhoff, *Kaspar Olevian und Zacharias Ursinus*, Elberfeld 1857; L.D.Bierma, *German Calvinism in the Confessional Age: the covenant theology of Caspar Olevianus*, Durham (N.Carolina) 1991; Baker and McCoy, op.cit., pp.36-39.

37 *De Substantia Foederis Gratuiti inter Deum et Electos*, Geneva 1585.

38 Ibid., p.16.

39 Ibid., p.26.

40 Ibid., pp.67-72.

41 Ibid.

42 See below, ch.11.

43 See Vuilleumier, op.cit., vol.2, pp.131-134, and F.W.Cuno, *Daniel Tossanus der Ältere: Professor der Theologie und Pastor 1541-1602* (2 vols.), Amsterdam 1898, vol.1 pp.239-246, for the course of the dispute at Bern. Also Adam, op.cit., pp.50-104 for the whole dispute, pp.58-67 for Huber's "christological protest" against the Reformed position at Montbéliard, and pp.79-90 for his understanding of predestination.

44 Adam cites Huber's four points on pp.58-59, from the Bernese Archives. Huber's view of the extent of the atonement, including its "unconditionalism", is clearly expressed in his *Theses*, Tübingen 1590: "We assert, both according to the teaching of divine Scripture, and according to the consensus of the whole of Christianity, that Christ suffered and died not for some only but for all the posterity of Adam, and, to put it very clearly, with no-one excepted from the whole universality of the human race, whether he should claim and apply salvation to himself through faith and remain in the accepted salvation, or whether, through unbelief, he should reject the offered salvation, and, on account of that, perish eternally." (Thesis 19, "Christum esse mortuum pro peccatis omnium hominum", cited in Adam, op.cit., p.94).

45 *The Articulus de Providentia Dei et Aeterna Praedestinatione sue Electione Filiorum Dei ad Salutem*, Frankfurt 1593, no pagination, is directed against Huber, with a lengthy preface against the predestination teaching of Daniel Tossanus of Heidelberg: "Calvinists hold to the absolute predestination of some, Huber of all...both without respect to faith."

46 Schaff, op.cit., vol.3, pp.181-189, esp. pp.185,189.

47 "A Piece of a Speech, concerning that Question, to whom properly doe the benefits of Christ's sufferings and death belong? And, How Christ is said to die for all?", pp.807-811 in *Theological Miscellanies of Dr.David Pareus*, London 1645, (pp.667-844 of *The Summe*). A fuller Latin version is in "Miscellanea" cols.39-44, in Ursinus' *Opera* 3.

48 Ibid., p.808. A note by Pareus' son Philip in the *Theological Miscellanies* (*The Summe*, p.697), indicates that his father had regularly used "the old distinction" in his treatment of the extent of the atonement, but that, when it was questioned at the Synod of Dort, shortly before his death, he began "to suppose that it was not altogether so necessary" and that the seeming contradictions of Scripture might be resolved without it. In the light of his previous habitual use of the sufficient/efficient formula (see n.52 below) it is not possible to guess what Pareus' revised view was.

49 Ibid., pp.808-811.

50 In his "Aphorismes of the Orthodoxicall Doctrine of the Reformed Churches" (*Miscellanies*, in *The Summe*, pp.689-736) and "Epitome of Arminianisme" (*Miscellanies*, in *The Summe*, pp.817-844) Pareus adopted the same arguments as used in the "Speech".

51 *Irenicum, sive, de unione et synodo evangelicorum concilianda liber votivus paci ecclesiae...*, Heidelberg 1615, pp.139-145.

52 In *Acta Synodi Nationalis...Dordrechti Habitae*, Dort 1620, 1.209-239.

53 For Tossanus, see Cuno, op.cit. Tossanus' correspondence, in vol.2, reveals his interest in the Montbéliard Colloquy and its aftermath. Vol.1 pp.239-258 deals with his conflict with Huber and Hunnius.

54 *Drei Christliche Predigten*, Heidelberg 1591; *Gegenbeweisung*, Heidelberg 1594; *Gülden Kleinot vom Todte Christi: das ist notwendige, gründtliche und richtige Erklärung der neuerregten Frage: ob Christus für alle Menschen gestorben sey oder nit*, Neustadt 1592. Adam, op.cit., mentions the *Gülden Kleinot*, the *Güldene Leyter*, both of which he believes to have been written by Tossanus. He also refers to Tossanus, *Disputatio An Jesus Christus esse mortuum pro omnibus*, 1589. It has not been possible to consult these two last mentioned rare works.

55 Information on Kimedoncius is scarce. Tossanus mentioned his appointment at Heidelberg, in a letter of January 1586, and described him as "once a disciple of Ursinus" (Cuno, op.cit., vol.2 p.119).

56 *Theses de Universalitate Redemptionis et Gratiae per Christum*, Heidelberg 1591, e.g. theses 2,5.

57 Ibid., theses 25,26,27,37,41,42; th.4.

58 J.Kimedoncius, *Of The Redemption of Mankind Three Bookes: wherein the controversie of the universalitie of redemption and grace by Christ, and of his death for all men, is largely handled*, London 1598.

59 Ibid., pp.31-38.

60 *Of the Redemption*, pp.39-46.

61 Ibid., p.56, "He truly gave himself a price of redemption sufficient for all, none excepted at all of the whole universalitie of men: but because the unbeleevers do not applie the redemption to themselves, the wrath of God abideth on them."

62 This danger in covenant theology has been identified by J.S.Coolidge, *The Pauline Renaissance in England: Puritanism and the Bible*, Oxford 1970, pp.99-140, esp. p.109: "The central problem of Federal Theology, then, is to keep the Covenant of Grace distinct from the Covenant of Works, while still showing it to involve that sense of human response and responsibility which is expressed by the conditionality of the Covenant of Works...The most obvious solution is to say simply that anyone who is in the Covenant of Grace will be moved by grace...". See also J.B.Torrance, "Covenant or Contract", op.cit., and "The Incarnation and 'limited atonement'", *EQ* 55(1983), pp.83-94.

The Sixteenth Century

Summary of Part One

John Calvin's theology gave an important place to God's predestination of some and his promise to all. He explained these two aspects of his teaching by reference to the existence, albeit in appearance only, of two wills in God. On the basis of these two sides to his soteriology he presented the atonement from both universal and restricted perspectives, though he did not give much specific attention to the issue of the extent of the atonement. His successor Theodore Beza picked up a tendency in Calvin to make the absolute will of God his ultimate reference point, and developed a logical supralapsarian system in which the design of the atonement related strictly to the elect. This view was a significant element in his controversy with the Lutherans at Montbéliard.

In Heinrich Bullinger there was a determination not to allow a predestinarian doctrine of grace to destroy the universality of the atonement, set within the framework of a universal, conditional covenant. His moderation on predestination was a source of strain in his relationship with Calvin. The doctrine of double predestination, deduced from the attributes of God, was prominent in the thought of Girolamo Zanchi. Within his predestinarian system, which gave pride of place to God's absolute will, Zanchi taught that Christ died for the elect only, though he granted that the atonement was in itself sufficient for all and conditionally available to all. Zanchi, even earlier than Beza, was involved in disputes with the Lutherans about restricting the scope of Christ's work.

In Heidelberg, Zacharias Ursinus made a significant advance in the construction of covenant theology, by positing a pre-fall, conditional *foedus naturale*. Ursinus' theology combined predestination with a universal, conditional *foedus gratiae*, and so he presented the atonement as having both universal and non-universal dimensions, making much of the formula that it is sufficient for all but efficacious for the elect only. He placed the particularity of the atonement in its application through faith, which is the gift of the risen Christ to the elect. Ursinus' immediate successors at Heidelberg were involved in arguments with the renegade Samuel

Huber and with the Lutherans over the extent of the atonement. Following Ursinus they presented the limitation of the atonement in terms of its benefits being conditional upon faith, rather than setting it in the immediate context of predestination, though they did hold, of course, that faith is granted in accordance with election. Ursinus' colleague Olevianus had a rather different approach, because he made God's covenant virtually equivalent to predestination. Its content is the promise of God to the elect. Faith, rather than being a condition required of all by the covenant, is a part of the promise of the covenant to those for whom it is intended. Accordingly, Olevianus stated fully and directly that the work of Christ was performed for the elect only.

Thus, while there was general agreement among the Reformed that predestination involves eternal and unconditional divine choice about who will be saved, there was considerable diversity in the way that predestination was related to the work of Christ. The differences already apparent in the sixteenth century would become more obvious and difficult to hold together in the seventeenth.

Part Two

The Synod of Dort

Chapter Seven

The Synod of Dort (1618–1619)

THE RISE OF ARMINIANISM

The scope of Christ's redeeming work had been discussed by the Reformed long before controversy was aroused by the teachings of Jacobus Arminius.[1] Bucer against Hoffman, Calvin against Pighius, Zanchi against Marbach, Beza against Andreae, and the Heidelberg theologians against Huber and Hunnius had all argued that the extent of Christ's work was limited in some sense by predestination. Amandus Polanus, who can be regarded as a representative Reformed theologian of the turn of the century, in his 1598 work on predestination, directed primarily against Cardinal Bellarmine, maintained that,

> "Christ did not die for them [those who reject him]."[2]

The rise of Arminianism, however, caused the Reformed to give greater attention than ever to this question. Arising from within its own ranks, and making its challenge across the fields of providence, predestination, the will and grace of God, human freedom, the nature of the new covenant and of justification by faith, and the nature and extent of the atonement, Arminianism posed a threat that drew down upon itself the full weight of "orthodox" opposition.

C.Bangs has traced the connections between Arminianism and an already existing moderate Dutch Protestantism which had been displaced increasingly by rigid Calvinism.[3] It is beyond the scope of this study to examine in detail the historical background to the development of the Arminian cause. It is important to understand, however, how closely national, political, ecclesiastical and theological issues intertwined in the United Provinces at the beginning of the seventeenth century. Having freed themselves from the combination of Spanish rule and Roman Catholic religion, through a long period of war and suffering, it was easy for the Dutch to seek their national identity in a religion that was the complete opposite of Catholicism. When Arminius seemed to be presenting a theological system with something more in common with Catholicism than orthodox Calvinism had, and when the Arminian party favoured the abandonment of the military struggle to drive the Spanish from the South, popular feeling against such "treachery" was quickly aroused. Arminianism found its adherents among the burgher class. Its political leaders were trying to retain some local independence over against an increasingly dominant central power, and the right of local magistrates to regulate the affairs of a church increasingly asserting its own autonomous authority. When Prince Maurice, the Stadholder, set about removing Arminian officials from power, authorised the calling of the Synod of Dort and executed for treason Oldenbarneveld, the Advocate of Holland and political leader of the Arminian party, he was attempting to establish a nation united under his rule, bound together by aggressively anti-Spanish feeling and directed by church ministers of uncompromising, anti-Roman theology.[4]

Arminius himself was well acquainted with extreme predestinarianism, having studied under Beza at Geneva. As a minister in Amsterdam from 1587, he aroused controversy between 1591 and 1593 by relating Romans 7 to the unregenerate, enlarging on the capabilities of the human will prior to regeneration, albeit enabled by grace. In 1597, in correspondence with the Leiden professor Franciscus Junius,[5] he sought to demonstrate inconsistencies in Junius' theses on predestination, which were typical of Reformed teaching on the subject. He claimed that the various ways Reformed theologians explained the order of the divine decrees were beset with problems, devoting special attention to Beza's supralapsarianism. Having become a professor of theology at Leiden in 1593, he took up the same theme in 1604, writing against theses on predestination by his fellow professor, Franciscus Gomarus.[6] Arminius' most comprehensive treatment of predestination is found in a reply to a pamphlet by the Englishman, William Perkins.[7] Perkins died in 1602, before the reply could be published, and, in fact, publication did not occur until 1612.

Perkins' presentation of predestination was along Bezan lines. Arminius criticized Perkins for allowing himself too much liberty in the use of reason in constructing his doctrine. In opposition to Perkins' supralapsarianism, he maintained that predestination relates to man as a sinner. But he went further, setting himself against all contemporary forms of Reformed predestination doctrine, by defining election as,

> "The preordination to life eternal of those sinners who shall believe in Christ."

To Arminius, this did not imply that certain people are preordained to become believers, but that predestination has respect to those God foresees will become believers, for,

> "The decree of predestination puts nothing in the predestinated person."

Predestination is to be distinguished clearly from providence. It is not a causal decree, is not to be understood in a way that makes God's will contradict itself and does not imply that Christ acted as the representative of the elect alone. God's saving will is universal and conditional. "Antecedently" God wills the salvation of all, "consequently" (with respect to foreseen faith) he wills the salvation of those who believe.

Arminius claimed that he made Christ central to his doctrine, chiding Perkins for giving an inadequate place to Christ:

> "But the Scripture puts Christ as the foundation, not of the execution only, but also of the making of election itself."

To be elect in Christ means to be chosen as a believer in Christ, for,

> "No-one is in Christ except by faith."[8]

For the Leiden professor, this meant an order of decrees as follows: first, the decree to create; second, the decree to send Christ; third, the decree ordaining that all who would believe in Christ would have eternal life; fourth, the decree electing those God foreknew would in fact perseveringly believe.

The mission of Christ proceeded from the universal philanthropy of God. Christ shared the common humanity of all and died for the common sin of all. If Christ had not come for all, there could be no way God would require faith from all. In itself, Christ's work brought about potential rather than actual reconciliation, for it removed the barrier to God's justice and so enabled him to be actually reconciled to human beings on whatever condition he might stipulate. In fact faith is the condition God has appointed.

Arminius died in 1609, but his ideas had gained sufficient ground that in the following year, on 23 November, 46 ministers drew up at Gouda the "Grand Remonstrance" to be presented to the States of Holland. They called for a national synod to revise the Heidelberg Catechism and Belgic Confession because, they claimed, some were misinterpreting these standards in support of extreme predestinarianism. 11 On March 1611 a conference of 6 members from each side commenced in the presence of the States of Holland in the Hague, at which a "Contra Remonstrance" was presented.[9] In spite of attempts at conciliation, the trend was towards greater polarisation. When, in 1617, Maurice openly declared his sympathies with the Contra-Remonstrants, the way was open for a synod which would not consider Remonstrant demands, but would bring about the exclusion of Remonstrant teaching from the church.

THE ARMINIAN VIEW OF THE EXTENT OF THE ATONEMENT

In order to appreciate some of the emphases made during the Synod of Dort, it is necessary to have in mind the Arminian position. Because Arminianism was a new and fast-developing movement, it encompassed a range of views, and it was easy for the orthodox to pick out from individual writings features they found most objectionable. A moderate statement is found, however, in the second article of the Grand Remonstrance, and in the "Opinions" presented to the Synod of Dort on 13 and 17 December 1618.[10] Concerning Christ's death the "Opinions" say:

1) The price of the redemption which Christ offered to God the Father is not only in itself and by itself sufficient for the redemption of the whole human race but has also been paid for all men and for every man, according to the decree...therefore no-one is absolutely excluded from participation in the fruits of Christ's death by an absolute and antecedent decree of God.

2) Christ has...so reconciled God the Father to the whole human race that the Father...has been able...to make...a new covenant of grace with sinners...

3) Though Christ has merited reconciliation with God and remission of sins for all men and for every man, yet no-one, according to the pact of the new and gracious covenant, becomes a true partaker of the benefits obtained by the death of Christ in any other way than by faith....

4) Only those are obliged to believe that Christ died for them for whom Christ has died....But all are obliged to believe....

Concepts of sufficiency, covenant and conditionality were already common currency in Reformed theology. An examination of the proceedings at Dort shows how these categories were used by the "orthodox".

CONCLUSIONS OF THE SYNOD

The Synod, which held its first session on 13 November 1618, was composed of deputations from other Reformed nations and from the regions of the United Provinces.[11] The deputations separately considered the Remonstrant positions and reported. On the basis of these reports, and the ensuing discussions, the final articles were drawn up. The Remonstrants did not make any active contribution to debate, but were questioned, and their writings examined. Resenting their position as the accused, they made no effort to assist the Synod's smooth running, so, early on, they were dismissed, and their views discussed and condemned in their absence.[12]

Predestination[13]

The Canons of Dort present a decidedly infralapsarian doctrine, relating predestination to the human race as fallen. A minority of deputies held to the opposite view, most notably Gomarus, long-standing colleague and opponent of Arminius at Leiden.[14] This difference did not threaten to cause a major split, however. Indeed, before and after Dort it was generally regarded as a matter of friendly but not fundamental disagreement among the Reformed.[15] The Canons defined election as,

> "The unchangeable purpose of God whereby, before the foundation of the world, out of the whole human race, which had fallen by its own fault out of its original integrity into sin and ruin, he has, according to the most free good pleasure of his will, out of mere grace, chosen in Christ to salvation a certain number of specific men...."[16]

The reference to "a certain number of specific men" is in harmony with the submissions of all the deputations, which prominently and repeatedly stated that election has to do with the salvation of "certain persons".[17] Election, according to Dort, is the ultimate explanation of why some, as opposed to others, are saved.

The Extent of the Atonement[18]

There was less of a consensus regarding the extent of the atonement. Agreement to the final articles was possible by including within them statements that were both disharmonious and unexplained.

The Canons begin by pointing out that God sent his Son into the world to save sinners and that the gospel should be preached. Election is introduced as the explanation of why some believe:

> "That some in time are given faith by God and that others are not given faith, proceeds from God's eternal decree."

Nevertheless, election is not merely the explanation of why some, in spite of the corruption of human nature, come to faith. The next article relates election to the purpose of God in sending Christ "whom He from eternity appointed the Mediator and Head of the elect".

Under the second heading,[19] the universal sufficiency of the death of Christ is asserted, but without clarification of whether or how this sufficiency is related to the will of God.

> "This death of the Son of God is the only and most perfect sacrifice and satisfaction for sins, of infinite value and worth, abundantly sufficient for expiating the sins of the whole world."

This infinite value is attributed to the "infinite being" of the Son of God and the "sense of the wrath and curse of God which we by our sins had deserved".

Immediately after the assertion of the universal sufficiency of the atonement the requirement to announce the promise of the gospel to all indiscriminately is acknowledged, though an explicit link between infinite sufficiency and indiscriminate preaching is avoided. It is denied that the perishing of those who do not believe is due to

> "any defect or insufficiency in the sacrifice of Christ...but through their own fault",

but no explanation is offered as to how the sufficiency of Christ's death relates to the non-elect.

A further article stating, conversely, that the salvation of those who do believe is to be attributed to the grace given them in eternity prepares the way for article 8, entitled "The efficacy of the death of Christ". Here it is the particular, electing will of God that is in view:

> "God willed that Christ, through the blood of the cross (by which he confirmed the new covenant) should effectually redeem out of every people, tribe, nation and tongue all those and only those who were from eternity chosen to salvation and were given to him by the Father."

There is no attempt to resolve the apparent contradiction between the assertion of universal sufficiency, preaching and inexcusability, on the one hand, and limited saving will and efficacy on the other. It should be observed, however, that the will of God is only mentioned in connection with efficacy: infinite sufficiency is the inevitable implication of the divine person of Christ, efficacy alone is presented as a matter of divine volition. The absence of an attempt to reconcile apparently opposite concepts is significant. As a result of the biggest disagreement of the Synod, it was impossible to find an acceptable way of relating universal and particular aspects of the atonement in the final document. It had to be left undecided whether the work of Christ had its sole basis in God's predestination of the elect to salvation or whether it also had another basis in a general but conditional love to all mankind. It may well be because of the ambiguities of the second section of the Canons that Strehle can conclude that it reflects the view of the majority while Godfrey decides that it represents a triumph for the minority. The underlying conflicts at Dort are revealed by scrutiny of the submissions from the individual deputations.[20]

SUBMISSIONS OF THE DEPUTATIONS

To explore the differences, we will sample the submissions of several of the deputations in response to the second article of the Remonstrance.

Great Britain[21]

The fact that the British submissions were always received in first place is indicative of the respect shown throughout to the British deputation: the Dutch obviously valued good relations with the king of England. Indeed, James, who had encouraged the calling of the Synod, took a keen interest in it, personally appointing the British deputies and instructing them as to the kind of settlement they were to pursue.[22] The British theologians played a very active role in the Synod, in open debate and informal negotiations, and political pressure was applied by the English ambassador at the Hague to the president of the Synod.

The British submission on the second article was itself a compromise, with John Davenant and Samuel Ward taking a more universalistic approach than the other three deputies. Without explicitly using the sufficient-efficient formula, the British submission was built upon it. The first part maintained that God willed efficiently to save the elect through the death of his Son:

> "From the special love and intention of God the Father and Christ, Christ died for the elect, so as to obtain for them, and infallibly confer, remission of sins and eternal salvation."

Arising from this special love, and through the merit and intercession of Christ, faith, and everything else necessary for the fulfilment of the covenant of grace, is given to the elect. Next, the universal sufficiency of Christ's sacrifice was asserted. As its particular effectiveness is traced to God's love to the elect, so its universal applicability is referred to God's "pity upon the fallen human race", out of which God

> "sent his Son, who gave himself as the price of redemption for the sins of the whole world".

The promise is founded on this universality. On the basis of an infinitely sufficient redemption, God has implemented a universal covenant to save all believers.

The twofold approach of the British submission is powerfully reminiscent of Ursinus' approach to the question of the extent of the atonement. It is more than likely that the British were influenced by it, since his exposition of the Heidelberg Catechism had been widely circulated in England during the previous 30 years. Indeed, it was almost word for word quotation when the British said,

> "We consider two things in this offering of Christ - the manner of calling people to actual participation, and the fruit."

The British explained that faith is both the manner of participation in, and the fruit of, Christ's death. By his death, faith has been established, in covenantal terms, as the means of participation for all, and is to be preached to all. But as the fruit of Christ's death, granted by the risen Lord through the Spirit, it is effectively given to the elect and is particular to them. Thus universality and particularity hinge at the point of faith, which God is free to give or withhold as he pleases.

> "In spite of this universal covenant of saving believers, God has made no covenant to communicate the gospel or saving grace to each and all."

The particularity of the atonement appears when viewed through the particularity of the response of faith, for

> "It is at this point that the secret decree of election makes itself known."

The Palatinate

Having found the British deputation drawing on the theology of late sixteenth-century Heidelberg, it comes as a surprise to find a quite different approach from the Palatinate itself.[23]

The Palatinate submission takes for granted the sufficiency of Christ's ransom, in itself, for all. Apart from this concession, the universality of the atonement is not developed, since

> "The whole question concerns the efficiency and efficacy of the ransom."

To the theologians of the Palatinate, the question was, for whom was Christ's saving work intended? In answer, they co-ordinated the intention behind the cross with election. Likewise they identified God's saving love with his predestinating will:

> "We judge that it [God's love] is not general but special, not for each and all in common, but properly for the elect."

Christ is subordinate to the decree of predestination:

> "God the Father ordained his Son Jesus Christ to be the Redeemer and Propitiatior for our sins, out of that love by which he specially embraced his elect for eternal life."

The effective redemption of the elect is the Redeemer's glory, and to represent his work as merely making possible a state of grace, on condition of faith and repentance, is unworthy.

Other objections to universal atonement were the absurdity of Christ dying for those already damned, and the co-extensiveness of the acquisition and application of salvation. Furthermore, it seemed to entail a move away from a substitutionary understanding of the atonement: "in our place" became merely "for our good". The Remonstrant use of foreseen faith also seemed to the Palatinate theologians to represent Christ as dying for the faithful, rather than for sinners.

Although certain arguments used against Huber by Ursinus' colleagues and immediate successors at Heidelberg recurred, and the spectre of Huber was raised, there was a remarkable divergence from the Ursinian theology in the decided imbalance in favour of the particular as opposed to universal way of viewing the atonement. The letter of the elderly Pareus to the Synod preserved the Ursinian approach in contrast with the submission of the Palatinate theologians at Dort. To them, the particularity of salvation was a primary consideration, rather than something to be pondered in view of the fact that faith is not granted to all. The covenant motif, used by Ursinus to establish the openness of salvation to all, appears in the Palatinate submission as a way of underscoring the eternal separateness of elect and reprobate.

Geneva

The Genevan submission contains one of the most particularistic treatments of the second article.[24]

Taking as their starting point the destination of Christ to be Mediator and Head of "a certain number of men", the six Genevan theses go on to set the atonement firmly in a particularistic predestinarian context. Christ was given for the elect. The universal statements of Scripture regarding the death of Christ are to be "restrained to the universality of the body of Christ". Though the acquisition and application of salvation may be distinguished, they cannot be separated: within the purpose of God, the one is the inevitable effect of the other.

Emphasising as strongly as they did the particularity of the atonement, the Genevans continued the Calvin-Beza tradition of lack of enthusiasm for the sufficient-efficient formula, and did not use it. Their whole concern was with the effectiveness of the atonement for the elect. At three points there seems to be a glimpse of something wider, but each time it becomes apparent that no room was being made for a universal element in the cross of Christ. The "infinite price" of Christ's death was mentioned, but referred to the will of Christ to die effectively for the elect. Secondly faith was called a condition, but only in the course of stating that faith is not only a condition, but also a gift of the covenant of grace and effect of union with Christ. Thirdly it was granted that the Bible's universal expressions relative to the death of Christ may refer to that administration of the new covenant in which all without external distinction are assembled into the church, and on which the general preaching of the gospel is founded. This, however, was further explained to mean merely that preachers do not have to make an external difference between persons, because election crosses the boundaries of race and class. So there is nothing in the entire Genevan submission that relates the death of Christ directly to all people.

Martinius of Bremen

By championing the universality of the atonement, Matthias Martinius made himself unpopular with many at the Synod. His views were sufficiently individual that his fellow deputies from Bremen, although they supported him as a colleague, made separate statements on the second article.[25] Martinius claimed that his submission was based on Ambrose's dictum:

> "Though Christ died for all, he especially died for us."

On this basis his submission was divided into halves, entitled, "Concerning the death of Christ for the elect alone", and, "Concerning the death of Christ for all men." Martinius argued for a general philanthropy in God and a general call of the gospel. On this basis, he held that a universal atonement was necessary, for,

> "This external calling necessarily pre-requires certain things, the promise and sending of the...Son, and redemption, that is, the payment of a price for the expiation of sins, pleasing God so that he requires no other sacrifice for the sins of any human being...provided..each apply this common and health-giving medicine to himself."

Martinius held that Christ's death has a universal sufficiency that cannot be detached from the will of God, otherwise it could not be the basis for preaching the gospel,

> "For how can a necessity of believing that a benefit pertains to me be deduced from a benefit that is indeed sufficient, but not destined to be such by a true intention?"

Christ's universal death is conditional, however, and in this sense it can be said that he did not make satisfaction for the persistently impenitent. Furthermore, the grace of God alone can supply the ability to fulfil the conditions. There is indeed a special decree of election, according to which Christ died effectively for some only, and Martinius believed that he could have both universal and particular redemption:

> "Christ died for all with the intention of saving all, and he did not so die."

He died so that all could be saved, but so that only believers would be, and divine election determines who will in fact believe.

Martinius gave as his reasons for maintaining that Christ died for all: to reconcile apparently conflicting Scriptures without twisting them; to maintain the glory of God in his truth, justice and mercy in the commands, promises and threats of the gospel "lest God should be judged to will or do something other than his words say"; and to attribute the blame for perishing to ourselves rather than any inadequacy in God's remedy.

As in the case of the British submission, the similarities to the Ursinian way of dealing with universality and particularity are noteworthy. Indeed, Martinius specifically claimed to be following Ursinus' Catechism on Christ's universal merit and sufficiency. Martinius closed by denying Huber's view that all have been restored to God's favour because Christ died for all as far as efficacy, as well as sufficiency, is concerned.

No attempt will be made to analyse individually the contributions of all the deputations. The submissions from Martinius and Geneva represent two extremes, those from Britain and the Palatinate are more moderate but still strikingly divergent positions. These comparisons are, of course, relative. Had the Remonstrants been allowed to participate as equals, Martinius would have been the moderate.

RECURRENT THEMES

To broaden our survey, and highlight some crucial issues, we will examine some recurrent themes in the range of submissions on the second article.

The Sufficient-Efficient Formula

The sufficient-efficient formula is implicit or explicit in most of the submissions. For Britain the sufficiency of Christ's sacrifice was the basis of the universal proclamation of the gospel, not *per accidens*, but as willed by God.[26] Similarly for Martinius, with an eye to the reality of the promise and command of the gospel, the satisfaction of Christ was divinely willed to be sufficient.[27] Also H.Isselburg of Bremen founded universal sufficiency on the eternal will of God, and so did Hesse:

> "...the dignity, force, value and price of the death of Christ is so great and inestimable that it is abundantly sufficient to expiate the sins of each and all, whoever has lived, lives or will live. For since Christ who suffered and died was not only a holy and just man but also true God...it is necessary that his passion and death were of infinite value. So each and all can be received into grace and favour provided they adhere to Christ with true faith. Therefore the gospel...is announced indiscriminately to elect and reprobates, and all are commanded to believe in him."

> "The ransom of Christ is sufficient in itself for expiating the sins of each and every one...Therefore God the Father willed from all eternity that it should be."

Universal salvation is, however, rendered a purely hypothetical possibility, ruled out by God's limited intention revealed in the event, according to Hesse:

> "Truly Christ has efficaciously merited, acquired and obtained reconciliation with God for his elect."[28]

Those from Switzerland, and Groningen, held that the sufficiency of Christ's death removes all excuse from unbelievers.[29] The Belgic (i.e. Dutch) Professors (Gomarus, Polyander, Thysius, Walaeus and Lubbertus), began their submission with reference to the merit and value of Christ's sacrifice,

> "not only sufficient to expiate all the sins of men but also of all the posterity of Adam".

As their second point they stated unequivocally,

> "It is not to be doubted that these things were done by the intention of God the Father...and of Christ."

Utrecht, too, maintained the universal sufficiency of Christ's work, but without building anything on it. Other deputations followed the Palatinate in admitting but minimising the significance of universal sufficiency:

> "The ransom of Christ is easily in itself sufficient for each and all. But it is efficacious to restore...and finally to communicate sufficient and efficient grace to all and only the elect."

South Holland and Zeeland fall into this category. The comment of South Holland was,

> "God decided that the satisfaction and merit of Christ's obedience and death, which sufficed in itself to redeem each and every one, should be the subordinate means...by which the elect...should be led to eternal salvation."[30]

The Nassau-Wetterau deputation recognized the sufficiency of Christ's ransom for all the world, and agreed that the universal statements of Scripture imply that the gospel offers a remedy to all. However, these theologians worked out their distinction between the sufficiency and efficiency of Christ's death to the following extraordinary practical conclusion:

> "The elect alone are obliged to believe simply that Christ died for them...Reprobates, however, are obliged to believe that the dignity of the merit of Christ is so great that it is also able to be profitable to them, and if they believe the gospel and are penitent it will indeed profit them."[31]

Geneva mentioned the "infinite price" within the confines of the particular divine purpose,[32] while others, such as Emden, Overijsel, North Holland, and Geneva did not use the efficient-sufficient formula at all. None of the deputations denied the universal sufficiency of Christ's death, for that would have seemed an attack on the dignity of the person of Christ, but South Holland spelt out what was implicit in many of the submissions, namely that even if Christ's sacrifice was sufficient, it was sufficient in itself and *per accidens*, not because of the will of God.

> "Wisely destined means do not exceed a suitable end."

So they denied

> "that the price of redemption was not only sufficient in and through itself for the redemption of the whole human race but that it was paid for each and every one by the decree, will and grace of God the Father".[33]

Martinius' challenge to those who would grant only an inherent sufficiency was,

> "It is sufficient and...God and Christ have willed it to be sufficient. For otherwise the command and promise of the gospel will be overturned."[34]

His opponents had no substantial reply to this point.

The distinction between the sufficiency and efficacy of the atonement was able to command the assent, if not the enthusiasm, of all the participants at Dort. It had the weight of tradition behind it, being, as Scottish deputy Balcanqual called it in his report to the ambassador, "the received distinction". So it could form the basis of the Canons on the second article. Its acceptance enabled Balcanqual to pronounce that the Synod had achieved substantial unity. It was, however, only an apparent unity, on the basis of a formula open to very different interpretations.

Covenant

The Remonstrant second article viewed the death of Christ as universal in that it had so atoned for sin that God had been able justly to make a new covenant with mankind, promising salvation on a less stringent condition than perfect obedience to his law, namely faith. While none of the "orthodox" could subscribe to this view, their own responses revealed two markedly different concepts of the covenant of grace.[35]

Several deputations condemned the implication of the Remonstrant position, that, through the death of Christ, all humanity has been transferred from the covenant of nature to that of grace. Nevertheless, some of them had much in common with the Remonstrants at this point.[36] They too maintained a conditional covenant, founded on the death of Christ, open to all, and with faith as the covenant condition. Others clearly regarded such a construction as dangerously prejudicing the grace of God, and preferred to regard the death of Christ as ratifying an already existing covenant between God and the elect. Thus some held covenant and predestination to be substantially distinct and self-contained modes of the divine activity, though operating through the same means, and though the actual fulfilment of the conditions of the covenant could only be as a result of election. Others viewed the covenant as virtually synonymous with, and designed to execute, predestination. The former used the conditionality of the covenant to claim that it was open to all. The latter, while not denying a conditional element, were quick to explain that the conditions should be understood as God's method of gathering in the elect. It was not so much a difference between a one-sided or two-sided covenant theology, as has sometimes been claimed, but between the ways the covenant was related to predestination, atonement and the gospel.

The way the British deputation approached the atonement through an understanding of covenant has already been touched upon: a conditional covenant has been established by Christ's death and made available to all, but not all are enabled to fulfil the conditions of the covenant.

> "Christ has...established the covenant."
>
> "Christ died for all in that, by means of faith, all and each would be able, by virtue of this ransom, to obtain remission of their sins and eternal life."
>
> "...the price paid for all, which certainly profits all who believe, does not profit all, however, because it is not given to all to fulfil this condition of the covenant of grace."[37]

As has already been observed, the British were closely following Ursinus' theology.

Martinius did not develop the covenant theme, but his whole position hinged on the conditionalism of faith, as in the Ursinus covenant tradition:

> "So it appears here that remission of sins and conditional salvation pertain to all, but not the promise to give the powers and arouse the abilities by which that condition is fulfilled."[38]

Nassau-Wetterau spoke of the condition of faith, though without relating this specifically to a covenant motif. Hesse stated,

> "All, if they adhered to Christ with true faith...would be received into grace and favour."

However, they distinguished the origin of the covenant from its administration when they insisted that Christ is the principal promise of the covenant of grace.[39] A narrower interpretation is represented by the Palatine assertion that Christ's death has efficacy

> "to restore and receive into grace, according to the tenor of the free covenant, and finally to communicate sufficient and efficient grace, only to all the elect".

The Palatinate rejected the kind of conditionalism contained in the positions of the Arminians (and some of the Reformed), that Christ's work does not reconcile people to God, but just renders them reconcilable.[40] For the Palatinate, the covenant of grace was virtually synonymous with predestination.

Emden also displayed a wish to stress the predestinarian context of the covenant, pointing out not just that Christ is its principal promise and gift, but asserting that, although the covenant of grace has conditions of repentance and faith,

> "God, the author of the covenant of grace, promises to give the faith and repentance he requires from his confederates."

> "Even if God requires faith and repentance from his confederates, his will is by no means conditional on that account. Nor does the will of God in applying the merit of Christ depend on the fulfilling of these conditions, since the fulfilling of the conditions is purely and perfectly the gift of God."

Conceding conditionalism in the divine will would make God seem weak, and reverse the proper order of causes by making the First Cause follow from a second.

Emden rejected, as Socinian and Pelagian, the Arminian view (shared by some of the Reformed) that through Christ's death,

> "God would be able to open the door of grace to sinners, so that through observing the conditions of the new covenant, whoever wants to should enter."[41]

Zeeland shared the tendency to equate covenant and predestination, in teaching, on the basis of Jeremiah 31, that the application of salvation is promised in the covenant of grace. Utrecht specifically denied that the covenant was made for everyone. Groningen pointed out that, like election, the accomplishment and application of redemption are unconditional.[42]

Clearly two concepts of the covenant were operating at Dort, one viewing the covenant primarily in terms of the preaching of the gospel and the other virtually equating it with election. The former of these reflects Ursinus' understanding, while the latter reflects that of Olevianus. Although not every deputation opted for one or other with total consistency, the presence of two essentially different concepts is not difficult to discern. Again with the proviso that some inconsistencies are to be found, it is broadly true that the deputations that made the most of the universal sufficiency of the atonement also saw the covenant in broadly universal terms.[43] Those that equated covenant with predestination either saw the universal sufficiency of the atonement as necessarily implied in the deity of Christ but not directly related to the will of God, or else ignored it.[44]

Covenant, Predestination and Christ

The Remonstrant view of the relationships between Christ and the covenant, and Christ and predestination, were controverted at Dort. It was repeatedly stated, for example by Hesse, Switzerland and Emden, that the covenant was not obtained by Christ, but rather that he confirmed it and was its principal gift.[45] This may appear to be a statement equating predestination with the covenant, and, for some, no doubt it was. It cannot be, however, that all meant it in that way, for even Martinius accepted the positive side of the statement. However, it is likely that, when he called Christ the principal promise of the covenant, he was thinking of Christ as necessitated and promised by God's conditional covenant.[46] From the same perspective, the British deputation taught,

> "On this merit of the death of Christ is founded the universal promise of the gospel."
>
> "Christ by his death has...established the covenant."[47]

As far as election was concerned, the participants in the Synod granted that, as Scripture says, election is "in Christ", and many stated that election is *in Christo* and *per* and *propter Christum.*[48] They also were agreed in rejecting the Remonstrant view that "chosen in Christ" means "chosen by virtue of being foreseen to be in Christ by faith". They were not so unanimous when it came to offering an alternative exposition. A number understood the phrase to refer to the giving of the elect to Christ by the Father, and the headship of Christ over them. Another explanation was that the elect do not become the recipients of saving benefits except through Christ. Several insisted, in contradiction of the Arminian position, that to be chosen in Christ means to be chosen *to be* in Christ by faith.[49]

In the Arminian order of the decrees the election of individuals presupposed the election of Christ.[50] The Dort deputations were anxious to point out that the Arminian designation of Christ as *fundamentum electionis* (foundation of election) was acceptable only if it meant that without Christ the decree of election could not be executed. So Emden, in an extended comment, stated,

> "We are elect in Jesus Christ, *theanthropos*, as in our head...But we want this to be understood not of the decree itself but of its execution."
>
> "The efficient cause of election must have been from eternity, but the merit of Christ was not from eternity."
>
> "The one elected to the office of mediator from eternity, to reconcile the elect to God, is not the cause but the effect of election...For God did not choose us indeed because Christ was to die for us, but he died because God chose us in him."[51]

In fact, there were many strong statements that Christ is a means subordinate to the decree of the election of a certain number of individuals of mankind. Gomarus, though singular in his supralapsarianism, was spelling out the position of most at the Synod when he said,

> "The giving of Christ is a means subordinate to the election of men to salvation."

Crocius made the same point. The Swiss, revealing how far Zurich had shifted from Bullinger, protested,

> "We abhor with serious and true detestation that which is said, that God predestined Christ to be mediator before having any will or intention to save anyone by name."

One of the reasons for insisting that Christ is subordinate to the decree was to ensure that Christ is understood as the expression of the unconditional love of God, as the Palatine theologians stated:

> "God the Father ordained his Son Jesus Christ to be our Redeemer and make propitiation for our sins according to that love by which he specially loved his elect to eternal life."[52]

In a sentence showing both a subordination of Christ to election and a linking of election and covenant, Groningen insisted,

> "The decree of giving and sending Christ follows election to salvation and, indeed, the decree concerning entering into a covenant of grace with sinners."[53]

Subordinating Christ to a decree of particular election could not but result in a limitation of his saving work to the elect, unless some other consideration were introduced. The British and Bremenese, however, spoke of God's "universal covenant of saving believers", which gave the work of Christ a basis outside the decree of particular election. Martinius maintained a universal divine philanthropy "by which he loves the whole fallen human race".[54] Martinius understood the preaching of the gospel to all to flow from this love. Without the death of Christ there could be no gospel command and promise, and so the work of Christ, too, finds its basis in the universal love and covenant of God. Giving the work of Christ a basis instead of or alongside particular election left room for Britain, Bremen and some others to assert a genuine universality in the atonement.

Debate in the Synod threatened to erupt into violence over Martinius' views. John Hales, the English ambassador's representative, reported that on the 22 January a clash took place between Gomarus and Martinius over whether Christ is the *fundamentum electionis.* According to Hales, Martinius wished Christ to be not only "the Effector of our election, but also the Author and Procuror thereof". Martinius spoke of Christ as the "meritorious cause of electability", giving Christ a logical priority over the election of individuals, within the plan of God. Martinius' order of the decrees fitted his conditional covenant theology, for it made election that which related to the fulfilment of conditions, the *ex post facto* explanation of why some believe. To Gomarus and many others, this order played into the hands of the Remonstrants. Martinius was far from making election dependent on faith, however, as the Remonstrants did.[55] The British submission was in considerable agreement with Martinius, in relating election to the fulfilment of the conditions of the universal covenant established by Christ's death:

> "It is here that the eternal and hidden decree of election appears, when the price paid for all...does not however profit all, because it is not given to all to fulfil the condition of the covenant of grace."[56]

Clearly the doctrine of election held by all the Contra-Remonstrants had a tendency towards a limited atonement. However, both the concept of universal sufficiency, and the location of the basis of the work of Christ at least partly in a universal conditional covenant, kept some away from that stark conclusion.

Actual or Potential Redemption

The submissions of all the deputations were pervaded by a conviction that the work of Christ was an effective work, a conviction enshrined in the Canons:

> "God willed that Christ through the blood of the cross...should effectively redeem...all those and only those who were from eternity chosen...."[57]

This effectiveness, however, was explained in different ways.

The will of God was understood to be a guarantee of the effectiveness of the atonement. Since the will of God had set as its end the salvation of the elect, and the cross of Christ was a means to that end, then the elect would be effectively redeemed.[58] Contrariwise, since the same will of God had decreed the reprobation of others, they would inevitably be condemned,[59] and thus the cross could not be understood as an instrument of the will of God for their redemption. Experience itself shows that not all believe and are saved, therefore it cannot have been God's will to save all through the cross.[60] South Holland expressed this confidently:

> "Since wisely destined means do not exceed their end...the satisfaction and merit of Christ should be effective both to acquire and apply redemption only to the elect."[61]

Many of the deputations were prepared to limit this discussion to the absolute will of God,[62] probably through an aversion to the Remonstrant use of the division of God's will into antecedent and consequent, but others followed the previously more common Reformed practice of also referring to the apparent existence of another will in God. Britain, Hesse, Nassau, Martinius and Crocius of Bremen, and the Belgic Professors fell into this category. Without denying an absolute and effective will operative through the death of Christ, they added another will. Thus Britain:

> "Therefore Christ died for all so that, by means of faith, each and all would be able, by virtue of this ransom, to have, through faith, remission of sins and eternal life."

Crocius:

> "The scope and intention is...to obtain for each and all sinful men...and promise that...if they repent and believe they can be reconciled to God."[63]

As well as tracing its source to the will of God, there was a desire to understand the work of Christ in itself as an actual rather than potential work. This emphasis was made most strongly among the Dutch provincial deputations, with North Holland insisting on the accomplishment of a "true and real reconciliation", and Utrecht maintaining that redemption necessarily implies acceptance into God's favour.[64] Many deputations specifically rejected the Arminian idea of the work of Christ achieving a new conditional covenant.[65] Friesland pointed out that it was reconciliation, not reconcilability, Christ obtained, and rejected the view that Christ died for anyone conditionally. South Holland refused to see the death of Christ as merely the opening of a door of grace, and also appealed, as did the Palatinate, to the substitutionary nature of the atonement: Christ dying not just for someone's good (*bono alicuius*) but on someone's account and in his place (*vice et loco alicuius*) must have achieved satisfaction actually.[66]

The point of these arguments in the context of the second article was that the extent of actual redemption must be capable of being measured by the number of those who, through faith, actually receive the gift of forgiveness. Actual reconciliation did not mean that persons are justified before God in advance of exercising faith, but that God would ensure that those for whom the reconciliation was made would exercise faith in due time. The acquiring of the gifts of the Spirit and faith were counted among the actual accomplishments of the cross, constituting a bridge between the acquisition and application of redemption. It therefore followed that Christ could not have died for those who are never granted the Spirit and faith.[67]

Even among those deputations that related Christ's death to a conditional will and covenant, there was concern to stress the actual accomplishments of the atonement, with Britain speaking of a redemption that "really (*re vera*) redeemed" and Hesse arguing,

> "Those for whom Christ...actually obtained remission of sins...are truly made partakers."[68]

However, these deputies also made room for a non-effective dimension to the work of Christ. Martinius could speak of Christ as the "foundation of electability", Samuel Ward of "redeemability", "reconcilability" and "procurability" (*impetrabilitas*) and the whole British deputation state that the benefits of Christ's death do not come to all for whom he died.[69]

Another way in which the effectiveness of Christ's death was maintained was by claiming that the unity of the whole work of Christ implied that the same prospective beneficiaries must have been in view from beginning to end.[70] What the crucified Christ obtained cannot be separated from what the risen, interceding Christ applies. Again, at this point, there was divergence of opinion.[71] For some, establishing this co-extensiveness was all that was necessary. For others, while granting such a co-extensiveness within the absolute intention of God, there was room for a wider scope to the work of acquisition than that of application. Redemption accomplished did not have to be co-extensive with redemption applied. For Martinius,

> "This redemption is the payment of a price for us captives, not that we go free in any way whatever, but that we are able to...if we believe in the Redeemer",

and,

> "Christ indiscriminately satisfied for all in such a way that their sins could be remitted, but obtained that the sins of the elect alone had to be remitted really in the event."[72]

For Nassau Wetterau,

> "This most divine remedy should be proposed to all generally, but none of its virtue is transfused into them unless applied by faith in Christ...In this sense Christ died for the elect only."[73]

A broad band of opinion was revealed in the attempt to insist on the effectiveness of the work of Christ. For some, and the Provincial deputations went furthest in this direction, Christ's work is effective in that it achieved precisely what God willed it to, and so, conversely, it is possible to judge the extent of the atonement by observing how extensively it proves effective in experience.[74] It is not a door open to all. Others, and the British and Martinius went furthest in this direction, while having no wish to lessen the effectiveness of the atonement, saw in it a certain universal potentiality. It is a medicine available even to those who refuse it. Others, coming somewhere in between these two poles, granted a universal potentiality, but were unwilling to present this as a significant part of the divine purpose.[75] Broadly these were the three positions on the atonement at Dort.[76]

CONFLICT

Nothing caused greater division at the Synod of Dort than the question, "For whom did Christ die?" The foregoing analysis of the submissions of the deputations has indicated the range of thought on this issue, and the problems inherent in the various positions adopted.[77] Looking beyond the official documents reveals that the divisions and difficulties were very much recognized and felt by those who were involved.

John Hales disclosed to the British ambassador the acrimony that existed. Gomarus' challenge to Martinius to fight a duel was not an incident attributable only to the former's undoubted hot temper.[78] After the contentious session on

22 January, there was a private meeting of the foreign divines with Martinius in the lodgings of the Bishop of Llandaff, in which Martinius was persuaded to promise moderation in the expression of his views for the sake of the unity of the Synod. Then on 28 January, immediately after Davenant had given an address on election, business was undertaken in private, for fear of dissension over the same issue. In this session Martinius once again asserted that Christ is the foundation of election. Llandaff made another approach to him, this time by letter.[79] However, it was not long before the British deputation itself was in disarray, to such an extent that Balcanqual, who had replaced Hales as correspondent to the ambassador, and, unlike Hales, was a member of the deputation, wrote on 9 February,

> "Concerning this second Article I beseech your Lordship, give me leave to express my grief, as there is difference touching it in the Synod, so there is much difference about it in our own Colledge."

Davenant and Ward had come out in favour of Martinius in holding that the biblical statements about Christ dying for all were to be understood "of all particular men", while the others adhered to the interpretation, "only...the elect, who consist of all sorts of men".[80] A compromise was worked out, and the British deputies managed to retain friendly relations among themselves while differing in their views.[81]

The same friendliness was not apparent in the treatment Martinius received from the Dutch provincial deputations, who began to "use Martinius very uncivilly". The opposition to Martinius culminated in what Balcanqual considered a plot to discredit the Bremenese, in which the Synod president was complicit, the Belgic professors Lubbertus and Gomarus were prominent, and Scultetus of the Palatinate also took part. Afterwards the British had to engage in peacemaking again.

Strife continued, however. Without enlarging upon his comment, Balcanqual noted that on 17 March, "The Palatines were very bitter about some of the things Ward said about the Second Article." Harmony seems to have been restored between the British and Palatines by 19 March, when they joined in seeking to exclude the more extreme views of the Provincials "especially on the second Article" from the canons. Balcanqual, who was on the more "particularist" side of the British deputation, was nevertheless appalled at what had come from the Dutch.

> "Some of the Provincials, especially Gelder and North Holland, who are the greatest in the president's books, have delivered such propositions on that Article, as I dare say, never any Divine in the world dreamed of but themselves: for my part I had rather lose my head than subscribe to them."[82]

A British call for the avoidance of "harshness and rigidity" in the framing of the canons was followed by a Dutch counter attack, with Gomarus and Lubbertus displaying "unheard bitterness against our College", so that the temperamentally moderate Davenant was provoked to attempt, but without being given leave, to make a defence. Strife again subsided, however, and Balcanqual was able to report on 14 April that the deputies appointed to frame the canons "have taken pains...to give our College satisfaction". On the 19th. conflict recommenced. The British argued the whole of the morning regarding certain aspects of the proposed canons and rejection of errors relating to the second article, the contention being whether the incarnation should be defined as an absolute rather than ordained necessity for the redemption of mankind. Only after several days were the proposals modified sufficiently to gain British agreement.[83]

OUTSTANDING PROBLEMS

Those who limited the atonement to the elect in the strictest manner, knew that they would have to answer the question, "Why is the gospel to be preached to all?" The fact that at least two deputations foreshadowed "Hyper Calvinism" by arguing that, in fact, there is no obligation to preach to all, is indicative of the extreme particularism of their thought. Friesland argued that God's call does not invite all, but is addressed to the "weak and heavy laden", and qualified by "whoever believes". The Gelderland deputies quoted the same text and referred to their own practice:

> "We do not command all indiscriminately to believe in Christ. We command all to repent and come to Christ...We say it is commanded to each and all the truly penitent to come to Christ, that is, to believe...It is of grace to be called to repent, but not Evangelical grace, which is only offered in Christ....It is falsely said, that the grace of the gospel is universal, that is, that the benefits acquired by Christ's death are offered to each and all to whom they are preached."[84]

Others, though not going this far, located the requirement for universal preaching merely in ministerial inability to distinguish elect from reprobate.[85] So, in striving for theological consistency, some of the more particularistic theologians were eroding a major part of the Reformed heritage, by qualifying and restricting the preaching of the word.

At the other end of the scale, the British and Bremenese, and others who resembled them to some degree, seemed to be trying to accommodate contradictory positions. A conviction that the gospel is to be preached to all, and that the minister's offer to all is nothing less than God's offer, compelled them to formulate the gospel in terms genuinely applicable to all, whilst maintaining that divine election has respect to certain persons only. The atonement was both accomplished and conditional, limited and universal. The salvation of all was willed and not willed, the work of Christ was rooted in a special love for the elect and a general philanthropy, the death of Christ purchased faith for the elect, yet faith is the condition without which that death is unavailing. These apparent contradictions had been with the Reformed from the beginning, but appeared at Dort more obviously and embarrassingly than before.

The development of conditional covenant theology made the contradictions more stark.[86] The position of those who espoused it was replete with the difficulties inherent in any attempt to combine absolute predestination with conditionalism. In so far as they made the conditional covenant basic to their system, they achieved a certain coherence, for predestination could then be given a role in supplying to incapacitated human beings the ability to fulfil the conditions. However, in assigning to predestination the role of merely enabling people to fulfil the conditions of God's covenant, the *extra nos* character of salvation, which predestination was supposed to underscore in Reformed theology, was overshadowed. Human beings take centre stage in the drama of salvation, as fulfillers of conditions on which everything hinges. The work of Christ is suspended upon these conditions, for they alone convert Christ's work from potentiality to actuality. Within this system the fact that it is grace allocated from all eternity that grants to certain people the ability to fulfil the conditions invests the individual's (divinely enabled) contribution to his own salvation with supreme importance: predestination puts the spotlight on what is done in us, not what was done in Christ. The point some of the deputations made against Arminianism could be brought against their "conditional covenant" Reformed colleagues, namely that to make Christ the purchaser of a new covenant, whose conditions we must fulfil, does not adequately magnify the grace of God in Christ. Gomarus' challenging of Martinius to a duel may be regarded as pictorial of the fundamental antagonism of the different principles at work among the Reformed.

JOHN DAVENANT (1572-1641)

John Davenant, Lady Margaret Professor of Divinity at Cambridge when he went to represent King James at the Synod of Dort and Bishop of Salisbury shortly after his return, is a neglected figure.[87] While it is true that Davenant's views on the universality of the atonement were in a minority at Dort, no deputation was more influential at the Synod than the British, and no member of the British deputation made a stronger impression on the Synod and its Canons than Davenant. For this reason he deserves special attention in this chapter. Not only does Davenant deserve to be better known, but he also should be better understood, in the face of the tendency of the Reformed of later centuries to portray him as an oddity because of his combination of unconditional election and universal atonement. Is W.R.Godfrey correct, in his thesis devoted to the extent of the atonement at Dort, to claim that Davenant's theology was intriguingly new?[88]

Davenant's loyalty to a Reformed doctrine of predestination cannot be doubted. He wrote a long treatise against the Arminian Samuel Hoard, strenuously asserting the doctrine of double predestination. His commitment to predestination is strikingly illustrated by the fact that he was required to appear before the Privy Council to explain why he had mentioned election in a sermon preached before the king at Whitehall. Although Davenant seems to have genuinely misunderstood the scope of a declaration by King Charles that no-one should dispute about predestination in preaching or in print, the fact that he had wanted to preach about such a politically sensitive subject is testimony of its importance to him.[89]

Davenant was just as convinced of the universality of the atonement, however. This is clear from his stance at Dort, from a number of lesser writings, and especially from his "Dissertation on the Death of Christ".[90] Far from putting forward a novel construction, this work echoed many of the themes we have already found in other Reformed theologians who had discussed the extent of Christ's redeeming work.

English Reformed theology had been heavily influenced throughout the sixteenth century by continental thinkers. After the initial impact of Luther, the theology of Zurich and Geneva took the lead, imported by returning exiles, by the printed page and by those who had studied abroad. Calvin and Beza were certainly influential, but so were W.Musculus and Bullinger.[91] Not surprisingly, the different emphases in continental Reformed theology were reproduced in England. As a result, at the beginning of the seventeenth century, there were those like William Perkins and William Ames whose predestinarianism ruled their formulation of the extent of the atonement.[92] At the same time, the immensely learned, respected and staunchly predestinarian James Ussher (1581-1656),[93] Archbishop of Armagh, contended for a universal atonement, conditional upon faith for its effect. Davenant belonged within this variety of Reformed thought.

In his treatment of the death of Christ, Davenant employed the familiar two wills distinction, giving to the *voluntas signi* a much more than external significance. He appealed to the sufficient-efficient dictum regarding the death of Christ, insisting that the universal sufficiency of the atonement was willed by God. The idea of a conditionally universal covenant went hand in hand with a universally sufficient atonement. The work of Christ logically precedes the decree of election, which, by supplying to certain persons the condition of faith, fits into the system as that which overcomes the human failure to respond to the gospel. The fact that universal atonement and particular predestination may not seem to be logically harmonious does not entitle us to dispense with one side of the truth.[94]

Davenant's thought on the extent of the atonement was shaped by a desire not to innovate: he made extensive use of the fathers and scholastics, as well as of the reformers. In his moderation and appeal to tradition he was a true Anglican. He also had a strong interest in international Protestant unity, and was alive to the offence caused to the Lutherans by those Reformed theologians who allowed predestination to govern their theology so far that it limited the scope of Christ's redeeming work.[95] It is interesting to see how very scholastic he was. Syllogisms and citations from the medievals abound as part of what his biographer calls "his cautious scholastic mode".[96] In Davenant's case, the combination of a scholastic approach and a "Calvinistic" doctrine of predestination certainly did not produce limited atonement.

This brief description of Davenant's understanding of the extent of the atonement and related themes indicates that he belonged, if not at the very centre, certainly well within the main stream of Reformed theology, whether English or continental. It is natural to see him as standing firmly in the traditions of Bullinger and Ursinus, and, as far as content but not method is concerned, as a forerunner of the theology of Saumur.

CONCLUSION

While scholars have generally thrown off the view that Dort represented Reformed orthodoxy at its most rigid, some, such as Godfrey, still emphasise the basic agreement reached.[97] It is true that agreed formulae were arrived at, and it is also true that the shared understanding of predestination, as the predetermination of certain individuals as opposed to others to be saved, was never in doubt. However, the present study has shown that the attempt to relate the extent of the atonement to this definition of predestination threw up all manner of inconsistencies. Cracks already long present in the Reformed consensus became menacingly obvious at Dort. Ecclesiastical and political necessity ensured that the cracks were papered over. But it was inevitable that in a short space of time, they would reappear.

Chapter Seven

Notes

1 For Arminius, see "Life of Arminius", in *The Works of James Arminius* (3 vols.), ed. W. Nichols, London 1875, vol.l; A.W.Harrison, *The Beginnings of Arminianism: to the Synod of Dort*, London 1926, pp.16-130; C.Bangs, *Arminius: A study in the Dutch Reformation*, Nashville 1971; C.M.Cameron, "Arminius: hero or heretic?", EQ 64(1992)3 pp.213-227; A.Skevington Wood, "The Declaration of Sentiments: the theological testament of Arminius", *EQ* 65(1993)2 pp.111-129.

2 A.Polanus, *A Treatise concerning God's Eternall Predestination*, Cambridge 1599, p.94. On Polanus, see R.W.Letham, "Amandus Polanus: a neglected theologian?" *SCJ* 21(1990)3 pp.463-476.

3 Bangs, op.cit., pp.51-55,83-109. See also, P.Y. de Jong, "The Rise of the Reformed Churches in the Netherlands", in P.Y. de Jong (ed.), *Crisis in the Reformed Churches: Commemoration of the Great Synod of Dort 1618-19*, Grand Rapids 1968, pp.1-21; A.Duke, "The Ambivalent Face of Calvinism in the Netherlands, 1561-1618", in Prestwich, op.cit., pp.109-134; A.Duke, *Reformation and Revolt in the Low Countries*, London 1990, esp. pp.269-293.

4 Bangs, op.cit., pp.185,265-306; Harrison, op.cit., pp.104-118,163,190-299; P.Geyl, *The Netherlands in the Seventeenth Century*, pt.1 1609-1648, London 1961, pp.38-63.

5 For the first round of strife and Arminius' views on Rom.7 see Bangs, op.cit., pp.138-152, 186-192; Harrison, op.cit., pp.27-29; L.Praamsma, "The Background of the Arminian Controversy", in De Jong, op.cit., pp.22-38. For the correspondence with Junius, see Bangs, op.cit., pp.199-205, and Harrison pp.33-35. The correspondence is printed in *Works*, op.cit., vol.3 pp.1-248. The entire discussion was conducted at a very philosophical level and in scholastic style. A work of 1596 by a Friesland minister, Gellius Snecanus, on Rom. 9, drew from Arminius an exposition of the same chapter. Snecanus won his approval by making predestination dependent on foreseen faith. For Arminius on Rom.9, see *Works*, vol.3, pp.485-519; Bangs, op.cit., p.193-198.

6 *Works*, vol.3 pp.521-658. See Bangs, op.cit., pp.261-264.

7 *Works*, vol.3 pp.266-484, on which the following exposition is based. See Bangs, op.cit., pp.206-221. For Perkins' view of predestination, see I.Breward (ed.), "Editor's Introduction", in, *The Work of William Perkins*, Abingdon 1970, pp.80-99; M.T.Malone, "The Doctrine of Predestination in the Thought of William Perkins and Richard Hooker", *ATR*, 52(1970)2 pp.103-117.

8 Arminius, *Works*, vol.3, pp.296-303.

9 Details of the preparation and presentation of the Grand Remonstrance, and of the Conference of the Hague, can be found in Harrison, op.cit., pp.157-160, 148-152, and in Praamsma, in De Jong, op.cit., pp.33-38. The 5 points of the Remonstrance are in Schaff, op.cit., pp.545-549. De Jong, op.cit., Appendix D, pp.210-213 has the Contra-Remonstrant articles.

10 De Jong, op.cit., Appendix H, pp.224-225, has the Remonstrant "Opinions". Cp. J.M.Hicks, "The Theology of Grace in the Thought of Jacobus Arminius and Philip van Limborch: a study in the development of seventeenth-century Dutch Arminianism", Ph.D. Westminster 1985, pp.71-77. See also H.D.Foster, "Liberal Calvinism: the Remonstrants at the Synod of Dort in 1618", *HTR* 16(1923)1 pp.1-37.

11 Schaff, vol.3, pp.558-560, gives the names of the deputies and the nations and provinces they came from.

12 "Letters From the Synod of Dort", in *Golden Remains of the ever Memorable Mr. John Hales*, London

1673, pp.74-77 (15th. January). The Remonstrants were dismissed on 14 January 1619. The English and other foreigners were disturbed by the severe and unilateral manner in which Bogerman, the president, sent them away.

13 The canons can be found in Schaff, op.cit., pp.550-597. The translation used here is that of A.A.Hoekema, *A New Translation of the Canons of Dort*, 1968, reprinted from *CTJ* 3(1968)2 pp.133-161. For a decidedly sympathetic exposition, see F.H. Klooster, "The Doctrinal Deliverances of Dort", in De Jong, op.cit., pp.52-94.

14 See letters dated 9 March and 26 March 1619, in "Letters", pp.124-130. Though Gomarus had no hope of writing supralapsarianism into the canons, he tried to exclude a specifically infralapsarian statement. George Carleton, Bishop of Llandaff, opposed him on behalf of the British deputation, maintaining that, as Gomarus was the only exception, "it was fitting for the Synod to deliver itself for *homo lapsus*". In the event, the only support Gomarus received was from South Holland, which also wished the point to remain undetermined. The "Letters" from 2 February 1919 onwards were written by Walter Balcanqual, who replaced Hales as correspondent to the British ambassador. Unlike Hales, he was a deputy at the Synod, the only Scot, sent as an afterthought by King James in response to a Dutch request for the Scottish Church to be represented. He took his seat on 20 December, and acted with the English as one "college". The official records of the Synod regularly refer to them as the "theologi Magnae Britanniae". See G.D.Henderson, "Scotland and the Synod of Dort", *AKG* 24(1931) pp.1-24; J.Platt, "Eirenical Anglicans at the Synod of Dort", in D.Baker (ed.), *Reform and Reformation: England and the Continent c.1500-c.1750*, Oxford 1979, pp.221-243.

15 In his correspondence with Arminius in Arminius, see *Works*, op.cit., vol.2 pp.1-248, Junius sought to minimise the differences between the two views. Zanchi had pronounced both constructions acceptable. A.Heidanus, cited in K. Barth, *Church Dogmatics*, Edinburgh 1957, II.2 p.127, maintained (1686) that the two views could be debated "without any loss of mutual love and brotherliness".

16 1.7.

17 *Acta Synodi Nationalis...Dordrechti Habitae*, Dort 1620, e.g. 2.4, 2.26, 2.43, 2.50, cp. Dort's "Rejection of Errors" 1.3, Schaff, op.cit., p.557, against those "who teach: That the good pleasure and purpose of God...does not consist in this, that God chose certain persons rather than others..." The *Acta* is in three parts, the first being a record of the proceedings, the second containing the judgements of the foreign deputations on the Remonstrant "Opinions" and the third being the judgements of the provincial deputations about the same.

18 Treatments of the way the Synod dealt with the scope of Christ's redeeming work are to be found in W.R.Godfrey, op.cit.; Strehle, "The Extent", op.cit., pp.216-235, and "The Extent of the Atonement at the Synod of Dort", *WTJ* 51(1989) pp.1-23; W.A.McComish, *The Epigones: a study of the theology of the Genevan Academy at the time of the Synod of Dort, with special reference to Giovanni Diodati*, Allison Park 1989, pp.85-105; N.R.N.Tyacke, *Anti Calvinists: the rise of English Arminianism 1590-1640*, Oxford 1989, pp.87-105; P.O.G.White, *Predestination, Policy and Polemic: conflict and consensus in the English Church from the Reformation to the Civil War*, Cambridge 1992, pp.187-192.

19 The Second Heading of the Canons is entitled, "Of the Death of Christ, and the Redemption of Men by it".

20 Godfrey, op.cit., p.268; Strehle, "The Extent", op.cit., p.18.

21 The British deputation was composed of George Carleton, Bishop of Llandaff and brother of the ambassador; John Davenant, Lady Margaret Professor of Divinity and Master of Queens College, Cambridge; Samuel Ward, Master of Sidney College, Cambridge; Joseph Hall, Dean of Worcester; Walter Balcanqual, royal chaplain. Hall was replaced by Thomas Goad, chaplain to the Archbishop of Canterbury, in January 1919 due to ill health.

22 James delivered instructions to his deputies in Newmarket, and subsequently Davenant and Ward had a two hour audience with him in Royston on October 8, before leaving for the Netherlands. The king had developed a strong opposition to the Remonstrant cause in the years immediately preceding the Synod. However, his main concern was to avoid innovation, extremism and Protestant disunity. His delegates were charged to oppose the granting of confessional status to any new article. The instructions and their background are given in M.Fuller, *The Life, Letters and Writings of Bishop Davenant D.D. 1572-1641*, London 1897, pp.74-77. See also White, op.cit., pp.175-180; C.Grayson, "James I and the Religious Crisis in the United Provinces", in Baker, *Reform*, op.cit., pp.195-219. For the kind of negotiation and persuasion that took place, see for example Balcanqual's letter of 17 March to Ambassador Carleton, "Letters", pp.134-135: "Frequent admonitions and exhortions from your Lordship to the President may hinder much indiscretion in this Synod." Cp. 19 March p.138. For the negotiation of a compromise among the British, see below. The British submission on the second article is found in *Acta*, 2.85-91, on which the following exposition is based.

23 The Palatine deputation was composed of Abraham Scultetus, Henry Alting and Paul Tossanus. The Palatine submission on the second article is in *Acta*, 2.91-96, on which the following exposition is based.

24 The Genevan deputies were John Diodati and Theodore Tronchin. Their submission is found in *Acta*, 2.110-113, on which the following exposition is based.

25 The Bremenese deputation was composed of Matthias Martinius, Ludwig Crocius and Henry Isselburg. Martinius (1572-1630) was professor and pastor at Herborn from 1595, then professor of theology at Bremen from 1610 until his death. For an understanding of Martinius' moderate theology, see J.Moltmann, *Christoph Pezel (1539-1604) und der Calvinismus in Bremen*, Bremen 1958. Crocius and Isselburg made separate submissions, not being able to go as far as Martinius did. Both went as far in his direction, however, as to accept that there is a gracious divine purpose with respect to both elect and non-elect behind the atonement (*Acta*, 2.118-128). Balcanqual reported that all three Bremen deputies were on the point of leaving because of the uncivil conduct of the Dutch towards Martinius, ("Letters" p.109, letter of 18 February). Martinius' submission is found in *Acta*, 2.113-118, on which the following exposition is based.

26 2.86: "Christ died for all, so that, by means of faith, all and each could, by virtue of this ransom, obtain remission of sins and eternal life."

27 See ante, p.137.

28 2.119-120: "This is the will and intention of God from eternity, that the death of Christ should be sufficient for all, in such a way that God requires nothing else as a sacrifice or satisfaction for the sins of men"; 2.97-100.

29 2.103 (Swiss), "Nor does this rule out that those who perish do not do so through any insufficiency in...the death of Christ, whose dignity and sufficiency we profess and believe is infinitely more abundant than all the enormity of all sins"; 3.152 (Groningen).

30 3.96; 3.128; 2.95; 2.110-111.

31 2.107,109.

32 2.111.

33 3.111-112.

34 2.114.

35 The way that the Arminian formulation of the covenant figured prominently in the thinking of the deputies is shown in the fact that, in the "Rejection of Errors" at the end of the canons, three of the seven points on the death of Christ specifically rule out the Arminian concept of the covenant, and another opposes the view that Christ's death acquired for the Father the possibility of accepting

sinners on easier conditions than those of the law.

36 Muller, *Dogmatics*, op.cit., vol.2, p.37, says, with respect to covenant theology, "Here, the near contact between the Reformed and their Remonstrant opponents was most obvious." See, on Arminian covenant theology, Hicks, op.cit., pp.92-95; R.A.Muller, "The Federal Motif in Seventeenth-Century Arminian Theology", *NAKG* 62(1982)1.

37 2.86-87.

38 2.116. See Letham, op.cit., p.261 for Martinius' covenant theology.

39 2.97,100.

40 2.95,93.

41 2.132.

42 3.124,128,125,136,155.

43 Notably Great Britain, Martinius and Crocius of Bremen, Nassau-Wetterau, Hesse.

44 Notably the Palatinate, Emden, Zeeland, Groningen, Utrecht.

45 2.100,105,131.

46 2.118.

47 2.86,87.

48 E.g. 2.25 (Hesse), 2.39 (Switzerland), 2.59 (Bremen), 3.3 (Belgic Professors).

49 The Swiss (2.39) had a combination of these explanations: "He is the foundation of the execution of election in such a way that there are no spiritual blessings except through and on account of Christ. And in this sense we are elect in Christ, that the Father gave us to Christ to be redeemed through Christ...he chose us that we should be in him, and that we might be saved through him." C.G.Berkouwer, *Divine Election*, Grand Rapids 1960, p.145, acknowledges that Dort's terminology regarding election and Christ was not "scientifically exact".

50 Arminius, *Works*, op.cit., vol.3 p.293, "For Christ, according to the Apostle, is not merely the medium by which the salvation already prepared by election is obtained, but, as it were, the meritorious cause in respect of which that election took place, and on account of which that grace has been prepared. For the Apostle says that we have been "chosen in Christ...."

51 2.71,74.

52 3.24, 2.105, 2.92.

53 3.155.

54 2.88; 2.113.

55 "Letters", pp.86-88, letter of Jan.25, "It hath been lately questioned, how Christ is said to be *Fundamentum Electionis*." See K.Barth, *Church Dogmatics*, 2.2. pp.68-70 for an analysis of the issue of the *fundamentum electionis* at Dort.

56 2.86.

57 2.8.

58 2.103 (Switzerland): "The will of God the Father, the election of those to be saved, the obedience and offering of the Son, the saving operation of the Holy Spirit, whether efficacious calling or sanctification, relate to the saints. For the Father has given the elect, whom alone he loves, to the Son, to ransom them alone." 2.110 (Geneva): "Christ himself willed and decreed to die for them...and with the infinite price of his death, to achieve a most effective and singular intention of his will."

59 3.111 (S. Holland): "The all-wise God did not have the intention in Christ's death to obtain forgiveness of sins and reconciliation for those he did not elect in his eternal counsel."

60 E.g. Hesse proved a divine decree to save certain persons through Christ from the known fact of experience that certain persons are saved through Christ: "Whatever God does in time he decreed to do from eternity." (1.25).

61 3.111.

62 E.g. S.Holland, 3.112, "We reject...that the price was not only sufficient in and through itself for redeeming the whole human race, but was paid for each and every man according to the decree, will and grace of God the Father."

63 2.86; 2.127.

64 3.119, 3.134.

65 E.g. 3.119 (N.Holland), 3.100 (Belgic Professors), 2.118 (Martinius), 2.134-135 (Emden).

66 3.138; 3.115; cp.2.99; 3.115; 3.114, 2.96.

67 3.150-151 (Overijsel): "If reconciliation was obtained for all, faith, adoption, regeneration, sanctification and conversion were obtained for all."

68 2.86.

69 2.98.

70 In a letter to the ambassador, Llandaff referred to Ward's attempt to avoid the implication of those Scriptures which put redemption and forgiveness together, by divising the terms *redimibilitas* instead of *redemptio reconciliabilitas* instead of *reconciliatio* and *impetrabilitas* instead of *impetratio*. Llandaff's view was, "This divising of Words makes me more to suspect the Doctrine; for I think a devised School term should not determine a Truth in Divinity" ("Letters", pp.179-182, letter of 8 Feb. 1619). Balcanqual reported that the Palatine deputies were very bitter about some of the things Ward had said in Synod concerning the second article. ("Letters", p.135, letter of 17 March 1619). Abbot, the Archbishop of Canterbury, referred to Ward's "giddy parts", see Tyacke, op.cit., p.101.

71 E.g. Nassau-Wetterau spoke of the error of the Remonstrants in separating the acquisition and application of redemption, for Scripture joins the two acts of the Mediator (2.95-96, cp.3.159-160). The unity of Christ's work of sacrifice and intercession was especially insisted on. See, for example, 2.102 (Hesse), 2.104 (Switzerland), 3.153 (Groningen), 3.181 (N.Holland).

72 2.115,116.

73 2.107-108.

74 E.g. 3.116 (S. Holland), "We say it is absurd that Christ died for those for whom death is not overcome, since in his passion he showed himself as the death of death (*mortis mortem*)." Was this striking phrase the inspiration for the title of John Owen's treatise on the extent of the atonement?

75 2.107.

76 Broadly, the three groups identified here correspond to those Godfrey, op.cit., pp.225-226, calls strict, moderate and mediating.

77 Strehle, "The Extent of the Atonement at...Dort", op.cit., pp.1-23, maintains (p.17) that there were two ways of defining limited atonement within the context of Dort. One way was to hold that "the cross itself by the intention of God was accepted...during its enactment for the elect alone". The other, that "God intended to apply its benefits efficaciously only to the elect when he first set out to devise it". This analysis is helpful in pointing to the key concepts of: the will of God behind the atonement, the conjunction of acquisition and application, and the insistence that Christ actually redeemed.

78 "Letters" pp.86-88, letter of 25 January 1619.

79 Ibid., p.91-92, letter of 28 January; letter of 29 January, "My Lord Bishop has taken pains with Martinius, to bring him from his opinion of universal grace."

80 Ibid., p.101, letter of 9 February. Bodleian Library "Tanner" Ms. 74 contains a number of letters relating to the Synod of Dort, including correspondence between Ward and Martinius, showing that the controversies brought the two men together.

81 From the tone of Balcanqual's letter, from the fact that he urged the ambassador to get a ruling from the Archbishop of Canterbury, and from the fact that LLandaff also wrote to the ambassador on this

point (8 February 1619), it is clear that the differences within the British deputation were deep. The eventual compromise was reached by Llandaff removing from the submission on the second article already prepared by Davenant and Ward those things he found most objectionable. Consequently a letter of 18 February to the Archbishop could proclaim the agreement of the British divines. The ability to reach a working compromise was no doubt partly due to awareness of the premium the king's instructions had placed on unity among his representatives, and to his charge that new terminology regarding Christ's death be avoided, and that the Synod should cause "as little distaste and umbrage to the Lutheran churches as may be". These instructions help to explain why Davenant and Ward had such success in getting their views into the English submission. A royal instruction via Secretary Nanton, that the British should be "as favourable to the general propositions as may be", and a somewhat conflicting instruction from the Archbishop, agreed by the king, both arrived too late to have much influence. See ibid., pp.100-106 (letters from Balcanqual to ambassador of 9 and 15 February), pp.179-182 (letter from Llandaff to ambassador of 8 February), pp.182-183 (letter from Llandaff to Archbishop of 18 February), p.134-135 (letter from Balcanqual to ambasador of 17 March). For the British at Dort, see Platt, in Baker, op.cit., pp.221-243; Tyacke, op.cit., pp.87-105; White, op.cit., pp.175-202.

82 Ibid., p.109, letter of 18 February; pp.110-115, letter of 23 February; p.138, letter of 19 March; cp. his similar comments on the judgements of Gelderland and Drenthe on the second article, ibid., p.132, letters of 15 and 17 March.

83 Ibid., p.140, letter of 25 March; p.143, letter of 14 April; pp.145-149, letter of 25 April, "What trouble we have had in these last Sessions none can conceive but those that were present in them."

84 *Acta*, 3.142; 2.109-110.

85 2.132. The Synod as a whole did not wish to restrict the scope of the preaching of the gospel, or regard it as a mere necessity because of the way the elect and reprobate are mixed up in the world. Canon 2.5, "This promise ought to be announced and declared indiscriminately...together with the command to repent and believe"; 2.8, "As many as are called by the gospel are seriously called." "Letters", p.132, letter of 15 March, "And so ended the judgements on the Second Article, in which there was not altogether so much uniform a consent both in regard of phrases and forms of speaking, and in regard of some propositions, as was in the first Article: yet certainly there was very great, more than could well have been expected from so great a number of learned men in so hard and controverted an Article."

86 In the light of difficulties over the understanding of the covenant, it is perhaps only to be expected that the Canons regarding the death of Christ do not use a federal framework, and avoid the term "condition", keeping rather to the safer, ambiguous terminology of the universal sufficiency of the death of Christ. Letham, op.cit., p.324ff., points out that whereas the Canons ruled out the Arminian interpretation of the covenant, they did not set out an "orthodox" position on the covenant.

87 For Davenant, see M.Fuller, op.cit.; J.Allport, "Life of Davenant", prefaced to vol. 1 of J.Davenant, *An Exposition of the Epistle of S. Paul to the Colossians* (2 vols), London 1831.

88 Godfrey, op.cit., p.182.

89 J.Davenant, *Animadversions upon a Treatise intitled Gods Love to Mankind*, Cambridge 1641. For the preaching incident, see Fuller, op.cit., pp.299-312.

90 J.Davenant, "Dissertation on the Death of Christ", appended to *Colossians*, op.cit.

91 See G.D.Cremeans, *The Reception of Calvinistic Thought into England*, Urbana 1949, pp.24-43; P.Christianson, "Reformers and the Church of England under Elizabeth and the Early Stuarts", *JEH* 31(1980) pp.463-482; C.M.Dent, *Protestant Reformers in Elizabethan Oxford*, Oxford 1983, pp.74-106. P.Collinson, "England and International Calvinism 1558-1640", in Prestwich, op.cit., pp.197-223;

Tyacke, op.cit., pp.248-265; White, op. cit, esp. pp.60-69,80-100. C.F.Allison, *The Rise of Moralism: the proclamation of the gospel from Hooker to Baxter*, shows Davenant in the context of the Reformed Church of England.

92 For Perkins, see n.7 above. Ames' views on the extent of the atonement emerge clearly in his writings relating to the Conference of the Hague and the Synod of Dort: *Coronis ad Collationem Hagiensiem*, London 1618; *Anti-Synodalia Scripta*, Amsterdam 1633.

93 For Ussher's views, see especially C.R.Elrington (ed.) *The Whole Works of the Most Rev. James Ussher D.D.*, Dublin 1864, vol.12, "The Judgement of the late Archbishop of Armagh, and Primate of Ireland, of the True Intent and Extent of Christ's Death and Satisfaction upon the Cross" (3 March 1617), pp.553-570.

94 This exposition is based on the "Dissertation", in *Colossians*, op.cit., and "Dr.Davenant Touching the Second Article, Discussed at the Conference at the Haghe [sic], of the Extent of Redemption", in "Letters", op.cit., pp.186-190.

95 *See Good Counsells for the Peace of Reformed Churches, by some reverend and learned Bishops and other Divines*, Oxford 1641.

96 Fuller, op.cit., p.247.

97 Godfrey, op.cit., p.269.

Part Three

The Saumur Theology and its Opponents

Chapter Eight

John Cameron (1579–1625)

INTRODUCTION

John Cameron[1] was one of many Scots who exercised a ministry in the French Reformed Church. He graduated from Glasgow University in 1599, having gained a reputation for his abilities, especially in languages. After a year as regent in Greek at Glasgow he moved to Bordeaux, and from there to the Academy of Sedan as professor of philosophy. Two years later the church at Bordeaux called him to be its pastor, sponsoring his pursuit of further studies on condition that he would eventually return to work there. A year as a tutor in Paris was followed by two as a student at the Academy of Geneva, and another one at Heidelberg. Returning to Bordeaux he worked alongside his compatriot Gilbert Primrose, until called to be professor of theology at Saumur in 1618. His work there had to be terminated in 1621 because Louis XIII would not allow him, as a foreigner, to serve the French Church. He moved to London, and then to Glasgow, having been appointed by King James as Divinity Principal there. Cameron's royalism, no doubt a factor in his appointment, meant that he had a cool reception in Glasgow, especially as the previous principal had been removed to make way for him. So he did not stay long, returning to France in 1623, and obtaining permission to teach at the Montauban Academy. After only two years, however, he was beaten while trying to pacify a riot, and died on 27 November 1625. The National Synod of Castres, 1626, showed its regard for him by awarding a generous pension to his wife, and instigating the publication of his works.

Perhaps as significant as the events of Cameron's life are the surviving indications of his character. His learning was widely recognized, and the fact that he could gain the friendship of, and engage in correspondence with, the renowned humanist scholar, Isaac Casaubon, is one indication of it. His remarkable ability to win the loyalty of students meant that after only three years at Saumur, he had left an indelible impression on those who would form the "triumvirate" of Saumur in the next generation, Moïse Amyraut, Louis Cappel and Josué de la Place. Cappel recorded Cameron's freedom in sharing his ideas with his students. It seems that the congregation at Bordeaux did not appreciate Cameron's talkativeness, for more than one member told their pastor that his sermons were long, tedious and full of irrelevant digressions. The comments of one of these, a lawyer, gives an insight into the pastor's unconventional character:

> "Being heated, by reason of his fervour and action in preaching, in ye midst of Sermon, He would unbutton his doublet, stretch out his hand kerchief as if it were a napkin or towell, rub away his Sweat before ye Auditory, and sometimes forgetting himself, He would take off his hat, and lay it down by him on ye pulpit. Theise actions of Monsr. Cameron's disgusted ye people..."[2]

The purpose in drawing attention to these details is to show that Cameron had a distinctive and original personality. It should not seem strange that theological innovation should come from such a man.

CAMERON STUDIES

Attention has been devoted to Cameron in recent years, as the enterprise of understanding the development of Reformed orthodoxy has been pursued, and also in the wider context of the study of the intellectual developments of the seventeenth century leading to the Enlightenment. In the latter context, Walter Rex has seen Cameron as introducing a new rationalism into Reformed theology. Jürgen Moltmann has presented him as an important contributor to the development of covenant-oriented *Heilsgeschichte*, and Brian Armstrong has understood him as a humanistic Calvinist, who had more in common with Calvin than the scholastic Reformed theologians who were his contemporaries. François Laplanche has studied Cameron's theology, seeing him, as do Moltmann and Armstrong, as the originator of most of the distinctive elements in the theology of Amyraut. More recently, Laplanche has sought to relate the Saumur scholarship to the social, cultural and political milieu in which the Huguenots of the seventeenth century found themselves. Axel Swinne has engaged in bibliographical research.[3]

Just over a decade after Cameron's death, he and Amyraut were being accused of innovation,[4] and to the present day their teaching that Christ died for all, but faith is given to the elect only, often designated "hypothetical universalism", is commonly referred to as "Amyraldism". J.I.Packer, for example, has written, "The position known as Amyraldism, after its leading exponent...originated with a Scots professor at Saumur, John Cameron." Moltmann, however, has pointed out the inadequacy of the approach, represented by A. Schweizer, of using the particularism-universalism dichotomy as a *"grille"* through which the Saumur theology should be studied.[5] This point is well made, but it should not be forgotten that no part of Cameron's legacy caused more controversy among the Reformed than his insistence that Christ died for all. The present work will examine the thought of Cameron against the Reformed theological background presented in previous chapters, and show that, although Cameron was a creative thinker, his doctrine of the extent of the atonement was not new, but rooted in an already existing Reformed tradition. Universal atonement was indeed important to Cameron and Amyraut, but they can neither be blamed nor credited with introducing it into Reformed theology.

CAMERON'S THEOLOGY

Helpful, concise accounts of aspects of Cameron's theology can be found in Armstrong and Moltmann.[6] Here we attempt to deal with those aspects which have a direct bearing on his understanding of the extent of the atonement.

Predestination

Some have considered that Cameron adopted a position mid-way between Reformed and Arminian soteriology.[7] Such a verdict depends on which elements are considered most vital to the "orthodox" and Arminian positions respectively. There can be no doubt that Cameron wrestled with Arminian concerns, and that he did not share the tendency of the orthodox to react by becoming more entrenched in opposite positions at every disputed point. His resolute rejection of Arminianism, however, should not be questioned, in that, for example in the lengthy *Amica Collatio*, he firmly maintained against the Arminian Tilenus the Augustinian view that God's saving grace is not based on, but rather produces, a right disposition in the individual. This view was entirely at one with the Reformed understanding of predestination, Cameron's own definition of election being:

> "A decree...by which God decided with himself from eternity to separate by efficacious calling and sanctify certain men."

It differs from calling as "cause from effect".

In harmony with this, Cameron denied that reprobates are such because they are worse than others. It is true that, considered "absolutely", their reprobation is as a result of their participation in sin, but considered "comparatively" it is not due to sin, that is, to their being more sinful than others, but to the distinguishing good pleasure of God, for which no reason can be given.[8]

This explanation was given to counter Tilenus' attempt to base reprobation on people's relative demerits, but it also implied a rejection of supralapsarian predestination, in that supralapsarianism denied that reprobation was dependent on sin "comparatively" or "absolutely". Cameron's firmly infralapsarian position brought him into conflict with Beza's view of predestination. It should not be forgotten, however, that Beza's supralapsarianism was the minority view among the "orthodox" of the early seventeenth century, as the discussions and canons of Dort revealed. A rejection of Bezan predestination, therefore, cannot be taken as evidence of a departure from contemporary "Calvinism".[9]

The Remonstrant controversy had made the order of the divine decrees a crux. To the Arminian, the decree to send Christ precedes the decree to save believers, which itself precedes the decree to elect specific individuals foreseen as believing in him. The "orthodox" responded by saying that the election of individuals to be saved is prior to the decree to send Christ, Christ being the means by which the decree of election is fulfilled. Cameron's distinctive order of the decrees was as follows:

(i) to restore the divine image upon human beings in a way that divine justice would be preserved,
(ii) to send the Son so that all who believe in him should be saved,
(iii) to render some people able to believe,
(iv) to save those who believe.

> "The first two decrees are general, the last two special and particular."[10]

Thus the divine predestination of specific persons relates to the giving of faith, rather than the sending of Christ.[11] This is the interpretation of predestination found in Davenant and Martinius. It was also characteristic of Ursinus and Bullinger to introduce predestination into their system in relation to effectual calling, although neither of them concerned themselves with a specific order of decrees.

In line with his order of the decrees, and with the positing of conditional as well as absolute decrees, Cameron distinguished two sorts of election, "election in Christ" and "election to Christ".[12] "Election in Christ" is the election of believers to salvation, "election to Christ" the election of certain individuals to become believers. While in this way Cameron was accommodating the Arminian insistence that union with Christ is foundational to election, he retained the view that union with Christ by faith is entirely the free gift of God.

We have already found the treatment of election at two levels, in a similar way, by Bullinger. It will be recalled that even Beza found it necessary to have two versions of election, "before and after" Christ. Although in neither of these forms was the human object of election considered as a believer, Beza's purpose in having two elections was, like Bullinger's and Cameron's, to preserve the scriptural "elect in Christ" while at the same time wanting election to have the function of explaining why some come to be "in Christ". In struggling to give meaning to the phrase, "chosen in Christ", that would accord with a definition of election as the foreordination of certain individuals to be saved, many of the orthodox of the beginning of the seventeenth century were explaining the Pauline phrase to mean "chosen to be in Christ".[13] Cameron's use of "chosen in Christ" to refer to believers, in a way distinct from unconditional predestination, amounted to an abandonment of the struggle, and the loss of a key predestinarian proof text (Ephesians 1.4). It is significant that the attempt to bring the concept of unconditional election into relation to Christ is notable by its general absence from Cameron's writings.

The Will of God

An element in Cameron's predestination teaching was the familiar division of the will of God.

> "My opinion indeed is this..., in Scripture the will of God is understood in two ways. For there is one will of God which decrees and one which commands. The first will is followed, necessarily indeed, by the effect, since the counsel of God cannot be in vain. But the other will...[is that] by which God either simply commands something to be done, or also delights in what he commands."[14]

The decretive will is absolute or antecedent, the other conditional or consequent. The antecedent will is operative in election to Christ, for it determines the gift of faith, the consequent relates to election in Christ, for it grants salvation as a consequence of faith-union with Christ.

In the light of the way this study has traced the use of the two wills distinction by various Reformed theologians, we cannot see this as a product of the Ramist penchant for dichotomizing.[15] Having said that, Cameron's adherence to the philosophy of Pierre Ramus may have helped him to feel comfortable in holding two apparently incompatible concepts of God's will. As the Ramist impulse was to categorize rather than harmonize knowledge, the Ramist Cameron may have felt no obligation to unify his thought by submitting the conditional will to the absolute. It is difficult to go very far in following Armstrong's view that the two wills device was a major new insight of the Saumur School, recovered from Calvin.[16] The two wills distinction, adopted from the medieval scholastics, was taken for granted in Reformed theology. One way in which Cameron did differ from many of his contemporaries, however, was that he insisted that the commanding will is not chiefly a merely external thing, but can proceed from a real delight of God in the thing commanded. This was in contrast with many of the "orthodox", for whom the non-decretive will merely supplies rules for human conduct, while the decretive will provides the deepest insight into the mind of God. Even when granting that the preceptive will could proceed from God's delight in the thing commanded, they easily slipped into speaking of it as a merely external device. Zanchi and Beza did so when they used God's command to sacrifice Isaac as a typical instance of the commanding will of God.[17] Cameron had a triple approach:

> "I indeed divide the divine will into that by which he has determined something (I have said that by this will God wills the conversion of some) and that by which God simply prescribes something (by which he ordered Abraham to sacrifice his son) or by which he not only simply prescribes something, but also truly delights over it (by this will I have said God wills the conversion of all)."[18]

The first and last categories were the most important to Cameron, and with respect to them he was content to allow a sharp dualism to remain in his predestination thought, never suggesting that the preceptive will is inferior to, or simply an instrument of, the decretive.

> "Scripture seems to assert and deny the same thing about God, that he plainly wants and does not want the salvation of all."[19]

The Threefold Covenant

Cameron's *Opera*, published posthumously in 1642, contain "De Triplici Dei cum Homine Foedere Theses".[20] These are accompanied by the note, "*Heidelbergae, pridie Nonas April. Anno 1608*". Swinne, having failed to discover any record of Cameron's having sustained these or other theses at Heidelberg, has concluded that the work is not genuine. He maintains that it must have been composed by the editors of the *Opera* (Amyraut, Cappel and Bochart) to show that their own covenant teaching was derived from Cameron. In view of the ravages suffered by the Heidelberg Library, the absence of reference to Cameron's theses need not require such an extreme explanation. Even if Swinne is correct in denying that the theses were defended at Heidelberg, Laplanche has pointed out that they may still have originated with him, and, as an accompanying note in the *Opera* claims, have been shown to many friends. Laplanche finds this a more credible explanation than to impute dishonesty to the editors.[21] Also, while it is correct that nowhere else in his works does Cameron make much of his three covenant idea in itself, it is not entirely confined to the "Theses".[22] Furthermore there is no evidence that any of the opponents of the Saumur theology ever disputed Cameron's authorship. They are accepted here, therefore, as at least embodying Cameron's own position.

Moltmann, Armstrong and Laplanche may be consulted for an exposition of Cameron's covenant teaching. Because of their work, only a brief survey, and comment, is given here.[23]

Cameron's three covenants are those of nature, grace and law (the subservient covenant). As its name indicates, the subservient covenant is not equal to the other two: "they are the chief". The covenant of nature was made with the human race in its unfallen state, requiring perfect righteousness in accordance with the principles of the moral law known from the beginning. It was a covenant Adam could have kept by his own natural ability, and promised him an everlasting life in an earthly paradise.[24] It was founded on creation, and declared the justice of God. The subservient covenant, introduced by Moses, was a repetition of the covenant of nature, in that it also required perfect obedience to the moral law, but it added ceremonial and civil regulations. The promise of this covenant was a happy life in Canaan, but its main purpose was to expose more fully human sinfulness and so prepare the way for the Saviour. Cameron explained that the subservient covenant was that after which the first part of the Bible was named in being called the Old Testament. The adjective "old" did not imply that it was chronologically prior, for the covenant of nature fully and the covenant of grace partly had been revealed before it. Rather it was old because defunct, since the coming of Christ.[25] The covenant of grace is that promise of eternal life through Christ to all who repent and believe. Unlike the subservient covenant, made with Israel, the covenant of grace is made with the whole human race.[26]

The obvious difference between this and other contemporary Reformed teaching on the covenant is that it was usual to have two covenants only: the original covenant of nature (or works), and the covenant of grace entering in from the fall. Calvin and Bullinger had thought principally in terms of two covenants, old and new, the old covenant being the Mosaic. To them, however, these covenants were the same in substance but different in administration,[27] in other words they were two forms of the covenant of grace. Ursinus could speak, as Calvin had, of two covenants the same in substance but different in administration, but at the same time he introduced a pre-fall covenant of nature. This meant that, although he never spoke of three covenants as such, he was in fact dealing with a covenant of nature, a covenant of grace, and a Mosaic covenant which was something of a mixture of the two. Cameron's position, asserting that the Mosaic was not the same in substance as that of the new covenant, can be regarded as completing the move, initiated by Ursinus, from Calvin and Bullinger. The novelty of Cameron's position, therefore, should not be exaggerated. The difficulty of fitting the Mosaic administration neatly into one or other category of "nature/works" or "grace" was widely recognized, and, without calling it a separate covenant, other Reformed theologians did treat it as a special case.[28] Furthermore, the distinctive role of the law, repromulgated in the ten commandments, in preparing the way for Christ by exposing the helplessness of the human condition, was a well established feature of Reformed theology.[29]

The "Theses" were published in English by Samuel Bolton in 1645, as an appendix to his own work against the Scilla and Charybdis of legalism and antinomianism. Bolton listed a number of ways the Reformed had tried to fit the Mosaic law into their covenant theology, noting the difficulties of subsuming it simply under either nature or grace. His introduction to the "Theses" claims that,

> "in the ensuing discourse, this doubt is resolved".[30]

Clearly he regarded Cameron's "Theses" not so much as a new departure but as essentially a statement of what the best theologians had been trying to say all along. Indeed, in all the posthumous criticisms of Cameron's "novelties", there was little complaint about his use of three covenants, although the idea that the reward of the first covenant was earthly did not find favour.

Cameron's presentation is not so much noteworthy, therefore, as a radical departure in terms of doctrinal content, but for its willingness to highlight the historical and progressive nature of the activity and revelation of God. Instead of having two covenants of nature and grace operating together, in various combinations, from the fall onwards, Cameron threw into sharp relief the progressive character of God's dealings with the human race, by presenting three successive covenants, leading up to the climactic covenant of grace. This does not mean that he denied that the covenant of grace was revealed before Christ, but he insisted on the obscurity of the revelation, and its gradual clarification until the work of Christ had been accomplished in time. Nor does it mean that he taught that the covenant of nature no longer has a place, for its standard of righteousness is unchangeable.[31]

Cameron's departure from the usual two-covenant scheme, then, was methodologically convenient as a way of dealing with the Mosaic dispensation more tidily than the two covenant theology could. However, as Moltmann has argued, Cameron's scheme embodied a concept of salvation-history, of the progressive development of the purposes of God in the human story. The conditional covenant theology which had flourished in Heidelberg involved a certain change of focus away from pretemporal decrees to the mutual relations between God and the human race in time, and this was the perspective Cameron was putting to greater use.

Armstrong may be correct in claiming that Cameron wanted to put a new emphasis on the gospel in the face of a tendency to legalism among the Reformed, arranging his system in such a way that the gospel was evidently the pinnacle of God's dealings with humanity.[32] However, it can also be said that the three covenant system gave greater scope to "nature", continuing the trend set by Heidelberg's introduction of the *foedus naturale*. Reformed contemporaries were working with two covenants, nature and grace. These covenants were at one, and yet in opposition. Their unity consisted in sharing the same basic structure of condition and promise, and in that the covenant of nature provides the pattern of life to which those taken into the covenant of grace are to conform themselves. Their opposition appears in that the former puts before people a standard of perfect obedience which is impossible for them, as fallen, to attain, and so is unable to bring salvation, whereas the latter is based on the work of Christ and the qualitatively different condition of faith. The Pauline opposition between works and grace was interpreted as an opposition between nature and grace, and the terms *foedus naturale* and *foedus operum* came to be used interchangeably. For Cameron, with three covenants, the opposition between law and grace does not relate immediately to the covenant of nature, but to the subservient covenant, and he avoided calling the covenant of nature a covenant of works. It would be tempting to conclude that this arrangement was meant as a protest against the prevailing view, in which God's original and legal covenant revealed that justice, narrowly defined, is his pre-eminent moral attribute. However, although Cameron insisted, in a way others did not, that God is under a necessity of his nature to exercise goodness as much as justice, he did say that the covenant of nature was intended primarily to demonstrate God's justice. His scheme of covenants may have softened the impression generally given by covenant theology that justice, punishing and rewarding, is the most basic element in God's dealings with the human race. What it certainly did for Cameron and the Saumur school, however, was remove from "nature" something of the suspicion bound to attach to it when set in opposition to the gospel. Cameron thus accented the positive scope and use of "nature".

Cameron taught that the subservient covenant is abolished but the covenant of nature remains essentially the same. It is unchangeable, as God's original order, expressing his own nature and the basic pattern of his relationship to humanity, and embodying a permanent moral standard.

> "The creature is unable not to owe piety to God, nor can God fail to favour piety or to hate sin. Since the covenant of nature is built on these two foundations, which are immovable and unshakeable, it is necessary that the covenant of nature itself is unchangeable. And God is unable not to love the person who fulfils the conditions, or not to be angry with the one who despises them."[33]

The covenant of grace is necessary for the sinner's justification, but it does not replace the basic pattern of the divine-human relationship established in the covenant of nature.[34] The covenant of grace too contains a promise and conditions, and the fulfilment of the conditions is rewarded according to the consequent love of God,

> "which is not only voluntary but also a naturall property in God, who according to his own nature inclines to the rewarding of a good man."[35]

God the law-giver continues to be bound by his own nature. Thus the covenant of nature sets the basic pattern according to which the covenant of grace is fashioned.

In fact, Reformed theology generally accepted that, though the covenants of works and grace are in opposition as far as justification is concerned, the content of the covenant of works remains God's standard for human conduct. The covenant of nature could thus be used as the common basis of the ethical life of society, composed as it is of the unregenerate still under the covenant of nature and the believing elect who are under the covenant of grace.[36] In formally giving the covenant of nature an existence independent of the Mosaic economy, Cameron was bringing into sharper definition positions which had already become part of the Reformed inheritance.

Cameron went further than other Reformed theologians in his teaching that saving grace is at work in the natural order.

> "God is said 'to have given Christ for the life of the world', 'to will the salvation of all' certainly in so far as he calls all to penitence, some by the law of nature, others by his written law, others by the gospel."[37]

Cameron did not work out in any detail the relationship between redemption and nature, or teach that anyone responds positively to the invitation of nature. However, when his student Amyraut did develop the connections between nature and grace, the "orthodox" protested as vigorously against this as against his assertion of universal atonement. According to Cameron, it is because God loved the world and Christ gave himself for it that the call to penitence goes out to all by the three means described above. Consequently, there are those who have never heard the gospel preached, yet,

> "have been invited to God by a more obscure grace of the Saviour".[38]

If the indiscriminate gospel required a universal atonement, then so did nature's universal call to penitence.

It is beyond the scope of this study to investigate fully the importance of the concept of nature to Cameron. Laplanche has shown its significance in Saumur's endeavour to provide for the Huguenots a basis for understanding their relationship, as a religious minority, to the social order.[39] Evaluations of the Cameronian covenant of nature need to take this wider perspective into account. Suffice it to say here that the degree to which Cameron saw a unity between nature and grace necessitated a certain universalism in his doctrine of redemption.

Conditional covenant

The novelty of Cameron's threefold division should not disguise the fact that he worked with a definition of covenant which had by that time become well-established, especially through the Heidelberg tradition. At the commencement of his "Theses" he stated that two sorts of covenant are conceivable, the absolute and the conditional.[40] The same terms could be applied to the will of God:

> "This distinction of the covenant, depends upon a distinction in the love of God."

Some divine covenants, such as "the covenant in which God promises to give faith and perseverance to the elect" are absolute, requiring nothing from human beings. The absolute covenant relates to the primary or antecedent love of God, the conditional to the consequent or secondary. There is, then, one sort of covenant which promises but does not make stipulations. This is equivalent to predestination. Having referred to this kind of covenant, Cameron makes no further use of it in the "Theses", nor does it have any prominence in his other writings. The three covenants of the "Theses" are those having stipulations. They are conditional. It is true that the existence of a covenant of grace itself, with such outstanding promises, is unconditional, deriving from the antecedent love of God, but in its operation conditionality is of its essence. The failure of the "Theses" to develop the theme of predestination as covenant is difficult to view as a convenient limitation of the field of study. It seems rather to reveal a priority in Cameron's own thought, explained by his statement that God's antecedent love is "altogether voluntary", whereas the consequent, rewarding love of God is a "naturall propertie of God, who of his own nature doth incline to the reward of good, as to the punishment of evil." This interest in what is natural to God is a strand running throughout Cameron's thought.

The strongly conditional flavour of his thought may have influenced Cameron in his rejection of the by then standard interpretation of justification as involving not only forgiveness through Christ's passive obedience, but also the imputation of Christ's active obedience. For the imputation of Christ's righteousness may seem to leave no condition left for people to fulfil as their side of the covenant. We raise this only as a possibility as far as Cameron was concerned, bearing in mind that in the covenant theology of Richard Baxter, which would have many similarities with the thought of Cameron, and for which Baxter had a high regard, the imputation of the active obedience of Christ was excluded from justification.[41] What is clear is that Cameron's notion of conditional covenant, deriving from the very nature of God, would be determinative for his treatment of the extent of the atonement.

Conversion

The bulk of the *Amica Collatio* is taken up with debate about how conversion is effected. Cameron and Tilenus agreed about the need for divine illumination as prerequisite to conversion. Tilenus maintained that the critical factor was the response of the human will to illumination. Cameron, however, made everything rest on the illumination, maintaining that there is a degree of divine illumination, granted to the elect, which always persuades the mind of the truth of the gospel. The force of this persuasion is such that the will inevitably follows it and embraces Christ. Cameron's assertion of the effectiveness of divine illumination was in contradiction of the Arminian position, but his view that conversion involves one divine act upon the mind, which inevitably moves the will, was at odds with the usual Reformed explanation of a double action on the understanding and the will. Cameron defended his view on the basis of a faculty psychology which presupposed that the will is always directed by the understanding. So, in the process of opposing

Arminianism, the Saumur professor aroused the suspicions of the orthodox. Consequently the theology professors at Leiden, where the work was being printed, wrote to express their regret that, unless he could qualify his position, they would be unable to give their commendation to it.[42]

It would be in line with Cameron's somewhat rationalistic approach to apologetics, and with his commitment to finding explanations for God's works without resorting to the hidden will wherever possible, to see his defence of the priority of the understanding over the will as further evidence of rationalism. It also was in harmony with his concern to see grace operating in accord with nature, for he regarded the mind's direction of the will as the natural order. However, Cameron's explanation was also in tune with the Reformation principle of the primacy of the word, and its concomitant that the work of the Spirit should not be separated from the word.

Cameron's insistence that the Spirit works on the mind through the word demanded a clear and directly applicable message. The connection between this and his view of the extent of the atonement was that the work of Christ has to be capable of being presented as a truth for the mind to be persuaded of, rather than for the will to opt into. A measure of assurance is necessary for conversion. Before their will can respond, people have to be persuaded that Christ died for them.

The Nature of the Atonement[43]

Cameron branched out from the usual Reformed interpretation of the atonement by employing the concepts of God as *rector*, *magistratus publicus* and *iudex mundi*. According to Cameron, God would be able to forgive sins, without any satisfaction, if sin were simply a private injury against him. However, sin is a "public" offence, because God's position is analogous to that of a magistrate. This does not mean that Cameron removed from God a necessity, arising from his nature, to punish sin, for it is God's justice that compels him to enforce his just and righteous laws, in the same way that a just ruler is not free to put just laws to one side.

> "It is essential to God to punish sin."

In answer to a supposed objection, that God's *dispensatio* is free, he replied,

> "In an action of power and wisdom, I concede; in an action of justice and mercy, I deny."

In a "private" capacity, however, God was never angry with us, but rather inclined to forgive. However, he was angry for the sake of the public good. It is because God deals with the offence as a "public" matter that he has the freedom to accept Christ's satisfaction in place of the punishment of those guilty of sin. Nevertheless, God does not have the liberty to change the penalty out of all recognition: an infinite penalty is required because the offence against God is infinite. So Christ could provide satisfaction because he is both man and infinite God. One drop of the blood of this infinite person would not be an adequate satisfaction, though, because the law requires that a very substantial penalty be borne.

Cameron was trying to explain, contrary to the Socinians, how the satisfaction of Christ was a divine necessity in order to make possible the forgiveness of sins, but how, at the same time, God could change the circumstances and duration of the penalty of the law, and the person who pays it. He was also explaining how God can command us to forgive without any satisfaction, when he does not do so himself. While relating the necessity for the atonement to God's governmental operations, he tried to show that those governmental operations were themselves demanded by the very nature of God. In the process of doing this he indicated yet another departure from the usual Reformed position by positing that mercy is as much, or even more, a necessity of God's nature than justice.

It is significant that these views were set out in Cameron's "Theses de Efficacia Gratiae Dei", his inaugural exercise at Saumur in 1618, the year following the publication by the Dutch jurist Hugo Grotius of the *Defensio Fidei Catholicae de Satisfactione Christi* against Faustus Socinus.[44] Grotius explained the death of Christ in terms of the manifestation of divine justice as part of the divine rule, rather than as a necessity of God's nature. This "rectoral" theory was quickly adopted by the Arminians. The fact that Cameron accepted and used much in that view, without abandoning the "orthodox" position, is typical of his habit of engaging genuinely with views most Reformed theologians preferred to reject out of hand.

Cameron's exposition of the nature of the atonement shared the tendency of Ursinus and others to give a rational and detailed explanation of its necessity, according to the concepts of infinite demerit, infinite punishment and infinite satisfaction, and according to the attributes of God. Founding the divine action on inner divine necessity was, in fact, a leading feature of Cameron's theology, and one which played a large part in determining his answer to the question of the extent of the atonement.

The Extent of the Atonement

The *Opera* contain a number of letters from Cameron's Bordeaux period, to Louis Cappel, in which his views on the extent of the atonement are expounded more fully than anywhere else.[45] These letters will be used as a basis for examining his treatment of this theme. There are other references scattered throughout his writings, however, and these will be used to supplement the correspondence.

To appreciate Cameron's perspective on the extent of the atonement, it is worth noting his commitment to spreading the faith. This is evident from the amount of attention he gave to apologetic writing, directed towards Roman Catholics. In comparison with the "encyclopaedic" character of contemporary French Reformed apologetics, there is a freshness of approach in his concentration on broad principles and appeal to his readers to recognize that all human beings are inclined to be blinded by prejudices, especially in religious matters. The impression received is that he really wanted to persuade his readers rather than merely attack them and justify his own position.[46]

Cameron was a preacher, as well as apologist. His concern for the proclamation of the gospel informed his approach to the extent of the atonement. The gospel is to be taken to all for,

> "God has not restrained the preaching of the gospel any more than the giving of alms or any of the other duties of godliness."

Indeed, unlike others, Calvin included, who were quick to see a sign of predestination in the fact that the gospel is not preached equally to all, Cameron pointed to the human failure to fulfil the God-given task.

The gospel promise is:

> "Jesus Christ died for you; but unless you believe you will receive no benefit from it, in fact the amount of your wickedness will increase. Believe, therefore, and you will live."

> "Consider the stated words of the covenant, Believe Christ died for you and you will live."

Others had attempted to present the gospel in this direct and personal way. Bucer and Zanchi had described the response to the gospel in terms of believing that Christ died for oneself, and they understood that this was tantamount to believing in one's election. They offered no answer to the logical difficulty of how people can be called to believe Christ died for them, when theology tells us he may not in fact have done so. Cameron proceeded on the assumption that people cannot be called upon to believe that Christ died for them, unless it is known to be true that he did. His call to believe in Christ was not, initially, a call to believe in one's own election.

The Remonstrants had exploited the inconsistency of those who called all who hear the gospel to believe that Christ died for them, whilst at the same time maintaining that Christ died for the elect only. Their attack was anticipated by William Perkins and others, who adopted the position that it is not the duty of everyone who hears the gospel to believe that Christ died for him.[47] By contrast, Cameron maintained boldly that hearers of the gospel are to believe that Christ died for them, because he did. He drew attention to those passages of the New Testament warning people about rejecting the blood of Christ, and asked how it was possible to reject a blessing which is not bestowed.

This perspective fitted well with Cameron's view of faith, in which the persuasion of the understanding was fundamental.[48] Such a view demands a clear, compelling object. To know that Christ has died for some, without knowing whether I am included in that number, cannot be the overwhelming, transforming persuasion of the love and mercy of God that Cameron's concept of faith demanded. It would require an act of will to "opt in" to the favoured circle, before I could have any persuasion of the love of God to me. Thus Cameron's concept of faith required a definition of the extent of the atonement in which everyone who hears the gospel can feel himself embraced.

> "I believe then that Christ satisfied for me because he did so truly. But I have recognized that this satisfaction is salvific for me because I am conscious of my faith."

Not only does this view of the extent of the atonement accord with Cameron's stress on communicating the gospel and with his definition of faith, it also fits his understanding of God's covenantal dealings with the world. The divine covenants with the human race have both promise and condition. Faith is the condition of the evangelical covenant. The covenant says, "Believe Christ died for you and you will live". Universal atonement does not guarantee universal salvation, but it does make universal preaching possible, leaving the outcome suspended on the fulfilment or non-fulfilment of the condition.

> "If you think that God wills the salvation of all, without any condition, you are very mistaken."

In human terms, it is like the payment of a ransom through which captives become entitled to go free, but will only experience freedom if they avail themselves of their opportunity.

The will of God for the salvation of all, asserted in 1 Timothy 2.4, is conditional, or "hypothetical", as the context concerning prayer for all people shows; we pray for all to be saved, but not to be saved without faith and repentance on their part. God has an antecedent (i.e. unconditional) love for the world, out of which he sends Christ into it. The "second step" of the antecedent love is to give faith to the elect, who on performance of the condition of faith, are actually saved, according to God's consequent will and love. From the perspective of the consequent will it can be said,

> "Christ is...given for the elect only, and wills to save only them."

Cameron's use of the sufficient-efficient formula continues this line of thought. Noting that divines have found the scriptural statements that Christ is the Saviour of the world rather sweeping, he pointed out that they have employed the distinction that,

> "Christ died sufficiently for all, but effectually for believers only."

He added immediately,

> "In this I do not differ."

Again,

> "Those who teach, Christ died *sufficiently*, as they say, for the ungodly, and *effectually* for believers, are right."

Aware, however, that some of those who accepted the formula did not admit that universal sufficiency implied any divine will for the salvation of all, he added,

> "But then, this term *sufficiency* seems to me to signify something wider in this argument than some think."

He meant a sufficiency intended by God, and having an important role in his purposes.

The efficacy of Christ's death is through faith, which is the gift of God to his elect.

> "I am not ignorant that Christ intercedes with the Father only for believers; but that belongs to the efficacy of Christ's death, which, I freely grant, belongs to believers. It is faith, then, which renders the death of Christ effectual."

> "Christ died for all, yet his death blesses only those who by faith embrace him...The fruit of his satisfaction only reaches those who become members of this head, that is, only believers."

The sun shines, but its light is seen only by those with open eyes.

It will be observed from the above that the intercession of Christ, as well as his sacrifice, was understood to depend upon faith:

> "As Mediator, he prays for believers."[49]

Throughout his treatment of the extent of the atonement, Cameron showed no sign of being worried about the implications for universal atonement of a doctrine of substitution. This is not surprising in view of the "governmental" aspects of his understanding of the nature of the atonement.

Implications of universal, conditional atonement[50]

Making the efficacy of the atonement dependent on faith posed the question, "Was not faith itself one of the fruits of Christ's death?" This was indeed the position of many of the deputations at Dort: Christ obtained the Spirit and faith for those he represented in his death, namely the elect, and as the ascended Lord bestows these gifts on those for whom they were obtained. Cameron's position, that the death of Christ was for all, could not allow that Christ's atonement won faith, or the hypothetical element would be threatened. So he stated,

> "Truly [faith is given] that you may participate in the merit of Christ. The death of Christ is properly the final [not meritorious] cause of faith."

Faith proceeds directly from the good pleasure of God.

Another question arising in the correspondence with Cappel was whether Cameron held the Lutheran "heresy" that Christ died as much for Judas as for Peter. This he denied. For Scripture speaks of Christ dying for the ungodly, but

> "not that Christ died as much for the ungodly as for the godly".

Cappel had to remember the difference between satisfaction and its fruit. Between the two must come the condition of faith. Christ cannot therefore be said to have died for all equally, because he has died conditionally, and the fulfilment of the condition turns out to be unequal. His death for the ungodly is none the less real, and even to such an extent that,

> "No-one can be condemned by the law, unless he is unbelieving...This belongs commonly to all, and is to be credited to Christ's death, which so far delivered all from the malediction of the law that no-one incurs it, except the one who does not believe that Christ died for him."

A third implication is that there seems to be an incompatibility between Cameron's understanding of faith and his covenant theology. The conditional covenant motif stresses the individual's contribution to his salvation. Even Christ's finished work could be spoken of as conditional:

> "Christ satisfied for you but on condition [*ea lege*] that you believe in him."

On the other hand, Cameron's view of faith tends to minimise the human contribution. Faith is not chiefly an act of the will, but a passive persuasion. The difficulty is at its most acute when it is borne in mind that Cameron conceived of God's recognition of faith in terms of a law-giver rewarding what his justice has no option but to reward. We have not found any record of Cameron having addressed the uncomfortable alliance of faith as covenant condition and faith as persuasion. However, in the course of expounding his system in which everything depends on faith, he did insist that faith is not a meritorious contribution to salvation.

> "It is faith, then, which renders the death of Christ effective, not from any dignity or merit in it, but because God willed that by it we should be united to Christ the head."

However, how this accepted and basic assertion of Reformed theology could coexist harmoniously with an atonement entirely conditioned upon faith, and a system of covenantal obligations and rewards arising directly from the moral character of God, was not explained.

These, then, were some of the difficult implications of Cameron's teaching, of which he himself was aware, even if, in the case of the third, only vaguely. Others would come to the fore when his teaching was amplified by Amyraut.

The Nature of God

Is Cameron's God thoroughly divided within himself? He wills the salvation of all, and of some only. He loves all people antecedently, but not consequently. He sent Christ to die for all, but makes no provision for the fruit of Christ's death to be applied to all. For Cameron, there was indeed a fundamental cleavage in God's works, some being constrained by his nature and others determined by his good pleasure. The atonement arises from the justice that is in God's very nature. His antecedent love for all people, his sending Christ for all, and his will for the salvation of all proceed from his goodness, by which he naturally desires the good of the creature.[51] On the other hand his granting faith to some, so that they may participate in the fruit of the atonement and be loved by his consequent love, proceeds from his absolute will, which is beyond human investigation.[52] Cameron vigorously asserted the existence of this undetermined will of God, for it was a defence against Pelagianism, a guarantee that in granting faith to someone, God is not moved by any consideration of justice, debt or merit. It was the ultimate bulwark of salvation by grace. However, this *beneplacitum* of God seems to have been used to fill gaps in Cameron's theology which might otherwise have been dangerous. His preference, and this is most obviously the case in his covenant teaching, was to work with the natural and predictable operations of God. It may be that the rise of Socinianism, building its denial of the need for atonement on a supposition of the absolute freedom of God, influenced Cameron in his construction of a theology dominated by the idea that God acts according to his nature.

The question of a Nominalist background to Cameron's thought has been raised by Armstrong.[53] He concludes that, although Nominalist theology gave prominence to God's covenantal dealing with mankind, the similarities between Cameron's thought and Nominalism are more apparent than real. It is worth adding to Armstrong's conclusion that there is a fundamental dissimilarity between Cameron and Nominalism, in that Nominalism was concerned with the absolute freedom of God. To the Nominalists, the covenant was a matter of voluntary condescension in which God placed limits, for the sake of mankind, on his absolute power, *potentia absoluta* becoming *potentia ordinata*. To Cameron, however, the covenants are an expression of the very nature of God, who cannot do other than reward those who observe certain intrinsically virtuous conditions.[54] In this connection he sometimes distinguished God's actions as law-giver, which proceed from his nature, pre-eminently his wisdom, justice and goodness, according to which he rewards and punishes, and as ruler, in which he can act according to his own unpredictable and incomprehensible good pleasure. Cameron's strong theological interest in the covenantal dealings between God and the world can be explained by reason of the fact that he saw these dealings as founded in and expressing the divine nature. To assert, as does Strehle, that Saumur's teaching on the extent of the atonement was dominated, as was all Protestant theology after Luther and Calvin, by Nominalist concepts, is, in our view, to miss the direction of the thought of Cameron and his followers.[55]

Cameron's place in the tradition

This chapter opened by pointing to the unconventional personality behind the theological originality. The devising of the three-covenant scheme, with its bold attempt to relate the Mosaic dispensation to the covenants of nature and grace in a more coherent way than Reformed theology had yet achieved, was his accomplishment. Samuel Bolton gave his judgement that no one had managed so successfully to avoid the twin errors of making the Mosaic law a version of the gospel, or of confusing with the law of nature a dispensation designed for man as a sinner. Cameron's work was,

> "The Key to the Gospel, and the best resolver that I have met with of all those intricate Controversies and Disputes Concerning the law."[56]

At a more fundamental level, Cameron deserves full credit for his grasp of the historical dimension of God's revelation and dealings with the human race. The covenant teaching of Heidelberg and Zurich, overlaid on a doctrine of static pretemporal predestination, had made some room for the historical dimension, but its sense of movement in history was limited by the view that the old (post fall) and new covenants were the same in substance and differed only in administration.

Cameron's thought, then, had a marked originality, but it should be said that Cameron's teaching on the extent of the atonement, the point at which he is so often regarded as having departed from the tradition, was not new. The same view was held by contemporaries such as Davenant and Martinius,[57] whose doctrine had been given some recognition in the Canons of Dort. It had previously been espoused by Bullinger, whose theme of the pre-eminence of the goodness of God Cameron also took up. Ursinus had dealt with the extent of the atonement in language almost identical to Cameron's, and Pareus, his colleague and successor at Heidelberg, had explained at length the sufficiency of the atonement for all, its efficacy for the elect, the conditionality attached to the universality of the atonement, and the gift of faith to the elect only. Cameron was a pupil of Pareus during his year at Heidelberg. As far as his teaching on the extent of the atonement is concerned, no further background need be sought. What does distinguish Cameron is his thoroughness in systematically relating the universality and conditionality of God's dealings with the human race to the divine nature, and the particularity of God's dealings to his inscrutable good pleasure.

Cameron's written works are not very extensive, partly because of his untimely death. It was left to Amyraut to expound and develop his teaching at greater length.

CONCLUSION

In his teaching on the extent of the atonement, the Scottish theologian followed the line already developed in the universal-conditional covenant tradition. He did this with great thoroughness, and with a consistent effort to root the universal and conditional elements in the nature of God, so tending to put the absolute, particular predestinating will of God into the background. In accepting and accenting the dualism of this already existing approach he abandoned the attempt to keep particular predestination and Christ together. Other Reformed theologians, unable to forget the biblical "chosen in Christ", had sensed that the gap in their theology between Christ and the decree of individual predestination was something they should attempt to bridge, and Dort produced a number of suggestions as to how this could be done. Cameron recognized the hopelessness of the task, and resigned himself to the existence of a chasm between the Christ who died for all, and the predestination which chose the few.

Chapter Eight

Notes

1 For biographical details see L.Cappel, "Icon", prefaced to Cameron's *Ta Sozomena sive Opera*, Frankfurt 1642; J. Quick, "Icones Sacrae Gallicanae" (MS in Dr.Williams's Library) vol.1 pt.1., pp.310-340; R.Wodrow, *Collections upon the Lives of the Reformers and Most Eminent Ministers of the Church of Scotland*, Glasgow 1848, vol.2 pt.2, pp.81-223; G.Bonet-Maury, "John Cameron: a Scottish Protestant Theologian in France", *SHR* 7(1910) pp.325-345; B.G.Armstrong, *Calvinism*, op.cit., pp.42-70.

2 Quick, op.cit., vol.l pt.1, pp.317-318,330. Quick explains that his negligence of "gait, habit and person" was imputed to "the incessant operations of his mind".

3 W.Rex, *Essays on Pierre Bayle and Religious Controversy*, The Hague 1965, pp.88-97; J.Moltmann, "Gnadenbund und Gnadenwahl: die Prädestinationslehre des Moyse Amyraut, dargestellt im Zusammenhang der heilsgeschichtlich-foederaltheologischen Tradition der Akademie von Saumur", Ph.D. Göttingen 1951, esp. pp.45-94 (summarized in Moltmann, "Prädestination und Heilsgeschichte bei Moyse Amyraut", *ZKG* 65(1954) pp.270-303; Armstrong, *Calvinism*, op.cit.; F.Laplanche, *Orthodoxie et Prédication: l'oeuvre d'Amyraut et la querelle de la grâce universelle*, Paris 1965; *L'Evidence du Dieu Chrétien: religion, culture et société dans l'apologétique protestante de la France classique (1576-1670)*, Strasbourg 1983; *L'Ecriture, Le Sacré et L'Histoire: érudits et politiques protestants devant la Bible en France au 17e. Siècle*, Amsterdam 1986, esp. pp.194-208; A.H.Swinne, *John Cameron, Philosoph und Theologe (1579-1625)*, Marburg 1968.

4 Pierre du Moulin coined the term "*Cameronisme*" early in the dispute. Swinne, op.cit., ch.2, traces the various terms employed to describe Cameron's teachings.

5 J.Owen (ed.J.I.Packer), *The Death of Death in the Death of Christ*, London 1959, editor's introduction, p.23. W. Cunningham identified Cameron as the first exponent of the particular election/universal atonement view, *Historical Theology* (2 vols.), Edinburgh 1862, vol.2 p.324. Charles Hodge saw it as a seventeenth-century introduction, associated chiefly with Amyraut, *Systematic Theology* (3 vols.), London 1872, vol.2, pp.321-322. B.B.Warfield, *Calvin and Calvinism*, New York 1931, p.363, refers to "the first important modification of the Calvinistic system...by the professors of the French school at Saumur". See Moltmann, "Gnadenbund", op.cit., pp.20-21. Moltmann's protest is endorsed by Laplanche, *L'Ecriture*, op.cit., p.17.

6 Armstrong, op.cit., pp.47-70; Moltmann, "Gnadenbund", op.cit., pp.23-94.

7 Moltmann observes that Cameron seems to occupy a position between Arminianism and "orthodoxy", op.cit., pp.29-30,81-82,93. Neuser, in Andresen, op.cit., p.238, says, "The school of Saumur developed a mediating theology for the reconciliation of Arminianism and orthodoxy". E. Léonard, *A History of Protestantism* (2 vols.), ed. H.H.Rowley, London 1965, vol.2 p.371, calls Amyraut and De la Place "representatives of moderate Arminianism".

8 *Amica Collatio de Gratia et Voluntatis Humanae Concursu in Vocatione*, in *Opera*, 612a-708b; 663b; 630a.

9 For Cameron's antipathy to Beza, see Quick, Icones, op.cit., p.335. Du Moulin called Cameron "Beza's Scourge", *De Mosis Amyraldi adversus Fridericum Spanhemium Libro Iudicium*, Rotterdam 1649, p.213. Armstrong, *Calvinism*, op.cit., pp.41-42,158-160, uses Cameron's criticisms of Beza to support his thesis that Saumur represented humanistic, as opposed to scholastic, Calvinism.

10 "De Ordine Decretorum Dei in Negotio Salutis Humanae I. Cameronis Sententia", in *Opera*, 529a-

529b, and *Myrothecium Evangelicum*, Geneva 1632, p.277 (on 1 Tim.2.4).

11 "Praelectiones de Ecclesia", in *Opera*, 207a-329b, in answer to the problem, "Why he gives repentance and faith to one rather than to another, since we are equal by nature", concludes, "It is for us to acquiesce in the will of God here" (212A).

12 "De Electionis et Oppositae Reprobationis Obiecto I. Cameronis Inchoata Tantum Disputatio", in *Opera*, 793a-796b. It is in this aspect of Cameron's predestination teaching that Moltmann has detected a middle way between the Reformed and Arminian positions, "Gnadenbund", op.cit., p.81.

13 See ante, p.143.

14 *Opera*, 642a, cp.361b.

15 Cameron's commitment to Ramism is not in doubt: André Rivet testified to his "addiction" to it since his Glasgow student days. See Armstrong, *Calvinism*, op.cit., pp.45-46, and Moltmann, "Gnadenbund", op.cit. pp.24-26. Ramism may have contributed a predilection for the "two wills" doctrine, but cannot be the origin of the two wills framework itself, since it is found, for example, in the pre-Ramist Calvin and the anti-Ramist Ursinus. For Ramism see H.Baker, *The Wars of Truth: studies in the decay of Christian humanism in the earlier seventeenth century*, London 1952, pp.98-110; J.Moltmann, "Zur Bedeutung des Petrus Ramus für Philosophie und Theologie in Calvinismus", *ZKG* 68(1957) pp.295-318; W.J.Ong, *Ramus: Method and the Decay of Dialogue. From the art of discourse to the art of reason*, Cambridge (Mass.) 1958, esp. pp.175-292; W. and M.Kneale, *The Development of Logic*, Oxford 1962, pp.300-306; Neuser, in Andresen, op.cit., pp.328-330; D.K.McKim, *Ramism in William Perkins' Theology*, New York 1987, pp.15-36.

16 Armstrong, *Calvinism*, op.cit., pp.188-195.

17 See ante, pp.54,93.

18 *Opera*, 693a.

19 *Myrothecium*, p.277, on 1 Tim.2.4.

20 *Opera*, 544a-551b.

21 Swinne, op.cit., pp.27-33; Laplanche, *L'Ecriture*, op.cit., pp.386-387.

22 In particular, an emphasis on the progressive nature of the covenants can be found outside the "Theses" (e.g. *Myrothecium*, pp.295,320-321,325-328).

23 Moltmann, *Gnadenbund*, op.cit., pp.32-94; Armstrong, *Calvinism*, op.cit., pp.47-56; Laplanche, *Orthodoxie*, pp.50-57; see also Strehle, *Calvinism*, op.cit., pp.198-205. Except where indicated, our exposition of Cameron's covenant teaching is based on the "De Triplici...Foedere Theses", in *Opera*, 544a-551b.

24 Ibid., th.80: "The covenant of nature is that by which God, by right of creation, requires perfect obedience from all mankind, promises a most blessed life in Paradise to those who render it, and threatens with eternal death those who withold it. This is in order that it may appear to all how virtue is attended by love and vice by hatred."

25 Ibid., th.81: "The old covenant is that by which God requires from the people of Israel obedience to the moral, ceremonial and civil law. To those who render it to him he promises all sorts of blessings in the possession of the land of Canaan, but threatens most severely with curses and death those who disparage it. Its purpose is to lead them to the coming Messiah."

26 Ibid., th.82: "The covenant of grace is that in which God promises, with the condition of faith in Christ proposed, forgiveness of sins in his blood and a heavenly life, in order to display the riches of his mercy". See *Opera*, 211a-212a, for the contrast between law and gospel.

27 *Institutes*, 2.10-11; Bullinger, *The One and Eternal Testament*, op.cit. For a presentation of a two covenant scheme contemporary with Cameron, see Johannes Wollebius (1586-1629), "Compendium Theologiae Christianae", 1.8,21, in J.W.Beardslee III, *Reformed Dogmatics*, New York 1965; Amandus

Polanus (1561-1610), *Partitiones*, one third of which is devoted to the covenant, as R.Letham points out in "Amandus Polanus", op.cit.

28 According to Strehle, *Calvinism*, op.cit., p.181, Bucanus (1602 *Institutes*) called the old covenant legal with respect to the Mosaic dispensation but gracious with regard to the promise to Abraham and his seed. Cameron's compatriot Robert Rollock's *A Treatise of God's Effectual Calling*, 1597/1603, in *Select Works of Robert Rollock*, ed.W.M.Gunn, Edinburgh 1849, vol.1, p.62, states that Moses wrote both legal and evangelical covenants, the former fully but the latter in its first outlines only. In a section appended to the same work, entitled, "Of the Means Whereby God from the Beginning Hath revealed Both His Covenants Unto Mankind", (pp.274-278) Rollock writes, "Q. How many ages, then, say you, are there of the Church? A. Three" These are explained to be from Adam to Moses, Moses to Christ and from Christ onwards. They differ in the measure and manner of revelation and in the fulness of the Holy Spirit, with a progressive increase of both." (p.281).

29 See A.J.Bandstra, "Law and Gospel in Calvin and Paul", in D.E.Holwerda (ed.) *Exploring the Heritage of John Calvin*, Grand Rapids 1976, pp.11-39, where Calvin's varied treatment of law and gospel, sometimes as opposed and sometimes as essentially one, is demonstrated. Similarly, I.J.Hesselink, "Law and Gospel or Gospel and Law", in R.V.Schnucker, op.cit., pp.13-32 shows that for Calvin law and gospel were to be both identified and distinguished.

30 "Certain Theses, or Positions of the Learned John Cameron, Concerning the Threefold Covenant of God with Man", appended to S.Bolton, *The True Bounds of Christian Freedom*, London 1645, Preface to "Certain Theses", no pagination.

31 "De Triplici...Foedere Theses", in *Opera*, 546a th.22; 544b th.8, 548b th.46, *Myrothecium*, p.330.

32 Armstrong, *Calvinism*, op.cit., pp. 55-56, followed by McGrath, *Iustitia Dei*, op.cit., vol.2 p.42.

33 *Opera*, 498a (cols. 498 a & b contain "Some explanations taken from what he [Cameron] said by word of mouth concerning the threefold covenant of God with mankind").

34 "De Triplici...Foedere Theses", in *Opera*, 544b th.8, 548b th.45.

35 Ibid., 544a th.5. Cp. "De Electionis...Obiecto Disputatio", *Opera*, 793b: "God's office towards man in this is twofold: as supreme and most just judge...he pronounces sentence from the law and the gospel..."

36 See ante, p.121 n.24.

37 *Opera*, 531b, in a letter to Louis Cappel, dated Dec. 1610. This is one of a series of letters of 1610-1612 to Cappel, answering questions about universal-particular grace, printed in *Opera*, 529-535b. They are reproduced in loose translation in R.Wodrow, op.cit., pp.94-105. Citations in this chapter are our own translation.

38 *Myrothecium*, p.277, on 1 Tim.2.4; "De Electionis...Obiecto... Disputatio", *Opera*, 794b.

39 Laplanche, *L'Ecriture*, op.cit., esp. pp.477-496 dealing with Amyraut's thought on the relationship between God's will, natural law, ethics, and politics. For the abundant use made of the concept of nature in France in the period immediately following Cameron's death see B. Tocanne, *L'Idée de Nature en France dans la Seconde Moitié du XVIe. Siècle*, Paris 1978. For the extent to which natural theology was given a place in Reformed theology see J.Platt, *Reformed Thought and Scholasticism: the arguments for the existence of God in Dutch theology 1575-1650*, Leiden 1982. Platt concludes that after an increased confidence on the part of Melanchthon and Ursinus in the ability of nature to yield truth about God, there was a renewed caution in this area among the Reformed. They reacted against the Arminians' positive view of the instruction of nature and consistently stressed the negative function of rendering all men inexcusable. Thus they would have been predisposed to be hostile to suggestions from Saumur of a more positive role for natural revelation. See esp. pp.177-241.

40 This section is based primarily on the "De Triplici...Foedere Theses", *Opera*, 544a-551b.

41 For Cameron on justification, and the controversy it caused at the National Synod, see Moltmann, *Gnadenbund*, op.cit., pp.65-75. For Baxter's "Neonomianism", and its similarities and connections with the Saumur teaching, see J.I.Packer, "The Redemption and Restoration of Man in the Thought of Richard Baxter: a study in puritan theology", D.Phil. Oxford 1954, pp.212-308. For Baxter's admiration of Cameron and Amyraut, see N.H.Keeble and G.F.Nuttall (eds.) *Calendar of the Correspondence of Richard Baxter* (2 vols.), Oxford 1991, vol.1 (1638-1660), pp.53,113 n.4,118,278. Baxter held to unconditional election and universal atonement, as did Cameron. See also A.C.Clifford, *Atonement*, op.cit.

42 *Amica Collatio*, in *Opera* 613a-615b. The correspondence is printed in *Opera*, 709a-712b.

43 The following exposition is based mainly on the "Argumenta In Disputatione Adversus Praecedentes Theses Proposita", in *Opera*, 355a-365b, relating to "Theses de Efficacia Gratiae Dei, et Usu Liberi Hominis Arbitrii in Negotio Salutis Humanae", in *Opera*, 331a-336b. See also 350a-352a.

44 For Grotius' theory, see Ritschl, op.cit., pp.309-314; Paul, op. cit, pp.115-116.

45 These letters are found in *Opera*, 529-535a. The following exposition, with citations, comes from them, except where indicated otherwise. They are analysed by Armstrong, *Calvinism*, op.cit., pp.56-59. The extent of the atonement is also dealt with in *Myrothecium*, pp.276-278 on 1 Tim.2.4-5, and in "Ad Questiones in Epistolam ad Hebreos illi Propositas, Responsiones", in *Opera*, 366a-415b, esp.389b-390a.

46 Cameron's most directly apologetic work was translated into English as *An Examination of Those Plausible Appearances which Seeme Most to Commend the Romish Church and to Prejudice the Reformed*, Oxford 1626. See Rex, op.cit., pp.8-22, who points out that Cameron was responsible for a new departure in commencing his argument in the realm of moral philosophy.

47 "Opinions" 2.4, in De Jong, op.cit., p.225: "Only those are obliged to believe that Christ died for them for whom Christ died. The reprobates, however, as they are called, for whom Christ has not died, are obligated to such a faith...In fact, if there should be such reprobates, they would be obliged to believe that Christ has not died for them". Perkins' subtle explanation was that God does not require everyone to believe that it is true that Christ died for him. Rather every man is to believe that it is true that God requires him to believe that Christ died for him. See Perkins, *Predestination*, op.cit., pp.102-105.

48 For the correlation in Reformed theology of limited atonement and faith as an act of the will, see Kendall, op.cit., pp.13-38.

49 "Praelectio de Ecclesia", *Opera*, 213a.

50 This section is based on the "Letters", in *Opera*, 529-535a, unless otherwise stated.

51 See, e.g. *Opera*, 363b, "God who loved us with his innate goodness and therefore was kindly disposed towards the wretched..."; 363a-363b,544a.

52 In "Praelectio de Ecclesia", *Opera*, 213a, the will of God in election and in justification are contrasted on the basis that the latter can be located by us in the nature of God, the former cannot: "It is not a merely free action with God to justify the believing and penitent...for there is a certain natural property in God, namely mercy, whose object is the one who...trusts the offered pardon. Clearly God is not able to deny the same."

53 Armstrong, *Calvinism*, op.cit., pp.51-52, accounts for Cameron's rigid distinction between *foedus hypotheticum* and *foedus absolutum* by reference to "his rigid adherence to the dichotomization so characteristic of Ramism", rather than to Nominalist influence. For Nominalism, see ante, pp.5-6,p.9 n.11. Nominalist theology traced God's dealings with mankind to the divine will considered as distinct from the divine nature. McGrath, *Intellectual Origins*, op.cit., pp.69-85, points to two characteristic elements in the thought of the (Nominalist) *Via Moderna*, the two powers of God, and voluntarism. The distinction of ordained and absolute powers of God was designed to maintain that God deals

with the world in a reliable manner *(potentia ordinata)* but not of necessity (*potentia absoluta*) i.e. he wills to act constantly, or covenantally, in certain matters but his will is not determined by his nature.

54 Moltmann has observed that Cameron's rejection of the absolute freedom of God for a position in which God's dealings with mankind are constrained by his nature was "Cameron's first distancing from the orthodox tradition". "Gnadenbund", op.cit., p.34, and see ibid., pp.32-34.

55 Armstrong, *Calvinism*, op.cit., p.52, rightly points out that, while Cameron distinguished absolute and conditional covenants, "the *foedus absolutum* does not seem to be of importance or use in his covenant teaching", but he does not place great emphasis on the significance of this observation, or trace the crucial connection with the nature of God. Strehle's analysis of the Saumur theology is found in "The Extent", op.cit. pp.250-271.

56 Bolton, op.cit., preface to "The Threefold Covenant" no pagination.

57 Moltmann, "Gnadenbund", op.cit., pp.200-202, associates the Saumur school with the German Reformed tradition, with which he also connects the English deputies at Dort, Davenant, Ward and Hall. There was a Protestant conditional covenant tradition in England going back as far as William Tyndale. See Møller, op.cit.; W.A.Clebsch, *England's Earliest Protestants 1520-1535*, New Haven 1964, pp.181-204; R.L.Greaves, "The Origin and Early Development of English Covenant Theology", *The Historian* 31(1968) pp.21-35; M.McGiffert, "William Tyndale's Conception of Covenant", *JEH* 32(1981)2 pp.167-184, and "Grace and Works: the rise and division of covenant divinity in Elizabethan puritanism", *HTR* 75(1982)4 pp.463-502, and "From Moses to Adam: the making of the covenant of works", *SCJ* 19(1988)2 pp.131-155; Strehle, *Calvinism*, op.cit., pp.323-328; Stoute, op.cit. pp.163-189. It was prominent in Dudley Fenner's *Sacra Theologia* (1585), which Cameron is likely to have known. The conditional covenant was represented in Scotland by another work with which Cameron is likely to have been familiar, R.Rollock's *De Vocatione Efficaci* (1597), which stated that,"all the word of God appertains to some covenant" and that "the covenant of God generally is a promise under some one certain condition", (*Works*, op.cit., vol.1 pp.33-34).

Chapter Nine

Moïse Amyraut (1596–1664)

INTRODUCTION

Just under a century after Calvin first published his *Institutes*, Moïse Amyraut,[1] professor of theology at the Academy of Saumur, issued a short work on predestination which initiated a major controversy. An extensive and often acrimonious literature was provoked, schism in the French Reformed Church seemed imminent several times, and severe strains were caused throughout international Calvinism.

Little information about Amyraut's early life is available. It is known that he finished studying law at Poitiers in 1616, and took up theological studies at Saumur probably in 1618. Significantly this was the same year John Cameron began teaching there. In 1626 Amyraut became minister at Saumur, a post he combined with lecturing at the Academy. From 1640 until his death he was its principal. Throughout his career Amyraut commanded widespread respect. A token of the esteem in which he was held by the Reformed as early as 1631 was his appointment by the National Synod of Charenton to wait upon the King on its behalf that year. He also had friends among the Catholic nobility, and was once approached, unsuccessfully, by an emissary of Cardinal Richelieu, with a view to making an alliance between the Reformed Church and French Catholicism. During Amyraut's time at Saumur the Academy was the best attended in France, and it is reckoned that most of the ministers in France were adherents of the Saumur theology by the time he died. His many works give evidence of concern to resist reunion with Roman Catholicism and promote union with the Lutherans, to stress the importance of the Protestant doctrine of justification, to uphold royal rule and oppose ecclesiastical independency (especially in view of events in England), to demonstrate the reasonableness of Christianity over against scepticism, and to supply the public with sermonic and devotional material. Running throughout, and often dominating, his work was his distinctive view of universal and particular grace.

Following François Laplanche, it is helpful to divide the dispute into three stages.[2] The first followed Amyraut's publication in 1634 of the *Brief Traitté de la*

Prédestination.[3] This led to his examination at the National Synod of Alençon (1637), with the result that he was pronounced orthodox, but warned to desist from using certain expressions that were causing offence.[4]

Open controversy subsided until Amyraut heard of and objected to theses being disputed under Friedrich Spanheim at Leiden in 1644, and which Amyraut regarded as an attack upon himself. He answered Spanheim, thereby entering a second period of conflict, leading to debate at the National Synod of Charenton (1644-5). It was decided that neither side should continue the controversy, and Amyraut was dismissed honourably to his post.[5] His colleague at Saumur, Josué de la Place did not fare so well, as his doctrine that Adam's sin is imputed to the human race by means of inherited corruption only, rather than directly, was condemned.[6] The Synod did not satisfy the "orthodox", who then put their hopes in what turned out to be an enormous work by Spanheim, the *Exercitationes de Gratia Universali,*which provoked a further round of literary warfare. This was brought to an end only by the intervention of the Protestant Prince de Tarente, who gathered Amyraut and some of the principal combatants, and persuaded them to sign on 16 October 1649 the "Acte de Thouars". A striking illustration of the status of the nobility in the French Reformed movement is afforded by this incident, in which bitter opponents, long convinced that their adversaries were shaking the very foundations of the faith, took only two days to agree to promote peace, with the understanding that any further complaints would be referred directly to the Prince.

The third period (1649-64) saw the refusal of the provincial Synod of Bas-Languedoc to accept for the ministry adherents to Amyraut's views. However, the tide was turning decisively in Saumur's favour, helped by major publications by the influential David Blondel and Jean Daillé.[7] The fact that Amyraut was cleared of all blame, this time without any restrictions being imposed, at the National Synod of Loudun (1659),[8] is an indication of the extent to which his views had gained acceptance. Outside France, however, opposition remained strong, and later the anti-Amyraldian position won a decisive, though short-lived, victory in the Swiss *Formula Consensus* of 1675.

Throughout the long debates, the issue was the extent of the grace of God, resolved chiefly into the questions, whether Christ died for all, and whether all have, through natural revelation, a call to repentance sufficient to lead them to salvation, should they be inclined to heed it.[9] Reformed consideration of the extent of the atonement had led to a variety of positions in the sixteenth century. At the beginning of the seventeenth the Synod of Dort had failed to clarify the doctrine, and throughout the Amyraldian debates both sides professed their loyalty to Dort. In fact, the impetus to compromise at Dort had resulted in canons which were eclectic and inconsistent at this point, not merely leaving room for further investigation, but positively demanding it.

Apart from the brief account just given, it is not intended to provide a sequential study of the Amyraldian controversy. This has been done well by Laplanche, and more recently by Van Stam, who has supplemented Laplanche's contribution by extensive research into unpublished correspondence. It is generally agreed that little, if any, significant theological development occurred during the disputes, both sides engaging in endless repetition, without fruitful interaction. For an introduction to Amyraut's theology, Brian Armstrong's outstanding work, the standard treatment in English, may be consulted.[10] The following analysis of Amyraut's theology is intended specifically to give an understanding of the frame of thought in which his uncompromising defence of universal atonement was set.

AMYRAUT'S THEOLOGY

It is difficult to dissent from Moltmann's judgement that Amyraut's theology is an "*absolut treue Kopie*" of Cameron's.[11] Amyraut himself often made that claim, and his works are peppered with admiring references to his master.[12] Indeed, another disciple of Cameron, Paul Testard, pastor at Blois, went into print before Amyraut on the theme of "hypothetical universalism", setting out almost exactly the same views, and was examined with him at the Synod of Alençon.[13] Amyraut lived longer than Cameron, and controversy forced him to express himself at greater length and in fuller detail than Cameron had, so his writings provide a more complete version than those of his mentor of what may be regarded as the Saumur theology. The pattern of the previous chapter will be followed and the unity of Cameron's and Amyraut's thought will be apparent.

Predestination

The *Brief Traitté de la Prédestination* was written in French as a simple and apologetic treatment of its theme. Nevertheless, comparison with other presentations of predestination by Amyraut shows that it may safely be taken as representative of his views, and so forms the basis of this section.

Predestination is introduced as a necessary outworking of God's goodness, which could not allow him to create the human race as "the chief work of his hand" without exercising his care over what would become of it. From the first, God aimed at the perfection of human beings, as rational creatures made in his own image, with the purpose of intelligently and voluntarily glorifying him. Amyraut began his exposition, then, in terms of the end God has in view for the human race, rather than with reference to "certain persons" or with causal decrees.

However, the intervention of sin

> "seems to have changed not only the whole face of the universe, but even the whole design of his first creation and, if one ought to say so, induced God to make new plans [*prendre de nouveaux conseils*]".[14]

In fact God's ultimate ends did not change, but new steps had to be taken in order to lead humanity to its original goal, and, indeed, to take it beyond original, natural holiness and happiness to a supernatural condition.[15] The *Traitté* continues that Scripture does not attribute the fall to God, and it is impossible to explain why God permitted it, but that we must remember God cannot be other than just, and should take account of the fact that his purpose in sending his Son into the world was to counter the effects of the fall. Foreseeing it, God from eternity had ordained Christ to restore the human race. Amyraut's explanation is clearly infralapsarian, in that the fall is not viewed as a pre-ordained means for fulfilling God's purpose. However, in that God's pre-fall aim in creation with respect to mankind as a whole continues to be pursued, albeit by new means, it shares the supralapsarian insight that the fall did not change God's ultimate purpose. Amyraut had, however, no sympathy for the usual supralapsarian placement of the election of individuals.[16]

Christ's ordination and mission had respect to all people, as did the original predestination, but his saving work requires faith as the condition upon which it is applied. Foreseeing that fallen human beings would be unable to fulfil this condition, God chose to enable some to fulfil it. Thus, a double election emerges, a conditional election of all to salvation and an absolute election of some to faith.[17] Amyraut conceded that the Bible uses the terms "election" and "predestination" of the latter only, because, he explained, it alone is effective.

> "Predestination to salvation being conditional, and having regard to the whole human race conditionally, and the human race being universally corrupted by sin and incapable of accomplishing this condition upon which salvation depends, it happens necessarily, not through any fault in predestination itself, but through the hardness of the heart...that this first predestination is in vain for those who do not have a part in the second."[18]

The "conditional predestination" terminology caused great offence and it was one of the ways of speaking Amyraut was forbidden to use by the Alençon Synod.

Amyraut had, in fact, extended the infralapsarian principle of allowing historical events (the creation and fall) logically to precede the decree of particular election. He went further in making the work of Christ, and human failure to believe in him, also precede that decree:

> "Such is the nature of man that if, in ordaining to send his Son into the world, God had not made further plans...both the sending and the suffering of his Son would have been useless to the human race."

In other words, Amyraut made particular election relate to the giving of faith, through the Spirit, and to nothing else whatsoever:

> "The force of election relates to...the creation of faith in us."

He believed that this presentation of election acquitted God of favouritism and of being the author of sin.[19]

Using Aristotelian categories of causality, Reformed thought viewed all historical events as means preordained by God for the accomplishment of certain ends. Somewhat reluctantly, but under pressure to absolve God from the charge of causing sin, infralapsarians attempted to present the fall as somehow exempt from this tight causal system, thus introducing one moment of genuine historical interaction between God and humanity. Amyraut sought to make room for extensive interaction between God and every individual in history, by making the decree of individual election and reprobation enter in only at the point of every person's failure to respond to God's call. Amyraut modelled the order of the decrees upon the order of history.[20] Whereas for the orthodox God triumphs by causing history, for Amyraut God triumphs in and in spite of history: God perseveres through every instance of human rejection, producing at the last moment the trump card of effectual calling.

> "Particular grace, when added to the common, will have such mighty strength, that there will be nothing in human corruption, nothing in the devil, nothing in the lure of sin, nothing, finally, in the devices of the world, whatever they may be, over which it will not triumph magnificently."[21]

Essential to Amyraut's order was the separation of predestination from Christ. He could, and occasionally did, use the "in Christ" terminology in connection with the conditional decree:

> "It was not therefore in vain when God destined salvation in Christ for all."

With respect to particular election, Amyraut expounded the Pauline "chosen in Christ" as "chosen...in order to be led to Christ", and claimed that *en auto* here was equivalent to *eis auton*,[22] so following through his decision to make the ordination of Christ logically prior to particular election. This was the best he could do in attempting to relate absolute predestination to Christ. In a system designed to enable the work of Christ to stand complete and valid without any reference to particular election, the connection between such election and the person and work of Christ could not have fundamental significance. The non-necessity of Christ's shedding light on particular predestination, or predestination on Christ, was basic to Amyraut's thought, and accounts for the fact that throughout his long treatments of the theme he hardly ever touches on the "chosen in Christ" motif. To him, absolute predestination was not in any sense the gospel. Predestination related entirely to the work of the Spirit in effectual calling and not to the redemptive work of Christ or its proclamation.

The Will of God

The "Theses Theologicae de Voluntate Dei"[23] provide a starting point for an exploration of Amyraut's teaching on the will of God. These theses, defended by J. Ricoltier in 1657, with Amyraut presiding, would have been drawn up by Amyraut and based on his lectures. The twofold division of the will of God is considered successively as revealed and hidden, of sign and of good pleasure, commanding and decreeing, ineffective and effective, conditional and absolute.

The "Theses" are directed against the Arminian rejection of the traditional Reformed division of the will of God in which, as the Arminians saw it, the revealed will was contradicted and nullified by the hidden.[24] Amyraut did not follow the Arminian abandonment of the concept of hidden will, but nor did he follow the lead given by other Reformed thinkers and attempt to resolve the dichotomy by showing that the revealed will really serves to advance the hidden. Rather, he aimed to give the revealed will a valid, independent content.

An example of Amyraut's insistence on the reality of the revealed will is his statement that the *voluntas signi* is not merely an external command or promise, but truly "signifies" something in God. He also used the word *serio*, taken over from the Arminians by the divines at Dort, in connection with the revealed will:

> "It is called voluntas signi not because it consists in a mere sign, with nothing existing in God to which the sign corresponds. For a sign clearly is a sign of something, and it is not credible that God signifies that he wills what he does not will."

> "It is true that God by nature vehemently delights in the fulfilment of those things he commands."

The "Theses" seem close to a breakthrough when they observe that in Scripture the good pleasure (*eudokia*) of God refers to

> "the things in which God delights, because there is some quality or condition in them that agrees with the nature of God",

and cites the description of Christ as *ho agapetos, en ho eudokesa* (Matthew 3.17). However, they return to the traditional scholastic use of the term in claiming that usually in Scripture it refers to the inscrutable decrees.

> "Eudokia is used of the decrees, or, so to speak, wishes, of God, concerning which no other explanation can be given, except that so it pleased God."

Although in human covenants, testaments and promises it is not invariably necessary for conditions to be stipulated,

> "In the covenants God has contracted with men, Natural, Legal and Evangelical, matters are otherwise."[25]

The conditions have their basis in the moral character of God. To have omitted them would have been to have violated his own majesty. Accordingly, Amyraut maintained elsewhere that God's will is conditional in itself, rather than merely a will to impose conditions. The freedom of God's absolute will is beyond doubt. Although the revealed will of God is determined by God's moral qualities, Amyraut says there is no threat to God's freedom, which resides chiefly in the absence of external constraint upon his will:

> "The conditional [will] is necessary, because...he was unable not to require this or that condition from the creature....Those who think otherwise seem not to have understood liberty, or the nature of God, and how necessarily, and at the same time freely, he is good."[26]

Throughout Amyraut's work much hinges on the conditionality of God's will for human salvation. God wills the salvation of all conditionally *(ea conditione, ea lege)* if (*si, modo*) they believe.

> "Since all theologians concede that evangelical promises have a perpetual condition attached, a condition, moreover, required from each and all...when therefore a promise is nothing other than a speech through which we declare our will with respect to some future good which we have bound ourselves to accomplish, we ask how God can promise conditionally and universally if he does not have a conditional or universal will?"[27]

Whether God's wanting all to be saved if they believe implies that he wants all to believe is a difficult point for Amyraut. To say so would amount to an admission that God's will fails to be accomplished, and Amyraut usually holds back from expressing himself so starkly, preferring to refer back to the condition: if they believe he wills their salvation, if they do not believe he does not will it. Either way, God's will is not frustrated. This position left him open to the charge that he might as well say that, according to his conditional will, God does not want anyone to be saved, because he knows that no-one will fulfil the condition. The fact is that Amyraut's main concern was to teach that God's goodness implies a divine willingness for all to have the possibility of salvation.[28]

In connection with God's conditional will is his "marvellous philanthropy". It is necessary to go beyond the "Theses" to investigate this theme. To Amyraut, philanthropy meant a love, universal by definition, for human beings as human beings. It was from this universal philanthropy that the sending of Christ, and his work of atonement, proceeded, so that, irrespective of the human response or lack of it, the goodness of God is revealed.

> "There are two affections in God concerned with procuring salvation for man: one is common because it embraces men as men, and therefore pertains to all indifferently. The other is particular...out of God's mere good pleasure."

> "God, impelled by his philanthropy and mercy to the human race, decreed from eternity to send his Son into the world. Having offered satisfaction for sins, he acquired forgiveness of sins and eternal salvation for all with this condition [*ea lege*], if they embrace him by faith..."[29]

Another reason why God's universal saving will is never in vain is that, even though it may not be universally fruitful, yet his goodness and mercy is universally revealed. Whatever the human response, God has acted in accordance with his nature.[30]

None of this was designed to cast doubt on the fact that there is also an absolute will, or special love, which decrees the salvation of a certain number, and is infallibly effective. There was a strong dualism, then, but the absolute will was kept in the background, and occupied a secondary place in the whole scheme, in that it was only brought in to deal with human unwillingness to appropriate salvation. Its function was to supplement a system perfectly self-contained and adequate for salvation, except that it did not take account of human inability to fulfil its conditions. While it is true that Amyraut sometimes said that the absolute will and love are supreme, the whole drift of his theology suggests that this should not be taken as a simple comparison between the two sorts of love and will. Rather the absolute is understood as containing the conditional, and going one step beyond it, but not in any sense moving it from the centre of God's dealings with the world.

Covenant[32]

The "Theses de Tribus Foederibus Divinis" were defended by J. la Rue in 1639, and commenced with a statement revealing the centre of Amyraut's theology:

> "It is necessary that all true religion should consist of some covenant which comes between God and men."[32]

These "Theses", although noting that Scripture does sometimes use the word "covenant" to refer to an unconditional promise of God, do not pursue that option, but turn immediately to Cameron's three conditional covenants of nature, law and grace. Amyraut denied the possibility of earning a reward by merit, even under the covenant of nature, but taught that the goodness of God, pleased with the moral perfection of the creature, would have granted a reward. In the legal covenant made with Israel, as in the natural covenant with all people, God acted as legislator, requiring the same conditions of natural morality, but with ceremonial duties added. The legal covenant is subservient to the evangelical, being intended to lead to Christ.

Unlike the law, the evangelical covenant serves not to reveal the vindicatory justice of God, but his mercy, and, unlike both predecessors, its promise does not depend upon moral perfection. It rests upon the work of the Mediator, but it does have a moral condition, namely faith, which may be considered as a duty:

> "The evangelical duty is placed in the one condition of faith."[33]

Amyraut drew on jurisprudence to establish that "a condition...is a law attached to a matter on which its outcome depends." He granted that the gospel covenant may be considered as absolute, but only once the condition has been fulfilled.[34] The fulfilment of the condition is made possible by the work of the Spirit in the elect. This greater work of the Spirit in connection with the new covenant is in proportion to the increasing clarity of the revelation of God's character, two features marking the superiority of the new covenant to the previous dispensations. However, it is distinctive of Amyraut's thought that, although the election by which the Spirit's activity is directed ensures the success of the covenant, particular election is not to be considered as part of the covenant of grace, which is universal:

> "Natural human blindness...is overcome by the election of God, which is outside the ambit of the covenant of grace."

Amyraut made it plain that the covenant is universal:

> "The covenant of saving grace was...made in Adam with each and every one...on condition of faith, so that if each and every one would believe, he would be made possessor of salvation granted by Christ."[35]

He frequently based the covenant on the universal philanthropy of God.[36]

Amyraut maintained the historical sequence of the three covenants, with gradually increasing revelation leading up to the full manifestation of the most excellent covenant of grace. However, he recognized some overlapping in what are, strictly speaking, entirely separate dispensations. Both law and gospel presuppose nature, in terms of the original ideal of communion between mankind and God, and the moral law. Traces of the gospel appear under both nature and law, in that the rudiments of the gospel were made known immediately upon the first sin, and were progressively clarified with the passing of time. Amyraut recognized his own continuity, in spite of appearances, with the Reformed tradition, which stressed the unity of the old and new covenants:

> "It should not seem strange if men of outstanding doctrine and piety teach that the legal and evangelical covenants are the same in essence."[37]

For, he explained, the tradition had highlighted the existence of evangelical promises under the law. In this it was showing a valid insight. However, "speaking strictly and accurately" there are three distinct covenants - of nature, law and gospel It was clearly because of his more historical approach that such a division seemed more accurate to Amyraut.

The "Theses" state that,

> "The gospel is not, strictly speaking, a law."[38]

This is because those who fail to fulfil its conditions are condemned by the justice revealed in the covenants of nature and law, rather than by anything distinctive to the evangelical covenant, the essence of which is mercy. It must be said, however, that its resemblance to a law, in having a condition, the fulfilment of which is a duty, is, hard to miss. Elsewhere, Amyraut said that God acts as legislator in the covenant of grace in so far as he requires faith. He made it clear that in all three covenants, God acts as legislator, in contrast to election in which he works as Father, a distinction he based on Calvin:

> "In illumining all by exterior preaching he performs the office of legislator, and so calls all men to life; at the same time he shows himself as Father only to his elect, regenerating them by his Spirit."[39]

The covenantal framework is, therefore, a legal one, and basic to it is a system of reward and punishment in response to morally pleasing or displeasing human endeavour. So, after stating that God cannot but show mercy to the penitent, Amyraut stated that the same principle of punishment and reward is operative in all three covenants:

> "The whole dispensation of God towards his creature, in that which concerns punishments and rewards, life and death, depends entirely on the covenants God has contracted with it."

The evangelical covenant imposes a "*lex credendi*" upon all who hear, a "law" which, although much easier than the conditions of the other two covenants, is still beyond the ability of fallen humanity. Consistent with this legal framework is the description of Christ as,

> "The Mediator of the covenant of grace, the legislator established by God to give his church its constitution and laws."[40]

Because the conditions of all three covenants correspond to qualities in the character of God, the promises are tied to the exercise of some human moral quality: perfect holiness, obedience to the commands of the law, or faith. This supposition of a legal framework and moral basis of even the evangelical covenant gives a rather hollow ring to Amyraut's caveat[41] that God does not want the evangelical covenant to rest on faith in its character as a moral virtue, but as an instrument.

In this connection it should be noted that, although the evangelical covenant is supreme, various concepts revolving around "nature" are very important to Amyraut, as signalled by his adherence to the term "covenant of nature" when "covenant of works" had become the more usual designation.[42] Nature lays the foundation for the evangelical covenant in several respects. One is that the pattern of condition and reward set in the covenant of nature is reproduced in the covenant of grace.[43] Another is that evangelical conversion results in the implementation of natural standards of morality in personal behaviour and social responsibilities.[44] Furthermore, Amyraut stressed that in conversion God works according to human faculties as originally constituted under the covenant of nature: "natural", though not "moral", ability remains.[45] Daringly, Amyraut also took up Cameron's "darker grace of Christ" and taught that the works of nature proclaim God's willingness to show mercy to the repentant sinner, and are objectively adequate to engender saving faith. This last point caused as much offence to the orthodox as his assertion of universal atonement.[46]

It is not possible to do justice here to the theme of nature in Amyraut, but only to point out its significance for the present work. The concept of nature implied orderliness and predictability, and the existence of a stable basis for rational thought.[47] Furthermore, Amyraut saw the natural order as an expression of the moral and comprehensible nature of God. The whole concept of "nature" in Amyraut signals therefore a determined preference for a theology worked out on the basis of God's predictable moral attributes to one constructed on the dictates of an unfettered divine will. We may venture to suggest that "nature" in Amyraut has a function parallel to that of "cause" in Beza as a means of understanding God's dealings with the world, with Amyraldian theology resting primarily upon the recognizable attributes of God, as that of Beza had rested on God's secret will.

One way in which Amyraut developed Cameron's covenant theology with some originality was in relating its successive phases to the persons of the Trinity, as set out in his *De Oeconomia Trium Personarum in Operibus Divinis Dissertatio* (1648) and *De Mysterio Trinitatis* (1661).[48] The latter work commences with a traditional, indeed scholastic, treatment of the unity and infinity of God, even including a discussion about the space occupied by angels.[49] It then breaks new ground in relating the progressive revelation of the Trinity to the three covenants identified by the Saumur school. The covenants of nature and law pertain chiefly to the Father as creator, judge and law-giver. The covenant of grace relates to the Son, who is its mediator, and the application of the covenant of grace belongs to the Spirit. This co-ordination of the Trinity with covenantal salvation history underlines the importance of the covenant motif to Amyraut's theology, and highlights its historical orientation. It also shows that the Spirit is more directly related than Christ to predestination in Amyraut's thought.

Conversion

Cameron's explanation of conversion as a persuasion of the mind by the word and Spirit, which in turn inevitably moves the will, was espoused by Amyraut. Faculty psychology held great interest for Amyraut, and he defended his position not only by theological considerations, but by abundant reference to the philosophers, and especially to Aristotle's *Ethics*. While holding to the corruption of the human will by original sin, Amyraut was anxious to stress that human faculties have not been destroyed.[50] So he followed Cameron's distinction between lost "moral" or "ethical", as opposed to remaining "natural" or "physical", ability. In conversion, the Spirit works according to the natural process of human psychology. Rightly constituted human nature invariably seeks the true and good. Sin, especially by means of the distorting influence of the passions upon the understanding, prevents people from seeing the truth that would lead them to the good. The Holy Spirit, however, removes the blindness, by bringing such a strong illumination and persuasion of the truth and goodness of the object (Christ) that the will cannot but embrace it.[51]

Amyraut's doctrine of faith as primarily an intellectual persuasion of an objective truth was significant for his understanding of the extent of the atonement. Such a persuasion, he contended, could only arise from the knowledge that Christ had died for all, and therefore for me.[52]

The Nature of God

Cameron's method of bringing the known and predictable nature of God to the fore, relegating God's absolute freedom to a secondary position, is reproduced in a much fuller way in Amyraut's writings. God's will is understood to operate in strict subordination to his character. The following statement is typical:

> "And if God be naturally inclin'd to provide for the happiness of man, because he is his Creator, he is likewise naturally inclin'd to execute vengeance upon his sin."[53]

The moral attributes of God - his wisdom, justice and goodness - receive frequent attention. God's goodness is undoubtedly his supreme characteristic[54] for Amyraut:

> "God's goodness is that which loves the perfect holiness of the creature and cannot but love it. It is a quality related to the condition of the creature. Thus God loved Adam in Paradise, and wished him to remain in that state...But there is in God a certain merciful goodness, exceeding ordinary goodness, in which he reveals that he loves the sinner if he repents, and does not love him if he does not. God is unable not to love the repentant sinner."[55]

The mission of Christ flowed from this higher level of goodness, or philanthropy. He interpreted John 3.16 in this way.[56]

Amyraut also spoke of two levels of mercy in God, one conditional and the other absolute:

> "Regarding these two degrees or sorts of mercy [the exercise of one is totally free]...The other is very different...He is his own law to himself. He cannot but love the good and hate the evil...So if the creature is good and holy he is unable not to love it...because he is infinitely good."

Likewise, he continued, if the creature is sinful God must hate it. But if it has recourse to his mercy,

> "he is unable not to have compassion on it".

It is on this conditional mercy, essential to the nature of God, that the evangelical covenant rests.

At one level, mercy is very close to justice in its operation. Whereas Reformed theology usually regarded the exercise of vindicatory justice as being a necessity to God, with the exercise of mercy being discretionary, Amyraut saw both as acting under a necessity of the divine nature:

> "For justice truly demanded a penalty, for we have already decided that it is unable not to exercise itself wherever there is sin. Mercy likewise...if people should repent of sin, was inclined to pardon it."[57]

Mercy operates in the evangelical covenant in the same way that justice does in the other two, namely by responding to some human moral exercise, the difference being that justice looks for perfection, while mercy requires only faith.[58] The proviso must be made that the reward of the evangelical covenant was made possible through the sacrifice of Christ. Though Amyraut repeated the accepted position that God was under no necessity to provide a saviour, he must have been thinking of the absence of external constraint. Otherwise it would be difficult to reconcile that statement with his view that God is under necessity to show mercy to the penitent,[59] since, for Amyraut, satisfaction for sin is absolutely essential to salvation.

Amyraut was aware of the way he was developing the tradition. In answering the criticisms of Spanheim he stated that it is possible to divide God's attributes into those dependent and those not dependent on a quality or condition in the creature. God's goodness in creation is an example of the latter, and his goodness in promising rewards to Adam if he should persevere in integrity represents the former. Acknowledging the disagreements among theologians, as to whether sin in the creature obliges God to punish, Amyraut aligned himself with those who asserted that necessity. Next he pointed out that the orthodox disagreed over whether God's mercy can be regarded in the same way. They all maintained a certain absolute mercy, over against the Arminians, but Amyraut stated that it was an undecided question whether

> "there is indeed in God a mercy whose use is necessarily determined to a certain quality, namely faith and penitence, to such an extent that according to it he cannot forgive sin except where that condition is present, and is unable not to forgive sin wherever that condition exists...I certainly have always been of the opinion that there is..."[60]

The same method of proceeding upon the basis of the attributes of God is found in Amyraut's ethical teaching, where he is sure that God's own nature obliges him to make and enforce certain laws.[61]

Amyraut did not dismiss the awesome and unfathomable freedom of God, but assigned it a place in the realm of predestination: no-one can give any reason for the rejection of one person and election of another other than the inscrutable good pleasure of God. Within the Reformed system, where predestination answers the question about why some believe and others do not, in a way that does not give any credit to human beings, there was no option but to refer to an inscrutable divine freedom. Without rendering it redundant, Amyraut removed predestination to the background and concentrated attention on the comprehensible, predictable, covenantal dealings of God with the world. For, he explained, it is the conditional will which

> "may be elicited from the properties of God, such as his goodness".[62]

In view of Amyraut's preference for starting with the nature rather than the omnipotent will of God, it is surprising to find that, in the excellent studies of Amyraldian theology by Laplanche and Armstrong, the formative influence of Amyraut's view of the divine nature is hardly emphasized. Even Moltmann only begins to explore its significance. Yet the firmness of Amyraut's defence of universal atonement cannot be properly understood without fully appreciating that, to him, it stood or fell with the very nature of God.[63]

The Nature and Extent of the Atonement

Amyraut took for granted the concept of satisfaction, viewing punishment of the sinner, or satisfaction on the sinner's behalf, as absolutely necessary in view of the divine justice. He stated that penal language about the atonement is more strictly accurate than the language of debt, for debts can be simply cancelled, but God is bound by his justice to exact punishment for sin. Echoing Cameron, he said that for God to do otherwise would be contrary to his nature and to his position as supreme judge, for sin is to be compared not to a private, but a public injury. God must act according to the eternal rules of his justice. The Nominalist "*acceptilatio*" therefore had no place. Amyraut frequently repeated the argument that an infinite satisfaction was required, and that this could only be provided by an infinite, that is, divine person, namely Christ. The humanity of Christ was also necessary to constitute him a suitable representative for the human race.[64]

It is appropriate to observe that Amyraut shared Cameron's apologetic concern. Of particular relevance is the fact that his *Brief Traitté* was written with an apologetic purpose. It was designed to help a nobleman who had embraced the Reformed faith, but was in danger of going back to Roman Catholicism because of a horror of the predestination doctrine.[65] Catholic polemic had no difficulty in caricaturing the Reformed doctrine as presenting a God who is a cruel and arbitrary tyrant, who created human beings in order to damn them, and who condemns without respect to sin and saves without regard to righteousness.[66] The *Traitté* shows that Amyraut was sensitive to the offence caused to Catholics who were genuinely trying to understand the Reformed position. He scarcely disguised his regret that Beza's supralapsarianism in particular was bound to distress the sensitive as well as provide ammunition to the hostile.[67] To him, the limitation of the extent of the atonement was a liability in the endeavour to make and keep Catholic converts.

Combined with his sensitive apologetic was the concern of the pastor and preacher. How could people believe unless they were persuaded that the atonement was, albeit conditionally, for them?

> "It is necessary that the mind...in order to perform the first act of faith, should judge that object to be universal by divine institution."

If the object of faith were not suitable to all, faith could not be commanded to all. The preacher, therefore, should declare the universal love of God and atonement of Christ, not mentioning election until after his hearers have come to faith.

> "For then we do not think of election, nor do we want anything about election to come into the minds of our hearers...We just want this: It is God's fixed and immutable will, and founded in the nature of the thing itself, that believers will have salvation."[68]

The fact that Amyraut's theology led to such artificiality must cast serious doubt upon it, but the pastoral concern that lay at its heart cannot be questioned.

In addition to meeting apologetic, pastoral and homiletic concerns, universal atonement fitted into the rest of the Amyraldian system. The examination of that system in the preceding pages has made it possible to show that his atonement teaching was integral to the rest of his theology. It was a necessary ingredient of the universal, conditional covenant, and expression of the universal, conditional, saving will and philanthropy of God:

> "Christ, by the will of the Father, and by his own philanthropy and charity to the human race, died for all, provided they believe."

> "Christ obtained salvation for all in order to confer it actually upon all equally if they believe. From that it is denied however that God, in the redemption made through Christ, had such a conditional end before his eyes that his will in redeeming men is not universal. Rather the contrary follows."

Universal atonement also matched his insistence that salvation is offered universally, more clearly by the word, less clearly, but nevertheless really, by natural revelation. In the same passage where he insisted that,

> "The sacrifice he offered for the propitiation of the sins of men was made equally for all",

Amyraut continued that, although not all people hear the gospel by distinct preaching, the goodness of God in providence

> "is a sufficient preaching for them, if they should be attentive".[69]

Amyraut described the atonement itself as conditional. It is the medicine whose effect in any particular case is dependent on application, the ransom now paid, but only making a difference to the captive when he walks free.[70]

> "For grace and propitiation are not called universal by us because he expiates all sins universally, without even the exception of unbelief, [but]...because he expiates the sins of all in the world provided they are not unbelieving or impenitent."[71]

Even for the elect the atonement can only be called absolute in so far that God foresaw that they would believe. This position prompted his opponents to ask how a conditional atonement can be regarded as an accomplished event and, indeed, how a past act can be described as conditional upon a future response.

The whole mission of Christ was entirely rooted in God's philanthropy, which, as a natural attribute of God, is exercised universally, for what is natural is unvarying. Amyraut regarded God as acting in the atonement in his capacity as benevolent legislator, dealing with humanity upon certain general principles of goodness and justice. Viewed in this way, equal dealings with the whole human race were of the essence. His use of the word "equal" in this respect caused great offence and he was enjoined at Alençon to abandon it.[72] Cameron, though teaching the same in substance, had cautiously rejected that "Arminian" term.

According to Amyraut, conditional covenant, divine philanthropy, the *voluntas signi*, the goodness revealed in creation, and the divine necessity to show mercy to the penitent are all founded on the very nature of God and therefore have universal significance. It is evident, therefore, that the atonement, interdependent with all these elements in his theology, is also universal and, as such, a necessary expression of the nature of God: God could not have provided a less than universal redemption.[73]

Amyraut also pointed out that the humanity of Christ was shared with the whole race and provided a presumption in favour of universal atonement.[74] He accepted, of course, the infinite sufficiency of Christ's sacrifice, based on the infinite value of his divine person. As did Cameron, however, he pointed out that it was not enough for theologians to concede this universal sufficiency unless they based it in the will of God.

> "For clearly, a ransom, however big, paid to a victor cannot be said to be absolutely sufficient to redeem a captive unless paid with the intention that the captive should be freed by the payment."[75]

Amyraut rarely alluded to the "Christ died efficiently for the elect" side of the scholastic formula, however. This was probably because he did not ground the atonement in election as well as a general saving will, but in the latter only. He subordinated particular election and effectual calling to the general saving will and atonement. Thus, only in a carefully qualified sense could Christ be said to have died for the elect.

> "The same Scripture which teaches us so distinctly that Christ died universally for the whole world also sometimes speaks in a way which seems to say that he died only for the small number of those elected to faith. It is necessary to distinguish carefully ways of speaking which arise from the consideration of results only and those which come from consideration of the plans of God."[76]

In other words, Christ died for all conditionally, but only the elect fulfil the condition; so Christ died for the elect with respect to result rather than intention.

A frequent distinction Amyraut used, in preference to the sufficient-efficient atonement formula, was that between sufficient external and efficient internal (or, sometimes, objective and subjective) grace. External grace consists in the work of Christ plus preaching, either by the word or natural revelation. No-one needs anything else done for him or made known to him than he already has, but does need something done in him, to enable him to appropriate external grace. This internal grace of the Spirit is particular and effective in contrast to universal and sufficient but ineffective external grace.[77]

CONCLUSION

The implications of Amyraut's teaching on the extent of the atonement will be explored in another chapter, in the light of the criticisms of his opponents. Two observations may usefully be made here, however. The first is that the doctrine which produced limited atonement in Reformed theology was unquestionably that of the absolute predestination of certain individuals. In refusing to give predestination a place in his system until, logically, after the external call, Amyraut prevented predestination from dominating the extent of the atonement.

The second observation relates to the charge frequently levelled at scholastic Calvinism, namely that it began with a concept of the absolute freedom of God in the exercise of omnipotent power. It then deduced its soteriology on that basis, presenting the plan of salvation as the inevitable outworking of incomprehensible decrees of election and reprobation. Limited atonement is seen by the critics of scholastic Calvinism as the most obvious result of this flawed procedure. Amyraut's method, by contrast, is described as "biblical".[78] It may be granted that Amyraut came closer to a biblical approach than did his opponents in ensuring that the interaction of God with the human race in history was not lost behind a theology of comprehensive eternal decrees. However, our survey of the Saumur teaching shows that, like their opponents, Cameron and Amyraut also began with a certain concept of God, and applied it logically to the field of soteriology. Unlike their opponents, it was a concept of God in which his moral attributes, pre-eminently goodness, are supreme, and control his dealings with humanity. An atonement made for all, offered to all, but beneficial only to those who fulfil certain ethical conditions, was derived from controlling concepts of the moral nature of God, and of the nature of things, with as much use of human logic and reason as employed by the "orthodox" in their deductions from a concept of God in which omnipotent will was pre-eminent. The doctrine that nature preaches the gospel to all people, including those who have never heard the name of Jesus, was as much a rationalistic projection as was the limited atonement of his opponents. In fact, to the same degree to which Amyraut marks a break with the scholastic logic of the past, his preoccupation with the comprehensibility of the moral character and requirements of God seems to foreshadow the rationalism of the future.[79]

Chapter Nine

Notes

1 For biographical details see Quick, "Icones", op.cit., vol.1 pt.2, pp.958-1028; E. and E. Haag (eds.), *La France Protestante*, new edition ed. H. Bordier (6 vols.), Paris 1877-1888, vol.1 cols. 185-206 (which also contain analyses of his major writings); Laplanche, *Orthodoxie*, op.cit., pp.58-83; Armstrong, *Calvinism*, op.cit., pp.71-119; R.Nicole, *Moyse Amyraut: a bibliography; with special reference to the controversy on universal grace*, New York 1981, pp.4-16.

2 Laplanche, *Orthodoxie*, op.cit.; T.M.Lindsay, "Amyraldism", in J.Hastings (ed.), *Encyclopaedia of Religion and Ethics*, Edinburgh 1925, vol.1, pp. 404-406; L. Proctor, "The Theology of Moïse Amyraut Considered as a Reaction against Seventeenth-Century Calvinism", Ph.D. Leeds 1952; Armstrong, pp.71-119; F.P. van Stam, *The Controversy over the Theology of Saumur, 1635-1650: disrupting debates among the Huguenots in complicated circumstances*, Amsterdam 1988.

3 M.Amyraut, *Brief Traitté de la Prédestination et de ses Principales Dépendances*, Saumur 1634.

4 J.Quick, *Synodicon in Gallia Reformata: or, The Acts, Decisions, Decrees and Canons of those Famous National Councils of the Reformed Churches in France*, (2 vols.) London 1692, vol.2, pp.352-357, 397-411, gives a record of the proceedings at Alençon concerning Amyraut and Paul Testard. They were required to avoid speaking of Christ's dying "equally" for all, and "of conditional, frustratory or revocable Decree[s]", to be careful in the use of anthropopathism, and not to call the knowledge of God which may be derived from creation "faith".

5 Ibid., p.455. Arguments among students about "unnecessary Questions, as concerning the Order of God's Decrees, of Universal Grace by the Preaching of Nature, which may lead and bring Men unto Salvation" were forbidden, and the decrees of Alençon were to be strictly observed by all.

6 According to Quick, "Icones", vol.1 pt.2, p.159, the three Saumur professors, Amyraut, De la Place and Louis Cappel were so closely identified as to be commonly regarded as "three Heads covered with one and ye same Night-cap".

7 David Blondel (1590-1655), see Haag and Haag op.cit., vol.2 cols. 623-631, was an outstanding ecclesiastical historian and three times assessor at National Synods. From 1650 Blondel lived in the Netherlands, where he attempted to quell opposition to Amyraldian theology. *His Actes Authentiques des Eglises Reformées de France, Germanie, Grande-Bretaigne, Pologne, Hongrie, Païs Bas, etc.*, Amsterdam 1655, was part of that effort. Jean Daillé (1594-1670), see Haag and Haag, op.cit., vol.5, cols.23-37, and Van Stam, op.cit., pp. 448-450, was Amyraut's predecessor at Saumur and then pastor at Paris. Laplanche, *L'Ecriture*, op.cit., pp.1-12 has demonstrated that Amyraut derived most of his support from North of the Loire, and refers to the "Saumur-Paris axis". The general support of the Paris (Charenton) church was decisive in preventing the condemnation of Amyraut at times when opposition was at its height.

8 Quick, *Synodicon*, vol.2, p.554.

9 See letter from the Paris pastor Charles Drelincourt to André Rivet of 13 Feb. 1637, cited in Van Stam, p.85 n.28. Drelincourt wrote that Amyraut's view on the possibility of salvation without the knowledge of Christ should be condemned, his speculation on what felicity could be obtained if it were possible to keep God's law forbidden, but that his opinion on the extent of grace could be tolerated.

10 op.cit., pp.158-262.

11 Moltmann, "Gnadenbund", op.cit., p.285. Rex, op.cit., p.89, claims, "Every important change which occurred in French Calvinism between 1634 and the Revocation can be traced eventually back to him [Cameron]."

12 E.g. M.Amyraut, *Specimen Animadversionum in Exercitationes de Gratia Universali*, Saumur 1648, pt.2, p.295, "my father, Cameron"; *Ad Reverendi Viri, G. Riveti, Ecclesiae Talleburgensis Pastoris, Responsioriam Epistolam Replicatio*, Saumur 1649, p.43, "my teacher, Cameron".

13 P.Testard, *Eirenikon seu Synopsis Doctrinae de Natura et Gratia*, Blois 1633.

14 *Brief Traitté*, op.cit., pp.5-9 (cp. p.30, "The end to which he destined man in his creation being to place his image upon him..."; p.46, "It pleased God to take advantge [*prendre occasion*] of his fall").

15 Ibid., pp.40-43,68-69.

16 Ibid., pp.31-32,36-38,46-47,72-73; See M. Amyraut, *De Secessione ab Ecclesia Romana deque Ratione Pacis inter Evangelicos in Religionis Negotio Constituendae Disputatio*, Saumur 1647, pp.163-165.

17 *Brief Traitté*, p.77, "The misery of men was equal and universal, and the desire God had of delivering them from it by means of such a great Redeemer proceeded from the compassion he had towards them as his creatures fallen into such great ruin, in that they are equally his creatures. So the grace of redemption, offered and procured for them, had to be equal and universal, provided that they should find themselves equally disposed to receive it."; p.78, "The salvation which he [Christ] has received from his Father...is destined equally for all, provided, I say, that the disposition necessary to receive it shall be equal on their part."; pp.83-119, "God deploys his power in such a way that it overcomes all that there is of corruption in his understanding and his will....It is in this plan, therefore, that that which is called election or predestination consists." (p.103).

18 Ibid., pp.163-165: "It is necessary to distinguish carefully predestination to salvation and predestination to faith, the latter being the means and condition through which we come to salvation." (p.163).

19 Ibid., pp.102-103,119-131; M.Amyraut, *In Orationem Dominicam Exercitatio*, Saumur 1662, p.184.

20 Ibid., pp.492-493, where the temporal order - the conditional offer, faith, the giving of salvation - corresponds to the eternal order - the will to save if people believe, the foreknowledge of who will through grace believe, the decision to give salvation absolutely.

21 *Specimen*, op.cit., Preface p.99.

22 Ibid., 2 p.81; M.Amyraut, *De Mysterio Trinitatis, deque Vocibus ac Phrasibus quibus tam in Scriptura quam apud Patres Explicatur, Dissertatio*, Saumur 1661, pp.254-255.

23 In L.Cappel, M.Amyraut, J. de la Place, *Syntagma Thesium Theologicarum in Academia Salmurensi Variis Temporibus Disputatorum*, Saumur 1665, (2 vols.), vol.2, pt.4, pp.105-116. The date of this and other theses, and other backgound, is supplied by L. Desgraves, "Les Thèses Soutenues a l'Académie Protestante de Saumur au XVIIe. Siècle", in *BSHPF* 125(1979) pp.76-97.

24 "Opinions", 3/4.8, in De Jong, op.cit., pp.226-227, cp. *Canons of Dort*, op.cit., 3/4.8.

25 *Syntagma*, pt.4, pp.111-115, theses 20,21,19,32.

26 Ibid., p.115, th.32: "God was unable not to add a condition, or else he would violate the great majesty of his attributes", cp. *Specimen*, op.cit., 2 p.69; *Syntagma*, pt.4, p.116 th.37.

27 M.Amyraut, "Doctrinae de Gratia Universali, ut ab Orthodoxis Explicatur, Defensio", p.105, in *Dissertationes Theologicae Quatuor*.

28 *Specimen*, 1 pp.188-189; "De Gratia Universali", pp.44-48.

29 *Specimen*, 1 p.134; "De Gratia Universali", pp.4-5.

30 *Specimen*, 2 p.81.

31 See J.von Rohr, *The Covenant of Grace in Puritan Thought*, Atlanta 1986, esp. pp.127-133.

32 In *Syntagma*, op.cit., pt.1, (pp.212-231), p.212 Th.1.

33 Ibid., p.221 th.37.

34 "Theses de Voluntate Dei" in *Syntagma*, pt.4, p.114 th.32; "De Gratia Universali", p.32: "The evangelical covenant ought to be considered either as absolute, with its condition discharged, or as conditional, that is, with respect to those from whom the condition, not yet discharged, is required. Cp. *Paraphrases sur les Epistres de l'Apostre S. Paul au Galates, Ephésiens, Philippiens, Colossiens, I Thessaloniciens, II Thessaloniciens*, Saumur 1645, pp.60-61.

35 "Theses de Tribus Foederibus Divinis", in *Syntagma*, pt. 1 p.223, th.45, cp. M. Amyraut, *Six Sermons de la Nature, Estendue, Necessité, Dispensation et Efficace de l'Evangile*, Saumur 1636, p.31-32, "The Evangelical covenant therefore has its correspondence with this other mercy, which requires the condition: if you believe, you will be saved"; "De Gratia Universali", p.87.

36 E.g. *Specimen*, 2 p.238.

37 "Theses de Tribus Foederibus Divinis", in *Syntagma*, pt.1, pp.224-231 theses 48-74.

38 Ibid., p.230 th.72.

39 *Eschantillon de la Doctrine de Calvin, touchant la Prédestination*, (prefaced to *Six Sermons*), cp. M.Amyraut, *Doctrinae Ioannis Calvini de Absoluto Reprobationis Decreto Defensio*, Saumur 1641, p.104.

40 *Six Sermons*, p.30; "De Gratia Universali", p.20; "Doctrinae de Gratia Particulari ut a Calvino Explicatur Defensio", pp.64-65, in *Dissertationes*; M.Amyraut, *Sermon du Voile de Moyse, sur I [in fact II] Corinthiens* 3.13,14,15,16, *avec Deux Autres Sermons sur les Textes Suivans*, Saumur 1651, p.114.

41 *Specimen* , 2 p.492.

42 E.g.in J.Wollebius, "Compendium Theologicae Christianae", (1626), ch.7, in Beardslee, *Reformed Dogmatics*, op.cit., p.64. McGiffert, "The Making", op.cit., p.136, says Dudley Fenner was the first to use the term "covenant of works" in his *Sacra Theologia* of 1585.

43 "Theses de Tribus Foederibus Divinis", p.225 th.56, in *Syntagma*, states that both legal and evangelical covenants are built on the covenant of nature.

44 In *Six Sermons*, pp.106-108, Amyraut says that in spite of election, natural human ties remain. According to Amyraut, *La Morale Chrestienne*, (4 parts in 6 vols.) part 4, Saumur 1659, pp.21, and pp.799-800: "Adam, Aristotle and Moses are those who begin and continue my Morale. But it is finished by our Saviour Jesus Christ. For it is from his teachings that I bring this work to perfection, and draw the fulness of a man's duties." See Laplanche's comments on Amyraut's use of natural morality, in *L'Evidence*, op.cit., pp.38-43,185-212, for the social dimension, and Laplanche, *L'Ecriture*, op.cit., pp.379-478, for the natural basis of Amyraut's political and social thought.

45 Cp.*Doctrinae Ionnis Calvini...Defensio*, pp.32-33, 91-96.

46 *Specimen*, 1 p.140; 2 p.202, "The difference consists in this, that the one [the gospel] has declared Christ most manifestly, the other [nature], set against such great light, very obscurely". Cp. *Brief Traitté*, pp.81-83. C.J.Betts, *Early Deism in France*, The Hague 1984, pp.35-36, refers to Amyraut's trouble over this matter and sets it against the background of the controversy, during the second quarter of the century, between the Catholics Arnauld and La Mothe Le Vayer, over the salvability of the heathen. Betts points out that Catholic theologians were generally inclined to be favourable to the possibility. B.Tocanne, *L'Idée de Nature en France dans La Seconde Moitié du XVIIe Siècle*, Klincksieck 1978, pp.207-235, explains that in seventeenth-century Catholic thought nature was being given an ever larger share in ethics, and that Christian morality was being increasingly identified with natural morality. He also describes the debates of the 1650s between Jansenists and Jesuits around the themes of the natural knowledge of God and the condition of human nature, see pp.250-275. It appears that Amyraut was in touch with the questions of his time discussed beyond the confines of Reformed theology.

47 Tocanne, op.cit., p.11, points out that the concept of nature, acted as "a normative principle of order and regularity".

48 "De Oeconomia Trium Personarum in Operibus Divinis, Dissertatio", in *Dissertationes*; and *De Mysterio Trinitatis*, op.cit.

49 *De Mysterio*, p.64.

50 E.g. *Doctrinae Ionnis Calvini..Defensio*, pp.32-37, 91-96.

51 *Brief Traitté*, p.157: "It is natural to man that the understanding, which perceives a truth clearly and certainly, acquiesces in it. We love it for its natural excellence and utility, which we recognize, because it is natural to man to ardently love the true and the useful." One of many full accounts of the process of conversion according to Amyraut is found in his vindication of Calvin from the charge of teaching Stoic necessity, in *Doctrinae Ioannis Calvini...Defensio*, pp.32-34.

52 *Specimen*, pref. p.4, cp. 2 pp.279-280,311-313,327.

53 M.Amyraut, *A Treatise Concerning Religions, in refutation of the opinion which counts all indifferent*, London 1660, p.446.

54 *Specimen*, 1 p.192, and 2 pp.78-79; 2 p.169.

55 "De Gratia Universali", pp.30-31,36-39; *Six Sermons*, p.24-30 ("The word of God presents his mercy to us to be considered in two ways", p.25).

56 *Six Sermons*, pp.27-29,31.

57 *Specimen*, 2, p.381, cp. "De Gratia Universali", p.92; *Doctrinae Ioannis Calvini...Defensio*, pp.269-270; *Specimen* 2 pp.308-309.

58 *Six Sermons*, pp.228-229.

59 *Specimen*, 2. p.389: *Doctrinae Ioannis Calvini...Defensio*, pp.240-242, esp.p.242: "In constituting the new covenant, God used no such freedom. He offered one and the same mercy to all..."

60 *Specimen*, 2 pp.378-38, cp. p.406.

61 *Doctrinae Ioannis Calvini...Defensio*, p.27; *A Treatise Concerning Religions*, p.420, 425.

62 *Six Sermons*, pp.267-268; *Doctrinae Ionnis Calvini...Defensio*, p.232; *Specimen*, pt.1, pp.168-169.

63 "Gnadenbund", op.cit., pp.33-35.

64 *In Orationem Dominicam Exercitatio*, Saumur 1662, pp.174-176. *Acceptilatio* is acquittal without the payment of an exact penalty, the concept revived by Grotius, see Müller, Dictionary, op.cit., pp.18-19; *De Mysterio Trinitatis*, pp.265-268, and, *In Orationem*, p.174; *Brief Traitté*, pp.72-73.

65 *Eschantillon*, op.cit., no pagination. An early and important apologetic work by Amyraut is *A Treatise Concerning Religions, in refutation of the opinion which counts all things indifferent*, London 1660 (first published Saumur 1631). For Amyraut's apologetics, see Laplanche, *L'Evidence*, op.cit., pp.38-43.

66 *The Doctrinae Ioannis Calvini...Defensio, op.cit.*, was written against such allegations, although from an Anglican rather than Roman source, ibid., pref. p.1.

67 Ibid., p.256 "As for that method of Beza...it should not in any way be ascribed to Calvin..."

68 *Specimen*, 2 p.311, cp. p.277; ibid., p.456.

69 M.Amyraut, *De Secessione, op.cit.*, pp.166-167; *Specimen*, pt.2, pp.187-188; *Brief Traitté*, p.81.

70 *Specimen*, 2 pp.418,487; 1.134; "Doctrinae de Gratia Universali", pp.102-103.

71 *Specimen*, 1 pp.189,218; ibid., 2 p.375, "The death of Christ...was absolute for them, not properly because they were elect as such, but because they believed", cp.ibid., p.359.

72 See *Syntagma*, p.214; *Doctrinae Ioannis Calvini...Defensio*, pp.103-105.

73 *Specimen*, 1 p.134.

74 *Brief Traitté*, pp.77-78: "The Redeemer was taken from their race and made participant of the same flesh and same blood with them all..."

75 "Doctrinae de Gratia Universali", p.99.

76 *Brief Traitté*, p.166.

77 M.Amyraut, *Eirenikon sive de Ratione Pacis, in Religionis Negotio, inter Evangelicos Constituendae, Consilium*, Saumur 1662, p.306, and *Specimen*, 2 pp.13,72,203,267,354,413.

78 E.g. Hall, in Duffield, op.cit., p.27; Armstrong, op.cit., p.137: "This synthetic methodology of the Reformed scholastics was responsible for another teaching in which Beza and Calvinism went beyond Calvin himself, the doctrine of limited atonement", see also pp.165-166.

79 See below, pp.213-219 and p.222 n.38, for Amyraut's rationalism.

Chapter Ten
The Roots of Amyraldism

INTRODUCTION

In view of Amyraut's claim to be following Calvin, his opponents identification of his teaching with Arminianism, and the practice of later Reformed historians to regard Amyraut's teaching as a new departure, some investigation of the origins of his thought is called for. Since Cameron was the greatest influence on Amyraut, the search for the roots of Amyraldism must include investigation of the influences upon Cameron.

AMYRAUT AND ARMINIANISM

Pierre du Moulin brought the charge that Amyraut's teaching amounted to Arminianism.[1] Other opponents, though critical, were not so sweeping in their judgement. Amyraut himself often asserted that his position was the same as that of Dort.[2]

There are many points at which Amyraut's views resemble those of the Arminians. Foremost among these is that God gives all people sufficient external grace for salvation, consisting of not only a universally suitable atonement, but also a universal offer of grace through creation and providence. He stopped short of the Arminian conviction that all are granted an ability to respond to this universal offer.

Amyraut's tendency, noted above, to develop his doctrines logically from a concept of the goodness of God was also characteristic of Arminianism, which, in A.Ritschl's phrase, referred "the idea of God to the standard of indulgent reasonableness".[3]

Amyraut shared the Arminian concern that the divine *voluntas signi* should not be merely an external instrument of the hidden, absolute will of God. In this connection, Amyraut's strong conditionalism was also redolent of Arminianism. The second layer of Amyraut's theology attributed faith wholly to the will of God, but the first and most prominent layer shared the Arminian method of making God's purpose dependent on human faith. Amyraldians and Arminians posited a conditional decree to save all believers, and made it logically prior to an absolute decree to save particular people. So, the basic form of the covenant of grace was the same in Arminianism and Amyraldism: God sent his Son to make possible the covenant of grace, in which Christ's saving benefits are given to those who fulfil the conditions of faith and repentance. In insisting, however, on the purely instrumental function of faith, Amyraut tried to avoid following the general trend of his thought too far, namely to present the covenant conditions as a new and modified law, as the Arminians did, and as the English Richard Baxter would do.[4]

To a degree Amyraut shared the Arminian defence of the integrity of human nature. For him this meant that human faculties remained intact after the fall, but with a corrupt *habitus* interfering with their right operation. Unlike the Arminians, he insisted on the need for irresistible grace, to enable the mind and will to rise above the corruption of human nature and respond to the gospel.

The Saumur theologians were at one with Arminianism in insisting on the universality of the atonement, arguing from the fact that the gospel calls upon all to believe that Christ died for them. Their opponents could not fail to hear in this argument, and in Amyraut's assertion that Christ died "equally" for all, echoes of Remonstrant teachings. In spite of a similar position on the extent of the atonement, however, Amyraut rejected the view that the atonement was not necessitated by the divine justice, whereas the Arminians, following Grotius, came to agree with the Socinian premise that God may in principle relax his law, so that Christ's atonement was not of absolute necessity.

This brief comparison should be enough to show that, although Amyraut was unfairly labelled by his more extreme critics, he did in fact have many points in common with the Arminians. Most fundamental among these was the commitment to demonstrate and make comprehensible the goodness and justice of God in dealing with the human race. There is evidence that Philippe Duplessis-Mornay, the founder and patron of the Saumur Academy, was willing to be more tolerant of Arminianism than Dort was. Furthermore, the Reformed Church of Paris, whose pastors became the most influential and committed defenders of Amyraut's theology outside Saumur itself, was disposed to welcome Arminian expatriates into its midst without making an issue of disputed points of theology.[5] It is not surprising that, in the atmosphere of alarm and suspicion generated by the Remonstrant conflict, there were widespread fears about the direction in which France's main Protestant Academy seemed to be moving.

AMYRAUT AND LUTHERANISM

Since the debates at Strasbourg and Montbéliard, it was understood that Lutherans and Reformed were divided over the extent of the atonement. Among those Reformed who thought of the limitation of the atonement chiefly in terms of its result, there was scope for reconciliation, as attempted by Pareus in his *Eirenikon.*

Du Moulin, the main anti-Amyraldian campaigner of the 1630s, had led an attempt to create a union among all Protestants in the years before the Synod of Dort. His plan, worked out in company with Duplessis-Mornay and James I, was approved in 1614 by the National Synod of Tonneins. It envisaged a union on the basis of a creed drawn from the Protestant churches, from which all contentious issues would be excluded. Du Moulin even professed himself willing to include the followers of Arminius in such a union. Due to lack of action on James' part, and in the face of the growing Remonstrant crisis, the plan failed to progress.[6] It is evidence, however, that, in the second decade of the seventeenth century, there was in France a willingness to regard differences with the Lutherans, including predestination and the extent of the atonement, as secondary.

After Dort, and the adoption of its formulations by the National Synod of Alès in 1620, a stricter orthodoxy prevailed.[7] Nevertheless, in 1631 the National Synod of Charenton approved a motion to receive Lutherans into communion, and accept marriage between Lutheran and Reformed.[8] In his *De Secessione* (1647), Amyraut defended Lutheran-Reformed intercommunion while maintaining that the same kind of union with Catholics was impossible. The work was dedicated to the Lutheran William VI, Landgrave of Hesse, whom he had met when the young prince had spent several months in the town of Saumur. Amyraut's *Eirenikon* (1662) was written in support of the measure of agreement reached at a Lutheran-Reformed colloquy in Cassel, called by William. The *Eirenikon* argued for union with the Lutherans on the basis of a statement of faith which would omit articles not considered to be essential. In discussing the differences, Amyraut acknowledged the offence caused to the Lutherans by Bezan predestinarianism, but claimed that most Reformed held the infralapsarian view. He then set out to show that some followed a mode of treating the doctrine (i.e. his own) in which the decree of unconditional election is brought in, logically, not only after the fall, but after the mission of Christ. Even though his formal definition of election was not the same as theirs, Amyraut suggested that this system could provide a basis for harmony with the Lutherans. For the function of election within it was to protect the truth that faith is the gift of God, a truth the Lutherans also held, nor did its use of election cancel the purposeful universal sufficiency of the atonement.[9]

To what degree Amyraut's whole doctrine of predestination and the extent of the atonement were shaped by concern to promote Protestant unity is difficult to ascertain. On the one hand, his distinctive views first appeared in print in a different context. On the other, as first a student then professor of the Saumur Academy he may well have been influenced by the Protestant-ecumenical outlook of Duplessis-Mornay. What is clear is that Amyraut regarded his own construction of the disputed doctrines as eminently advantageous in the search for peace among Evangelicals, a search which must have appeared all the more important as the position of the French Reformed as a minority community, living under the provisions of the Edict of Nantes, was made increasingly difficult through ever growing state-imposed restrictions.[10]

Amyraut referred several times to the Confession of Thorn, drawn up by the Polish Reformed in 1645 to show their agreement with the Lutherans at a time when both were under pressure from Catholicism. In it they professed to hold universal atonement in such a way that they were not in disagreement with the Council of Trent's position. Amyraut cleverly challenged his opponent Spanheim, that if he would state his agreement with Thorn, the controversy on the extent of the atonement could be regarded as closed. To Amyraut, Thorn was proof that universal atonement was not at variance with Reformed theology at its best, and a model for Reformed-Lutheran co-operation.[11]

It is also of interest in this connection to note that leading Anglican proponents of moderate predestination and universal atonement were also eager participants in attempts at Reformed-Lutheran unity.[12]

AMYRAUT AND CALVIN

On deciding to enter the ministry, Amyraut began to study Calvin's *Institutes*, and his works reveal considerable familiarity with the reformer's writings.[13] From the outset of the predestination controversy, Amyraut made frequent appeals to Calvin. Indeed, he was criticized for so doing by Du Moulin, who demanded why he should not also refer to such men as Beza and Zanchi, who were not inferior to Calvin.[14] After his *Brief Traitté* Amyraut published, in 1636, *Six Sermons*, prefaced by an *Eschantillon de la Doctrine de Calvin Touchant la Prédestination*. This was followed in 1641 by the *Doctrinae Ioannis Calvini de Absoluto Reprobationis Decreto Defensio*. The publication of these works was shrewd, as it served to underline Amyraut's orthodoxy by identifying him with Calvin. The *De Absoluto Decreto* was not by any means limited to defending a certain view of reprobation, and an examination of it enables a comparison between the predestination teaching of Calvin and that of Amyraut to be made.[15]

In sixteen chapters Amyraut considered and refuted various objections brought against Calvin's predestination doctrine. The first chapter summarized what Amyraut considered to be Calvin's view. It claimed that he presupposed mankind as a corrupt mass, in other words, that Calvin favoured infralapsarianism.

> "God was so affected towards mankind that he willed to send his one and only Son into the world, who made satisfaction by his death to the inexorable justice of the Father, with this condition [*ea lege*] attached, that whoever, without any exception, believes should share in the benefits of his propitiatory work."

This gospel is to be preached indiscriminately, and, should a question arise concerning the reason for, say, Paul's salvation as opposed to Judas' condemnation, it would be adequate to answer in terms of the faith of Paul and the unbelief of Judas. However, it is also possible to go farther, recognizing that faith is granted by the power of the Holy Spirit, operating according to a distinction between people, which is wholly in God and not in the qualities of the people themselves. This is election. Its opposite, reprobation, is purely negative, the passing over of certain people. Calvin, Amyraut maintained, had indicated that the cause of reprobation is twofold, depending on the way it is considered. Absolutely, it is caused by human sin, comparatively, because there is no difference between the sin of the elect and the reprobate, by the will of God alone.[16]

Was Amyraut's theology a faithful representation of Calvin's? Scholars have disagreed sharply about whether Calvin can be said to have believed in natural revelation at all.[17] It is generally agreed that, even if he allowed a possibility of deriving some knowledge of God from creation, his only use for this possibility was to emphasise human inexcusability.[18] Amyraut went farther by assigning a positive role to natural revelation, claiming that God wills natural revelation to be salvific, if rightly used.

It may be questioned whether Amyraut was correct in "clearing" Calvin of supralapsarianism. He specifically dissociated Calvin from Beza,[19] and certainly Calvin was not the consistent supralapsarian Beza was. However, while it is easy to find passages in Calvin which relate predestination to fallen humanity, there are others implying that the fall itself was subordinate to the decree of twofold predestination.[20]

Amyraut was justified in citing some of Calvin's statements about a universal promise and a Christ whose saving death is offered to all. He was perceptive in making much of Calvin's distinction between two wills in God, and pointing out that Calvin was content never to reconcile fully a universal, non-effective, saving will with a particular, effective, saving will.[21] In examining Calvin's dual approach, however, our conclusion was that a tendency to subordinate the revealed, universal will to the hidden, predestining will can be detected at several points. So when Beza developed a consistent supralapsarian, limited atonement view he was taking the direction already signposted by Calvin. Amyraut's use of the two wills device, in which he preferred to concentrate on the revealed will, cannot therefore be said to be a more legitimate version of Calvin's theology than was Beza's, and could even be regarded as less faithful.

The distance between Calvin and Amyraut is well illustrated by their different interpretation of the love of God that lay behind the sending of Christ. As has been seen, Calvin closely related this love to the divine *beneplacitum*, the absolute, incomprehensible will. Amyraut concentrated rather on the general goodness and universal philanthropy of God, quite distinct from election. This is not to suggest that Calvin never spoke of the saving love of God in a more general sense, or that Amyraut never spoke of goodness and love in connection with predestination, but there was certainly a difference of emphasis in explaining what lay behind the mission of Christ. Accordingly, Calvin often spoke about election in Christ our head, Amyraut hardly at all. The Genevan reformer regarded Christ as the mirror of election; the Saumur professor was heir to a tradition that distinguished universal, conditional covenant from absolute, particular predestination, and he had followed Cameron in placing Christ in connection with the former, and having virtually nothing to say about Christ's connection with the latter.

In taking this view, we are departing from B.G.Armstrong's seminal work. Armstrong concluded that Amyraut's own claim to be reproducing Calvin's teaching was substantially justified, though he indicated that the relationship between the two demanded further investigation.[22] It is indeed true that it was not characteristic of Calvin to systematize all doctrine under the organizing concept of predestination. Nevertheless, neither did he, Amyraut-fashion, labour under a compulsion to harmonize as much doctrine as possible with a preconceived idea of general philanthropy, considered to be a necessity of God's nature. Our conclusions coincide to a considerable degree with those of Jonathan Rainbow, in his recent refutation of Amyraut's claim to be following Calvin. Though Rainbow does not appear to have made an extensive study of Amyraut, and portrays a Calvin who is much more consistently particularistic and predestinarian than we can recognize, he successfully shows that Christ, predestination and the love of God are substantially united in Calvin's thought, while deliberately disjointed in Amyraut's.[23]

A related form in which the difference of outlook emerges is in the two theologians' statements about the incomprehensibility of God. Armstrong praised Amyraut for following Calvin in the recognition that much about God is inscrutable, and that theologians must be prepared to accept that they cannot explain everything. But this reverent acknowledgment was not peculiar to Calvin and Amyraut. All Reformed theologians regularly appealed to it when they reached a point of being unable to give a convincing explanation of any doctrine! Amyraut's opponents appealed to it quite as often as he did, and reproached him, as eagerly as he condemned them, for prying into God's secrets.[24] The significant question to ask is where they located the boundary of the inscrutable. For Calvin and Beza, it was usually found at the point where the explanation of God's works made God sound shockingly unjust. Thus, throughout his chapters on predestination, and especially in the context of reprobation, divine hardening of the heart and active divine rule over (as opposed to permission of) evil, Calvin repeatedly rebuked the human instinct to question. We are to be satisfied with the explanation that,

> "The will of God is the supreme rule of righteousness, so that everything which he wills must be held to be righteous by the mere fact of his willing it."

Though he denied giving "countenance to the fiction of absolute power", he explained that, as far as human understanding is concerned, God's will and justice are incomprehensible.

> "We deny that he is bound to give an account of his own procedure; and we moreover deny that we are fit of our own ability to give judgement in such a case."

Calvin concluded the *Institutes*' section on predestination with reference to Romans 9.20,

> "'Nay but, O man, who art thou that repliest against God?' Truly does Augustine maintain that it is perverse to measure divine by the standards of human justice."[25]

Amyraut may seem to occupy the same ground as Calvin in employing a Nominalist dictum to warn against carnal reason:

> "He is infinitely elevated above his creatures and is not obliged to anyone in anything whatsoever."

If God should throw all into hell without regard to their deeds, it would be for his creatures to acquiesce.[26] However, the immediate context of this uncharacteristic remark, as well as the method of the *Brief Traitté* in which it is found, made it clear that such a possibility is unthinkable, and Amyraut proceeded to demonstrate that God's dealings with the world, including predestination, are eminently and comprehensibly good. It is the conviction that the works of God are substantially ethically comprehensible, that divides Amyraut's theology from Calvin's. Walter Rex's perceptive comment needs to be firmly grasped by students of Amyraldian theology:

> "The burning question in "hypothetical universalism" concerns not merely the purpose of Christ's mission, but also the relationship between mystery and comprehension...for the first time in French Calvinist orthodoxy, without denying the incomprehensible, [there is] a new consciousness of the reasonable criterium of ethics in interpreting the Scripture..."[27]

At the same time Amyraut did warn against human reason drawing logical deductions from known truths.

> "If Adam's sin happened through the providence of God, God was therefore its author; if it is said that God hardened Pharaoh's heart, then he punishes sins and vices he himself created; if God wanted to reprobate the greater part of mankind, he therefore does not want to save all; if he declares to us he wants to save all, there is therefore no absolute, precise election and predestination of a certain small number only; if Jesus Christ died for all, therefore the gospel must be preached equally clearly through the whole earth; if the gospel is not preached equally clearly, however, God therefore does not lead the rest of mankind to repentance; if by means of his providence he truly leads people to repentance...therefore it is for nothing that he causes his gospel to be preached...Good God! When God's word teaches on the one hand that some are reprobated...and when on the other side the same word teaches me God wants all to be saved...even though my reason should find there things which seem to clash...I will not stop holding the doctrines as true..."[28]

This revealing passage, in which Amyraut anticipates one of the main charges of his opponents, namely absurdity, shows that he recognized the intellectual difficulty caused by a system in which he sought to hold apparently contradictory doctrines together. It will be taken either as a reverent caution regarding the limits of human reason, or an excuse for an incoherent system, largely according to the sympathies of the reader. It should be recognized, however, that Amyraut did indeed seek to reconcile contradictions, not so much in the interests of logical but of ethical consistency: his scheme of God's hypothetical and conditional dealings with the world was the instrument by which he sought to vindicate divine goodness and justice and establish human responsibility. But in seeking a certain ethical acceptability he displayed the opposite of Calvin's tendency to leave doctrine in rugged and often offensive form, to be submitted to, though not understood. Amyraut sought to show as far as possible the ethical comprehensibility of God's works. To Calvin and "orthodox" Calvinism, much of God's work is ethically incomprehensible and unacceptable to human reason. To Amyraut it is ethically comprehensible provided the right method is followed, but often appears logically contradictory. Thus when they warned against scrutinizing God's ways, Calvin and the "orthodox" were allowing for an ethical incomprehensibility, while Amyraut was leaving room for logical incomprehensibility.[29] Again, therefore, there is good reason to see Amyraut not as closer to Calvin, but as further from him, than were other seventeenth-century Calvinists. In terms of the extent of the atonement, this means that, in spite of superficially similar statements in both theologians regarding the death of Christ for all, the very different standpoints from which they made these statements must be carefully borne in mind.

THE GERMAN TRADITION

Amyraut's claims to be following Calvin can divert the researcher in the quest for antecedents. As has been demonstrated, Cameron carried the German covenant tradition to Saumur, and it was this tradition which shaped so much of Amyraut's thought.[30] Though Calvin was most frequently cited, Amyraut often gave the names of others in whose steps he considered himself to be treading. One of those most frequently referred to was Bullinger. Spanheim correctly observed that Calvin, Musculus and Bullinger were the theologians Amyraut appealed to most.[31] Bullinger's caution regarding predestination, his tendency to regard the proper function of that doctrine as to explain the origin of faith, his couching of the atonement in universalistic terms and his stress on the conditional nature of God's universal promises mark him as closer to the Saumur theology than was Calvin.

Since Ursinus was the first to systematize German conditional-covenant theology it is surprising that Amyraut only refers to him occasionally. Nevertheless, Ursinus' closest disciple, Pareus, whose moderation was apparent in his seeking to build theological bridges to the Lutherans, is cited frequently and with emphasis.[32] Amyraut was also well aware of the Bremenese and British contributions at Dort, and defended his own orthodoxy by appeal to their positions on universal atonement. Reference has already been made to his appeal to the Polish Confession of Thorn.[33]

Amyraut's supporter Jean Daillé wrote a lengthy work, in which he established a pedigree for the Amyraldian tenets. He devoted 31 pages to Wolfgang Musculus, and 11 to Bullinger, theologians whose influence on the German tradition was formative, compared with 10 to Bucer, 5 to Peter Martyr Vermigli and 1 to Beza. David Blondel pointed mainly in the same direction when he made mention of the British and Bremenese at Dort who "held the same hypotheses that are still held by the Reformed of Poland, Brandenburg, Hesse, Bremen, Saumur and others".[34]

HUMANISM

Brian Armstrong has argued that Amyraut had roots in a French humanistic tradition which gave his theology a quite different orientation from that of his scholastic contemporaries. Armstrong is certainly right in sensing a different atmosphere in the works of Amyraut from that in the productions of his opponents. However, there are difficulties in defining "scholasticism" and "humanism", and it is important to recognize that these are terms that refer to different and often complementary rather than conflicting fields. Beza, for example, was both a humanist (in his literary work) and scholastic (in his Aristotelian logic).[35] Nevertheless, Armstrong has successfully demonstrated that, in many respects, Cameron and Amyraut departed from the Aristotelian scholasticism of many contemporaries, in seeking to exclude speculative logic from their theology and to avoid constructing a strict causal system.

The question remains whether "humanism" is an adequate category to indicate the distinctiveness of Amyraut's approach. An ethical rationalism appears prominently in Cameron and Amyraut, and it is significant that both, following Duplessis-Mornay, were leaders in the field of apologetic addressed to Roman Catholics. Their apologetic work was less aggressive and detailed than that of other Reformed writers, concentrating on broad themes and appealing to reason and nature. It had to combat the Pyrrhonic scepticism of those Catholics who taught that nothing could be established by human reason, and that therefore Christian doctrine had to be accepted on the basis of authority. It sought to assail the doctrine of transubstantiation which the Reformed regarded as patently absurd. Moreover, there had been a century of failing to win over Catholics by using biblical arguments and Aristotelian deductions, and, furthermore, the reality of the Huguenot situation was that they had to share the same nation as the Catholic majority, and relate to its intellectual life. It is perhaps not surprising that a new kind of rationalism developed.[36] Although Descartes did not go into print early enough to shape Amyraut's thought, the Saumur theologians seem to have imbibed to some degree the confidence in human reason which Descartes was to enunciate.[37] This rationalistic strand could be followed to the heterodox pupil of Amyraut, Claude Pajon, and through the Amyraldian professors at Geneva in the late seventeenth century to the obviously rationalistic professors of that city at the beginning of the eighteenth.[38]

Returning to the question of the extent of the atonement, the rationalistic and apologetic concern to show that God is fair to everyone had its share in shaping the Saumur doctrine of universal atonement. This influence should be viewed not as creating a new doctrine, but as giving new life to one which had not yet been banished from the arena of Reformed theology in spite of all the onslaughts of logical predestinarianism.

CONCLUSION

Amyraut relied on Calvin for the two wills distinction. The conditional covenant and universal atonement teaching came to him from Bullinger and the Heidelberg theologians, among whom Pareus was an outstanding influence. In Amyraut's own lifetime the "liberal" wing at Dort showed the way for his theology. All these influences were mediated by John Cameron, as well as imbibed directly by reading.

Cameron left his own distinctive mark on the doctrine of universal, conditional covenant and atonement, viewing it in some sense as a necessary expression of the goodness and justice of God, and adding to it the universal call to salvation by the voice of nature, themes which Amyraut explored in greater depth. The result was that universal atonement became embedded in a more rationalistic system than previously. However, the conditional covenant system was already in place in all its main aspects, and its concomitant universal atonement had already received plentiful recognition. Furthermore, the two wills motif had a long and distinguished pedigree. With his historically based order of decrees, and his placing of the conditional universal covenant at the centre of God's dealings with the human race, Amyraut put the decree of predestination firmly into the background. Thus his doctrine of the universality of the atonement was less balanced by predestinarian considerations than in the systems of those theologians who sought to root the atonement in both a universal saving will, and election.

Saumur, then, gave a new prominence, and a more thorough and rationalistic grounding in the moral nature of God, to universal atonement. It would be just as incorrect, though, to represent the Saumur doctrine of the extent of the atonement as a new and odd departure from a monolithic Reformed tradition as it would to view it as simply a rediscovery of Calvin's Calvinism after years of neglect. It was rather an ambitious attempt to restate in an emphatic way, in the face of an orthodoxy in the process of excluding positions that were too close to those of the Arminian enemy, a doctrine that could be discovered in Calvin and seen clearly in Musculus and Bullinger, and that had been maintained in the German tradition. The fact that Amyraut's doctrine of the extent of the atonement caused so much controversy, whereas Cameron's almost identical position had gone unchallenged, must be attributed chiefly to his more forthright statement of it, partly to the more obviously rational-ethical character of Amyraut's presentation, and partly to the direction of post-Dort "orthodox" thought, rather than to the supposed novelty of a universal atonement position as such.

Chapter Ten

Notes

1 Du Moulin constantly compared the teaching of Amyraut with Arminianism in his *De Mosis Amyraldi Adversus Fridericum Spanhemium Libro Iudicium*, Rotterdam 1649 and see below, p.2424 and 5. Van Stam, op.cit., p.96, points out that André Rivet, though a firm opponent of Amyraut's teaching, clearly distinguished it from Arminianism.

2 *Specimen*, pref. p.98, cp. Daillé, *Apologia*, op.cit., 972-978, 1138; Blondel, *Actes*, op.cit., pp.12-14,77.

3 Ritschl, op.cit., pp. 245-246. Cp. F.Platt, "Arminianism", in Hastings, op.cit., vol.1, pp.807-816.

4 See ante, p.172, andp.185 n.41.

5 For Duplessis-Mornay's attitude, see Laplanche op.cit., p.5; for the Paris Church's leniency towards Arminians see Van Stam, op.cit., pp. 19-21.

6 See Quick, *Synodicon*, op.cit., vol. 1 pp. 434-437; L.G.Tait, "Pierre du Moulin (1568-1558), Huguenot theologian", Ph.D. Edinburgh 1955, pp.200-207; L. Rimbault, *Pierre Du Moulin 1568-1658: un pasteur classique de l'âge classique. Etude de théologie pastorale sur les documents inédits*, Paris 1966, pp.71-79; M. Mousseaux, "Pierre du Moulin", *BSHPF* 109(1963) pp.160-179; B.G.Armstrong, "The Changing Face of French Protestantism: the influence of Pierre du Moulin", in *Calviniana*, op.cit. pp.131-149.

7 Quick, *Synodicon*, op.cit., vol.2 pp.37-49, Armstrong, *Calvinism*, op.cit., pp.132-136.

8 Quick, *Synodicon*, op.cit., vol.1, p.297. For the historical background, see R.Stauffer, *Moïse Amyraut, un précurseur Français de l'Oecuménisme*, Paris 1962, pp.17-22.

9 *Eirenikon*, p.298-313, cp. *Specimen*, 1 pp.103-105.

10 For example, no royal permission was forthcoming for national synods between Charenton (1644-5) and Loudun (1659). No official correspondence was allowed between the French and foreign churches at or after Charenton. Daillé especially was inclined to point out the danger that the state would use division in the Reformed Church as an excuse for eroding its already limited liberties. See the extract from an undated letter from Daillé to A.Rivet, in Van Stam, op.cit., p.74: "Our adversaries will seize the occasion to break our unity and exclude one party from the Edict of Grace."

11 *Specimen*, pref. pp.59-64. See also Amyraut, *Adversus Epistolae Historicae Criminationes Defensio*, Saumur 1649, pp.139-143, *De Secessione*, pp.170,179. Cp. Blondel, op.cit., p.77, Daillé op.cit., pp.979-98.

12 See, for example, Good Counsells, op.cit., with sections by Davenant, Ussher, Joseph Hall (Bishop of Exeter), Thomas Morton (Bishop of Durham).

13 Armstrong, *Calvinism*, op.cit., p.75.

14 Du Moulin, *Examen*, p.103.

15 The work against which Amyraut addressed himself was the same one Davenant opposed, Samuel Hoard's, *God's Love to Mankind Manifested by Disproving His Absolute Decree for their Damnation*, London 1633. See Armstrong, *Calvinism*, op.cit., p.99 n.102.

16 *Doctrinae Ioannis Calvini...Defensio*, pp.4-6.

17 Niesel, op.cit., ch.3, denies this, whereas Dowey, op.cit., pp.48-80, sees a limited natural knowledge of God taught by Calvin.

18 E.g. Dowey, op.cit., p.53; Warfield, op.cit., pp.33-48.

19 *Doctrinae Ioannis Calvini...Defensio*, p.256; *De Secessione*, pp.164-166.

20 See ante, pp.13-23.

21 See Armstrong, in Armstrong and McKee, op. cit, pp.142-146, for the "hypothetical structure of Calvin's thought".

22 Armstrong, *Calvinism*, op.cit., p.269, "I would offer a judgement on the persistent claim by Amyraut that his teaching was consistent with the emphases of Calvin. On the basis of all that I have learned I would maintain that his claim is substantially correct."

23 Rainbow, op.cit., esp. pp.64-100, 181-185.

24 See below, p.237.

25 *Institutes*, 3.23.2, 3.24.17. See Stauffer, *Dieu*, op.cit., pp.116-124, for Calvin on God's "double justice". Laplanche, *L'Ecriture*, op.cit. p.382, observes the considerable difference in the concept of justice in Amyraut and Calvin.

26 *Brief Traitté*, pp.38-39.

27 Rex, op.cit., p.91. See also the important article by D.Sabean, "The Theological Rationalism of Moïse Amyraut", *ARG* 55 (1964) pp.204-216.

28 *Six Sermons*, sermon 1 on Ezek.18.32.

29 J-P.Pittion, "Intellectual Life in the *Académie* of Saumur (1633-1685): a study in the Bouhéreau Collection", Ph.D. Dublin 1969, pp.42-47, seems to be hinting at the same distinction when he states that Amyraut's originality lay in his existential rather than ontological purpose.

30 Moltmann, "Gnadenbund", op.cit., pp.188-202.

31 F.Spanheim, *Exercitationes de Gratia Universali*, (3 vols.), Leiden 1646, vol.1, Dissertatio, 6, no pagination; see Amyraut, *Specimen*, pref., pp.79-81, 1 p.141; *De Secessione*, p.166.

32 E.g. *De Secessione* pp.167,170, *Ad Reverendi Viri, G. Riveti, Ecclesiae Talleburgensis Pastoris, Responsioram Epistolam Mosis Amyraldi Replicatio*, Saumur 1649, pp.54-55, 61-62.

33 E.g. *Specimen*, pref., p.98.

34 J.Daillé, *Apologia*, op.cit., pp.998-1108; D.Blondel, op.cit., p.12.

35 Armstrong, *Calvinism*, op.cit., esp. pp.14-16. Caution regarding a distinctively French tradition is advisable, in view of the facts that the biggest immediate influence on Amyraut (and De la Place and Cappel) was Cameron, a Scot, who mediated a German covenant tradition, and that Amyraut appealed often to the English contribution to Dort and the Polish Confession of Thorn, not giving French theologians, except Calvin and, partially, Daniel Chamier, a prominent place in his lists of "supporters", while consistently distancing himself from (the French) Beza. For humanism and scholasticism, see ante, p.60 n.2.

36 For the character of the Protestant-Catholic polemics see J.Rivière, op.cit., pp.4-19; Armstrong, *Calvinism*, op.cit., pp.4-13; Laplanche, *L'Evidence*, op.cit., pp.114-117.

37 Descartes published his *Discourse on Method* in 1637, and *Meditations* in 1641. In view of Amyraut's ethical concerns, as evidenced in his monumental *Morale*, op.cit., it is interesting to note that Descartes intended to produce a major ethical treatise, but was prevented by death, see D.C.Potts and D.G.Charlton, *French Thought Since 1600*, London 1974, p.9.

38 For the movement towards rationalism by Amyraut and those influenced by him, see Pittion, op.cit., esp. p.v; E.Labrousse, *Bayle*, Oxford 1983, pp.42-43; Laplanche, *L'Ecriture*, op.cit., p.721 (with respect to ethics, but contrast ibid., p.731); M.Heyd, *Between Orthodoxy and Enlightenment: Jean-Robert Chouet and the Introduction of Cartesian Science in the Academy of Geneva*, The Hague 1982; J.M.Pope, "Aspects of the Controversies concerning the Doctrine of Grace Aroused by the Teachings of Claude Pajon", Ph.D. St.Andrews 1974; J.W.Beardslee, "Theological Development at Geneva under Francis and Jean-Alphonse Turretin", Ph.D. Yale 1956. For Cartesianism and Reformed theology more generally, see J.Bohatec, *Die cartesianische Scholastik in der Philosophie und reformierten Dogmatik des 17. Jahrhunderts*, vol.1 Leipzig 1912; E.Bizer, "Reformed Orthodoxy and Cartesianism", *JTC* (1965)2

pp.20-82; M.I.Klauber, "Reason, Revelation and Cartesianism: Louis Tronchin and enlightened orthodoxy in late seventeenth-century Geneva", in *CH* 59(1990)3 pp.326-329, and *Between Reformed Scholasticism and Pan-Protestantism: Jean-Alphonse Turretin (1671-1737) and Enlightened Orthodoxy at the Academy of Geneva*, Selinsgrove 1994.

Chapter Eleven

Amyraut's Opponents and the Swiss Consensus of 1675

INTRODUCTION

The opposition to Amyraut's theology was intense and prolonged. Controversy raged not only in the French Reformed Church, but throughout international Calvinism. André Rivet and, later, Friedrich Spanheim, professors at Leiden, led the onslaught in the Netherlands. Already in 1637 letters of dire warning were sent from the pastors and professors of Geneva, who claimed that their anxiety was shared by all the Swiss, and from professors of Leiden, Franeker and Groningen, to the Synod of Alençon. In England, at the Westminster Assembly, 1643-1647, there were disagreements about the extent of the atonement, informed by the controversy in France.[1] Of the many theologians who put pen to paper over this issue, four of the most prominent have been selected here as representative.

BIOGRAPHICAL BACKGROUND

Pierre du Moulin (1568-1658)[2]

Pierre du Moulin's erudition and position among the French Reformed were such as to make him an opponent to be feared. He was the son of parents of the Huguenot nobility, experienced from his earliest days in suffering for the Reformed faith. As a young man he became pastor of the influential Paris church. It was Du Moulin who, along with Duplessis-Mornay, had promoted a scheme for European Protestant Unity in the second decade of the century, in the course of which he had engaged in personal negotiations with James I in London. Du Moulin was one of the deputies appointed to the Synod of Dort, and, though a last minute prohibition from Louis XIII prevented French representation, his views were made known to the Synod in a lengthy letter, and, to the wider public, in his *Anatome D'Arminianisme.*[3]

It was under Du Moulin's presidency that the Synod of Alès not only ratified the Canons of Dort, but made subscription to them compulsory for all ministerial *proposants.* Incurring the displeasure of the King of France because of his negotiations with foreign powers, he had to quit the country, and became professor of theology and principal of the Protestant Academy in the Duchy of Sedan. Du Moulin applied his skills as an implacable controversialist, honed in continual polemics with Rome, to contending against Amyraut's theology. He persistently presented Amyraut's ideas in the worst possible light.[4] To him, Amyraut was *Arminius redivivus.*[5]

Friedrich Spanheim (1600-1649)[6]

According to David Blondel, Spanheim oversaw the printing of Cameron's works in 1642 in Geneva, while he was pastor there.[7] He became convinced, however, that the Saumur theology was a deadly threat to the Reformed faith. As professor of theology in Leiden, he circulated among his students some theses, which became known to Amyraut. Amyraut considered them as an attack on himself, though Spanheim maintained that they dealt with Bremenese theology. In fact, the closeness of the theology Martinius had promoted in Bremen to that emanating from Saumur made this defence somewhat academic.[8] Amyraut defended himself in *Doctrinae de Gratia Universali ut ab Orthodoxis Explicatur Defensio*, whereupon Spanheim determined to produce a massive work that would crush Amyraldism for ever. Friends of Spanheim awaited this work with anticipation. As several promised publication dates came and went, and as the work grew and grew, even Spanheim's friends grew nervous about the kind of weapon being forged. Eventually, however, his *Exercitationes de Gratia Universali*, of some 2000 quarto pages, was issued in 1646, followed by a *Vindicia.*[9] Everything, from Amyraut's grammar to the main points of his theology, was criticized, with the leading arguments against him repeated endlessly. Spanheim's early death prevented further contributions to the debate.

John Owen (1616-1683)[10]

John Owen, who became the leading theologian of the English Independents, Vice-Chancellor of Oxford University and Chaplain to Oliver Cromwell, published *The Death of Death in the Death of Christ* in 1648. It was directed against Arminian and Amyraldian views of the extent of the atonement. Being written in English it does not seem to have received much notice on the continent, but was a sign of English Calvinistic anxiety about Amyraldism, and shows that the same arguments were used in England against a "general ransom", as on the continent. Owen was aware of, and referred to, the contributions of Du Moulin and Spanheim.[11] Since *The Death of Death* has been reprinted in the present century, and is sometimes regarded as the standard Reformed treatment of the extent of the atonement,[12] it is useful to place it in the context of the European debate. Later, Owen debated the extent of the atonement and related issues with Richard Baxter, who admired Amyraut and espoused a similar theological system.[13]

Francis Turretin (1623-1687)[14]

Francis Turretin belonged to an influential Italian family living in exile in Geneva. He is justifiably regarded as the last great systematician of the period of Reformed orthodoxy. After him, Reformed theology increasingly limited its field of interest, his son Jean-Alphonse being one of those leading the movement away from speculative and polemical systematics. Francis Turretin did not engage in direct literary warfare against Amyraut, and, countering Saumur theology in his *Institutio*,[15] his tone is calm and the survey of the points at issue quite objective. Nevertheless, his rejection of the theology of conditional universal grace was firm. Turretin was one of the architects of the 1675 *Formula Consensus*, intended to defend the Swiss against encroachments of the Saumur theology, which by then was dominant in France.

Because the opposition to Amyraut was substantially united, the views of these four theologians can be considered together.

THE CHARGES AGAINST AMYRAUT

Absurdity

At the forefront of the attack on Amyraut was the charge of absurdity. Selected citations cannot demonstrate the frequency with which this charge was made. The following are representative only. Du Moulin wrote that Amyraut's works were "full of a thousand absurdities and a thousand complicated contradictions".

> "Amyraut's habit is to tire out his reader...The Redeemer wills to redeem men conditionally, provided they are not what they are and have grace which they do not have and which he does not will to give them. So Christ wills to redeem conditionally those he wills to perish absolutely. This is...pitiful theology."[16]

Spanheim endlessly repeated parodies like the following:

> "Christ came to save on condition of faith those reprobated by the Father, whose unbelief and resulting damnation is inevitable."

Amyraut makes God's will "inane" and "illusory".[17] Owen, too, was driven to the limits of frustration by his opponents' failure to see how obviously absurd their system was:

> "Now, I ask, Whether anyone, not bereaved of all spiritual and natural sense, can imagine that Christ, in his oblation, intended to purchase life and salvation for all them whom he knew to be damned many ages before...?"[18]

The mature judgement of Reformed orthodoxy was expressed by Turretin, who referred to the "grave absurdities" of a conditional will for the salvation of all and absolute will for the salvation of some. Turretin listed the following absurdities of universal atonement: Christ would have died for many already in hell when he died; Christ would have died conditionally for many who never hear of him; Christ would have died for those he knew to have been reprobated; Christ would be a "saviour" of those never able to be saved.

It would be a mistake to discount this charge of absurdity as a cheap way of expressing disagreement. Rather, it goes to the heart of the orthodox position, which was one of pursuing logical consistency by means of deductions from predestination and the attributes of God. On the basis of God's omnipotent will, there could be no conditions in the decrees. In answering in the negative the question, "Whether some conditional will, or universal plan of mercy to the whole human race...ought to be attributed to God," Turretin explained,

> "We prove that there is not such will or plan in God (1) from the decree of election and reprobation...(There is) one single and absolutely simple act of will [in God]."[19]

It was argued that double predestination, acknowledged by Amyraut, rendered absurd the suggestion of a universal saving will of God, for how could God will to save those he had from eternity reprobated? Because God's will is joined with omniscience, he has always willed and known the non-universal outcome of the plan of salvation, so that it would have been pointless for him to have conditionally willed the salvation of all. It was not that the anti-Amyraldians objected to conditions attached to the appropriation of salvation, but to describing the will of God itself as conditional.

Omnipotent will and immutability render absurd any representation of God as changing his plans or willing what does not come to pass. [20] Owen set these points in the unmistakable framework of an Aristotelian discussion of ends and means, cause and effect, stating that,

> "The end is the first, principal, moving cause of the whole",

and concluding that if God's end in the death of Christ was to save all, experience shows that God must fail,

> "which to assert seems to us blasphemously injurious to the wisdom, power and perfection of God".[21]

The anti-Amyraldians even appealed, though less persuasively, to the attribute Amyraut made his starting point. God's goodness, they argued, made it inconceivable that he should tantalize us by promising such a great benefit as salvation on an impossible condition.[22]

The logical predestinarian system clearly revealed some of its tendencies in the debate with Amyraut. In order to maintain the omnipotence and immutability of the will of God certain other things had to be modified or denied. The "all"s of the Bible had to be explained as "all sorts", "all the elect" or "all the church" in the by then familiar way. The anthropopathic statements of Scripture had to be referred to facets of God's dealings with the world, but not his inner attitude towards it. In other words, biblical portrayals of God's grief over the lost could mean no more than that God requires sinners to repent. More generally, the revealed will of God, which most Reformed theologians had given a real, albeit subservient and occasionally precarious, existence, was reduced to an external statement of human duty.

> "The command to believe and repent shows us what God wills to require, but not that he has any intention or will that what he requires should take place."

In its address to all the gospel does not disclose a decree to save all. Rather,

> "It indicates...what is the duty of those who wish to be made partakers of salvation."

> "We must exactly distinguish between human duty and God's purpose, there being no connection between them."[23]

In addition to this caution, the point was made that God does not want people to believe immediately that Christ died for them, but mediately, that is, after certain degrees of repentance and faith have been attained. Strictly speaking, the call to believe is not addressed directly to all people, but to all the penitent. Penitence, as a gift of God and sign of election, indicates an entitlement to the atonement. Turretin divided the act of faith into a first (direct) and second (indirect) act. The direct act consists of "fly[ing] to Christ and embrac[ing] his promises", and is subdivided into assent to the promises "as true to all who repent and fly to Christ by living faith", and actually flying to Christ. The second (or third) step is a reflex act by which "I discover that I have indeed believed, and the promises of the gospel belong to me". These acts precede the belief that Christ died for me, and presuppose repentance:

> "Each and all are not commanded simply to believe, but those who are burdened, heavy-laden with the weight of their sins...the penitent, who acknowledge their wretchedness."[24]

In this way, high predestinarianism was combined with fully developed conditionalism. These statements show how far predestinarian logic could, and perhaps had to, lead away from the initial Reformation proclamation of grace.

There is no clearer way of showing that the orthodox were dominated by a logical predestinarianism than to examine their charge that Amyraut's system failed the test of predestinarian logic, and to see how willing they were to make the data of the

Bible, and of the Reformed tradition itself, conform to this logic. In their exaltation of logic, they professed that the Arminians deserved more respect than did the Amyraldians, for the former argued more consistently from their principles than did the avowedly predestinarian Amyraut.[25] The previous chapter has shown how Amyraut anticipated this charge, and admitted that he was prepared to live with logical inconsistency. His system was shaped rather by historical and ethical considerations. Indeed, within the limits of what Amyraut was trying to do, his system has consistency. It is primarily a description of God's historical, covenantal dealings with the human race. Predestination has its coherent place within that system only as the *ex post facto* explanation of how the conditions of the covenant are fulfilled. Whether this satisfies the biblical data about predestination is another question. It may also be asked why a concern to present conversion as being entirely of grace needs to go beyond a doctrine of effectual calling, to a system of pretemporal decrees concerning the fixed destiny of all individuals. Nevertheless it is not necessary to accuse Amyraut of absurdity, within the limited objective he set himself. The reason the "orthodox" saw only absurdity, is that they did not share his ethical and historical perspective. They expected his system to make sense in terms of the logic of a total predestinarian explanation, with no loose ends and, in accordance with their Aristotelian philosophy, no possibility that an omnipotent cause could fail to produce its desired effect.

However, although the charge of absurdity from the "orthodox" points partly to their own failure to appreciate a different perspective, it also draws attention to a deeper problem, namely the apparent inconsistencies already present in the Reformed system: the two divine wills, an atonement simultaneously for all and for some only, a gospel designed both to offer Christ seriously to all and to separate those preordained to be saved from the reprobates. Amyraut accepted these already existing difficulties and used them to construct a dichotomous system. He believed he could resolve the problems by making everything hinge on conditional and hypothetical elements in God's dealings with the world. Specifically, the predestinarian and covenantal sides of his system meet in the fulfilment of the conditions of the covenant. Conditionality facilitates the movement from universal to non-universal salvation. If at this point Amyraut fails to convince, and serious objections can be raised to giving conditionality such a crucial role in what is meant to be a theology of grace, it may be judged that his achievement was to bring into sharp focus the incompatible elements already within Reformed theology.

If it is true that Amyraut was more effective in exposing the problems of their common heritage than resolving them, the vehemence of his brethren in opposing him is easy to understand. Their charge of absurdity might have been better directed, however, not chiefly at his system, but at those contradictory elements of already existing Reformed theology which he so boldly brought to the fore. In this connection, Laplanche's judgement deserves more attention than it has received: "It does not seem an exaggeration to say that the effect of his system was to underline further the difficulties inherent in the beliefs he wanted to defend...the system of Amyraut deserves interest more for its intentions than its results."[26]

Each side exposed the weaknesses of the other's positions, but neither provided a satisfying way forward. Amyraut's opponents found it necessary to labour to remove the inconsistencies in Reformed theology more thoroughly than had been done before, except perhaps by Beza and the minority who adhered to his supralapsarianism. By carrying their systematization to such lengths, Du Moulin, Spanheim and their allies helped to fuel the reaction, which set in towards the end of the century, to all forms of Reformed systematics.

A Threat to Divine Freedom and Grace

One of the main objections levelled at the Arminians had been that their system, and in particular their use of antecedent and consequent decrees, made God dependent upon man, thus limiting divine freedom. There was a difficulty here for the orthodox, for most of them had espoused the infralapsarian construction, which viewed God's plan of salvation as a response of God to the world, in the single instance of the fall. It was the fear of doing this, and of the way this procedure could be extended, which had driven Beza to supralapsarianism. He had seen that there is no logical stopping point, once it is accepted that God can be thought of as responding to human beings, until the Bolsec position, in which election is God's response to human faith, is reached. It is possible that infralapsarians like Du Moulin and Turretin protested against Amyraut's willingness to make the decree of predestination consequent upon human rejection of the gospel partly through alarm that the principle behind their own infralapsarianism was being shown to be dangerously adaptable: if Amyraut could make the decree of election dependent on human rejection of the gospel (as they made the decree dependent on man's freely chosen fall), how could an appeal to the absolute nature of divine decrees serve as a defence against the Arminian understanding of election as dependent on human acceptance of the gospel?

The infralapsarians were being somewhat inconsistent, then, in accusing Amyraut of overthrowing God's freedom, understood as his independence from and determination of human actions, and, since the Reformed understanding of grace was bound to this view of God's freedom, of threatening the doctrine of grace. The freedom of God's will, in this sense, had become so basic to the logic of Reformed theology, that in fact the anti-Amyraldians regarded it as being worth maintaining for its own sake, irrespective of the need to defend the doctrine of grace. It was for this reason that Du Moulin declared that Amyraut "proposed with the Arminians universal conditional decrees...the whole controversy is about the decrees". Turretin, though a convinced infralapsarian, stated that,

"There are no conditional decrees, because they are eternal, immutable, dependent on God's pleasure alone, and because [conditional decrees would] make God dependent on man...There is no *scientia media*."

He went on to state that this was why the French synods had condemned the notion of conditional decrees. There was no objection to speaking of God's promises and warnings as conditional, provided it was understood that the human response was pre-ordained. From the human point of view there are conditions but from the divine, the "conditions" are simply "means", otherwise God's freedom is threatened. Du Moulin regarded it as intolerable that Amyraut should try to define God's actions as more or less free, and discuss whether God's actions are in accordance with his nature.[27]

It is interesting in this connection to note that both Owen and André Rivet, another leading opponent of Amyraldism, raised the question of whether the death of Christ was the only way satisfaction could be made, and both refused to answer in the affirmative. Owen frequently attacked Socinianism, and, probably through pondering the conclusions Socinians drew concerning the nature of the atonement from their premise of the absolute freedom of God, he later committed himself to the necessity of the atonement.[28] However, the fact that he and Rivet could suggest in the context of the Amyraldian debate that God might have acted otherwise is indicative of their preference for rooting the divine activity in the inscrutable divine will rather than in the moral attributes.

A Distortion of the Covenant

Different concepts of the covenant of grace had been apparent at Dort among the Contra-Remonstrants. Amyraut followed the tradition which excluded predestination from the covenant. The other tradition, followed by his opponents, made the covenant of grace co-extensive with election, as its means of execution. Thus, according to the anti-Amyraldians, faith is both a requirement and gift of the covenant. In making this point, Owen also revealed that he located the freeness of salvation not primarily in the form of the covenant, but in the empowering of the elect to fulfil its difficult conditions:

"Is it not as easy for someone by his own strength to fulfil the whole law, as to repent and savingly believe the promise of the gospel? This, then, is one main difference of these two covenants, - that the Lord did in the old only require the condition; now, in the new, he will also effect it in all the federates."

In the Saumur theology, faith is a requirement of the covenant, but a gift of predestination, regarded as a separate category. In the Amyraldian controversy, the anti-Amyraldians made it clear that faith is required of all people in so far as it is a natural duty, but not because the covenant applies to all.[29] Amyraut was criticized for viewing the indiscriminate call to faith as a matter of grace as well as duty. At the same time he was blamed for excluding the gift of faith from the covenant of grace, and thus from the benefits of the atonement, even making faith prior to the reception of the Spirit.[30] His opponents view was that,

> "Salvation, indeed, is bestowed conditionally; but faith, which is the condition, is absolutely procured."[31]

The objection of the orthodox, then, was that Amyraut was removing grace from the covenant of grace - grace became a supplement to the covenant, enabling its fulfilment. The impression that Amyraut made the gospel a kind of law was heightened by his pointing out that, initially, the gospel fails, exactly as the Mosaic law does, through human inability.[32] In fact, each side could be considered guilty of reducing faith to a kind of legal requirement, Amyraut because he made it a condition on which the covenant of grace was suspended, and the orthodox because, as far as the non-elect are concerned, and as far as the not yet converted elect can see, the requirement to repent and believe is purely a matter of duty.[33] In practice, in spite of variations within their covenant theology, both sides confronted the seeker of salvation with a condition he had to fulfil, and the work of divine grace was understood as enabling persons to fulfil the condition. Neither side could preach, "Christ died for you", without qualification. Both sides could only say, albeit with different meaning, "Christ died for you if you believe". Both positions, then, cast a heavy shadow of conditionalism over grace. Whilst Amyraut's pastoral concern to have a gospel applicable to all can be admired, the theological instinct of the "orthodox" may have been more sound. For if the original purpose of the predestination doctrine in Reformed theology was to safeguard and highlight the grace of God in the gospel, Amyraut was abandoning a fundamental insight in trying to make a radical separation between predestination on the one hand and the covenant and gospel on the other.

An Empty Atonement

In addition to the above criticisms, the orthodox directly attacked Amyraut's universal atonement teaching along the following lines:

a) The atonement could not have been made for all, since many were already in hell when Christ died. To suffer for such would have been useless.[34]

In making this point the orthodox seemed to have forgotten their own explanation of how Old Testament saints were justified, namely that the atonement was available and effective backwards as well as forwards in time, for, in the eternal purpose and knowledge of God, Christ was "the Lamb slain from the foundation of the world". It was hardly consistent of Du Moulin and the others to deny on chronological grounds the potential usefulness of the atonement to the non-elect who lived before Christ, when they taught its actual usefulness to the elect of the pre-Christian era. Perhaps they used this argument more for its vivid imagery than its consistency.

b) The sacrifice, intercession and resurrection of Christ, and the giving of the Spirit, are various stages in his one work, and must all relate to the same persons.[35]

Turretin made this often expressed point when he wrote that Christ's intercession is said in John 17.9 to be "not for the world", which he understood to mean the eternally reprobated portion of the world. Since, therefore, Christ prayed only for the elect, his sacrifice too must have been for them.[36] In similar vein it was constantly repeated that the acquisition and application of salvation must be co-extensive. Amyraut answered that the intercession of Christ was indeed in accord with his sacrifice: neither are for the unbelieving world actually, though both are potentially, since both are conditional:[37] all the saving acts of Christ are dependent on the human response, and therefore on the sovereign will of God, for their actualization.

Owen perceived that the connection between Christ's earthly and heavenly work could be turned against him, however, for it could be argued that Christ's universal lordship must imply a universal atonement. He therefore denied explicitly that Christ's kingly office is founded upon his death in the same way that his priestly office is.[38]

c) If Christ died for all sins, he died for unbelief. Therefore unbelief cannot be made the principle upon which some are excluded from the atonement. The exclusion must reside in the sovereign will of God.[39]

The tendency of this argument, suggested by Beza at Montbéliard, seems contrary to the statement of Dort, that none "perish in unbelief [because of]...any defect or insufficiency in the sacrifice of Christ offered on the cross, but through their own fault".[40] It also treats faith as if it were only a meritorious act (and unbelief as only an act meriting divine punishment, and calling for atonement), whereas Reformed theology had always insisted that, in justification, the significance of faith is instrumental rather than meritorious.

d) God cannot exact a double payment for sin.

This argument, first employed by Beza, and repeated at Dort, surfaced again in the Amyraldian debate. Spanheim wrote,

> "If Christ died absolutely for reprobates, then he died in their place as well as for their good, and therefore their sins are expiated. Justice cannot demand a further penalty."[41]

It is possible that an increased emphasis, due to the Socinian challenge, on a strictly substitutionary atonement in which Christ died not only "for our good" but "in our place",[42] gave this argument a greater prominence than in the past. Rejecting Grotius' view that Christ had offered an equivalent payment to that which was due, Owen argued for an identical payment (*solutio eiusdem*):

> "It was a full, valuable compensation, made to the justice of God, for all the sins of all those for whom he made satisfaction, by undergoing that same punishment which, by reason of the obligation that was upon them, they

> themselves were bound to undergo. When I say *the same*, I mean essentially the same in weight and pressure, though not in all accidents of duration and the like....Is it probable that God calls any to a second payment, and requires satisfaction of them for whom, by his own acknowledgement, Christ hath made that which is full and sufficient?"[43]

Later Owen argued that Christ suffered the same (*idem*, not just *tantundem*) penalty due to sinners, against the Amyraut-like Richard Baxter.[44] The Scot Samuel Rutherford made the same point forcefully in his 1647 work on the death of Christ.[45]

It is not surprising that, concentrating on the amount of suffering Christ endured for a certain number of people, Owen did not give prominence to the universal sufficiency of Christ's death. Unexpectedly, however, he did say that he made "this innate sufficiency of the death of Christ...the foundation of its promiscuous proposal to the elect and reprobate". Nevertheless, in granting that the "value, worth and dignity" of Christ's ransom was sufficient to benefit millions more than actually exist, he still maintained the atonement was not made for the non-elect. Turretin, Du Moulin and Spanheim also held that sufficiency alone is an empty concept. It must be linked with intention, and God's intention has reference to the elect only. Consistent with their stress throughout on God's will, these writers emphasized what Christ's work was willed to be, rather than what it may have been in itself. Du Moulin warned that the mere concept of sufficiency could easily lead to debate about whether the atonement was sufficient for horses and beetles![46]

However clumsy some of the above arguments may be, and though they threatened to move away from some of the prime concerns of earlier Reformed theology, they expressed a basic conviction that the atonement is an accomplished fact. It should be understood as having achieved something in the relationship between God and humanity, and not merely as having a potentiality awaiting the human response. So Spanheim bracketed Amyraut with the Arminians in teaching that Christ acquired conditional rather than actual remission of sins, and Turretin argued,

> "Christ did not die just to remove obstacles, or else he would have procured for us only the possibility of being saved...The words of Scripture imply actuality."[47]

Amyraut's assertion that Christ died for all if all should believe seemed to suspend the work of Christ on the human will, in distinction from biblical statements that Christ has redeemed, reconciled and propitiated. Amyraut's atonement merely removed the barriers to reconciliation. The movement from potentiality to actuality depended entirely on human faith. What, the orthodox demanded, was God's will in sending his Son? If it was only that all would be saved if they should believe, it would be equally true that his will was that none should be saved if none should believe.

> "To have willed life under an impossible condition is the same as not to have willed it."

Owen opposed the position of Grotius, shared by Amyraut and Baxter, that "we have no benefit from the death of Christ, except on performance of a condition, not absolutely procured by the death of Christ", and put forward his understanding of "actual deliverance":

> "That the Lord Jesus, by the satisfaction and merit of his death and oblation, made for all and only his elect, both actually and absolutely purchased and procured for them all spiritual blessings of grace and glory; to be made out unto them, and bestowed upon them, in God's way and time, without dependence on any condition to be by them performed, not absolutely procured for them thereby."

To speak of Christ dying for us conditionally is to rob his work of its objectivity.

> "It is nowhere said in Scripture, nor can it reasonably be affirmed, that if we believe, Christ died for us, as though our believing should make that to be which otherwise was not, - the act create the object."[48]

A Reformed dilemma was being pin-pointed: actual atonement seemed to render the call to faith superfluous and to be necessarily limited to the elect, in whom its reality is eventually seen. Universal atonement, ineffective until a condition is fulfilled, seemed to rob the work of Christ of its character as an objective accomplishment. The lonely Samuel Huber, at the end of the 16th. century, seeking to establish an actual, universal atonement, without necessarily entailing universal salvation, had been rejected, and no-one on either side of the Amyraldian debate sought to find a way out of the impasse by drawing inspiration from him. In fact, Amyraut's opponents sometimes accused the Saumur professor of approximating to Huber's views,[49] but Amyraut's conditionalism both cleared him of this charge, and prevented him from using the biblical terminology of accomplished redemption. Had Amyraut borrowed from the vocabulary of Samuel Ward, and spoken of *reconciliabilitas* etc., as he could have done, his departure from the biblical terminology would have been more obvious, and would have underlined the dubious nature of his solution.

e) The atonement and the love of God.

The Saumur school, in terms very similar to those used a century earlier by Heinrich Bullinger, had traced the atonement to its source in the love which is the very nature of God, a philanthropy which is, by definition, universal. Owen sharply countered this:

> "That God hath any natural or necessary inclination, by his goodness, or any other property, to do good to us, or any of his creatures, we deny. Every thing that concerns us is an act of his free will and good pleasure, and not a natural, necessary act of his Deity."

Similarly Du Moulin wrote,

> "Love in God is not an affection, nor passion, nor inclination of the minde, nor any desire: for God is not touched by these passions...so love in God is a certaine and sure will of doing good to the creature. Whence it cometh to passe, that hee may rightly be said to be loved by God, to whom he hath given or hath decreed to give more and better good things."[50]

God's love was identified with his will to save certain persons, as was election. Thus, for Amyraut's opponents, the mission of Christ proceeded from God's electing will, and so was necessarily limited in its scope. Accordingly Owen rejected the Amyraldian interpretation of John 3.16:

> "By 'love' in this place our adversaries agree that *a natural affection and propensity in God to the good of the creature, lost under sin, in general, which moved him to take some way whereby it might possibly be remedied,* is intended. We, on the contrary, say that *love* here is...an *act of his will.*"

Owen made "the purpose of sending or giving Christ to be...subordinate to God's love to his elect...in respect of our apprehension".

> "Christ's mission is traced from particular not general philanthropy...the mission of Christ proceeds from election."[51]

There is a basic difference here between Amyraut's preference to see God's acts as flowing necessarily from his nature and his opponents to see them arising from an undetermined will. It was in fact the continuation of a debate going back at least as far as the divide between the *Via Antiqua* and the *Via Moderna* of the medieval period.

f) Biblical texts favour limited atonement

It should be pointed out that the opponents of Amyraut believed that, as well as their reasoned theological arguments, they had statements of Scripture that were clearly on their side, such as those which speak of Christ dying for his sheep, his bride and his church.[52]

Novelty

Vying with the charge of absurdity was that of novelty. Amyraut and his followers were the "new methodists"[53], and the Alençon Synod detected and forbade their new ways of speaking.[54] Amyraut admitted that his "method" was different from the one currently popular, but claimed that it was the method only, and not the substance of his teaching, that was new. His most determined opponents rejected this defence, claiming that the Saumur method overthrew the orthodox faith itself.[55]

Reliance upon Reason

Amyraut was blamed for his use of reason. In return, he recognized his opponents as champions of logic and criticized them for their attempts, by means of logic, to pry into God's secrets. While he blamed them for trying to render the ways of God logically comprehensible, they condemned his attempts to render them ethically acceptable. He blamed them for their deductions from the omnipotence of God, they blamed him for his from the goodness of God. His attack was directed against their scholastic orientation, theirs against his human-centred approach. In other words, two different kinds of rationalism were at work.[56]

Universal Saving Revelation

Amyraut's teaching about a universal, potentially saving revelation in nature was strongly condemned as undermining the uniqueness of the gospel, rendering the knowledge of Christ unnecessary, and being wholly inconsistent with the historic stance of Reformed theology. It was recognized that this universal revelation was needed by Amyraut's ethically based system, in order to complete a picture of a universal, saving goodness of God towards lost humanity. Du Moulin, Spanheim and the rest were not slow to point out that this aspect of Amyraut's system was evidence that he was striking out into territory hitherto unknown to the Reformed, and betraying the weakness of his whole system. It was not acceptable, they insisted, to build grace upon nature.[57]

Separation of Christ and Predestination

In the "orthodox" system, Christ and predestination were necessarily connected: the Mediator is executor of the decree of election, and head of the elect.

> "The good pleasure of God alone is the foundation of election. Christ is the primary means."
>
> "The fountain and cause of God's sending Christ is his eternal love to his elect, and to them alone."[58]

In this system, Christ could not be the revealer of the whole meaning of the decree of election, for that decree had a secret element, having to do with "certain persons" whose identity could only be disclosed in individual experience. Nevertheless, at least Christ and predestination were intimately linked. In the work of redemption, the appointed head represented the elect members of his body.[59] Divine election necessitated and governed the Mediator and his work, and so, conversely, Christ at least partially embodied and revealed election. This appears as a strength in comparison with Amyraut's system, in which predestination is a kind of "plan B", brought in to prevent redemption turning out to be fruitless, but from which Christ's work stands entire and separate. Using the Amyraldian approach, it is impossible to interpret predestination christologically. It is regrettable that, in fact, neither side saw a need to construct the doctrine of predestination from a strictly christological starting point. However, at least the "orthodox" kept Christ and predestination together, whereas Amyraut's entire system rested on dividing them. By separating Christ and predestination, he diverted attention from the possibility of a christocentric understanding of predestination, and gave up all hope of viewing Christ as complete expression of the eternal will of God.

THE FORMULA CONSENSUS HELVETICA (1675)[60]

The Genevans took an active interest in the Amyraldian controversies from the outset, sending a letter calling for the condemnation of the new teaching to the Synod of Alençon. From the time of the Synod of Charenton (1644-5), Basel, Bern, Schaffhausen and Zurich began to consult about the situation in France, and, indeed, Zurich had withdrawn its students from Saumur as early as 1636. In 1645 the Bernese government forbade the Lausanne Academic Council to send students to Saumur. In the next few years, three letters were sent from the Swiss churches to the church at Paris, critical of the Saumur teaching. In spite of defensive replies, and a lengthy letter from Amyraut to Irminger of Zurich, they were not pacified. Meanwhile, the company of pastors would only certify the orthodoxy of Alexander Morus, who had succeeded Spanheim to one of the chairs of theology but in 1649 wished to leave Geneva, after he had signed anti-Amyraldian theses based on the strict Genevan submission at the Synod of Dort. The theses, which included the assertion that Christ had died for the elect only, were then given the status of an official standard of the Genevan Church. On 11 June 1669, at a pastors' meeting, two professors, Louis Tronchin and Charles Mestrezat, refused to impose the 1649 articles on a French *proposant*, Charles Maurice. Their colleague Turretin petitioned the Genevan authorities to see to it that the rule should be upheld, and wrote to J.H.Heidegger of Zurich to suggest the adoption of a creed for the whole of Switzerland. Gernler of Basel wrote around, urging support for the project. There was reluctance on the part of some, but eventually the *Formula Consensus*, drawn up by Heidegger, was approved by the Swiss Evangelical Diet in March 1675. Divisions in Geneva meant that it was not accepted there until January 1679, and, even then, Tronchin and Mestrezat only agreed to be bound by the Formula in their official lectures. Within a few years, the influx of French refugees as a result of the revocation of the Edict of Nantes in 1685, most of whom were Amyraldian, made the Formula difficult to maintain. Furthermore, a lack of confidence in speculative theology, and a determination to concentrate on fundamental, commonly held, truths was setting in by that time. So, the Formula did not remain in force for long, being suppressed in Basel, for example, in 1687 through the influence of the Elector of Brandenburg, and falling out of use in Geneva in 1706. It lasted longest - to 1758 - in Lausanne.

The Formula has been rightly called "the most precise and exclusive of Calvinist symbols"[61]. Although adopting a clearly infralapsarian stance, it presented a doctrine of grace wholly subordinated to predestination, understood as an absolute and inevitable decree relating to the destiny of individuals.

> "He elected a certain and definite number."

The work of Christ was firmly subordinated to this overarching concept of predestination.

> "In that gracious decree of Divine Election, moreover, Christ Himself is included, not as the meritorious cause, or foundation anterior to Election itself, but as being Himself also elect...and accordingly, as the first requisite of the execution of the decree of Election."

> "The Holy Scriptures...declare...the appointment and giving of Christ, our Mediator, to proceed from the strenuous love of God the Father to the world of the elect."

> "The appointment, also, of Christ, as Mediator, equally with the salvation of those who were given to Him...proceeds from one and the same Election, and does not underlay Election as its foundation."

In harmony with these statements the covenant of grace is conceived as relating only to the elect.

> "He was made Surety of the new Covenant only for those who, by the eternal Election, were given to Him as His own people."

The inescapable consequence of these positions is that,

> "He encountered dreadful death instead of the elect alone...and these only He reconciled to God."

The elect were actually reconciled by Christ, with whom they were united and in whom they died and rose. For them, and not the world, Christ intercedes. Continuing the tightly logical scheme, the gifts of the Spirit and faith are declared to have been merited by Christ's death for the elect. The fact that the call of the gospel also reaches the non-elect, who do not respond, is explained as in no way implying that God does not achieve what he wills, for he wills that the non-elect should know that they have a duty to believe, and that, in this way they should be rendered inexcusable.

> "For God always accomplishes His will."

The Amyraldian teachings about universal "philanthropy", and "a kind of conditioned willing", and the placing of election as logically posterior to the redemptive work of Christ are dismissed as "in no wise insignificant deviations", because of the explicit particularism of Scripture, for example regarding Jacob and Esau, and because they contradict God's immutability.

> "For God is infinitely removed from all that human imperfection which characterizes inefficacious affections and desires, rashness, repentance and change of purpose."

Other aspects of Saumur teaching were outlawed: the three covenant scheme, with the assertion that what was promised under the first two covenants was earthly happiness only; the call of nature and providence to salvation; the terminology of "moral" and "natural" ability; the denial of the imputation of Christ's active righteousness. Also condemned were De la Place's mediate imputation of original sin, and Cappel's denial of the divine inspiration of the vowel points of the Hebrew Old Testament.[62]

The Formula cannot but impress with its logic and consistency, within its own terms of reference. The subordination of the whole doctrine of grace, including the work of Christ, to particular predestination, eliminates untidiness, and produces a solid structure of doctrine. This impression is, indeed, the most significant thing about it, its coherence standing in contrast to the dichotomies of Amyraut's system. By the same token, the Formula presents in the plainest terms a theology starting with the hidden God of predestination rather than with the God revealed in Christ and his cross. The gospel call has been turned into an announcement of duty rather than a proclamation of grace: the grace can only appear after the duty has been complied with, for only then can a person conclude that he is one of those for whom Christ died.

Conclusion

The main argument brought against the Amyraldian construction of the doctrine of grace was "absurdity". This criticism is its own comment on the place of predestinarian logic in the system of the "orthodox", but also indicates that Amyraut highlighted contradictions inherent in the Reformed tradition. Amyraut thought that the way to resolve the contradictions was to emphasize the hypothetical nature of God's saving will and the conditionality of the gospel: Christ died for those who would fulfil the conditions of repentance and faith. This emphasis made the gospel resemble the law. It is true that Amyraut went on to talk about the gracious, effectual work of the Spirit attached to the gospel, but explicitly stated that this was something additional, and not essential to the covenant itself, as well as having reference to the elect only. Baxter's similar construction became known in England, not without reason, as Neonomianism.[63]

A criticism which was not prominent among the charges made by his opponents, but which arises by comparison with their system, was Amyraut's willingness to separate Christ and predestination.

Direct arguments against universal atonement had as their core the conviction that Christ's work actually accomplished something for those for whom he died, whereas Amyraut's theology emptied the atonement of objective accomplishment. In this respect the orthodox had the biblical terminology on their side.

In historical terms, no-one "won" the controversy over universal grace. Amyraut's views became general in France, but the French Church was dispersed by the revocation of the Edict of Nantes in 1685. Anti-Amyraldian views were enshrined in the Swiss Consensus, but this statement was far from wholeheartedly received, and the issues were soon to be largely lost sight of on the eve of the Enlightenment. In England, in spite of the fact that a number of deputies at the Westminster Assembly (1643-1647), including Calamy, Seaman, Arrowsmith and Vines, favoured universal redemption, the Confession set the redeeming work of Christ in the context of particular election, and co-ordinated the acquisition and application of salvation.[64] Nevertheless, as the century progressed, the Baxterian middle way gained a wide following among the Presbyterians, while the Anglican bishops of the Restoration generally shared a distaste for all forms of predestinarianism. The "Marrow" controversy in Scotland at the beginning of the eighteenth century saw conflict and division over the same issues again. It seems fair to conclude that the question of the extent of the atonement, already handled ambiguously by the Synod of Dort, was never satisfactorily answered by the Reformed Churches throughout their early and classical period.

In theological terms too, it is hard to award the prize to Amyraut or his opponents. Both systems had grave weaknesses, and rendered the inconsistencies of earlier Reformed theology more obvious. Our evaluation is that, while Amyraut bravely tried to free the atonement from the shackles of the particular predestinarianism of the "orthodox", many of their criticisms of his alternative were substantial. It is very difficult to conclude that he solved the problem of the extent of the atonement.

Notes

1 See Van Stam, op.cit., for detailed examination of the development of the controversy; Quick, *Synodicon*, op.cit., vol. 2, pp. 397-411, for letters to the Synod of Alençon. For "Amyraldism" at the Westminster Assembly, see A.F.Mitchell and J.Struthers (eds.), *Minutes of the Sessions of the Westminster Assembly of Divines*, Edinburgh 1874, pp. xxv-xxvi, xlvii-lxiii, 152-158 (Sessions 522-523, October 22-24 1645).

2 For Du Moulin, see ante, p.221 n.6, esp. Rimbault op.cit., pp.161-166, for his part in controversy with Amyraut. See also C. Bost, "Pierre du Moulin et Amyraut", *BSHPF* 77(1928).

3 The letter is found in *Acta*, op.cit., pp.289-300. *The Anatome D'Arminianisme*, Leiden 1619, was soon published in English as *The Anatomy of Arminianisme*, London 1620.

4 E.g. in his summary of the twelve leading points of the Amyraldian theology in *Examen de la Doctrine de Messieurs Amyrault & Testard...touchant la prédestination & les points qui en dépendent*, Amsterdam 1638, pref., no pagination.

5 *De Mosis Amyraldi adversus Fridericum Spanhemium Libro Iudicium*, Rotterdam 1649 p.28. The whole of chapters 10-13 (pp.24-44) enlarge upon this charge.

6 For Spanheim's part in the controversy, see ante, p.188. Spanheim was professor of theology at Geneva, then Leiden.

7 D.Blondel, *Actes*, op.cit., pp.17-18. Swinne, op.cit., pp. 88ff. denies Spanheim's role in the publication of the *Opera*, but it seems unlikely that the outstanding historian Blondel would have been mistaken about this comparatively recent event. It should be remembered that the publication of Cameron's works had the full weight of the National Synod of Castres (1626) behind it.

8 The anti-Amyraldian André Rivet acknowledged the similarily between Bremen and Saumur, letter to Claude Sarrau cited Van Stam, op.cit., p.19.

9 Amyraut's work was the "Doctrinae de Gratia Universali Defensio", in *Dissertationes*, op.cit. Spanheim's *Exercitationes de Gratia Universali* was published in Leiden in 1646, and contains the theses which had renewed the controversy (pp 1-19). The *Vindicia pro Exercitationibus Suis* was published in Amsterdam in 1649.

10 For Owen, see A.Thomson, "Life of Dr. Owen", in *The Works of John Owen*, ed.W.H.Goold, vol.1; P. Toon, *God's Statesman: the life and work of John Owen, Pastor, Educator, Theologian*, Exeter 1971; D.D.Wallace, *Puritans and Predestination: Grace in English Protestant Theology*, Chapel Hill 1982, pp.144-157; for his interest in the Amyraldian debate see J.I.Packer's Introductory Essay to *The Death of Death in the Death of Christ*, London 1959, pp.23,24, and Owen's references to Amyraut and Cameron in the same work, pp.37,110,117.

11 Ibid., p.297. The original title of Owen's work was, *Salus Electorum, Sanguis Iesu, or, The Death of Death in the Death of Christ*, 1648. The 1959 reprint is used here.

12 Ibid., Introductory Essay, pp.22-23.

13 For Baxter's admiration of Cameron and Amyraut, see N.H.Keeble and G.F.Nuttall (eds.), *Calendar of the Correspondence of Richard Baxter* (2 vols), vol.1 (1638-1660), pp.53,113 n.4,118,278. For the similarities between Amyraut and Baxter, see J.I.Packer, "The Redemption and Restoration of Man in the Thought of Richard Baxter: a study in puritan theology", D.Phil. Oxford 1954 pp.212-225, 254-270; A.C.Clifford, *Atonement*, op.cit., Oxford 1990, pp. 26-28,154.

14 For Turretin, see G.Keizer, *François Turrettini, sa vie et ses oeuvres, et la Consensus, Lausanne 1900;* J.W.Beardslee, "Theological Development", op.cit., and (ed.) *Reformed Dogmatics*, op.cit., Editor's Introduction, pp.14-25; D.Grohman, "The Genevan Reactions to the Saumur Doctrines of Hypothetical Universalism 1635-1685", Th.D. Knox College, Toronto, 1971, pp.51-124; M.I.Klauber, "The Helvetic Formula Consensus (1675): an introduction and translation", *TJ* 11(1990)1, pp.103-123.

15 *Institutio Theologicae Elencticae*, in *Opera* (4 vols.), Edinburgh 1847. Parts of this work relating to the Amyraldian debate are published in English in Beardslee, *Reformed Dogmatics*, op.cit., pp.335-359, and we have used Beardslee's translations where possible.

16 Du Moulin, *Iudicium*, pp.163,117-118.

17 Spanheim, *Exercitationes*, vol.3 p.2101, vol.1 pp.136,121.

18 Owen, op.cit., pp.226-227.

19 Turretin, 14.14.7; cp.4.18.20; 14.14.35; 4.17.14-15.

20 Du Moulin, *Examen*, pp.10-12; Turretin, 4.3.6; Spanheim, *Exercitationes*, p.136; Du Moulin, *Iudicium*, pp.84-85.

21 Owen, op.cit., pp.48,47.

22 Spanheim, *Exercitationes*, vol.2 pp.1501-1508. The alternative title to Du Moulin's *Iudicium* was, *Pro Dei Misericordia, & Sapientia, & Iustitia Apologia.*

23 Owen, op.cit., pp.218-256; Spanheim, *Exercitationes*, vol.2 p.1568; Turretin, 4.17.41; 14.14.53; Owen, op.cit., pp.187-189.

24 Turretin, 14.14.45-49, CP. 4.15.365.

25 Du Moulin, *Iudicium*, pp.29-30.

26 Laplanche, *Orthodoxie*, op.cit., pp.296-297.

27 Du Moulin, *Iudicium*, pref. (no pagination); ibid., p.73; Turretin, 4.3.6, 7.

28 A.Rivet, *Synopsis Doctrinae de Natura et Gratia*, Amsterdam 1649, pp.98-100; Owen op.cit., p.93: "[It is] false and erroneous [to say] that God could not have mercy on mankind unless satisfaction were made by his Son." By 1653, his view had changed, as the anti-Socinian work, *De Divina Iustitia Dissertatio*, (Works vol.10), published that year in Oxford, shows. See also the anti-Socinian *Vindiciae Evangelicae* of 1654, esp. pp.490-496 (Works vol.10).

29 Owen, *Death of Death*, pp.124-125; cp. Spanheim, *Exercitationes*, vol.1 p.104; Du Moulin, *Anatomy*, p.356. On the meaning of covenant conditionality, see Coolidge, op.cit. pp.99-140, and G.J.McGrath, "Puritans and the Human Will: voluntarism within mid-seventeenth century English puritanism as seen in the works of Richard Baxter and John Owen", Ph.D. Durham 1989, pp.184-202.

30 Spanheim, *Exercitationes*, vol.1 pp.531,633, vol.2 pp.1000-1001; Du Moulin, *Iudicium*, p 38; Owen, *Death of Death*, pp.137-146

31 Owen, *Death of Death*, p.123, cp. ibid., pp.144-145.

32 Amyraut, *Deux Sermons de la Matière de la Justification et de la Sanctification*, Saumur 1658, pp.12-16.

33 Du Moulin, *Iudicium*, pp.17-18; Spanheim, *Exercitationes*, vol.2 pp.1063-1064.

34 Owen, *Death of Death*, pp.61,135-136; Du Moulin, *Anatomy*, p.228.

35 Du Moulin, *Anatomy*, pp.238-242, *Iudicium*, p.38; Owen, *Death of Death*, pp.67-88.

36 Turretin, 14.14.38.

37 Spanheim, *Specimen*, vol.2 pp.313-314.

38 Owen, *Death of Death*, pp. 91-93: "Christ hath a power and dominion over all, but the foundation of this dominion is not in his death for all."

39 Spanheim, *Exercitationes*, vol.1 pp.81-82, vol.2 pp.953,941-969.

40 Canons of Dort 2.6.

41 Spanheim, *Exercitationes*, vol.1 p.441, cp. Turretin, 14.14.18,26.

42 Spanheim, *Exercitationes*, vol.1 pp.441; vol.3 pp.1726,2103-2115; Owen, *Death of Death*, p.61.

43 Owen, *Death of Death*, pp.157-158.

44 Owen, *Of The Death of Christ: the price he paid, and the purchase he made*, pp.438-448. For this debate about the nature of the atonement, including Owen's contribution to it, see W.Cunningham, op.cit., vol.2 pp.301-323.

45 S.Rutherford, *Christ Dying and Drawing Sinners to Himselfe*, London 1647, p.372, "Christ told downe a definite and certaine Ransome, as a told summe of money, every penny reckoned and layed, and he knew who was his own, and whom, and how many, by the head and name, he bought." Though chiefly directed against Arminianism, Rutherford wrote with an awareness of Amyraut's teaching (ibid., p.475).

46 Owen, *Death of Death*, pp.264,271-272; Turretin,14.14.9; Spanheim, *Exercitationes*, vol.2 p.1614, vol.3 p.2058; Du Moulin, *Anatomy*, p.255.

47 Spanheim, *Exercitationes*, vol.1 p.81, Turretin, 14.14.18, cp. Owen, *Death of Death*, pp.94-95.

48 Spanheim, *Exercitationes*, vol.1 pp.136-137; Owen, *Of the Death*, p.450; *Death of Death*, p.123.

49 A.Rivet, *Opera*, vol.2 c.1167b.

50 Owen, *Death of Death*, p.115; Du Moulin, *Anatomy*, p.262.

51 Owen, *Death of Death*, pp.209,119 (cp. Spanheim, *Exercitationes*, vol.1 pp.59,95,101; Turretin, 14.14.9.

52 E.g. Owen, *Death of Death*, pp.96-109.

53 Du Moulin, *Iudicium*, p.234; Spanheim, *Exercitationes*, vol.3 p.2079; Swinne, op.cit., pp.15ff, traces the use of this and other names for the followers of Cameron.

54 Quick, *Synodicon*, op.cit., vol.2 pp.354-61.

55 Van Stam, op.cit., pp.309-310 cites a letter of March 1647 from Zurich to Paris, saying, "We do not regard it as only a matter of certain emphases. We see the principal doctrines of the faith in peril."

56 Spanheim, *Exercitationes*, vol.1 pp.921-925; Letter of A.Rivet to the Doctors and Professors of Leiden, in *Synopsis*, p.232. On Amyraut's rationalistic tendency, see ante, p.244 n.56.

57 Spanheim, *Exercitationes*, vol.1 p.667; Du Moulin, *Iudicium*, pp.94-95. Alençon required Amyraut not to speak of possible natural knowledge as faith, but to reserve that term for use in connection with "distinct knowledge of Christ", Quick, *Synodicon*, vol.2, op.cit., p.360.

58 Turretin, 4.10.1; Owen, *Death of Death*, p.119.

59 Spanheim, *Exercitationes*, vol.1 p.278.

60 For the historical background to the Consensus see Keizer, op. cit, pp.96-200; Laplanche, *Orthodoxie*, op.cit., pp.221-227; Beardslee, "Theological Development", op.cit.; Grohman, op.cit. pp.125-421; M.I.Klauber, "The Helvetic *Formula Consensus*", op.cit., pp.103-123, and *Between Reformed Scholasticism*, op. cit, pp.17-34, and, for the demise of the Formula, ibid., pp.143-164.

61 Léonard, op.cit., vol.2 p.280.

62 For the text of the *Formula Consensus*, see A.A.Hodge, *Outlines of Theology*, Grand Rapids 1949, pp.651-663; Klauber, "The Helvetic", op.cit., pp.103-123. The citations in the following exposition are from Hodge's translation.

63 British and American Antinomianism may be seen as a reaction against the conditionalism which was intrinsic to covenant theology, and Baxter's Neonomianism as a counter-reaction. See Packer, "The Redemption", op.cit., p.227; Wallace, op.cit., pp.114-153; D.C.Lachman, *The Marrow Controversy 1718-1723; a historical and theological analysis*, Edinburgh 1988, pp.36-54.

64 See the *Westminster Confession of Faith*, ch.8, "Of Christ the Mediator", in Schaff, op.cit., pp.598-673. For the Marrow Controversy, see Lachman, op.cit.

Part Four

Conclusion

Chapter Twelve

Conclusion

SUMMARY: A REFORMED DILEMMA

The foregoing survey of the way the extent of the atonement was understood in the first 150 years of Reformed theology has revealed a variety of positions. Calvin presented the atonement as both universal and restricted, depending on whether it was viewed from the perspective of the promise or of election. He had little interest in the "sufficient for all, efficient for the elect" formula, which did not specifically take into account the will of God, either "hidden" or "revealed". Beza, pushing certain elements in Calvin's thought to logical conclusions, taught an atonement limited in intention to the elect only. He too, had little use for the scholastic formula, for the concept of universal sufficiency would only be of use, as far as he was concerned, had God decreed that redemption would be universally applied. By contrast, Bullinger maintained universal atonement, conditional on faith for its application, within a potentially universal, covenantal scheme. He was much more interested in understanding God's works in the light of God's nature as love than was the Genevan school, in which the "hidden" will of God was given greater prominence. In harmony with Bullinger, a German tradition, centred on Heidelberg, emerged in the second half of the sixteenth century, making the "sufficient for all, efficient for the elect" formula central to its statement of the extent of the atonement. Zanchi, too, who spent the latter part of his career at Heidelberg, kept this statement central to his discussions, though his preoccupation with the attributes of omniscience, immutability and will of God meant that he usually stressed the particularistic side of the formula.

The teaching of Bullinger and the German school on the extent of the atonement went hand in hand with caution about predestination, and an unwillingness to be as extreme as the Genevans. This was demonstrated right through from Bullinger's unhappiness about Calvin's handling of Bolsec to the way that the Heidelberg theologians Pareus, Kimedoncius and Tossanus consistently made faith rather than election the factor which limited the extent of the atonement. A theology of conditional covenant emerged, clearly articulated in Ursinus' commentary on the

Heidelberg Catechism. This was not opposed to, but balanced against predestination. Predestination was that which enabled corrupt human beings to fulfil the conditions of the universal covenant. It was thus characteristic of the German Reformed tradition to speak of the atonement as being designed for those who would fulfil the condition of the covenant, namely believers. Whilst this approach enabled the work of Christ to be presented as relevant to all people, giving such prominence to the fulfilling of conditions imparted to it a legalistic flavour. With such concentration on conditions, it could be asked why, if the electing grace of God was revealed in giving the ability to fulfil the difficult condition of faith attached to the gospel, would not the grace of God have been magnified even more by giving the ability to fulfil the even harder conditions of the law? The Reformed contention that salvation is by faith because faith in its very nature is that which does not set out to work for God's favour was in danger of being turned on its head by this conditionalism. In fact, the conditional covenant system became generally accepted among the Reformed, but a difference was maintained between those who, true to the German school, saw the covenant as having primarily a universal purpose, but with a limited application, and those who saw it purely as a means for gathering in the elect, and so limited in intention from the outset.

The rise of Arminianism, which could be seen as a radical modification of Reformed predestinarianism by Reformed conditionalism, necessitated the calling of the Synod of Dort. There, the different strands of Reformed teaching on the covenant, and the extent of the atonement, encountered each other directly, and could not be consistently reconciled. The result was that the Canons of Dort presented a mixture of the conditional-universal, and the absolute-restricted interpretations of the atonement. The unsatisfactory nature of this compromise guaranteed that there would be further debate. Cameron and Amyraut took up the issue. The Saumur school followed the German Reformed conditional covenant teaching, but went further than many had done by making the universal conditional covenant, with its implication of universal atonement, primary, and predestination secondary, in God's dealings with the world.

In the controversy which Amyraut provoked, the main uniting factor among the opponents of Amyraut was a concern for logical consistency on the basis of the doctrine of predestination and the attributes of God. It was clear that predestination was not one doctrine among many, but had come to occupy a dominant position. Amyraut, on the other hand, was concerned for ethical consistency and historical order. Amyraut's opponents were also united in wanting to maintain an atonement which actually and objectively accomplished something in the relationship of God with the world, something proceeding wholly from God's grace and initiative, and not dependent on a human response. In spite of the short-lived Consensus of 1675, it cannot be said that the controversy was properly resolved. Nor can it be claimed, on the basis of a survey of the Reformation and classical period that there was ever such a thing as a coherent and agreed "Reformed position" on the extent of the atonement. This is the most obvious conclusion to emerge from all the detail of the present survey, and one which challenges the view frequently asserted or assumed of monolithic agreement on this point existing, if not from Calvin, at least from Beza onwards.

Why did so much controversy and attention fail to result in agreement? The answer lies partly with an inner conflict between elements within Reformed thought from the beginning. The free promise, the unrestricted preaching of grace and the summons to all to believe were deeply embedded in the Reformed consciousness, as foundational principles of the Reformation itself. But a doctrine of the eternal predestination of certain individuals, as opposed to others, also quickly established itself as part of the Reformed inheritance, for it seemed to safeguard the truth that, even in the human response to the gospel, divine grace rather than human merit is what counts. One set of principles seemed to require a universal atonement, the other, a limited one. These two sets of principles could not easily be reconciled.

At times, though not always, the Reformed theologians showed an awareness that it was crucial for them to define their doctrine of election in relation to Christ. Three approaches to coupling Christ and election can be identified, though it must be appreciated that many of the theologians covered in this study were not wholly consistent. One approach was to subordinate Christ to election. Beza, Spanheim and the Consensus represented this view. It had the advantage that it kept predestination and Christ together. However, it had problems in relating the gospel to the non-elect, turned the call to faith into a mere duty or even denied that any were to be called to faith before they had repented, and made it necessary for people to become assured of their election before they could believe that the love and grace of God displayed in Christ were for them. It also had difficulties with the phrase, "chosen in Christ". Beza referred it to a secondary election, following the decree appointing which persons would be saved and the appointment of Christ to be their mediator. Others had to supply the gloss that the phrase means "chosen to be in Christ". Furthermore, this whole approach enshrined an attempt to understand Christ from the point of view of predestination, rather than the other way around.

The opposite approach was to subordinate predestination to Christ, an approach typical of German covenant theology, shared by English thinkers like Davenant and Ward, and given sharp definition by Cameron and Amyraut. In this system, God acted as if he intended to save the entire world, on condition that the world believes the gospel. Knowing, however, that the world would not believe, God determined to give faith to some as a gift, election being that decision of the divine mind about who would receive the gift of faith. The problems here were that the conditionalism of the covenant made the gospel seem like another law which human beings in their fallen state cannot keep: even in salvation law appears to be God's chief means of dealing with the human race, with grace coming in as an unfortunately necessary supplement; election was treated as if it were just another name for the doctrine of effectual calling; the normal New Testament description of election as being "before the foundation of the world", emphasising the firmness of God's eternal purpose, gave way to an understanding of election as that which steps in when all else fails, to rescue the work of Christ and the covenant from being useless. Furthermore, this presentation also failed to approach predestination through Christ, for it made predestination additional and supplementary to the being and work of the Mediator. Again, "chosen in Christ" was reduced to mean "chosen to be in Christ". Bullinger had indicated a different way of subordinating predestination to Christ when he spoke of the chosen in Christ, not as those who will infallibly believe in Christ, but as those who are actually in him by faith. While speaking in this way Bullinger still asserted that faith is the gift of God. This was the kind of approach Lutherans like Andreae followed, focussing on Christ and, while regarding faith as the gift of God, refusing to speculate further or give the question of why some believe and others do not a key position in the theological enterprise. Bullinger's position was not taken up by the Reformed, however, and even Bullinger did not speak in that way consistently. The fact that Arminians spoke of the election of those who believe in Christ made it unlikely that Bullinger's way of speaking could ever be acceptable to the Reformed of the seventeenth century.

Some theologians cannot be easily classified as subordinating Christ to election or vice versa. Most notable among these was Calvin. He could speak of election as logically following the work of Christ, determining "to whom he gives himself to be enjoyed", but he could also speak of the whole work of Christ as flowing from particular election. It is difficult to avoid concluding that he was simply inconsistent, and had not followed through the implications of his theology at these points. The apparently arbitrary expositions of the "all" and "world" and "many" of the Bible is one indication of the incompleteness of his thought. It is significant, however, that he showed a preference to give pride of place to the absolute will of God as over against the revealed, and that the tendency of his thought was therefore towards placing limits on the scope of the work of Christ.

It has been demonstrated, then, that, in spite of unity in defining election as the eternal and unconditional selection of certain persons to be granted faith and salvation, there was great diversity among the Reformed when it came to pronouncing on the scope of the work of Christ. As far as the extent of the atonement is concerned, theories about a division between Calvin and Calvinists, or about a Reformed consensus, unbroken except for the Amyraldian exception, are untenable.

REFORMULATION: BARTH ON THE DOCTRINE OF ELECTION

It was against this background of variety and inability to agree that, in the present century, Karl Barth re-examined the Reformed doctrine of predestination.[1] While recognizing the desire of the reformers and their followers, in adhering to their doctrine of predestination, to assert the freedom of God and the priority of grace, he could not follow them in maintaining an absolute, pre-temporal decree of election and reprobation concerning certain individuals, an element in the definition of predestination over which all the old Reformed theologians had been agreed. His main criticism of the tradition was that it had thought it could know God apart from Christ, and its doctrine of predestination was the product of this illegitimate knowledge. In Luther's terms, it had attempted to know *Deus absconditus* as separate from and in addition to *Deus revelatus*; it had embarked upon a *theologia gloriae* instead of a *theologia crucis.* Beginning from the position that Christian knowledge of God comes exclusively through Christ, and appealing to those biblical texts that speak of Christ as God's Elect, he reformulated the doctrine of election so as to make it focus primarily on the Father's appointment of the God-man Jesus Christ. According to Barth, the election of the human race, of the church and of individuals must be understood as implicit in the election of Christ, and not as truths that can in any sense stand in their own right. Thus the doctrine of election is not to be regarded as the explanation of why certain persons believe, but as God's gracious decision to say "yes" in Christ to humanity, which he could justly have rejected. This election, manifested most clearly in Christ's death for all humanity, in which he became the one true reprobate, encompasses the whole human race, and by Christ's death all are reconciled. Sovereignty and grace shine in the fact that this election stands firm, irrespective of the human response to it. At the same time, only those who believe begin to live as, look like and enjoy the benefits of being "the elect", and hence that designation is reserved for them. Why faith is granted to some and not others is not revealed, but it is not the issue at the heart of the doctrine of election. Nor is it legitimate to base our theology on the data of experience, such as the existence at a given moment of certain persons as believers and others as non-believers. Rather theology must base itself on the word of God. Barth's position is summarized in the following words:

> "How can we have assurance in respect of our own election except by the Word of God? And how can even the Word of God give us assurance on this point if this Word, if Jesus Christ, is not the electing God, not the election itself, not our election, but only a means whereby the electing God - electing elsewhere and in some other way - executes that which He has decreed concerning those whom He has - elsewhere and in some other way - elected?

> The fact that Calvin in particular not only did not answer but did not perceive this question is the decisive objection we have to bring against his whole doctrine of predestination. The electing God of Calvin is a *Deus nudus absconditus*. It is not the *Deus revelatus* who is as such the *Deus absconditus*, the eternal God. All the dubious features of Calvin's doctrine result from the basic failing that in the last analysis he separates God and Jesus Christ..."[2]

R.A.Muller has contested Barth's claim that the Reformed tradition failed to interpret election in a christocentric way.[3] He has shown how successive theologians pointed out that the Son of God was associated with the Father as author of election, and that in his human nature he was first of the elect, so that Christ was both subject and object of election. But proving that Reformed theology recognized that there is an election by Christ and of Christ as well as an election of other individuals scarcely meets Barth's point, which is that the being of Christ as divine-human mediator itself constitutes the electing will of God, according to which all other aspects of election must be strictly subordinated and understood.

The present study has demonstrated the Reformed inability to come to an agreed position on the extent of the atonement. It has indicated that the inability was inevitable in the light of the inconsistency of its doctrine of predestination with its other concerns, and its failure to take Jesus Christ as the starting point for the doctrine. In doing so, it proposes that an attempt such as Barth's to find a new way of understanding predestination deserves careful consideration by all who claim to stand in the Reformed tradition.

Chapter Twelve

Notes

1 K.Barth, *Church Dogmatics*, op. cit., 2.2, ch.7, "The Election of God". Emil Brunner subjected the traditional Reformed doctrine to similar criticisms, though arriving at a somewhat different formulation of the doctrine from Barth's. See, *The Christian Doctrine of God*, op.cit., pp.303-353.

2 Barth, op.cit., p.111.

3 *Christ and the Decree*, op.cit., esp. pp.149-160, 172-173.

Abbreviations Bibiography and Index

Abbreviations

ARG	Archiv für Reformationsgeschichte
ATR	Anglican Theological Review
BS	Bibliotheca Sacra
BSHPF	Bulletin de la Société de l'Histoire du ProtestantismeFrançais
CH	Church History
CO	Ioannis Calvini Opera Quae Supersunt Omnia, ed. G Baum, E Cunitz and E Reuss, Brunswick 1863-1900 (59 vols), in Corpus Reformatorum
CTJ	Calvin Theological Journal
EQ	Evangelical Quarterly
HTR	Harvard Theological Review
JEH	Journal of Ecclesiastical History
JETS	Journal of the Evangelical Theological Society
JR	Journal of Religion
JTC	Journal for Theology and the Church
NAKG	Nederlands Archief voor Kerkgeschiedenis
RTJ	Reformed Theological Journal
RTP	Revue de Théologie et de Philosophie
SCJ	Sixteenth Century Journal
SHR	Scottish Historical Review
SJT	Scottish Journal of Theology
TJ	Trinity Journal
VE	Vox Evangelica
WTJ	Westminster Theological Journal
ZKG	Zeitschrift für Kirchengeschichte

Translations from non-English titles are by the author unless otherwise indicated.

The Extent of the Atonement

Bibliography

PRIMARY SOURCES

Bodleian Library Tanner Ms.74 contains a number of letters to and from the English deputies at Dort, relating to the Synod.

Acta Synodi Nationalis Dordrechti Habitae, Dort 1620

Ames, W *Corona ad Collationem Hagiensem*, Leiden 1618

— *Anti-Synodalia Scripta*, Amsterdam 1633

Amyraut, M *Brief Traitté de la Prédestination et de ses Principales Dépendances*, Saumur 1634

— *Eschantillon de la Doctrine de Calvin Touchant la Prédestination*, Saumur 1636

— *Six Sermons de la Nature, Estendue, Necessité, Dispensation, et Efficace de l'Evangile*, Saumur 1636

— *De l'Elévation de la Foy et de l'Abaissement de la Raison en la Créance des Mystères de la Religion*, Saumur 1640

— *Doctrinae Ioannis Calvini de Absoluto Reprobationis Decreto Defensio*, Saumur 1641

— *Paraphrase sur les Epistres de l'Apostre S. Paul aux Galates...etc.*, Saumur 1645

— *Dissertationes Theologicae Quatuor*, Saumur 1645

— *Fidei Mosis Amyraldi circa Errores Arminianorum Declaratio*, Saumur 1646

— *Adversus Epistolae Historicae Criminationes Defensio*, Saumur 1649

— *Ad Reverendi Viri, G.Riveti...Responsoriam Epistolam, Mosis Amyraldi Replicatio*, Saumur 1649

— *Deux Sermons de la Matière de la Justification et de la Sanctification*, Saumur 1658

— *Exposition des Chapitres VI et VII de l'Epistre de S. Paul aux Romains et du Chapitre XV de la Première aux Corinthiens*, Charenton 1659

— *De Mysterio Trinitatis, deque Vocibus ac Phrasibus quibus tam in Scriptura quam apud Patres Explicatur Dissertatio*, Saumur 1661

— *Eirenikon, sive de ratione pacis, in religionis negotio, inter Evangelicos constituendae, consilium*, Saumur 1662

— *In Orationem Dominicam Exercitatio*, Saumur 1662

— *In Symbolum Apostolorum Exercitatio*, Saumur 1663

— *A Treatise conerning Religions, in refutation of the opinion which accounts all things indifferent*, London 1660 (1631)

— *The Evidence of Things not Seen. Or, Diverse Scriptural and Philosophical discourses concerning the state of good and holy men after death*, trans. J.G., London n.d.

Amyraut, M; Cappel, J; De la Place, J *Syntagma Thesium Theologicarum in Academia Salmuriensi Variis Temporibus Disputatarum*, Saumur 1665

Aquinas, T *Summa Theologica*, trans. by the Fathers of the English Dominican Province, London 1922
Arminius, J *Works* (3 vols.) trans. and ed. J.Nichols, London 1852
Arrowsmith, J *Armilla Catechetica: a chain of principles*, Cambridge 1659
— *Theanthropos*, London 1660
Aymon, J *Tous les Synodes Nationaux* (2 vols.), The Hague 1710
Beza, T *A Brief and Pithie Sum of the Christian Faith*, trans. R.F., London 1572
— *A Booke of Christian Questions and Answers*, trans. A.Golding, London 1572
— *Tractationes Theologicae*, 3 vols., Geneva 1570 & 1582
— *The Treasure of Trueth*, trans. J.Stockwood, London 1576
— *Novum Testamentum*, London 1574
— *Ad Acta Colloquii Montisbelgardensis Tubingae Edita Responsionis Pars Altera*, Geneva 1588
— *Correspondance de Théodore de Bèze*, collected H.Aubert, ed.A.Dufour, F.Aubert, H. Meylan, Travaux d'Humanisme et Renaissance 40, Geneva 1960
— *Cours sur les Epitres aux Romains et aux Hébreux* 1564-1566, *d'après les notes de Marcus Widler*, ed. P.Fraenkel et L.Perrotet, Travaux d'Humanisme et Renaissance 226, Geneva 1988
Beza, T and **Faius, A** *Propositions and Principles of Divinitie, propounded and disputed in the Universitie of Geneva*, Edinburgh 1591
Blondel, D *Actes Authentiques des Eglises Reformées de France, Geramanie, Grande Bretagne, Pologne, Hongrie, Païs Bas*, Amsterdam 1655
Bolton, S *The True Bounds of Christian Freedom*, London 1645
Bucer, M *Common Places*, trans. and ed. D.F.Wright, Abingdon 1972
Bullinger, H *In Sanctissimam Pauli ad Romanos Epistolam Commentarius*, Zurich 1533
— *Inluculentum Sacrosanctum Evangelium Domini Nostri In Divinum Iesu Christi Domini Nostri Evangelium secundum Ioannem, Commentariorum Libri x*, Zurich 1548
— *Iesu Christi Secundum Lucam*, Zurich 1548
— *Isaias Excellentissimus Dei Propheta...Expositus Homiliis cxc*, Zurich 1567
— *The Olde Fayth*, trans. M.Coverdale, London 1547
— *A Brief Exposition of the One and Eternal Testament or Covenant of God (1534)*, in C.S.McCoy and J.W.Baker, *Fountainhead of Federalism: Heinrich Bullinger and the Covenant Tradition*, Louisville 1991
— *Commonplaces of Christian Religion*, trans. J.Stockwood, London 1572
— *The Decades*, trans. H.I., ed.T.Harding, Cambridge 1849
— *Werke*, ed.F.Busser, Zurich 1972-
Calvin, J *Christianae Religionis Institutio*, Basel 1536
— *Institutes of the Christian Religion*, trans. F.L.Battles, ed. J.T.McNeill, Library of Christian Classics vols.20-21, London 1960
— *Old Testament Commentaries* (Calvin Translation Society), Grand Rapids 1948-1950
— *Harmonia ex Tribus Evangelistis Composita*, Geneva 1560
— *New Testament Commentaries*, ed.D.W. and T.F.Torrance, Edinburgh 1960-1972
— *Concerning the Eternal Predestination of God*, trans. and ed. J.K.S.Reid, London 1961
— *Sermons on Deuteronomy*, London 1583
— *Sermons on Isaiah's Prophecy of the Death and Passion of Christ*, trans. and ed. T.H.L.Parker, London 1956
— *Sermons on the Epistle to the Ephesians*, trans. A.Golding (1577), Edinburgh 1973
— *Sermons of M.John Calvin on the Epistles of S. Paule to Timothie and Titus*, London 1579

— *Thirteene Sermons Entreating of the Free Election of God in Jacob, and of Reprobation in Esau*, trans. J.Fielde, London 1579
— *An Answeare to Certaine Slaunders and Blasphemyes, appended to Thirteene Sermons*, 1579
— *Tracts and Treatises*, trans. H.Beveridge, Grand Rapids 1958
— *Theological Treatises*, trans. and ed. J.K.S.Reid, Library of Christian Classics, vol.22, London 1954

Cameron, J *Ta Sozomena, sive Opera*, Frankfurt 1642
— *Myrothecium Evangelicum*, Geneva 1632
— *An Examination of those Plausible Appearances which seeme most to commend the Romish Church, and to prejudice the Reformed*, Oxford 1626

Cappel, L *Icon*, prefaced to Cameron's *Opera*, 1642

Cochrane, AC *Reformed Confessions of the Sixteenth Century*, London 1966

Daillé, J *Apologia pro Duabus Ecclesiarum in Gallia Protestantium Synodis Nationalibus...adversus Friderici Spanhemii Exercitationes de Gratia Universali*, Amsterdam 1655
— *Vindiciae Apologiae...adversus Epicritam Gratiam Dei Universalem Oppugnantem*, Amsterdam 1657

Davenant, J *An Exposition of the Epistle of S. Paul to the Colossians with a Dissertation on the Death of Christ* (2 vols), trans. J.Allport, London 1831
— *Animadversions upon a Treatise Intitled, Gods Love to Mankind*, Cambridge 1641

Davenant, J *et.al*, *Good Counsells for the Peace of Reformed Churches*, Oxford 1641

Grotius, H *Defensio Fidei Catholicae de Satisfactione Christi*, 1617

Hales, J *Golden Remains of the Ever Memorable Mr. John Hales*, London 1673

Hodge, AA *Outlines of Theology* (contains *Formula Consensus Helvetica*, pp.651-663), Grand Rapids 1949

Hoekema, AA *A New English Translation of the Canons of Dort*, n.pl. 1968

Hottinger, JH *Historiae Ecclesiasticae Novi Testamenti*, Tom.VIII Sec. XVI Pars IV, Zurich 1667

Huber, S *Theses*, Tübingen 1590

Hunnius, A *Articulus de Providentia Dei et Aeterna Praedestinatione seu Electione Filiorum Dei ad Salutem*, Frankfurt 1593

Kimedoncius, J *Theses de Universalitate Redemptionis et Gratiae per Christum*, Heidelberg 1591
— *Of the Redemption of Mankind Three Bookes: wherein the controversie of the universalitie of redemption and grace by Christ, and of his death for all men, is largely handled*, trans. H.Ince, London 1598

Kingdon, M and Bergier, JF *(eds)*, *Registres de la Compagnie des Pasteurs de Genève au Temps de Calvin*, Travaux d'Humanisme et Renaissance, 55 and 107, Geneva 1962, 1964, 1969

Lombard, P *Sententiae*, in J-P.Migne (ed.), *Cursus Completus Patrologiae*, Paris 1845

Luther, M *Lectures on Genesis*, in *Works* (vol.5), ed.J.Pelikan, St.Louis 1968
— *The Bondage of the Will* (1525), trans. J.I.Packer and O.R.Johnston, London 1957

Melanchthon, P *Melanchthon on Christian Doctrine: Loci Communes 1555*, ed. C.L.Manschreck, New York 1965

Mitchell, AF and Struthers, J *(eds)*, *Minutes of the Sessions of the Westminster Assembly of Divines*, Edinburgh 1874

Moulin, P du *The Anatomy of Arminianisme*, London 1620
— *Esclaircissement des Controverses Salmuriennes*, Leiden 1648
— *De Mosis Amyraldi adversus Fridericum Spanhemium Libro Iudicium*, Rotterdam 1649

Musculus, W *Common Places of Christian Religion*, London 1563

Olevianus, G *De Substantia Foederis Gratuiti inter Deum et Electos*, Geneva 1585
— *An Exposition of the Symbol of the Apostles, or rather of the Articles of Faith*, London 1563
Owen, J *Works*, ed. W.H.Goold (1850-1853), London 1965-1968
— *The Death of Death in the Death of Christ*, with introductory essay by J.I.Packer, London 1959
Pareus, D *Eirenikon, sive, de unione et synodo evangelicorum concilianda liber votivus paci ecclesiae*, Heidelberg 1615
— *Miscellanea*, in Z.Ursinus, *Opera*, vol.3.
— *Theologicall Miscellanies*, in Z.Ursinus, *The Summme*
Perkins, W *A Christian and Plaine Treatise of Predestination*, London 1606
Polanus, A *A Treatise Concerning God's Eternall Predestination*, London 1599
Rivet, A *Synopsis Doctrinae de Natura et Gratia*, Amsterdam 1649
Rollock, R *Select Works*, ed.W.M.Gunn, Edinburgh 1849
Rutherford, S *Christ Dying and Drawing Sinners to Himself*, London 1647
Schaff, P *The Creeds of Christendom*, vol.3 "The Creeds of the Evangelical Protestant Churches", London 1877
Spanheim, F *Exercitationes de Gratia Universali* (3 vols.), Leiden 1646
— *Vindiciae pro Exercitationibus suis de Gratia Universali...adversus Amyraldi partes duae*, Amsterdam 1649
Tappert TG *(ed), The Formula of Concord: the Confessions of the Evangelical Lutheran Church*, Philadelphia 1959
Testard, P *Eirenikon, seu synopsis doctrinae de natura et gratia*, Blois 1633
Tossanus, D *Disputatio an Iesus Christum Esse Mortuum pro Omnibus*, Heidelberg 1589
— *Drei Christliche Predigten*, Heidelberg 1591
— *Gülden Kleinot Vom Todte Christi. Das ist: Notwendige, gründtliche und richtige Erklärung der neuerregten Frage: Ob Christus für alle Menschen gestorben sey oder nit*, Neustadt 1592
— (?)*Güldene Leyter*, Heidelberg 1592
— (?)*Gegenbeweisung*, Heidelberg 1594
— *Doctrina de Praedestinatione, brevibus ac perspicuis questionibus comprehensa*, Hanover 1609
Turrettini, F *Institutio Theologiae Elencticae*, in *Opera* (4 vols.), Edinburgh 1847
— *Institutio Theologiae Elencticae* (selection), in *Reformed Dogmatics*, trans. and ed. J.W.Beardslee, New York 1965
— *The Atonement of Christ*, trans. J.R.Wilson, Grand Rapids 1978
Ursinus, Z *Opera Theologica*, ed. Q.Reuter, (3 vols.), Heidelberg 1612
— *Doctrinae Christianae Compendium, seu Commentarii Catechetici*, London 1586
— *The Summe of Christian Religion*, trans. H.Parry, London 1645
Ussher, J *The Whole Works*, ed. C.R.Elrington, (17 vols.), Dublin 1864
Vermigli, PM *The Common Places*, trans.A.Marten, n.pl.1574
Zanchi, G *Opera Theologica* (3 vols.), Geneva 1613

SECONDARY SOURCES

Abray, LJ *The People's Reformation: magistrates, clergy and commons in Strasbourg 1500-1598*, Oxford 1985

Adam, G *Der Streit um die Prädestination im ausgehenden 16. Jahrhundert*, Beiträge zur Geschichte und Lehre der reformierten Kirche 30, Neukirchen 1970

Allbeck, WD *Studies in the Lutheran Confessions*, Philadelphia 1952

Allison, C *The Rise of Moralism*, New York 1966

Allport, J *Life of Davenant*, in J.Davenant, *Colossians*,vol.1

Althaus, PAWH *Die Prinzipien der deutschen reformierten Dogmatik im Zeitalter der aristotelischen Scholastik*, Leipzig 1914

Andresen, C *Handbuch der Dogmen- und Theologiegeschichte* (3 vols.), Göttingen 1980

Armstrong, BG *Calvinism and the Amyraut Heresy: Protestant scholasticism and humanism in seventeenth-century France*, Madison 1969

Baird, HM *Theodore Beza, counsellor of the French Reformation*, New York 1970

Baker, D *(ed), Reform and Reformation: England and the Continent c.1500-c.1750*, Ecclesiastical Historical Society, Oxford 1979

Baker, H *The Wars of Truth: studies in the decay of Christian humanism in the earlier seventeenth century*, Gloucester (Mass.) 1969

Baker, JW *Heinrich Bullinger and the Covenant: the other Reformed tradition*, Athens (Ohio) 1980

Bangs, C *Arminius: a study in the Dutch Reformation*, Nashville 1971

Barth, K *Church Dogmatics*, ed. G.W.Bromiley and T.F.Torrance, vol.2, "The Doctrine of God"(2), Edinburgh 1957

Bastide, C *Anglais et Français du dix-septième siècle*, Paris 1912

Bauke, H *Die Probleme der Theologie Calvins*, Leipzig 1922

Bavinck, H *The Doctrine of God*, Edinburgh 1971

Beachy, AJ *The Concept of Grace in the Radical Reformation*, Bibliotheca Humanistica et Reformatorica 17, Nieuwkoop 1977

Beardslee, J *(ed), Reformed Dogmatics*, New York 1965

Beck, LJ *The Metaphysics of Descartes*, Oxford 1965

Beeke, JR *Assurance of Faith: Calvin, English puritanism and the Dutch second reformation*, American University Studies 7, Theology and Religion 89, New York 1991

Bell, M C *Calvin and Scottish Theology: the doctrine of assurance*, Edinburgh 1985

Benedict, P *The Huguenot Population of France 1600-1685: the demographic fate and customs of a religious minority*, Transactions of the American Philosophical Society 81.5, Philadelphia 1991

Berkouwer, GC *Divine Election*, Grand Rapids 1960

Berte, F *Historical Introduction to the Book of Concord*, St.Louis 1965

Betts, CJ *Early Deism in France: from the so-called 'deistes' of Lyon (1564) to Voltaire's 'Lettres Philosophiques' (1734)*, The Hague 1984

Bierma, LD *German Calvinism in the Confessional Age: the covenant theology of Caspar Olevianus*, Studies in Historical Theology 4, Durham (N.Carolina) 1991

Bizer, E *Frühorthodoxie und Rationalismus*, Theologische Studien ed. K.Barth und M.Geiger 71, Zurich 1963

Blanke, F and Leuschner, I *Heinrich Bullinger: Vater der reformierten Kirche*, Zurich 1990

Bohatec, J *Die cartesianische Scholastik in der Philosophie und reformierten Dogmatik des 17 Jahrhunderts*, vol.1, Leipzig 1912
Bohatec, J *(ed), Calvinstudien: festschrift zum 400. Geburtstag Johan Calvins*, Leipzig 1909
Bouvier, A *Henri Bullinger, réformateur et conseilleur oecuménique, le successeur de Zwingli, d'après sa correspondance avec les reformés et les humanistes de langue française*, Neuchâtel 1940
Bouwsma, WJ *John Calvin: a sixteenth-century portrait*, New York 1988
Bray, JS *Theodore Beza's Doctrine of Predestination*, Nieuwkoop, 1975
Breward, I *(ed), The Work of William Perkins*, Abingdon 1970 (Editor's Introduction pp.1-131)
Brosché, F *Luther on Predestination: the antinomy and unity between love and wrath in Luther's concept of God*, Studia Doctrina Christianae Upsaliensia 18, Uppsala 1978
Brunner, E *The Christian Doctrine of God*, London 1949
Budé, E de *Vie de François Turrettini, théologien Genevensis, 1623-1687*, Lausanne 1874
Busson, H *Le Rationalisme dans la Littérature française de la Renaissance 1533-1601*, Paris 1957
Carruthers, SW *The Everyday Work of the Westminster Assembly*, Philadelphia 1954
Chenu, MD *Toward Understanding St. Thomas*, trans. A.M.Landry and D.Hughes, Chicago 1964
Clasen, CP *The Palatinate in European History*, Oxford 1963
Clebsch, WA *England's Earliest Protestants*, New Haven 1964
Clifford, AC *Atonement and Justification: English evangelical theology 1640-1790. An evaluation*, Oxford 1990
Coolidge, JS *The Pauline Renaissance in England*, Oxford 1970
Copinger, WA *A Treatise on Election, Predestination and Grace*, London 1889
Costello, WT *The Scholastic Curriculum at Early Seventeenth-Century Cambridge*, Cambridge (Mass.) 1958
Cremeans, GD *The Reception of Calvinistic Thought into England*, Urbana 1949
Cunningham, W *Historical Theology: a review of the principal doctrinal discussions in the Christian Church since the apostolic age* (2 vols.), Edinburgh 1862
Cuno, FW *Daniel Tossanus der Ältere, Professor der Theologie und Pastor 1541-1602* (2 vols.), Amsterdam 1898
Curtis, MH *Oxford and Cambridge in Transition 1558-1642*, Oxford 1959
Dent, CM *Protestant Reformers in Elizabethan England*, Oxford 1983
Deppermann, K *Melchior Hoffman: social unrest and apocalyptic visions in the age of the Reformation*, Edinburgh 1987
Dillistone, FW *The Christian Understanding of the Atonement*, London 1968
Donnelly, JP *Calvinism and Scholasticism in Vermigli's Doctrine of Man and Grace*, Leiden 1976
Dorner, IA *A History of Protestant Theology, particularly in Germany* (2 vols.), trans. G.Robson and S.Taylor, Edinburgh 1871
Dowey, EA *The Knowledge of God in Calvin's Theology*, New York 1965
Duffield, GE *(ed), John Calvin*, Abingdon 1966
Duke, A *Reformation and Revolt in the Low Countries*, London 1990
Elert, W *The Structure of Lutheranism*, trans. W.A.Hansen, St. Louis 1962
Elrington, CR "Life of Ussher", in *Works* vol.1
Elton, GR *Reformation Europe 1517-1559*, London 1972
Elton, GR *(ed), The New Cambridge Modern History*, second edition, vol.2: "The Reformation 1520-1559", Cambridge 1990
Fatio, O *Méthode et Théologie: Lambert Daneau, les débuts de la scholastique reformée*, Geneva 1976
Fraenkel, P *De l'Ecriture à la Dispute: la cas de l'Académie de Genève sous Théodore de Bèze*, Lausanne 1977

Fuchs, E *La Morale selon Calvin*, Paris 1986

Fuller, M *The Life, Letters and Writings of Bishop Davenant D.D. 1572-1641*, London 1897

Furcha, EJ *(ed) In Honour of John Calvin 1509-1564: papers from the 1986 Calvin Symposium*, Montreal 1987

Gäbler, U and Herkenrath, E *(eds) Heinrich Bullinger 1504-1575. Gesammelte Aufsätze zum 400. Todestag* (2 vols.), Zürcher Beiträge zur Reformationsgeschichte 7,8, Zurich 1975

Ganoczy, A *The Young Calvin*, trans. D.Foxgrove and W.Provo, Philadelphia 1987

Gardy, F *Bibliographie des Oeuvres Théologiques, Littéraires, Historiques et Juridiques de Théodore de Bèze*, Geneva 1960

Geiger, M G *Die Basler Kirche und Theologie im Zeitalter der Hochorthodoxie*, Zurich 1952

Geisendorf, PF Théodore de Bèze, Geneva 1949

Gerrish, B Reformers in Profile, Philadelphia 1967

Geyl, P *The Netherlands in the Seventeenth Century* (2 vols.), pt. 1: 1609-1648, London 1961

Gilson, EA *History of Christian Philosophy in the Middle Ages*, London 1955

Gouhier, H *Cartésianisme et Augustinisme au XVII Siècle*, Paris 1978

Grensted, LW *A Short History of the Doctrine of the Atonement*, Manchester 1920

Gründler, O *Die Gotteslehre Girolamo Zanchis*, Beiträge zur Geschichte und Lehre der reformierten Kirche 20, Neukirchen 1965

Haag, E and E *La France Protestante* (9 vols.), Paris 1847-1859

Haag, E and E, and Bordier, H *La France Protestante*, revised (6 vols.), Paris 1877-1892

Harrison, AW *The Beginnings of Arminianism to the Synod of Dort*, London 1926

Helm, P *Calvin and the Calvinists*, Edinburgh 1982

Heppe, HLJ *Reformed Dogmatics*, ed. E.Bizer, London 1950

— *Dogmatik des deutschen Protestantismus im sechzehnten Jahrhundert* (3 vols.), Gotha 1857

Heron, AIC *(ed) The Westminster Confession in the Church Today*, Edinburgh 1982

Hesselink, I J *Calvin's Concept of the Law*, Princeton Theological Monographs 30, Allison Park 1992

Heyd, M *Between Orthodoxy and Enlightenment: Jean-Robert Chouet and the introduction of Cartesian science in the Academy of Geneva*, The Hague 1982

Hodge, C *Systematic Theology* (3 vols.), London 1972

Hollweg, W *Neue Untersuchungen zur Geschichte und Lehre des Heidelberger Katechismus*, Neukirchen 1961

Holtrop, PC *The Bolsec Controversy on Predestination, from 1551-1555: statements of Jerome Bolsec and the responses of John Calvin, Theodore Beza and other Reformed theologians* (2 vols.), Lewiston 1993

Holwerda, DE *(ed) Exploring the Heritage of John Calvin*, Grand Rapids 1976

Hoogland, M *Calvin's Perspective on the Exaltation of Christ*, Kampen 1966

Hunter, AM *The Teaching of Calvin*, Glasgow 1920

Jacobs, P *Prädestination und Verantwortlichkeit bei Calvin*, Neukirchen 1937

Jansen, JF *Calvin's Doctrine of the Work of Christ*, London 1956

Jewett, PK *Election and Predestination*, Grand Rapids 1985

de Jong, PY *(ed) Crisis in the Reformed Churches: essays in the commencement of the great Synod of Dort, 1618-1619*, Grand Rapids 1968

Keeble, NH *and* Nuttall, GF *(eds) Calendar of the Correspondence of Richard Baxter* (2 vols.), Oxford, 1991

Keizer, G *François Turrettini: sa vie et ses oeuvres, et la Consensus*, Lausanne 1900

Kelly, JND *Early Christian Doctrines*, New York 1958

Kendall, RT *Calvin and English Calvinism to 1649*, Oxford 1979
Kickel, W *Vernunft und Offenbarung bei Theodor Beza*, Beiträge zur Geschichte und Lehre der reformierten Kirche 25, Neukirchen 1967
Kingdon, RM *Geneva and the Coming Wars of Religion in France 1555-1563*, Geneva 1956
— *Geneva and the Consolidation of the French Protestant Movement 1564-1572*, Geneva 1967
Klauber, MI *Between Reformed Scholasticism and Pan-Protestantism: Jean-Alphonse Turretin (1671-1737) and Enlightened Orthodoxy at the Academy of Geneva*, Selinsgrove 1994
Kneale, W and M *The Development of Logic*, Oxford 1972
Koch, J *Die Theologie der Confessio Helvetica Posterior*, Beiträge zur Geschichte und Lehre der reformierten Kirche 27, Neukirchen 1968
Kristeller, PO *Renaissance Thought*, New York 1961
— *Medieval Aspects of Renaissance Learning*, Durham 1974
Kristeller, PO and Wiener, PP *(eds) Renaissance Essays*, New York 1968
Labrousse, E *Pierre Bayle* (2 vols.), The Hague 1963,1965
— *Bayle*, trans. D.Potts, Oxford 1983
Lachman, DC *The Marrow Controversy 1718-1723: a historical and theological analysis*, Edinburgh 1988
Lang, A *Der Evangelienkommentar Martin Butzers und die Grundzüge seiner Theologie*, Leipzig 1900
Laplanche, F *Orthodoxie et Prédication: l'oeuvre d'Amyraut et la querelle de la grâce universelle*, Paris 1965
— *L'Evidence du Dieu Chrétien: religion, culture et société dans l'apologétique protestante de la France classique (1576-1670)*, Strasbourg 1983
— *L'Ecriture, Le Sacré et l'Histoire: érudits et politiques protestants devant la Bible en France au xviie. siècle*, Amsterdam 1986
Leith, JH *Assembly at Westminster: Reformed theology in the making*, Richmond 1975
Lenoble, R *Esquisse d'une Histoire de l'Idée de Nature*, Paris 1968
Léonard, EG *A History of Protestantism* (2 vols.), trans. and ed. H.H.Rowley, London 1965
Locher, GW *Zwingli's Thought: new perspectives*, Leiden 1981
McComish, WA *The Epigones: a study of the theology of the Genevan Academy at the time of the Synod of Dort*, Princeton Theological Monographs 17, Allison Park 1989
McCoy, CS *History, Humanity and Federalism in the Theology and Ethics of J.Cocceius*, Philadelphia 1980
McGrath, AE *Iustitia Dei: a history of the Christian doctrine of justification* (2 vols.), Cambridge 1986
— *The Intellectual Origins of the European Reformation*, Oxford 1987
— *Reformation Thought: an introduction*, Oxford 1988
— *A Life of John Calvin: a study in the shaping of Western culture*, Oxford 1990
McKee, EA and Armstrong, BG *(eds) Probing the Reformed Tradition*, Louisville 1989
McKim, DK *Ramism in William Perkins' Theology*, American University Studies series 3, Theology and Religion 15, New York 1987
— *(ed) Major Themes in the Reformed Tradition*, Grand Rapids 1991
McLelland, JC *The Visible Words of God: an exposition of the sacramental theology of Peter Martyr Vermigli 1500-1562*, Edinburgh 1957
— *Peter Martyr Vermigli and Italian Reform*, Ontario 1980
McNair, PMJ *Peter Martyr in Italy: an anatomy of apostacy*, Oxford 1967
McNeill, JT *The History and Character of Calvinism*, New York 1954

Martini, M *Fausto Socino et la Pensée Socinienne: un maître de la pensée religieuse (1539-1604)*, Paris 1967

Maruyama, T *The Ecclesiology of Theodore Beza: the reform of the true church*, Travaux d'Humanisme et Renaissance 166, Geneva 1978

Mettey, E *Etude sur Jean Daillé*, Strasbourg 1863

Metz, W *Necessitas Satisfactionis? Eine systematische Studie zu den Fragen 12-18 des Heidelberger Katechismus und zur Theologie des Zacharias Ursinus*, Zurich 1970

Miller, PGE *The New England Mind: from colony to province*, Cambridge (Mass.) 1954

— *Errand into the Wilderness*, Cambridge (Mass.) 1956

Milner, BC *Calvin's Doctrine of the Church*, Studies in the History of Christian Thought 5, Leiden 1970

Mitchell, AF and Struthers, J *Minutes of the Sessions of the Westminster Divines*, Edinburgh 1874

Moltmann, J *Prädestination und Perseveranz: Geschichte und Bedeutung der reformierten Lehre 'de perseverantia sanctorum'*, Beiträge zur Geschichte und Lehre der reformierten Kirche 12, Neukirchen 1961

— *Christoph Pezel und der Calvinismus in Bremen (1539-1604)*, Bremen 1968

Mours, S *Les Eglises Reformées en France*, Paris 1958

— *La Protestantisme en France au XVIIe. Siècle, 1598-1685*, Paris 1967

Mozley, JK *The Impassibility of God: a survey in Christian thought*, Cambridge 1926

Müller, G *(ed) Theologische Realenzyclopadie*, Berlin 1990-

Muller, RA *Christ and the Decree: christology and predestination in Reformed theology from Calvin to Perkins*, Durham (N.Carolina) 1986

— *Dictionary of Latin and Greek Theological Terms, drawn principally from Protestant scholastic theology*, Grand Rapids 1985

— *Post Reformation Reformed Dogmatics*, vol.1, "Prolegomena to Theology", Grand Rapids 1987

Neuser, WH *(ed) Calvinus Ecclesiae Doctor*, Kampen 1979

— *Calvinus Ecclesiae Genevensis Custos*, Frankfurt 1984

— *Calvinus Sacrae Scriptura Professor: Calvin as Confessor of Holy Scripture*, Grand Rapids 1994

Neve, JL *A History of Christian Thought* (2 vols.), Philadelphia 1943

Nicole, R *Moyse Amyraut: a bibliography*, New York 1960

Niesel, W *The Theology of Calvin*, Philadelphia 1956

Nygren, A *Agape and Eros*, pt.2, "The history of the Christian idea of love", London 1939

Oberman, HA *The Harvest of Medieval Theology: Gabriel Biel and late medieval Nominalism*, Cambridge (Mass.) 1963

— *Forerunners of the Reformation: the shape of late medieval thought*, London 1967

— *The Dawn of the Reformation*, Edinburgh 1986

— (ed.) *Itinerarium Italicum: the profile of the Italian Renaissance in the mirror of its European transformations*, Leiden 1975

Ong, WJ *Ramus: method and the decay of dialogue. From the art of discourse to the art of reason*, Cambridge (Mass.) 1958

Otten, H *Calvins theologische Anschauung von der Prädestination*, Munich 1938

Overfield, JH *Humanism and Scholasticism in Late Medieval Germany*, Princeton 1984

Ozment, SE *Mysticism and Dissent: religious ideology and social protest in the sixteenth century*, New Haven 1973

— *(ed) The Reformation in Medieval Perspective*, Chicago 1971

Pannier, J *L'Eglise Reformée de Paris sous Louis XIII de 1621 à 1629*, Paris 1931
Parker, THL *Calvin's Doctrine of the Knowledge of God*, Edinburgh 1969
— *Calvin's New Testament Commentaries*, London 1971
— *Calvin's Old Testament Commentaries*, Edinburgh 1986
— John Calvin, Edinburgh 1975
Partee, C *Calvin and Classical Philosophy*, Leiden 1977
Paul, RS *The Atonement and the Sacraments: the relation of the atonement to the sacraments of baptism and the Lord's supper*, London 1961
— *The Assembly of the Lord*, Edinburgh 1985
Penny, DA *Freewill or Predestination: the battle over saving grace in mid-Tudor England*, Royal Historical Society Studies in History 61, Woodbridge 1990
Peterson, RA *Calvin's Doctrine of the Atonement*, Phillipsburg 1983
Pfister, P *Le Colloque de Montbéliard*, Geneva 1873
Pitassi, MC *De l'Orthodoxie aux Lumières: Geneva 1670-1737*, Geneva 1992
Platt, J *Reformed Thought and Scholasticism: the arguments for the existence of God in Dutch theology 1575-1650*, Studies in the History of Christian Thought 29, Leiden 1982
Polman, P *L'Elément Historique dans la Controverse Religieuse du 16. Siècle*. Universitas Catholica Louvaniensis 2.23, Gembloux 1932
Popkin, RH *The Philosophy of the Sixteenth and Seventeenth Centuries*, New York 1966
Potts, DC and Charlton, DG
— *French Thought since 1600*, London 1974
Prestwich, M *(ed) International Calvinism 1541-1715*, Oxford 1985
Preus, RD *The Theology of Post Reformation Lutheranism* (2 vols.), St. Louis 1970
Quick, J "Icones Sacrae Gallicanae, or The History of the Lives of Fify Famous Ministers" (2 vols.). Ms. belonging to Dr. Williams's Library, London
— *Synodicon in Gallia Reformata: or, the Acts, Decisions, Decrees and Canons of those Famous National Councils of the Reformed Churches in France*, London 1692
Rainbow, JH *The Will of God and the Cross: an historical and theological study of John Calvin's doctrine of limited redemption*, Allison Park, 1990
Raitt, J *The Eucharistic Theology of Theodore Beza*, Chambersburg 1972
— *The Colloquy of Montbéliard: religion and politics in the sixteenth century*, New York 1993
— (ed.) *Shapers of Religious Traditions in Germany, Switzerland and Poland 1560-1600*, New Haven 1981
Rex, W *Essays on Pierre Bayle and Religious Controversy*, International Archives of the History of Ideas 8, The Hague 1965
Rimbault, L *Pierre du Moulin, 1568-1658: un pasteur classique de l'âge classique*, Paris 1916
Ritschl, AA *Critical History of the Christian Doctrine of Justification and Reconciliation*, Edinburgh 1972
Rivière, J *Le Dogme de Rédemption: au début du moyen âge*, Paris 1934
Rolston, H *John Calvin versus the Westminster Confession*, Richmond 1972
Scharlemann, R *Thomas Aquinas and John Gerhard*, New Haven 1964
Scheld, S *Media Salutis, zur Heilsvermittlung bei Calvin*, Stuttgart 1989
Schmid, H *The Doctrinal Theology of the Evangelical Lutheran Church*, Minneapolis 1961
Schnucker, RV *(ed) Calviniana: the ideas and influence of Jean Calvin*, Sixteenth-Century Essays and Studies 10, Kirksville 1988
Schrenk, G *Gottesreich und Bund im älteren Protestantismus, vornehmlich bei Johannes Cocceius*,

Gütersloh 1923
Schweizer, A *Die protestantischen Centraldogmen in ihrer Entwicklung innerhalb der reformierten Kirche* (2 vols.), Zurich 1854-1856
Sell, APF *The Great Debate: Calvinism, Arminianism and salvation*, Worthing 1982
Shepherd, VA *The Nature and Function of Faith in the Theology of John Calvin*, Macon 1983
Siggins, IDK *Martin Luther's Doctrine of Christ*, New Haven 1970
Staedtke, J *Die Theologie des jungen Bullinger*, Studien zur Dogmengeschichte und systematischen Theologie 16, Zurich 1962
Stankiewicz, WJ *Politics and Religion in Seventeenth-Century France: a study of political ideas from the monarchomachs to Bayle, as reflected in the toleration controversy*, Berkeley 1960
Stauffer, R *Moïse Amyraut: un précurseur français d'oecuménisme*, Paris 1962
— *Dieu, la Création et la Providence dans la Prédication de Calvin*, Bern 1978
Steinmetz, D *(ed) Reformers in the Wings*, Philadelphia 1971
Stephens, WP *The Theology of Huldrych Zwingli*, Oxford 1986
— *The Holy Spirit in the Theology of Martin Bucer*, Cambridge 1970
Strehle, S *Calvinism, Federalism and Scholasticism: a study of the Reformed doctrine of covenant*, Basler und Berner Studien zur historischen und systematischen Theologie 58, Bern 1988
Sturm, EK *Der junge Zacharias Ursin: sein Weg vom Philippismus zum Calvinismus (1534-1562)*, Beiträge zur Geschichte und Lehre der reformierten Kirche 33, Neukirchen 1972
Sudhoff, K *Caspar Olevianus und Zacharias Ursinus*, Leben und ausgewählte Schriften der Väter und Begründer der reformierten Kirche 8, Elberfeld 1857
Swinne, AH *John Cameron, Philosoph und Theologe (1579-1625)*, Marburg 1968
Tedeschi, JA *Italian Reformation Studies in Honour of Laelius Socinus*, Florence 1965
Thomson, A "Life of Dr. Owen", in Owen's *Works*, vol.1, London 1850/1965
Tocanne, B *L'Idée de Nature en France dans la Seconde Moitié du XVIIe. Siècle*, Strasbourg 1978
Toon, P *The Emergence of Hyper-Calvinism in English Nonconformity, 1689-1765*, London 1967
— *Puritans and Calvinism*, Swengel 1973
— *God's Statesman: the life and work of John Owen*, Exeter 1971
Torrance, TF *(ed) The School of Faith: the Catechisms of the Reformed Church*, London 1959
Trensz, A *Situation Intérieure de l'Eglise Evang.-Luthérienne de Strasbourg, sous la Direction de J. Marbach, Président du Convent Ecclésiastique (1557-1581)*, Strasbourg 1857
Tyacke, NRN *Anti-Calvinists: the rise of English Arminianism 1590-1640*, Oxford 1989
Van Buren, P *Christ in our Place: the substitutionary character of Calvin's doctrine of reconciliation*, Edinburgh 1957
Van Stam, FP *The Controversy over the Theology of Saumur 1635-1650: disrupting debates among the Huguenots in complicated circumstances*, Amsterdam 1988
Vignaux, P *Justification et Prédestination au XIVe. Siècle*, Paris 1934
Visser, D *Zacharias Ursinus, the reluctant reformer*, New York 1983
— *Controversy and Consolidation: the Reformation and the Palatinate 1559-1583*, Pittsburg Theological Monographs 18, Allison Park 1986
Voeltzel, R *Vrai et Fausse Eglise selon les Théologiens Protestants Français du XVIIe. Siècle*, Paris 1956
Von Rohr, J *The Covenant of Grace in Puritan Thought*, Atlanta 1986
Vos, A *Aquinas, Calvin and Contemporary Protestant Thought: a critique of Protestant views on the thought of Thomas Aquinas*, Grand Rapids 1985
Vuilleumier, H *Histoire de L'Eglise Reformée du Pays de Vaud sous le régime Bernois* (4 vols.), Lausanne 1928-1933

Wallace, D *Puritans and Predestination: grace in English Protestant theology 1525-1695*, Chapel Hill 1982

Walser, P *Die Prädestination bei Heinrich Bullinger, in Zusammenhang mit seiner Gotteslehre*, Studien zur Dogmengeschichte und systematische Theologie ll, Zurich 1957

Warfield, BB *Calvin and Calvinism*, New York 1931

Weber, HE *Reformation, Orthodoxie und Rationalismus*, Beiträge zur Forderung christlicher Theologie 37, Gütersloh 1937

Weir, DA *The Origins of the Federal Theology in Sixteenth-Century Reformation Thought*, Oxford 1990

Wendel, F *Calvin: the origins and development of his religious thought*, trans. P.Mairet, London 1974

White, P *Predestination, Policy and Polemic: conflict and consensus in the English Church from the Reformation to the Civil War*, Cambridge 1992

Wilbur, EM *A History of Unitarianism: Socinianism and its antecedents*, Cambridge (Mass.) 1948

Willis, ED *Calvin's Catholic Christology*, Studies in Medieval and Reformation Thought 2, Leiden 1966

Wodrow, R *Collections upon the Lives of the Reformers and Most Eminent Ministers of the Church of Scotland* (2 vols.), Glasgow 1948

ARTICLES

Anderson, MW "Peter Martyr, Reformed Theologian (1542-1562): his letters to Heinrich Bullinger and John Calvin", *SCJ* 4(1973)1 pp.41-64

Barclift, PL "Predestination and Divine Foreknowledge in the Sermons of Pope Leo the Great", *CH* 62(1993)1 pp.5-21

Beeke, JR "Faith and Assurance in the Heidelberg Catechism and its Primary Sources: a fresh look at the Kendall thesis", *CTJ* 27(1992)1 pp.39-67

Bell, MC "Calvin and the Extent of the Atonement", *EQ* 55(1983) pp.115-123

Bierma, LD "Federal Theology in the Sixteenth Century: two traditions?", *WTJ* (1983) pp.304-321

— "Covenant or Covenants in the Theology of Olevianus?", *CTJ* 22(1987)2 pp.228-250

— "The Role of Covenant Theology in Early Reformed Orthodoxy" *SCJ* 21(1990)3, pp.453-462

Bizer, E "Reformed Orthodoxy and Cartesianism", *JTC* (1965)2 pp.20-82

Boersma, H "Calvin and the Extant of the Atonement", *EQ* 64(1992)4 pp.333-355

Bonet-Maury, G "John Cameron, A Scottish Protestant Theologian in France", *SHR* 7(1910), pp.325-345

Bost, C "Pierre du Moulin et Amyraut", *BSHPF* 77(1928)

Boughton, LC "Supralapsarianism and the Role of Metaphysics in Sixteenth-Century Reformed Thought", *WTJ* (1986) pp.63-96

Burchill, CJ "On the Consolation of a Christian Scholar: Zacharias Ursinus (1534-1583) and the Reformation in Heidelberg", *JEH* 37(1986) pp.565-583

— "Le Dernier Théologien Reformé: Girolamo Zanchi. De officio docentium et discentium in scholis", *BSHPF* 135(1989) pp.54-63

Cameron, CM "Arminius - hero or heretic?", *EQ* 64(1992)3 pp.213-227

Christianson, P. "Reformers and the Church of England under Elizabeth and the Early Stuarts", *JEH* 31(1980), pp.463-482

Clifford, AC "John Calvin and the Confessio Fidei Gallicana", *EQ* 58(1986)3 pp.195-206
— "Geneva Revisited or Calvinism Revised: the case for theological reassessment", *Churchman* 100(1986)4 pp.323-331
Dantine, J "Les Tabelles sur la Doctrine de la Prédestination par Théodore de Bèze", *RTP* 16(1966), pp.365-377
Delval, M "Orthodoxie et Prédication: Théodore de Bèze", *BSHPF* 134(1988), pp.693-697
Desgraves, L "Les Thèses Soutenues a l'Académie Protestante de Saumur au xviie. Siècle", *BSHPF* 125 (1979) pp.76-97
Deyon, S "Les Académies Protestantes de France", *BSHPF* 135(1989) pp.77-86
Donnelly, JP "Italian Influences in the Development of Calvinist Scholasticism", *SCJ* 7(1976)1 pp.81-101
— "Scholasticism Protestant and Catholic: Francis Turretin on the Object and Principles of Theology", *CH* 55(1986)2 pp.193-205
Foster, HD "Liberal Calvinism: the Remonstrants at the Synod of Dort in 1618", *HTR* 16(1923)1 pp.1-37
Freeman, MS "The Doctrine of Predestination from Augustine to Peter Lombard", *BS* 47(1890) pp.645-668
Gerrish, BA "To the Unknown God': Luther and Calvin on the hiddenness of God", *JR* 53(1973) pp.263-292
Greaves, RL "The Origin and Early Development of English Covenant Theology", *The Historian* 31(1968) pp.21-35
Hagen, K "From Testament to Covenant in the Early Sixteenth Century", *SCJ* 3(1972)1
Harper, GW "Calvin and English Calvinism to 1649: a review article", *CTJ* 20(1985)2 pp.255-262
Helm, P "Calvin and the Covenant: unity and continuity", *EQ* 55(1983) pp.65-81
Henderson, GD "Scotland and the Synod of Dort", *NAKG* 24(1931) pp.1-24
Hoekema, AA "A New English Translation of the Synod of Dort", *CTJ* 3(1968)2 pp.133-161
Jinkins, M "Theodore Beza: continuity and regression in the Reformed tradition", *EQ* 64(1992)2 pp.131-154
Karlberg, MW "The Original State of Adam: tensions within Reformed theology", *EQ* 59(1987)4, pp.291-309
Kittelson, JM "Marbach versus Zanchi: the resolution of the controversy in late Reformation Strasbourg", *SCJ* 8(1977)3 pp.31-44
Klauber, MI "Reason, Revelation and Cartesianism: Louis Tronchin and the Enlightened Orthodoxy in late seventeenth-century Geneva", *CH* 59(1990)3 pp.326-339
— "The Helvetic *Formula Consensus* (1675): an introduction and translation", *TJ* 11(1990)1
— "Continuity and Discontinuity in Post-Reformation Reformed Theology: an evaluation of the Muller thesis", *JETS* 33(1990)4 pp.467-475
Lane, ANS "Calvin's Doctrine of Assurance", *VE*11(1979) pp.32-54
— "The Quest for the Historical Calvin", *EQ* 55(1983) pp.95-113
Leahy, FS "Calvin and the Extent of the Atonement", *RTJ* (1992), pp.54-64
Letham, RWA "Theodore Beza: a reassessment", *SJT* 40(1978)
— "The *Foedus Operum*: some factors accounting for its development", *SCJ* 14(1983) pp.457-467
— "Amandus Polanus: a neglected theologian?", *SCJ* 21(1990)3
Lillback, PA "Ursinus' Development of the Covenant of Creation: a debt to Melanchthon or Calvin?", *WTJ* 43(1981) pp.247-288
Lindsay, TM "Amyraldism", Encyclopaedia of Religion and
— Ethics, ed. J.Hastings, vol.1, pp.404-406, Edinburgh 1925

Lods, A "Les Actes du Colloque de Montbéliard 1586: une polémique entre Théodore de Bèze et Jacques Andreae", *BSHPF* 1897 pp.192-215
McCoy, CS "Johannes Cocceius: federal theologian", *SJT* 16(1963) pp.352-370
McGiffert, M "Grace and Works: the rise and division of covenant divinity in Elizabethan Puritanism", *HTR* 75(1982) pp.463-502
— "William Tyndale's Conception of Covenant", *JEH* 32(1981) pp.167-184
— "From Moses to Adam: the making of the covenant of works", *SCJ* 19(1988)2 pp.131-155
McGrath, AE "John Calvin and Late Medieval Thought: a study in late medieval influences upon Calvin's theological development", *ARG* 77(1986) pp.58-78
Malone, MT "The Doctrine of Predestination in the Thought of William Perkins and Richard Hooker", *ATR* 52(1970) pp.103-117
Møller, JG "The Beginnings of Puritan Covenant Theology", *JEH* 14(1963) pp.46-57
Moltmann, J "Prädestination und Heilsgeschichte bei Moyse Amyraut", *ZKG* 65(1954) pp.270-303
— "Zur Bedeutung des Petrus Ramus für Philosophie und Theologie in Calvinismus", *ZKG* 68(1957), pp.295-318
— "Föderaltheologie", *Lexicon für Theologie und Kirche* 4 pp.190-192, Freiburg 1960
Mousseaux, M "Pierre du Moulin", *BSHPF* 109(1963) pp.160-179
Muller, RA "The Federal Motif in Seventeenth-Century Arminian Theology", *NAKG* 62(1982), pp.102-122
— "*Fides* and *Cognitio* in Relation to the Problem of Intellect and Will in the Theology of John Calvin", *CTJ* 25(1990)2 pp.207-224
Murray, J "Covenant Theology", *Encyclopedia of Christianity*, vol.3 pp.199-216, ed. P.E.Hughes, 1972
Nicole, R "John Calvin's View of the Extent of the Atonement", *WTJ* 47(1985) pp.197-225
Nineham, DE "Gottschalk of Orbais: reactionary or precursor of the Reformation?", *JEH* 40(1989)1 pp.1-18
Oberman, HA "Some Notes on the Theology of Nominalism", *HTR* 53(1960) pp.47-76
Partee, C "Calvin's Central Dogma Again", *SCJ* 18(1987)2 pp.191-199
Pernoud, MA. "The Theory of *Potentia Dei* according to Aquinas, Scotus and Ockham", *Antonianum* 47(1972) pp.69-95
Platt, F "Arminianism", *Encyclopaedia of Religion and Ethics*, ed. J. Hastings, vol.1, pp.807-816, Edinburgh 1925
Pollard, JE "The Impassibility of God", *SJT* 8(1955)pp.353-364
Reardon, PH "Calvin on Providence: the development of an insight", *SJT* 28(1975)6 pp.517-533
Reid, J K "The Office of Christ in Predestination", *SJT* 1(1948) pp.1-19, 166-183
Rist, G "Modernité de la Méthode Théologique de Calvin", *RTP* 18(1968)1 pp.19-33
Sabean, D "The Theological Rationalism of Moïse Amyraut", *ARG* 55(1964) pp.204-216
Shepherd, N "Zanchi on Saving Faith", *WTJ* 36(1974) pp.31-47
Staedtke, J "Der Zürcher Prädestinationsstreit von 1560", *Zwingliana* 9(1953) pp.536-546
Strehle, S "The Extent of the Atonement at the Synod of Dort", *WTJ* 51(1989) pp.1-23
— "Universal Grace and Amyraldism", *WJT* 51(1989) pp.345-357
Summers, KM "Theodore Beza's Classical Library and Christian Humanism", *ARG* 82(1991) pp.193-207
Torrance, JB "The Incarnation and 'Limited Atonement'", *EQ* 55(1983) pp.83-94
— "Covenant or Contract: a study of the theological background of worship in seventeenth-century Scotland", *SJT* 23(1970) pp.51-76
Trinterud, LJ "The Origins of Puritanism", *CH* 20(1951) pp.37-57

Tylenda, JN "Girolamo Zanchi and John Calvin", *CTJ* 10(1975) pp.101-141
Venema, CP "Heinrich Bullinger's Correspondence on Calvin's Doctrine of Predestination", *SCJ* 17(1986)4 pp.435-450
Visser, D "The Covenant in Zacharias Ursinus", *SCJ* 18(1987) pp.531-544
Wawrykow, J "John Calvin and Condign Merit", *ARG* 83(1992) pp.73-90
Wood, AS "The Declaration of Sentiments: the theological testament of Arminius", *EQ* 65(1993)2, pp.111-129

UNPUBLISHED DISSERTATIONS

Anderson, JW "The Grace of God and the Non-Elect in Calvin's Commentaries and Sermons", Th.D. New Orleans Baptist Seminary 1976
Beardslee, JW "Theological Development at Geneva under Francis and Jean-Alphonse Turretin", Ph.D. Yale 1956
Burchill, CJ "Girolamo Zanchi in Strasbourg 1553-1563", Ph.D. Cambridge 1979
Chalker, W "Calvin and Some Seventeenth-Century English Calvinists: a comparison of their thought and examination of their doctrines of the knowledge of God, faith and assurance", Ph.D. Duke 1961
Daniel, C "Hyper-Calvinism and John Gill", Ph.D. Edinburgh 1983
Delval, L "La Doctrine du Salut dans l'Oeuvre Homéletique de Théodore de Bèze" (2 vols.), Lille 1982
Godfrey, WR "Tensions within International Calvinism: the debate on the atonement at the Synod of Dort", Ph.D. Stanford 1974
Grohman, D "The Genevan Reactions to the Saumur Doctrines of Hypothetical Universalism 1635-1685", Th.D. Toronto (Knox College) 1971
Grundler, O "Thomism and Calvinism in the Theology of Girolamo Zanchi", Th.D. Princeton 1963
Hicks, JM "The Theology of Grace in the Thought of Jacobus Arminius and Philip van Limborch: a study in the development of seventeenth-century Arminianism", Ph.D. Westminster 1985
Ives, RB "The Theology of Wolfgang Musculus, 1497-1563", Ph.D. Manchester 1965
Karlberg, MW "The Mosaic Covenant and the Concept of Works in Reformed Hermeneutics: a historical-critical analysis with particular attention to early covenant eschatology", Th.D. Westminster 1980
Letham, RWA "Saving Faith and Assurance in Reformed Theology to the Synod of Dort" (2 vols.), Ph.D. Aberdeen 1979
Lillback, PA "The Binding of God: Calvin's role in the development of covenant theology", Ph.D.Westminster 1985
McCoy, CS "The Covenant Theology of J.Cocceius", Ph.D. Yale 1956
McGrath, GJ "Puritans and the Human Will: voluntarism within mid-seventeenth century English puritanism as seen in the works of Richard Baxter and John Owen", Ph.D. Durham 1989
McPhee, I "Transformer or Conserver of Calvin's Theology? A study of the origins and development of Theodore Beza's thought", Ph.D. Cambridge 1980
Moltmann, J "Gnadenbund und Gnadenwahl: die Prädestinationslehre des Moyse Amyraut, dargestellt im Zusammenhang der heilsgeschichtlich-föderaltheologischen Tradition der Akademie von Saumur", Göttingen 1951

Packer, JI "The Redemption and Restoration of Man in the Thought of Richard Baxter", D.Phil. Oxford 1954

Pittion, JP "Intellectual Life in the *Académie* of Saumur, 1633-1685: a study in the Bouhéreau Collection", Ph.D. Dublin 1969

Pope, JM "Aspects of the Controversies concerning the Doctrine of Grace Aroused by the Teaching of Claude Pajon", Ph.D. St. Andrews 1974

Priebe, VL "The Covenant Theology of William Perkins", Ph.D. Drew 1967

Proctor, L "The Theology of Moïse Amyraut, considered as a reaction against seventeenth-century Calvinism", Leeds 1952

Stoute, DA "The Origins and Early Development of the Reformed Idea of Covenant", Ph.D. Cambridge 1979

Strehle, S "The Extent of the Atonement within the Theological Systems of the Sixteenth and Seventeenth Centuries", Th.D. Dallas 1980

Tait, LG "Pierre du Moulin (1568-1658); Huguenot Theologian", Ph.D. Edinburgh 1955

Tipson, LB "The Development of the Puritan Understanding of Conversion", Ph.D. Yale 1972

Veninga, JF "Covenant Theology and Ethics in the Thought of John Calvin and John Preston" (2 vols.), Ph.D. Rice 1974

Wiley, DN "Calvin's Doctrine of Predestination: his principal soteriological and polemical doctrine", Ph.D. Duke 1971

Index

Abraham 54, 73–74, 93, 114, 167
Adam 15–16, 22, 27, 45, 47, 53, 73, 104–105, 109, 139, 167, 188, 195, 198–199, 217
Affections, Divine 24, 193–194, 235–236, 240
Alençon, Synod of 188–190, 202, 224, 236, 238
Alting, H. 155
Alès, Synod of 212, 225
Ambassador to the Hague, English 134, 140, 144, 147–148, 154–155, 157–158
Ambrose 91, 137
Ames, W. 151
Amsterdam 129
Amyraldism 4, 21, 163, 187–189, 205, 210–211, 213, 215, 217–219, 223, 225, 229, 231, 233–242
Amyraut, M. 2–3, 21, 23, 66, 162–164, 167, 171, 178, 180, 187–204, 210–220, 224–241, 249–250
Anabaptists 8
Anselm 5–6, 26, 56, 109, 121
Anthropopathism 205, 228
Antinomianism 168, 244
Aquinas, Thomas 5, 15, 47, 53, 90,93,97, 99
Aristotelianism 43–45, 48, 59, 90, 92, 99, 191, 197, 207, 219, 227, 229
Arminianism 12, 66, 128–129, 130–131, 136, 138, 140–144, 146, 150–151, 164–165, 172–175, 192, 199, 202, 210–212, 220, 225, 229–230, 234, 251
Arminius, J. 128–130, 132, 212, 225
Armstrong, B.G. 3, 12, 21, 41, 163–164, 166–167, 169, 179, 189, 200, 215, 218–219
Arrowsmith, J. 241
Assurance, 16, 18, 58, 97–98, 112, 173, 250, 252
Atonement
– **actual/accomplished** 30, 34, 57, 76, 112, 130, 140, 142, 145–147, 149–150, 169, 180, 191, 202, 232–235, 239, 241, 249
– **application of** 19, 21, 29–34, 57–58, 72, 75–76, 110–113, 116, 118, 124, 134–137, 142, 145–147, 149, 173, 190, 202, 225, 232–233, 241, 248–249
– **availability of** 5, 27, 124, 141, 147, 232
– **classical theory of** 3–4, 26–27
– **'dynamic'** 4
– **effective** 5–6, 25, 30–33, 39, 57–58, 96–97, 110–112, 115–118, 124, 133–141, 145–147, 156–157, 177–178, 180, 203, 229, 232–236, 248
– **expiation** 26, 28–30, 57, 75, 116, 132, 137–139, 202, 233
– **governmental theory** 41, 173–174, 211, 233, 235
– **intention behind** 16, 34, 54, 57, 134–135, 137–139, 144–145, 147, 202–203, 226, 228, 234, 248–249, 250
– **limited (particular redemption)** 3, 5–7, 12–13, 18, 21–23, 26, 29–35, 47, 51, 54–58, 68, 72, 76, 80, 93, 97, 99, 112, 114–118, 123–124, 128, 132–140, 144–152, 163, 200–203, 215, 217, 226–229, 232–236, 248–253,
– **payment of debt** 26, 114, 200, 233
– **penal substitution** 3–4, 26–27, 56, 109, 111, 135, 146, 173–174, 177, 199, 233–234
– **propitiation** 29–32, 56, 97, 111, 135, 144, 202, 214, 234
– **ransom** 4, 32–33, 74, 111, 114, 116, 118, 135, 138–139, 141, 145, 176, 202, 225, 234
– **reconciliation** 7–9, 17, 25, 27–32, 76, 108, 130–131, 139, 146, 182, 212, 234
– **satisfaction** 5, 26–27, 39, 50, 56–57, 76, 109–114, 132, 137–139, 145–146, 149, 173–174, 176–178, 194, 199–200, 214, 231, 233–235
– **sufficiency** 5–6, 30–33, 57, 96–97, 111–118, 131–142, 145, 151, 176–177, 180, 202–203, 212, 234, 248
– **universal** 3–5, 7–8, 12–13, 26–34, 56–59, 66, 68, 74–76, 81, 110–118, 124, 130–152, 163–164, 174–178, 180–181, 189–190, 193, 195, 197, 200–203, 210–213, 218–220, 225, 232–236, 240–241, 248–250, 252
Attributes, Divine 52–53, 59, 66, 68, 74–76, 81, 90–92, 110–112, 115–118, 124, 130–152, 163–164, 174–178, 180–181, 197–200, 204, 227, 231
Augustine 4–7, 12, 16, 32, 44, 54, 64, 72, 75, 91, 93, 110, 164, 216
Aulen, G. 26
Baker, J.W. 81
Balcanqual, W. 140, 148–149
Baptism 73
Barth, K. 252–253
Bas-Languedoc 188
Basle 78, 115, 238–239
Bauke, H. 13
Baxter, R. 172, 211, 226, 234–235, 241
Bellarmine, R. 128
Berne 9, 38, 41, 63, 114–115, 238
Beza, T. 3, 6, 25, 41–59, 67–69, 71–72, 74, 77, 80–81, 87, 94, 98–99, 104, 106, 114–115, 117–118, 124, 128–129, 136, 151, 164–166, 197, 201, 212–216, 218, 230, 233, 248, 250
Bibliander, T. 69, 78–79
Blois 189
Blondel, D. 188, 218, 225
Bochart, S. 167
Bodleian Library 117

Bolsec, J. 14–15, 34, 42–44, 48–49, 61, 68, 71–72, 77–79, 230, 248
Bolton, S. 168, 180
Bordeaux 162–163, 174
Bray, J.S. 41, 47
Breitinger, J.J. 66
Bremen 137–138, 144–149, 218, 225
Britain 21, 134–135, 138, 141, 143–150
Bucer, M. 6–8, 12, 20, 87, 97–98, 112, 128, 175, 218
Bullinger, H. 4, 42–43, 66–87, 87, 94, 105, 112, 124, 143, 151–152, 165, 168, 180, 218, 220, 235, 248, 251
Buren, P. van 12, 26–28
Calamy, E. 241
Calling 22, 34, 71, 110, 134, 137, 164–165, 191, 203, 229, 251
Calvin, J. 2–4, 8–10, 12–35, 38, 41–44, 47–51, 53–54, 56–59, 66–69, 72, 74, 76–81, 87, 105, 113–114, 117, 124, 128, 136, 151, 163, 166, 168, 175, 180, 187, 196, 210, 213–218, 220, 248, 250–253, 256–259, 261–272
Calvinism 2–3, 12, 23, 79, 105, 115, 128, 149, 152, 163, 165, 187, 203, 216–217, 220, 224–225, 239, 251
Cambridge 150
Cameron, J. 3, 162–181, 187, 189, 194, 197–198, 200, 202, 204, 210, 215, 218–220, 225, 249–250
Cappel, L. 162, 167, 174, 178, 240
Carleton, G. 154–155
Casaubon, I. 162
Cassel 212
Castellio, S. 30, 42, 48–51, 54
Castres, Synod of 162
Catechism,
– **Heidelberg** 104, 109, 113, 130, 134, 138, 248
– **Luther's Little** 13
– **Ursinus' Major** 107
Catholicism, Roman 80, 116, 128, 174, 187, 200–201, 212–213, 219
Causality 14–18, 43–52, 55, 59, 71–72, 81, 89–94, 99, 106–107, 128, 130, 142–144, 189, 191, 197, 212, 219, 227, 237, 239
Charenton, Synod(s) of 187–188, 212, 238
Charles V Emperor 87
Charles I King of England 151
Christ
– **foreordination of** 41, 113, 130, 132, 134, 237, 239, 250, 252
– **kingship/lordship of** 34, 148, 233
– **mediator** 16–18, 22–23, 26, 45, 55–56, 58–59, 107–108, 110–113, 132, 136, 143–144, 177, 194, 196–197, 237, 239, 244, 250–251, 253
– **merit of** 4–6, 26, 111–112, 131, 134, 138–139, 142–145, 177–179, 233, 235, 239
– **mirror of election** 16–17, 215
Christocentrism 7, 13, 16, 18, 41, 70, 80, 94–95, 99, 238, 253
Church 13, 27, 30–32, 88–89, 94, 97, 106–107, 115, 118, 129–130, 136, 196, 228, 236, 238, 252–253
Clifford, A.C. 12
Cocceius, J. 264
Colloquy
– **of Berne** 114
– **of Cassel** 212
– **of Montbéliard** 42, 51–52, 59, 63, 212, 266
Complexio oppositorum 13, 34
Conditionality 28–29, 54, 68, 74, 76, 81, 91–93, 96–97, 105, 108–118, 121, 124–125, 130–137, 140–151, 165, 172, 176–181, 210–211, 214–218, 220, 226–235, 240, 248–250
Conference of the Hague 130
Confession
– **Augsburg** 87
– **Belgic** 130
– **Bernese** 115
– **Second Helvetic** 71, 79
– **Thorn** 213, 218
– **Westminster** 241
– **Zanchi's** 91–92
Consensus
– **Strasbourg** 89
– **Swiss** 2, 188, 224–241, 249–251
Conversion 16, 21–23, 43, 48, 106, 113, 167, 172–173, 196–198, 229, 232
Council
– **of Orange** 5
– **of Trent** 28, 213
Covenant 15, 29, 32, 66, 73–74, 76, 81, 93–94, 104–105, 107–109, 111–114, 118, 120–121, 124–125, 131, 133–136, 140–146, 150–151, 163, 167–172, 175–176, 178–181, 192, 194–197, 199–202, 211, 215, 218, 220, 229, 231–232, 239–240, 248–251
Creed, Apostles 13, 91, 106
Crocius, L. 143, 145
Cromwell, O. 225
Crypto–Calvinism 115
Davenant, J. 134, 148, 150–152, 165, 180
Decrees, Divine 7, 13–15, 17–18, 20, 23, 25, 34, 43–45, 47–49, 51–53, 55–56, 59, 69–71, 74, 77–78, 89–90, 91–94, 96–97, 105–106, 111–112, 118, 129–132, 135, 137, 140, 143–145, 151, 164–167, 169, 181, 189–192, 194, 203–204, 211–212, 214, 220, 227–231, 236–237, 239, 248, 250, 252–253
– **execution of** 17, 44–45, 47, 49, 51, 55, 59, 90, 94, 106, 130, 140, 143, 198, 231, 237, 239, 252
Denck, H. 8
Descartes, R. 219
Deus
– ***absconditus*** 5–6, 34, 75, 92, 252–253
– ***revelatus*** 5–6, 252–253
Devil 22, 57, 67, 89, 191
Dort
– **Canons of** 132, 150, 165, 180, 188, 225, 249
– **Synod of** 2, 66, 116, 127–152, 165, 177, 180–181, 188, 192, 210–212, 218, 220, 224–225, 231, 233, 238, 241, 249, 257, 259, 263–264, 269–271
Duplessis–Mornay, P. 211–213, 219, 224
Durham 36, 122, 221, 243, 261, 264–265, 271
Dutch 39, 117, 119, 128, 134, 139, 146, 148, 153–155, 174, 184, 261, 266
Election
– **Christ as Foundation of** 61, 130, 132, 143–144, 146, 148, 156, 232, 237, 239, 251

– as *ex post facto* explanation of conversion 21, 23, 34, 48, 144, 229
Emden 139, 141–143, 156–157
England 77, 87, 129, 134, 144, 151–152, 168, 187, 189, 211, 224–225, 241, 250
Enlightenment, The 163, 241
Erasmus, D. 6, 72
Esau 240
Eschatology 88
Ethics 109, 170, 197–198, 200, 204, 216–217, 219, 229, 237, 249
Experience 7, 17, 20–22, 28–29, 69, 91, 96, 98, 106, 145, 147, 176, 227, 237, 252
Faculty psychology 172, 197–198
Fall 22–23, 27, 43–45, 47, 53, 67, 69–70, 72, 89–90, 104–105, 109, 168–169, 180, 190–191, 211–212, 214, 230
Foreknowledge, Divine 6, 8, 23, 43–45, 53, 70, 89, 130
Foresight, Divine 4, 14–15, 31, 42–43, 62, 69–71, 78, 88, 115, 129, 130, 136, 143, 165, 190, 202
Forgiveness 58, 73, 75, 108, 121, 131, 134, 141, 145–147, 155, 172–174, 194, 199, 234
Formula
– **of Concord** 7, 52, 55, 88
France 3, 41, 162, 175, 187–189, 211–213, 216, 218–219, 224–226, 231, 238, 241
Franeker 224
Frederick III, Elector Palatine 104
Frederick, Duke of Württemberg 52
Friesland 146, 149
Gap, Synod of 181
Gelderland 148–149, 158
Geneva 8, 14–15, 41, 44, 60–63, 77, 87, 99, 104, 107, 129, 136, 138–139, 151, 162, 219, 224–226, 238–239
Georgius 12, 15, 31
Germany 66, 80, 105, 115, 218, 220, 248–250, 261
Gernler, M. 238
Glasgow 162
Godfrey, W.R. 4, 12, 133, 150, 152
Gomarus, F. 129, 132, 139, 143–144, 147–148, 150, 154
Good pleasure, Divine 15, 18, 23, 26, 48, 53, 67–68, 90, 92–93, 106, 132, 164, 178–180, 192–193, 200, 235, 237
Goodness, Divine 20, 33, 54, 66–70, 74–75, 77, 81, 89, 106, 112, 170, 179–180, 189, 193–194, 198–200, 202, 204, 210–211, 215–217, 220, 227, 235, 237
Gospel 7–8, 15, 18–19, 21–25, 30, 33–34, 51–54, 58–59, 67–68, 70–75, 77–78, 87, 89, 91, 93, 95–99, 105, 107–111, 113, 118, 132–133, 135–144, 149, 151, 158–159, 169–172, 175–176, 180, 191, 195, 202, 204, 211, 214, 217, 228–232, 237, 239–240, 249–250
Gottschalk 5, 12,
Gouda 130
Grace 4–8, 16, 18–23, 28–29, 33, 52, 70, 72–76, 78, 89–90, 93, 95, 105–108, 110–114, 118, 124, 128–129, 131–142, 144–146, 149–150, 164, 167–173, 179–180, 187–188, 191, 194–197, 202–203, 210–211, 226, 228–232, 235, 237, 239–241, 249–252
– **irresistible** 69, 211
Graubünden 87
Gregory 91
Groningen 139, 142, 144, 224
Grotius, H. 174, 211, 233, 235, 259
Grundler, O. 90, 93–94
Grynaeus, J. 117
***Gutachten*, Zurich** 80
Hague, The 130, 134
Hales, J. 144, 147–148
Hardening (of reprobate), 89, 90, 217
Heidegger, J.H. 238
Heidelberg, 4, 87, 94, 104–107, 109, 111, 113, 115, 117–118, 128, 130, 134–136, 162, 167, 169, 171, 180, 220, 248, 259–260
Heppe, H. 104
Heshusius, T. 39
Hesse, 138, 141–142, 145–146, 212, 218
Hincmar (of Rheims) 5
History 59, 73–74, 109, 118, 180, 191, 197, 204
Hoard, S. 151
Hoffman, M. 8, 97, 128
Holland 129–130, 139, 145–146, 148
Huber, S. 114–118, 125, 128, 136, 138, 235
Hubner, P. 114
Humanism 3, 41, 77, 162–163, 218–219
Hunnius, A. 114–115, 117–118, 128
Hyper–Calvinism 149
Illumination 16, 20, 22, 72, 172, 196, 198
Image, Divine 69–70, 165, 189
Immutability, Divine 20, 52–53, 59, 89–93, 106, 132, 170, 201, 227–228, 231, 240, 248
Imputation
-of Christ's righteousness 172
-of sin 188,240
Impute 167
Imputed 182, 188
Inability, Human 22, 81, 107–108, 150, 190, 194, 198, 232
Incarnation 17, 26–27, 55, 68, 75–76, 113, 143, 149, 258
Incomprehensibility, Divine 18, 22, 25, 47–48, 81, 89, 106, 179–180, 192, 200, 203, 215–217, 231
Infralapsarianism 90, 132, 164, 190–191, 212, 214, 230, 239
Intercession 33, 56, 70, 96–97, 114, 134, 146, 177, 233, 239
Intercommunion 212
Interim, Augsburg 87
Irminger 238
Isaac 54, 93, 162, 166
Israel 29, 51, 73, 168, 194
Isselburg, H. 138
Italy 87
Jacob 240
Jacobs, P. 13
James I, King of England 134, 150–151, 162, 212, 224
Jews 32–33
Judas 178, 214
Junius, F. 129
Justification 6, 14, 16, 94, 108, 120, 128, 146, 170, 172, 187, 232–233
Kendall, R.T. 3, 12, 33, 41
Kimedoncius, J. 117–118, 248
Laplanche, F. 163, 167, 171, 187, 189, 200, 230
Lausanne 41–42, 44, 238–239

Law 23–24, 50, 53, 70, 73–74, 91, 105, 107–108, 118, 140, 167–168, 170–171, 173–174, 178–179, 180, 187, 192–198, 200, 211, 231–232, 240, 249–251
Leiden 129–130, 132, 173, 188, 224–225
Leo, Pope 5
Llandaff, Bishop of 148
Logic 35, 41, 43–44, 48, 51, 53, 56–57, 63, 92, 98–99, 118, 204, 217, 219, 227–230, 237, 240, 248–249
Lombard, Peter 5, 30, 92
London 162, 224
Loudun, Synod of 188
Louis VI, Elector Palatine 9
Louis XIII, King of France 162, 224
Love, Divine 17–20, 23–24, 27– 29, 48, 52, 56, 58, 61–62, 64, 66–67, 70, 74–75, 77–78, 84, 89, 91–93, 95, 97–98, 106–107, 133–135, 144, 149, 156, 170–172, 176, 179, 193–194, 198, 201, 215, 235–237, 239, 248, 250
Lubbertus, S. 139, 148
Luther, M. 3–4, 6–7, 13, 43, 151, 180, 252
Lutheranism 3, 6–7, 42, 52, 55, 59, 79–80, 87–88, 96–99, 105, 108, 115–116, 124–125, 178, 187, 212–213, 218, 251
Marbach, J. 87–89, 91, 94–95, 97, 128
Martinius, M. 137–138, 140–142, 144–148, 150, 165, 180, 225
Medieval theology 4, 12, 30, 60, 152, 166
Melanchthon, P. 6–7, 77, 87, 104
Mercy, Divine 16-17, 20, 22–23, 43, 45, 56–57, 66–67, 69, 74, 77, 88–89, 91–92, 95, 106, 113, 137, 173–174, 176, 194, 196–199, 202, 227
Moltmann, J. 163–164, 167, 169, 189, 200
Montauban 162
Montbéliard, Colloquy of 42, 51–52, 55, 57–59, 99, 114–115, 117, 124, 212, 237
Morus, A. 238
Mosaic dispensation 105, 120, 168–169, 171, 180, 232, 271
Moulin, P. du 210, 212–213, 224–226, 230–232, 234, 236–237
Musculus, A. 114
Musculus, W. 105, 112, 151, 218, 220
Myconius 78–79
Nantes, Edict of 213, 238, 241
Nassau–Wetterau 139, 141, 145, 147, 156–157
Neonomianism 241
Netherlands 224
Neustadt 87, 105
Newmarket 155
Niesel, W. 13, 16
Nominalism 4–5, 9, 26, 102, 179–180, 200–216
Oldenbarneveld, J. 129
Olevianus, C. 94, 113–114, 118, 125, 142
Omnipotence, Divine 5, 14, 47, 52–53, 59, 67, 69, 74, 81, 90–94, 99, 106, 200, 203–204, 227–229, 237
Omniscience, Divine 227
Overijsel 139
Owen, J. 114, 225–227, 231, 233–236
Oxford 117, 225
Packer, J.I. 163
Pajon, C. 219
Palatinate 104–105, 109, 135–136, 138–139, 141, 144, 146, 148
Pareus, D. 109–110, 115–116, 136, 180, 212, 218, 220, 248
Paris 9, 162, 211, 224, 238, 259
Parry, H. 110
Pelagianism 4, 12, 32, 142, 179
Perkins, W. 129–130, 151, 175
Perseverance 88, 91, 97, 109, 130, 171
Persuasion 29, 98, 172–173, 176, 178, 188, 197–198
Pharaoh 51, 217
Philanthropy 67, 130, 137, 144, 149, 193–195, 198, 201–202, 215, 235–236, 240
Pighius, A. 12, 15, 21, 128
Place, J. de la 162, 188, 240
Poitiers 187
Poland 147, 213, 218,
Polanus, A. 128
Polyander, J. 139
Potentia absoluta/ordinata 49, 63, 179, 270
Preaching 19–22, 24–25, 51, 58, 70, 72, 95–97, 108, 133, 136–137, 142, 144, 149, 151, 163, 175–176, 196, 202–203, 250
Predestination 2, 4–8, 12–16, 20–25, 27, 31–32, 34, 41–45, 47–49, 51–52, 55–59, 69–72, 75–86, 88–91, 93–95, 97–99, 104–107, 109–110, 113–118, 124–125, 128–130, 132–133, 135–136, 140–144, 150–152, 164–167, 172, 175, 180–181, 187, 189–191, 197, 200–201, 203, 212–220, 227–232, 237–241, 248–253
Presbyterians 241
Primasius 5
Primrose, G. 162
Promise, Divine 18–20, 23–24, 26, 31–34, 51, 54–55, 57–59, 72–78, 81, 83, 88, 91, 99, 107–113, 116, 124–125, 133–134, 137–138, 140–145, 148, 167–172, 175–176, 192–196, 199, 214, 218, 227–228, 231, 248, 250
Prosper of Aquitaine 5
Providence 14–15, 23–24, 34, 45, 47–48, 53–54, 59, 68–69, 76–77, 83, 89–90, 94, 106, 115, 128, 130, 202, 210, 217, 240
Pyrrhonism 219
Rainbow, J.H. 3–4, 12, 18, 25, 215
Ramus, P. 166
Rationalism 41, 163, 173, 204, 219–220, 222, 237
Redemption 3, 5, 8, 12–13, 16–18, 21, 26–34, 67, 75, 90, 92, 98, 111–112, 115, 117–118, 128, 131, 134–135, 137, 140, 142, 145–147, 149, 151–152, 171, 201–202, 235, 237, 241, 248
Regeneration 88, 90, 129, 157, 196
Remonstrance, Grand 130–131, 134
Remonstrants – see Arminianism
Repentance 8, 20, 22, 55, 89, 91, 108, 110, 113, 116, 135, 139, 141–142, 145, 149, 158, 168, 171, 176, 188, 196–199, 202, 211, 217, 228, 231–232, 240, 250

Reprobation 14, 20, 22–25, 30–32, 34, 42–45, 47–49, 51–54, 71, 77, 88–90, 93, 96, 99, 106, 112, 114, 136, 138–139, 145, 149, 164, 191, 203, 213–214, 216–217, 226–227, 229, 233–234, 252
Resurrection 3, 34, 111–112, 114, 135, 146, 233
Reuter, Q. 109
Revelation
– **natural** 171, 197, 214, 237
Rex, W. 216
Rhineland 87
Richelieu, Cardinal 187
Ritschl, A.A. 210
Rivet, A. 224, 231
Rutherford, S. 234
Sacraments 42, 52, 54, 88–89, 108
Sanctification 14, 16, 58, 75, 164
Saumur 3, 72, 152, 162–163, 166–167, 170–171, 173–174, 180, 187–189, 197, 204, 211–213, 215, 218–220, 225–226, 231, 235–236, 238, 240, 249
Scepticism 187, 219
Schaffhausen 115
Schmalkaldic League 87
Scholasticism 2, 3, 6, 12, 23, 30–31, 41, 53, 72, 76–77, 80, 96, 98–99, 104, 109, 111, 114, 117, 119, 151–152, 163, 166, 192, 197, 203–204, 218–219, 237, 248
Schweizer, A. 13, 163
Scotland 140, 162–163, 181, 241
Scotus, Duns 5
Scultetus, A. 148
Seaman, W. 241
Sedan 162, 225
Simplicity, Divine 90, 92–93
Sin 3–5, 14–15, 17, 26–27, 29–33, 43–45, 47, 49, 50, 56–59, 67–78, 88–91, 106, 108, 111–114, 116, 129–132, 134–142, 144–147, 164, 168, 170, 173–174, 180, 188–191, 194–195, 197–202, 214, 217, 228, 233–234, 236, 240, 244
Socinianism 42, 142, 174, 179, 211, 231, 233
Socinus, L. 38, 174
Spain 128–129
Spanheim, F. 188, 199, 213, 218, 224–226, 230, 233–234, 237–238
Spirit, Holy 14, 19–22, 28, 31, 72, 88–89, 95, 98, 107–108, 112–114, 135, 146, 173, 177, 190–191, 195–198, 203, 214, 232–233, 239–240
Stoicism 68
Strasbourg 7–8, 12, 79, 87–88, 91–92, 96, 99, 115, 212
Strehle, S. 3–4, 12, 26, 133, 180
Summum bonum 66–67
Supper, Lord's 41, 52, 79, 88, 91, 101, 266
Supralapsarianism 43–45, 48–49, 51–52, 59, 69, 90, 124, 129, 143, 164–165, 190, 201, 214–215, 230
Swinne, A.H. 163, 167
Switzerland 87, 139, 142–143, 224–241
Syllogism, Practical 58, 98, 116
Table, Beza's 44–47
Tarente, Prince of 188
Testard, P. 189
Thouars, Acte de 188
Thysius, A. 139
Tilenus 164, 172
Tossanus, D. 117
Traheron, B. 77–78
Transubstantiation, 219
Trinity 197
Tronchin, L. 238
Turks 33
Turretin, F. 114, 226–228, 230, 233–234, 238
Universalism (**universal salvation**) 8, 115
Universalism, Hypothetical 2, 112, 130, 145–147, 150, 163, 176–177, 189, 216–217, 229, 232, 234, 240
Ursinus, Z. 94, 104–115, 118–124, 134, 136, 138, 141–142, 152, 165, 168, 174, 180, 218, 248
Ussher, J. 151
Utrecht 139, 142, 146
Vermigli, Peter Martyr 44, 78–80, 87, 218
Via moderna/antiqua 64, 158, 185, 236
Vines, R. 241
Viret, P. 41
Visitation Articles, Saxon 115
Voluntas beneplaciti – see **'Good pleasure'**
Voluntas signi 23, 53–54, 93, 151, 192, 202, 210
Walaeus, A. 139
Wendel, F. 15, 26
Whitehall 151
Wittenberg 6
Württemberg 52, 115
Zanchi, G. 4, 6, 78–80, 87–99, 112, 124, 128, 166, 175, 213, 248
Zeeland 139, 142
Zurich 42, 66, 73, 77–80, 82–83, 85–87, 115, 143, 151, 180, 238, 244
Zwingli, H. 15, 66, 68, 71

Studies in Christian History and Thought

(All titles uniform with this volume)
Dates in bold are of projected publication

David Bebbington
Holiness in Nineteenth-Century England
David Bebbington stresses the relationship of movements of spirituality to changes in their cultural setting, especially the legacies of the Enlightenment and Romanticism. He shows that these broad shifts in ideological mood had a profound effect on the ways in which piety was conceptualized and practised. Holiness was intimately bound up with the spirit of the age.
2000 / 0-85364-981-2 / viii + 98pp

J. William Black
Reformation Pastors
Richard Baxter and the Ideal of the Reformed Pastor
This work examines Richard Baxter's *Gildas Salvianus, The Reformed Pastor* (1656) and explores each aspect of his pastoral strategy in light of his own concern for 'reformation' and in the broader context of Edwardian, Elizabethan and early Stuart pastoral ideals and practice.
2003 / 1-84227-190-3 / xxii + 308pp

James Bruce
Prophecy, Miracles, Angels, *and* Heavenly Light?
The Eschatology, Pneumatology and Missiology of Adomnán's Life of Columba
This book surveys approaches to the marvellous in hagiography, providing the first critique of Plummer's hypothesis of Irish saga origin. It then analyses the uniquely systematized phenomena in the *Life of Columba* from Adomnán's seventh-century theological perspective, identifying the coming of the eschatological Kingdom as the key to understanding.
2004 / 1-84227-227-6 / xviii + 286pp

Colin J. Bulley
The Priesthood of Some Believers
Developments from the General to the Special Priesthood in the Christian Literature of the First Three Centuries
The first in-depth treatment of early Christian texts on the priesthood of all believers shows that the developing priesthood of the ordained related closely to the division between laity and clergy and had deleterious effects on the practice of the general priesthood.
2000 / 1-84227-034-6 / xii + 336pp

Anthony R. Cross (ed.)

Ecumenism and History

Studies in Honour of John H.Y. Briggs

This collection of essays examines the inter-relationships between the two fields in which Professor Briggs has contributed so much: history—particularly Baptist and Nonconformist—and the ecumenical movement. With contributions from colleagues and former research students from Britain, Europe and North America, *Ecumenism and History* provides wide-ranging studies in important aspects of Christian history, theology and ecumenical studies.

2002 / 1-84227-135-0 / xx + 362pp

Maggi Dawn

Confessions of an Inquiring Spirit

Form as Constitutive of Meaning in S.T. Coleridge's Theological Writing

This study of Coleridge's *Confessions* focuses on its confessional, epistolary and fragmentary form, suggesting that attention to these features significantly affects its interpretation. Bringing a close study of these three literary forms, the author suggests ways in which they nuance the text with particular understandings of the Trinity, and of a kenotic christology. Some parallels are drawn between Romantic and postmodern dilemmas concerning the authority of the biblical text.

***2006** / 1-84227-255-1 / approx. 224 pp*

Ruth Gouldbourne

The Flesh and the Feminine

Gender and Theology in the Writings of Caspar Schwenckfeld

Caspar Schwenckfeld and his movement exemplify one of the radical communities of the sixteenth century. Challenging theological and liturgical norms, they also found themselves challenging social and particularly gender assumptions. In this book, the issues of the relationship between radical theology and the understanding of gender are considered.

***2005** / 1-84227-048-6 / approx. 304pp*

Crawford Gribben

Puritan Millennialism

Literature and Theology, 1550–1682

Puritan Millennialism surveys the growth, impact and eventual decline of puritan millennialism throughout England, Scotland and Ireland, arguing that it was much more diverse than has frequently been suggested. This Paternoster edition is revised and extended from the original 2000 text.

***2007** / 1-84227-372-8 / approx. 320pp*

July 2005

Galen K. Johnson

Prisoner of Conscience

John Bunyan on Self, Community and Christian Faith

This is an interdisciplinary study of John Bunyan's understanding of conscience across his autobiographical, theological and fictional writings, investigating whether conscience always deserves fidelity, and how Bunyan's view of conscience affects his relationship both to modern Western individualism and historic Christianity.

2003 / 1-84227-223-3 / xvi + 236pp

R.T. Kendall

Calvin and English Calvinism to 1649

The author's thesis is that those who formed the Westminster Confession of Faith, which is regarded as Calvinism, in fact departed from John Calvin on two points: (1) the extent of the atonement and (2) the ground of assurance of salvation.

1997 / 0-85364-827-1 / xii + 264pp

Timothy Larsen

Friends of Religious Equality

Nonconformist Politics in Mid-Victorian England

During the middle decades of the nineteenth century the English Nonconformist community developed a coherent political philosophy of its own, of which a central tenet was the principle of religious equality (in contrast to the stereotype of Evangelical Dissenters). The Dissenting community fought for the civil rights of Roman Catholics, non-Christians and even atheists on an issue of principle which had its flowering in the enthusiastic and undivided support which Nonconformity gave to the campaign for Jewish emancipation. This reissued study examines the political efforts and ideas of English Nonconformists during the period, covering the whole range of national issues raised, from state education to the Crimean War. It offers a case study of a theologically conservative group defending religious pluralism in the civic sphere, showing that the concept of religious equality was a grand vision at the centre of the political philosophy of the Dissenters.

***2007** / 1-84227-402-3 / x + 300pp*

Byung-Ho Moon

Christ the Mediator of the Law

Calvin's Christological Understanding of the Law as the Rule of Living and Life-Giving

This book explores the coherence between Christology and soteriology in Calvin's theology of the law, examining its intellectual origins and his position on the concept and extent of Christ's mediation of the law. A comparative study between Calvin and contemporary Reformers—Luther, Bucer, Melancthon and Bullinger—and his opponent Michael Servetus is made for the purpose of pointing out the unique feature of Calvin's Christological understanding of the law.

***2005** / 1-84227-318-3 / approx. 370pp*

John Eifion Morgan-Wynne

Holy Spirit and Religious Experience in Christian Writings, c.AD 90–200

This study examines how far Christians in the third to fifth generations (c.AD 90–200) attributed their sense of encounter with the divine presence, their sense of illumination in the truth or guidance in decision-making, and their sense of ethical empowerment to the activity of the Holy Spirit in their lives.

***2005** / 1-84227-319-1 / approx. 350pp*

James I. Packer

The Redemption and Restoration of Man in the Thought of Richard Baxter

James I. Packer provides a full and sympathetic exposition of Richard Baxter's doctrine of humanity, created and fallen; its redemption by Christ Jesus; and its restoration in the image of God through the obedience of faith by the power of the Holy Spirit.

2002 / 1-84227-147-4 / 432pp

Andrew Partington,

Church and State

The Contribution of the Church of England Bishops to the House of Lords during the Thatcher Years

In *Church and State*, Andrew Partington argues that the contribution of the Church of England bishops to the House of Lords during the Thatcher years was overwhelmingly critical of the government; failed to have a significant influence in the public realm; was inefficient, being undertaken by a minority of those eligible to sit on the Bench of Bishops; and was insufficiently moral and spiritual in its content to be distinctive. On the basis of this, and the likely reduction of the number of places available for Church of England bishops in a fully reformed Second Chamber, the author argues for an evolution in the Church of England's approach to the service of its bishops in the House of Lords. He proposes the Church of England works to overcome the genuine obstacles which hinder busy diocesan bishops from contributing to the debates of the House of Lords and to its life more informally.

***2005** / 1-84227-334-5 / approx. 324pp*

Michael Pasquarello III

God's Ploughman

Hugh Latimer: A 'Preaching Life' (1490–1555)

This construction of a 'preaching life' situates Hugh Latimer within the larger religious, political and intellectual world of late medieval England. Neither biography, intellectual history, nor analysis of discrete sermon texts, this book is a work of homiletic history which draws from the details of Latimer's milieu to construct an interpretive framework for the preaching performances that formed the core of his identity as a religious reformer. Its goal is to illumine the practical wisdom embodied in the content, form and style of Latimer's preaching, and to recapture a sense of its overarching purpose, movement, and transforming force during the reform of sixteenth-century England.

***2006** / 1-84227-336-1 / approx. 250pp*

Alan P.F. Sell

Enlightenment, Ecumenism, Evangel

Theological Themes and Thinkers 1550–2000

This book consists of papers in which such interlocking topics as the Enlightenment, the problem of authority, the development of doctrine, spirituality, ecumenism, theological method and the heart of the gospel are discussed. Issues of significance to the church at large are explored with special reference to writers from the Reformed and Dissenting traditions.

2005 / 1-84227-330-2 / xviii + 422pp

Alan P.F. Sell

Hinterland Theology

Some Reformed and Dissenting Adjustments

Many books have been written on theology's 'giants' and significant trends, but what of those lesser-known writers who adjusted to them? In this book some hinterland theologians of the British Reformed and Dissenting traditions, who followed in the wake of toleration, the Evangelical Revival, the rise of modern biblical criticism and Karl Barth, are allowed to have their say. They include Thomas Ridgley, Ralph Wardlaw, T.V. Tymms and N.H.G. Robinson.

***2006** / 1-84227-331-0 / approx. 350pp*

Alan P.F. Sell and Anthony R. Cross (eds)

Protestant Nonconformity in the Twentieth Century

In this collection of essays scholars representative of a number of Nonconformist traditions reflect thematically on Nonconformists' life and witness during the twentieth century. Among the subjects reviewed are biblical studies, theology, worship, evangelism and spirituality, and ecumenism. Over and above its immediate interest, this collection provides a marker to future scholars and others wishing to know how some of their forebears assessed Nonconformity's contribution to a variety of fields during the century leading up to Christianity's third millennium.

2003 / 1-84227-221-7 / x + 398pp

Mark Smith

Religion in Industrial Society

Oldham and Saddleworth 1740–1865

This book analyses the way British churches sought to meet the challenge of industrialization and urbanization during the period 1740–1865. Working from a case-study of Oldham and Saddleworth, Mark Smith challenges the received view that the Anglican Church in the eighteenth century was characterized by complacency and inertia, and reveals Anglicanism's vigorous and creative response to the new conditions. He reassesses the significance of the centrally directed church reforms of the mid-nineteenth century, and emphasizes the importance of local energy and enthusiasm. Charting the growth of denominational pluralism in Oldham and Saddleworth, Dr Smith compares the strengths and weaknesses of the various Anglican and Nonconformist approaches to promoting church growth. He also demonstrates the extent to which all the churches participated in a common culture shaped by the influence of evangelicalism, and shows that active co-operation between the churches rather than denominational conflict dominated. This revised and updated edition of Dr Smith's challenging and original study makes an important contribution both to the social history of religion and to urban studies.

***2006** / 1-84227-335-3 / approx. 300pp*

July 2005

Martin Sutherland

Peace, Toleration and Decay

The Ecclesiology of Later Stuart Dissent

This fresh analysis brings to light the complexity and fragility of the later Stuart Nonconformist consensus. Recent findings on wider seventeenth-century thought are incorporated into a new picture of the dynamics of Dissent and the roots of evangelicalism.

2003 / 1-84227-152-0 / xxii + 216pp

G. Michael Thomas

The Extent of the Atonement

A Dilemma for Reformed Theology from Calvin to the Consensus

A study of the way Reformed theology addressed the question, 'Did Christ die for all, or for the elect only?', commencing with John Calvin, and including debates with Lutheranism, the Synod of Dort and the teaching of Moïse Amyraut.

1997 / 0-85364-828-X / x + 278pp

David M. Thompson

Baptism, Church and Society in Britain from the Evangelical Revival to *Baptism, Eucharist and Ministry*

The theology and practice of baptism have not received the attention they deserve. How important is faith? What does baptismal regeneration mean? Is baptism a bond of unity between Christians? This book discusses the theology of baptism and popular belief and practice in England and Wales from the Evangelical Revival to the publication of the World Council of Churches' consensus statement on *Baptism, Eucharist and Ministry* (1982).

***2005** / 1-84227-393-0 / approx. 224pp*

Mark D. Thompson

A Sure Ground on Which to Stand

The Relation of Authority and Interpretive Method of Luther's Approach to Scripture

The best interpreter of Luther is Luther himself. Unfortunately many modern studies have superimposed contemporary agendas upon this sixteenth-century Reformer's writings. This fresh study examines Luther's own words to find an explanation for his robust confidence in the Scriptures, a confidence that generated the famous 'stand' at Worms in 1521.

2004 / 1-84227-145-8 / xvi + 322pp

Carl R. Trueman and R.S. Clark (eds)
Protestant Scholasticism
Essays in Reassessment

Traditionally Protestant theology, between Luther's early reforming career and the dawn of the Enlightenment, has been seen in terms of decline and fall into the wastelands of rationalism and scholastic speculation. In this volume a number of scholars question such an interpretation. The editors argue that the development of post-Reformation Protestantism can only be understood when a proper historical model of doctrinal change is adopted. This historical concern underlies the subsequent studies of theologians such as Calvin, Beza, Olevian, Baxter, and the two Turrentini. The result is a significantly different reading of the development of Protestant Orthodoxy, one which both challenges the older scholarly interpretations and clichés about the relationship of Protestantism to, among other things, scholasticism and rationalism, and which demonstrates the fruitfulness of the new, historical approach.

1999 / 0-85364-853-0 / xx + 344pp

Shawn D. Wright
Our Sovereign Refuge
The Pastoral Theology of Theodore Beza

Our Sovereign Refuge is a study of the pastoral theology of the Protestant reformer who inherited the mantle of leadership in the Reformed church from John Calvin. Countering a common view of Beza as supremely a 'scholastic' theologian who deviated from Calvin's biblical focus, Wright uncovers a new portrait. He was not a cold and rigid academic theologian obsessed with probing the eternal decrees of God. Rather, by placing him in his pastoral context and by noting his concerns in his pastoral and biblical treatises, Wright shows that Beza was fundamentally a committed Christian who was troubled by the vicissitudes of life in the second half of the sixteenth century. He believed that the biblical truth of the supreme sovereignty of God alone could support Christians on their earthly pilgrimage to heaven. This pastoral and personal portrait forms the heart of Wright's argument.

2004 / 1-84227-252-7 / xviii + 308pp

Paternoster
9 Holdom Avenue,
Bletchley,
Milton Keynes MK1 1QR,
United Kingdom
Web: www.authenticmedia.co.uk/paternoster

July 2005

www.ingramcontent.com/pod-product-compliance
Lightning Source LLC
LaVergne TN
LVHW020538100826
845148LV00010B/1525